Canio
in Pagliacci

P9-CFP-695

Duke of Mantua
in Rigoletto

Richard
in A Masked Ball

Edgar
in Lucia di Lammermoor

Turiddu

Don Alvaro
in La Forza del Destino

AA OP
12⁵⁰
AA

The
Bluebird
of Happiness

ALSO BY ALAN LEVY

Good Men Still Live!
Rowboat to Prague
God Bless You Real Good
The Culture Vultures
Operation Elvis

THE BLUEBIRD OF HAPPINESS

The Memoirs of Jan Peerce

by Alan Levy

HARPER & ROW, PUBLISHERS

New York Hagerstown San Francisco London

Out of traditional religious deference,
the name of the Lord will appear herein as G-d.

Grateful acknowledgment is made for permission to reprint the following:

Lyrics quoted on pages 107–108, 110 reprinted from "Blue Bird of Happi-
ness" by Edward Heyman and Sandor Harmati. Copyright © 1934 T. B.
Harms Company. Copyright renewed. All rights reserved. Used by permis-
sion of the publisher.
Excerpt on page 313 from *New York Times.* © 1975 by The New York Times
Company. Reprinted by permission.
Excerpt on page 313 reprinted by permission of The New York Daily News.
Excerpt on page 119 reprinted from New York Post.
Excerpt on page 248 from *New York Herald Tribune.* Reprinted by permission
of IHT Corporation.

THE BLUEBIRD OF HAPPINESS: THE MEMOIRS OF JAN PEERCE. Copyright ©
1976 by Alan Levy and Jan Peerce. All rights reserved. Printed in the United
States of America. No part of this book may be used or reproduced in any
manner whatsoever without written permission except in the case of brief
quotations embodied in critical articles and reviews. For information address
Harper & Row, Publishers, Inc., 10 East 53rd Street, New York, N.Y. 10022.
Published simultaneously in Canada by Fitzhenry & Whiteside Limited,
Toronto.

FIRST EDITION

Designed by Dorothy Schmiderer

Library of Congress Cataloging in Publication Data

Peerce, Jan, 1904–
   The bluebird of happiness.
   Includes index.
   1. Peerce, Jan, 1904–   2. Singers—United
States—Biography.   I. Levy, Alan, joint author.
II. Title.
ML420.P38A3   782.1'092'4 [B]   75–25055
ISBN 0–06–013311–2

76 77 78 79 80 10 9 8 7 6 5 4 3 2 1

TO ALICE K. PEERCE
without whom this life could not have
been lived the way it was

Contents

Illustrations follow pages 150 and 246

Overture

January 1966: Jan and Alice Peerce are coming to cocktails. Carmel champagne and knishes, to keep it kosher. Three bottles are already on hand and will soon be on ice. And I am on jury duty at the New York County Courthouse, earning six dollars and two subway tokens per day for doing nothing but answering roll calls, reading Tolkien, eating tea lunches in Chinatown, and knocking off at 2 P.M.—a free-lance writer's dream. Today it will be Chinese dumplings at noon on Pell Street, Jewish dumplings at 5 P.M. on Perry Street. On my way uptown to our Greenwich Village brownstone, I'll pick up the knishes at Yonah Schimmel's bakery on Houston Street: a dozen kasha (buckwheat) knishes, a dozen potato knishes, and a dozen liver puffs. We'll serve them on paper plates, since the Levy family doesn't keep kosher. All is in order, with time to spare.

But . . . *but!* Returning from lunch for the usual afternoon roll call and dismissal, I am selected for a jury. Me impaneled! What the hell kind of democracy is this anyway? But there I am, my card stuck in slot number seven on the board, assigned to "a complicated case." How can I plead "Jan Peerce is coming for knishes" to wiggle out of it?

After several aborted thrusts ("I'm a feature writer." "Fine!"), I accept my fate. The defense attorney begins an agreed-upon presentation of the basic facts of the dispute.

1

"The plaintiff used to live in a one-room basement apartment on upper Seventh Avenue, to the left of the building's main entrance. His only ventilation was a long, narrow, slitlike casement window that he had to keep open if he wanted any air. To the right of the building's main door was another long slit and inside it was the coalbin for the whole house. Early one warm day, the plaintiff was awakened by the sound of a truck backing up, and as he opened his eyes, he saw a coal chute poking its way through his window. He fled the apartment just as a whole truckload of coal was dumped into his bedroom and now he is suing for damages to the apartment, relocation costs, and a nervous condition induced by . . ."

As he drones on with the facts, I begin to stop feeling sorry for myself and start taking an interest. True, we'll have to postpone the Peerces, but surely they allow jurors one phone call before they go on trial. Maybe I can reach Valerie before she puts the champagne on ice. And do I have the Peerces' number in New Rochelle?

The presentation is finished. The opposing counsel stands up to ask if anybody has good cause to be excused. Nobody does. Almost conversationally, he turns to me and asks, "Juror Number Seven, would it affect your judgment of the case any if I told you that the plaintiff is black?"

Without thinking, I blurt out, "Well, only if—I mean, was he black *before* this incident?"

"Challenge! Challenge!" Both sides' challenges ring out like hunters' shots in the jury room.

By 8 P.M. the knishes are warm and dwindling, the champagne is cold and diminishing, our fireplace is glowing and it illuminates Jan Peerce dandling one of our daughters on his knee while Alice Peerce holds the other on hers. Valerie has stopped serving; we pour and help ourselves whenever we wish. For an evening with the Peerces is always informal and relaxed. But for all their looseness, nothing about the Peerces is flabby or sprawling. Both are perfectly compact and composed people, just as alert to others as they are to themselves. Which is why a name is seldom forgotten, an address in another city is always recorded and often looked up, a letter or gift is always acknowledged, and new acquaintances quickly become old and cherished friends. A backstage introduction at Lewisohn Stadium two summers earlier had been followed by invitations to other concerts and an occasional opera at the Met, a warm note of congratulations when the second baby was born, and the taking up of an offer to "come and see both girls for yourself sometime." And now, after a couple of hours of chatting, Jan Peerce, who likes to talk in parables, is nonetheless coming to a point.

"I did an as-told-to article ten years ago with Stanley Frank," Jan is saying, "and when it came out it sounded like me. Stanley Frank had absorbed a lot of my expressions and mannerisms. So when I thanked him, we got to talking and I said to him, 'How about doing a book about me?'

"Stanley Frank was a kind of rough-and-tumble professional—hard-boiled on the outside, always ready to fight because his own nature was so sweet and generous he had to defend himself against giving in to it—so he came snarling back at me with, 'Whaddya wanna book for?'

"I said at the time, 'I don't know. All sorts of people are having books written about themselves. Here you and I are coming off so well—you're learning so much about me, my childhood, my early beginnings—that I thought maybe you could come through with something good for both of us.'

"Frank said, 'What have you got to tell the world? Why should you tell all the things you've got to hide?'

"I got mad and said, 'What have I got to hide?'

"And he said, 'Exactly! Then you have no book!'

"Now I got madder. 'You mean because I didn't sit in jail, because I didn't commit a crime, because I didn't steal or at least wasn't caught, because I didn't marry seven times and never raped anybody, my story isn't worth telling?'

"He said, 'Yeah. Any one of those would make you much more interesting to a publisher. So unless you feel you have a special contribution to make to the world, let's forget about it.' "

In the 1960s New York media explosion, Stanley Frank makes perfect sense to me. Resisting the overture, I tell Jan that my eyes are turned eastward—toward living in Europe—and, er, well, my wife and I are both Jewish, but we just aren't, er, you know, Jewish enough. So I suggest other writers.

"You may not know it yet," says Jan Peerce, "but you're the right person to do this book. Although you're not even practicing the Jewish religion, you're raising your family by its values. The time will come when you'll appreciate what's behind everything you've done, when you'll appreciate your own parents' roots on the Lower East Side, and when you'll want to learn more and write more about these things. You're young yet; the time will come—and I hope I'm here to see it."

On the way home to Westchester, I learn later, Jan tells Alice as she drives the Rolls-Royce, "Well, at least he listened."

My wife and daughters and I move in 1967 from Perry Street to Prague, Czechoslovakia, where something happens to fulfill Jan Peerce's prophecy.

A saintly politician named Alexander Dubcek illuminates the world in 1968 with his heretical notion that communism and decency (what he calls "socialism with a human face") can coexist in society. It takes half a million Russian soldiers and thousands of tanks that August to prove him naïve, if not wrong, and another three years before the roof finally falls in on the American Family Levy. In 1971 we are expelled and deported from Prague. We settle in Vienna, where opera is no archaic spur of the culture beat, but a vital throb in the city's pulse. Singers and singing become our friends and excellence more than ever our concern—along with the values we cherished under adversity in Prague and that Jan Peerce has brought to both his life and his career. His ethnic roots and ours are in Eastern Europe. Having survived a different kind of pogrom from the ones that drove Peerce's ancestors and mine to the Lower East Side, I have come to love human decency the way I love Mozart or Rembrandt or my own children's special moments: as a rarity, but a reality, not as an abstraction or an ideology. And when it flowers —particularly in public, whether out of the treacherous soil of politics or in opera—then, as a writer and as a man, I feel it should not merely be praised and preserved, but sung about, written about, and even preached about.

Before Jan Peerce and I hold a reunion in Vienna, I visit New York in early 1972 and go backstage at the Broadway Theatre to talk with him after a matinee of *Fiddler on the Roof,* in which he is playing Tevye. We talk some more—in New Rochelle, Vienna, and Paris—during that year, and late in 1972 the book at last begins to take shape. In 1973 it is begun: a book about being decent and Jewish in the twentieth century while becoming an opera star, a public figure, and a successful man—a life story told in more or less chronological sermons and parables, reminiscences and vignettes, by a wise man who happens to be a great artist, to a younger disciple who will reshape the words that are transmitted and the vibrations I feel: an autobiography orchestrated with rhythmic meditations, recitatives, an occasional duet, and sustained solo arias on the aspects of life that matter. The voice throughout is the earthy tenor of Jan Peerce. Listen to Peerce, in his seventies, telling me what he wants the book to be and not to be:

"Jan Peerce, warts and all—that's what it's gotta be. I'll tell you everything. I'll take you back to Orchard Street, where I was born, and Madison Street, where I lived my childhood, and I'll try to make you see the Lower East Side the way it was, but I want you to see as much as you can through your own eyes. And I want you to talk to others about me—not just the people I'll send you to, but people I don't know and people I do know who'll talk to you behind my back. And if there's something I don't tell you, it won't be on purpose, so if you find it out in your research, don't be afraid to face me with it. Or to put it in. And if there's something you don't like about me, try to show it—no cosmetics.

"I don't expect everybody to love me. Why should I? I don't love everybody either. I think it's a sickness to want to be loved by everybody or to say, 'I love everybody.' When I walk out on the stage in front of an audience, I know there's someone in those one or three or ten thousand people who doesn't like me from the moment I walk on, even if I sing like four angels. That's human.

"I'm not out to decorate the bookstores with another anemic memoir, with a show-biz chronology of names and numbers. I don't even want to pretend I sat down and wrote a book. But listen, I don't want it to read like a transcript of some spliced-up tape recordings. If it reads like me, *then* it'll sound like me.

"I'm not ashamed or afraid to talk about anything that's happened in my life. I don't want to sound like a robot who never raised his voice, and was shoved around by lesser creatures. The things you leave after you when you're dead are the things you built in your life. And if there are two or three people who can say something good about you as a human being after you're gone—not just because you were their father or her husband—that's enough to justify a good, decent life."

1

Jacob Pincus Perelmuth

To the New and Whorish World

In the beginning there was a people and from that people there came a man and a woman. My mother was Anna Posner from the tiny Jewish village of Horodetz, in Russia, an overnight ride east from Warsaw. My father, Louis Perelmuth, grew up in Hyakuvka, near Kobrin, not far away from Horodetz. But my father and mother didn't meet until after he had served his stint in the czar's army.

Many people we knew came to America to escape serving in the Russian army. We heard of men who chopped off a finger or two to get out of it. Not my father. He was one of six brothers, who actually wanted to serve and see a little of the world—or at least of Russia—beyond Kobrin.

He went off to the Russian army with a group of his fellow Orthodox Jews from Kobrin. They knew they were in for an ordeal, particularly at mealtime, for they had vowed to eat only kosher food.

On their first day as soldiers they marched a little, and when they came in for supper, big vats were opened and lids were lifted and the scent of cabbage borscht filled the Russian air. But it wasn't kosher, so the Jewish conscripts of Kobrin would have none of it. Instead they settled for black bread and tea.

The second day was colder and harder: more marching, more hard work, and military maneuvers, too. They came back to camp, the vats were opened, the lids were lifted—and this time the smell of borscht got to them. Yes, it smelled good, but no, they were kosher. So it was black bread and tea again.

But an army travels on its stomach, and how far could a Jewish soldier in the Russian army go on black bread and tea? Finally my father and his fellow soldiers consulted the written teachings of our religion, which say that where a question of health is involved, one is permitted exceptions to the dietary laws. These generally refer to matters of life or death. Two and a half years in the army on a diet of bread and tea would have been fatal with so great a work load. True, they were strong young men, but the kind of work the army demanded would have taxed strong young oxen.

So they held a meeting. They decided that, starting the next day, they would have just the liquid from the soup, which should be a little more sustaining. They did that for a week, but it wasn't enough as they went deeper into soldiering, working harder and growing weaker from hunger.

Again they had a meeting. They resolved that it was all right to munch on the soup bones. They had more and more meetings until finally they decided that if they wanted to live, they had to have sustenance. And they came to the conclusion that G-d would forgive them if they ate the food that was prepared for them.

They prayed to G-d every morning and evening, and on the day they were sent home, every one of them went right back on the kosher regimen. Years later, when my father told me about this, he would whisper, "You know, for two years I ate nonkosher food—and do you know something? It was very good."

My father visited the *shtetl* of Horodetz, where he met and married my mother. I couldn't tell you about their courtship because I wasn't there, but I can tell you she was madly in love with him for all the years I knew her —and he with her. I would even go so far as to say that my father was always such a good-looking and appealing man that my mother was often jealous of him.

My mother's father had emigrated to America before her marriage in search of a better life and his first letter home said succinctly: "It's a whorish world" (*kurvehsheh welt,* in Yiddish). Now, my Grandfather Berel was a very quiet, soft-spoken man, so his wife, Chashe Freda, was flabbergasted. She wrote back: "What's happened to you? Are you out of your mind?" And he answered in the mail: "I am sending for you soon. When you come to

America, you will see for yourself." And a year or two later, when he brought her over, my little grandmother agreed. If someone told her a child stole from its parents or a father beat a mother, Chashe Freda would say almost with pride, "I'm not shocked. My husband found it in America the very first day."

It was natural that having been in the army, my father outgrew his little world, and his in-laws' odyssey gave him and my mother a path to follow. They had a daughter who died as a baby in an epidemic in Russia. And before my father and then my mother left for America in the dawn of the new century, they had a son named Mot'l. In our family it was unlucky to be born in Russia. Mot'l died on the Lower East Side of New York City when he was six and I was three. He hooked a ride with some other boys on the back of an ice wagon. When they decided to get off, he was the last to jump—and a horse drawing a trolley car hit him. With that, I became the oldest child and all the family's ambitions were concentrated in me. In this respect, though I don't remember my older brother and never met my older sister, their deaths had a great influence on my life: I had to fulfill what my folks missed out on in them. I do remember, very hazily as in a dream, the mourning and weeping for my brother Mot'l, the family sitting *shivah* for him on boxes for seven days, and the sadness that went on for years. It took my mother a long time to get over Mot'l.

When my father landed on the Lower East Side around 1902, he had some difficulty getting started even though his in-laws were already there to help ease his way. He found work in the sweatshops, and it wasn't easy—as I realized when he told me once: "Back when I came to America, you could get a good meal in a restaurant on Essex Street for six cents. But the trick was, where did you get those six cents?"

"Hey, Pinky!"

I was named after the doctor who brought me into this world on Friday, June 3, 1904, in our cold-water walk-up apartment on Orchard Street in Manhattan. Nobody went to the hospital to have babies. You had them in the privacy of your own bedroom, with one of the "Broome Street doctors"—from a nearby branch of the Lying-In Hospital—in attendance. (Friends and neighbors were always around to help, so the doctor wasn't really necessary until the next day or the day after, when you had to give him a name to enter with the Board of Health.)

The Broome Street doctor came back to examine my mother and get my name. My mother had been in America barely a year, and even when she was here much longer, she spoke only a few words of English. After he got through to her what he wanted, she gave him my Hebrew name: Yehoshua Pinchus, which, Biblically speaking, should have been Joshua Phineas in English.

Doctors in those days were just as hurried as immigration officers. What he should have done was have my mother pronounce it and then gone to somebody knowledgeable and said, "Look, this is the name. What is its English translation or nearest English equivalent?"

Instead he made my mother a proposition: "Look, Mrs. Perelmuth, I'm Jewish. I'm not religious, but believe me, I come from a nice family. So you call him in Hebrew whatever you want—the kids'll call him something else anyway—and I'll list him as Jacob Pincus." Pincus was as close as you could come, but when my mother asked why Jacob, he explained, "It's a beautiful Biblical name. In fact, it happens to be *my* first name." Not even my mother could argue with that.

The doctor was right that the kids would call me something else. It was "Hey, Pinky!" this and "Hey, Pinky!" that. But my mother and father called me by the Yiddish diminutive of Pincus: Pinye, which sounds like a fruit drink. And if I did something my father especially liked or enjoyed or appreciated, he would call me Pinyele, the diminutive of a diminutive. With that I knew I was in. For in Yiddish, the more diminutives, the bigger you are.

In my concerts, I love to sing a song called "A Dudele," in which a rabbi expresses such love and affinity for the Lord that he addresses Him not just in the familiar *Du* form, but in the ultimate diminutive: *Dudele.* I always think of how when I pleased my father I was Pinyele.

For the last forty years I've been called Jan. But the name Pinky is a private, treasured thing with me. Pinky was I. I was born Jacob *Pincus* Perelmuth and if someone who knew me before Samuel "Roxy" Rothafel began tinkering with my name calls me Pinky, I have no objection. But if a stranger or a casual acquaintance says, "Hey, Pinky!" that's exactly what I'd like to give him: my pinkie, maybe my thumb, in his eye.

Children of the New World

Many years ago, as most people do eventually, I decided to revisit my birthplace on Orchard Street. With a friend, I came into a long, dark hallway from the bright afternoon sun, and we had taken only three or four steps when I slipped on a banana peel. I didn't go any farther because I knew already it was no longer the same. There would never have been a loose banana peel in any house my mother lived in.

My part of the Lower East Side is now mostly Puerto Rican. In the summer of 1974 I toured the East Coast in a musical version of Leo Rosten's delightful dictionary, *The Joys of Yiddish,* to which the librettist, Arnold B. Horwitt, had added a plot and some observations about "The New Greenhorns," as he called the Puerto Ricans. I had a speech at the end of the play in which I said that on Delancey, Rivington, and Hester Streets, you still find greenhorns. And with this, a Puerto Rican son says to his mother, "And thees ees the place you breeng me from San Juan to leeve in?" with an inflection not very different from that in which the grownups used to say, during my boyhood on Madison Street, "For this I came from Russia?"

Of my youth on the Lower East Side, I say often that "I wouldn't have missed it for the world, but I wouldn't repeat it for a million." The impression you get now—that everybody loved each other and everybody had a wonderful time—is a myth. Life down there was no more peaches and cream for us in those days than it is for the newer greenhorns now.

We knew we weren't rich, although we never thought of ourselves as poor, but sometimes our only consolation was that we knew someone who was worse off. Some people had to put a quarter in the meter to get gaslight, but we were ahead of them because we had the privilege of paying the bill at the end of the month. To keep the meter reading low, though, I did my homework by kerosene lamp, which was the cheapest form of illumination.

In winter we woke up half frozen. We didn't know what steam heat meant. I never lived in a steam-heated apartment until after I was married. My father would get up at five in the morning, throw coals on the stove, and get a fire going. Or if he was running late for his job as head presser in a garment factory, he'd turn on the gas range. My mother would get up with him to serve that chicory they called coffee—or maybe a plate of hot dairy soup, made of rice or meal with milk—and a roll. (An egg was a luxury reserved for Sundays, when you might have a herring, too.)

We had no electricity. Two rooms in our apartment had gas heaters. If you took the gas tip (used for light) out of the chandelier and connected the gas pipe up there, you could bask in the warmth of the little heater. But the gas would wane or sometimes the cat would pull out the pipe; many fires occurred and many lives were lost from gas asphyxiation on the Lower East Side.

There were several respects in which we were rich in comparison to others:

First and foremost, we had a bathroom in the apartment. Others had to use toilets in the hall or outhouses in the yard. Just imagine living on the third or fourth floor with a toilet down in the yard when you had to answer the call of nature on a cold winter day. Or think of toilet-training your kid.

In addition, ours was a relatively modern tenement with stone steps. Most of the tenements on the East Side had wooden steps and were firetraps.

We even had "fireproofing" in the hallways, where the walls were covered halfway up by pressed metal painted brown. If we had a fire, it wouldn't burn as fast as wood alone.

For the holidays of Passover in the spring and Rosh Hashonah in the fall, our parents always wanted us to have something new to wear. Shopping in the stores was out of the question. So we went to the pushcarts and open-air stands of Hester Street, where they sold not just fruits and vegetables, but hats and materials. My mother would buy a "remnant," a piece of cloth big enough for a pair of knickers. It was a great gift: new clothing to wear!

My parents never let us feel we were poor. There was always enough food; they figured out ways to feed us so we didn't need so much. To this day, I love soup at any time of year; even in the best hotel in Paris, a good soup and a piece of bread can be the equivalent of a steak dinner to me. Why? In my childhood, the soup was the meal.

Jewish mothers generally didn't know anything about the value of vegetables. We ate potatoes because they were filling. We ate barley because it was filling. We ate kasha because it was filling. We ate bread because it was filling. We ate potato pancakes and potato pudding because they were thick and full of chicken fat. One or another of these things, they made your meal, many meals.

We never knew what broiled meant. Everything was fried. Steak, lamb chops, chopped meat. All drained of the blood, too, as kosher slaughter prescribes. But fried meat was tasty—and we ate it in any form anytime we could. We'd go downstairs to play a little on a winter evening right after supper. An hour or two in the cold night air, and when we'd go back up, everybody was hungry. There was no refrigerator. If you had an icebox, you used it only in summer. For winter, there were the window sills.

Even though we'd finished supper barely two hours earlier, we'd make a grab for the fried cutlets or fried whatever. By then the chicken fat around them had turned gray. If we could control ourselves, we'd warm them up and dissolve the grease. But most of the time we ate them as they were—cold— or we'd slap each slab between two slices of corn bread and eat the sandwich, grease and all; wash it down with a glass of cold water; eat a piece of fruit; and go to bed. If we forgot the fruit, my mother would race around to our beds and drop an apple or a pear or some grapes down our mouths as if we were slot machines. This was the balanced diet we followed. Nobody I know died from it.

There wasn't anyone you could envy on the Lower East Side. Some people were better off than others, but this was only a question of degree, of privacy and plumbing. Everybody knew what everyone else had—and it was so little better than what you had that you could aspire to it rather than envy it.

On Orchard Street or later on Madison Street, you knew everything about everybody. And you shared with one another. Almost everybody was kosher. So if Mrs. Rabinowitz's child came down and said, "My mother made stuffed cabbage today and she would like you to have some of it," you'd accept it without question. And when the chance came, I'd knock on Mrs. Rabinowitz's door and say, "My mother made meat blintzes today and we thought you'd like to have some." That's how we lived. You learned to share, to live and let live, but most of all you learned to be happy with what you had.

I was my family's first child of the New World. Four years after me (one year after my big brother Mot'l's death) came Michoil (a name that also belongs to one of heaven's angels), later known as Max and now as Mac. A year and a half after Mac came Sender, which is usually an abbreviation for Alexander, but my brother's real name is Sender, as in "Return to Sender." For a while he was called Samuel or Sammy, but now he's Sender again. Four years after Sender (ten years after me) came my sister, Sara. Around 1936, Sara married Richard Tucker, a great tenor who had a great career as an opera singer. Because of family misunderstandings, we were never close.

Perhaps I should say here and now that this is all you're going to hear from me about my sister Sara and her late husband. I could tell you how I took Tucker to his first teacher, Paul Althouse, and encouraged him to study singing. I could tell you how, when Tucker was the cantor in a Passaic, New Jersey, synagogue, I convinced cantorial teacher Zavel Zilberts that two dollars a lesson was the most Tucker could pay him. During World War II, my late brother-in-law was in textiles—selling lining materials to the fur trade —as well as studying singing; it was a hard time to lay hands on supplies to sell, but I helped him find what he needed from some people I knew. I could tell you about that or about how I recommended him as my replacement whenever I could and introduced him to Leopold Spitalny of the NBC Symphony. But then Richard Tucker couldn't tell you his side of the story. So let's just say that we saw each other rarely, only on special family occasions, but even if you're family, it doesn't mean you have to get along—and we didn't. I might add that, when a little-known, but intensely gossiped-about feud between two noted tenors is mentioned, you expect maybe grand opera passions and singing rivalries, not petty family disputes. Well, you're wrong. Maybe it would be kinder to say that with two strong family men, for better or for worse, family is all.

When I became the oldest son, at age three, not only my parents' ambitions, but their frustrations, were focused in me. My mother had always dreamed of playing a musical instrument, but in her little *shtetl* of Horodetz there was nobody who could afford one and nobody who could give lessons —not even a fiddler on the roof. But it was part of my mother's culture that a person should grow up on speaking terms with an instrument. And this was part of what she expected from the New World for her child.

A piano was too expensive for the Perelmuths, even though a piano in the parlor was a status symbol second to none. It meant credit at the grocer's and the landlord calling monthly instead of weekly for the rent because a family with a piano wasn't going to disappear overnight. But we had to settle for a fiddle. Paying for lessons, however, was a luxury we couldn't afford. Fifty cents a lesson? Twice a week? A dollar a week? How were we going to get that kind of money?

My mother had a solution. She opened a private restaurant in our apartment. She charged twenty or twenty-five cents for a five-course meal. Her customers were mostly shopgirls and single men who came recommended; often they were Chasidic Jews wanting good kosher food, and always they were decent people struggling to live on measly salaries, for whom my mother was a godsend. I can't remember a family dinner without at least eight paying guests.

Sometimes one of her regulars would bring a friend. This was good for business, but we weren't a commissary and we had only enough to go around. Besides, the pots were only so large. We could add a little more hot water to the soup, but we didn't want the customers—particularly the new one!— to complain about the portions. So we'd have a family conference in the kitchen and agree not to eat much or any of the meat. Or my father would ask me, "Do you mind giving up a piece of meat today and then you can have a little more soup and an extra piece of corn bread?" He was that rare kind of man who would not only ask a child a question, but also listen to and heed the answer. In this case, the answer was always yes. I didn't feel done out of anything. Corn bread was a treat and so was more soup.

The black-seeded corn bread really was almost as good as we remember it now. The crust was great, but we boys only played with the soft inside part.

To this day, I don't care much for the inside of a roll. But it certainly was filling. The soup was *krupnik*, barley with beans. The rest of the meal would be meat, applesauce or stewed prunes, a piece of cake and a cup of tea. Chicken was a once-a-week luxury—on Friday nights for the beginning of the Sabbath. Otherwise it was only for weddings, bar mitzvahs, and holidays.

After a couple of years of violin lessons, my fiddle teacher came around to the house and told my mother, "You know, I can't teach Pinky any more. I'd like to, but there's nothing more he can learn from me. He needs a better teacher."

My mother asked, "What does a better teacher mean?"

"Someone who knows more than I do. I can recommend someone. His name is H. M. Shapiro. But he's all the way uptown on 110th Street and he'll be more expensive than I am."

H. M. Shapiro cost three dollars a lesson, plus at least a dime for the round-trip carfare. My mother's answer right away was yes, for while she never thought of my making a career or even a living from music, she wanted to promote my cultural development as well as to be able to say to other mothers and their daughters, "Look, he's a refined young man who can play the violin." Thus the only question, once again, was where would the three dollars a week come from? No private restaurant could enable her to clear that much regularly. Three dollars a week meant a fortune back when six cents was a luxury. So my mother took in boarders.

We had a five-room apartment: two bedrooms; a living room, which was called the front room in those days; a dining room; and a kitchen. My father and mother always had the bedroom off the "front." The other bedroom was used by my maternal grandparents, Chashe Freda and Zeyde Berel. Two of us boys slept in the dining room on beds put together from chairs and cushions. The third boy slept in the dining room on a black leather couch called the "lunge" for lounge. There were also a couple of uncles living with us. Boarders meant one or two of us children sleeping near the stoves (coal in the kitchen and a gas heater in the living room) on cushions covered with the kind of feather quilt (we called it *perene*) you still get in Austrian hotels. Then, as now, the feathers often traveled down to one end and you wound up covering yourself with just the linen bag.

Our first boarder, Yeshua, was such a find that we practically ended up paying him to stay with us. He had studied for the rabbinate in Europe; here he worked in a clothing factory. In exchange for teaching us boys Hebrew and Talmud and history, he received his food free and his bed at such a discount that it couldn't pay my way to H. M. Shapiro's violin lessons. Eventually two working-girl boarders moved in. We bought a couple of cots and pulled up more chairs by the stoves—musical chairs, whose purpose was to enable me to make music.

The game of musical chairs that taking in boarders became was nothing compared to the battle of just going crosstown on Madison Street from the Jewish quarter of the Lower East Side to the subway station at Park Row. I had to pass through an Italian, a Greek, and an Irish neighborhood. In each there were older boys who had something to tell you.

Jefferson, Rutgers, Pike, Market, Catherine, Oliver, James: each street meant a different danger. Market to Catherine was Italian, which meant if you ran into a gang (or if just a couple of tough kids picked on you) you had to fight your way through. Oliver to James was Irish territory, where you had every chance of being mugged. From James to New Bowery was a demilitarized zone populated by Greeks, who were content to sit there savoring their coffee and admiring your bruises—but you'd better keep moving.

A mugging in those days was a punch-and-run affair of three kids surrounding you and taking whatever you had. It was better just to turn open your pockets and give them everything; they'd hit you harder if they had to search you. Whatever you had—a piece of string, a penny or two, a pencil, or maybe even an ink pen—wasn't worth losing a tooth for. That's why, to me, the muggings and holdups and attacks one hears about in New York today are nothing new; they've just gathered momentum.

I remember one incident still. At public school I was told I had bad vision and sent to the eye clinic at Gouverneur Hospital to be examined. I needed glasses and came back for a fitting. I had to return once more to collect the glasses. My mother had told me to wait there for her to bring me home.

She was a little late and I grew tired of waiting. Anyway, I'd bump into her on the way home. No sooner had I left the dispensary and walked some two hundred feet when three Irish kids surrounded me and began asking the usual three questions.

"Where ya from?"

They knew the answer—that I was from enemy territory—but my saying "Madison Street" at least marked me as a truthful enemy.

"What're ya doing here?"

The glasses I'd come for were already on my face. I didn't want to call attention to them or they might take them. So I said, "To see a doctor."

They showed no interest in my health, but went on to the third and, for them, crucial question: "Whaddya got?"

As I started to relinquish the top that I had in one pocket and the two pennies I had in another, my new glasses helped me see my mother approaching in the distance. So I didn't offer them the pencil I had sticking out of another pocket. When they asked for that, I refused. By this time my mother —seeing her son surrounded by three bigger boys—had put on steam, and just as they took the pencil from me, she banged their three heads together so hard that they dropped the top and pencil and pennies and ran off with three good headaches to remember us by.

If I had to go west to the subway, I was often tempted to cross all three zones by hooking a ride on the back of a truck. But because my brother had died that way, I'd promised my parents never to do it. Once, however, I broke that promise.

I wasn't at all experienced at it, and besides, I was a fat, near-sighted, not very athletic kid. Other kids just stepped on and stepped off. Not me. I barely managed to jump onto a slow-moving truck, and once I was on, I couldn't lift myself up. As I bounced along with my feet nearly grazing the pavement, I prayed I wouldn't fall off and thought that if only I had listened to my parents, I wouldn't be where I was. There were no traffic lights in those days, so getting on and off had to be done while the truck was in motion. I had to hope for a traffic jam or, at least, my truck slowing down for another truck coming at it—but neither happened, so I couldn't jump off until I was just as far past the subway station as I was when I'd started out for it. And a little more scared and perhaps a little wiser.

During my boyhood the open horse-drawn streetcars on Madison Street were gradually replaced by closed electric trolleys that ran on batteries and were staffed by a motorman and a conductor. This form of transport we called the *Pavolye* line—from a word of Russian-Jewish origin, I think, meaning slow, very slow. It also swayed and was very hot and cost a nickel—three good reasons not to travel via *Pavolye.*

Still, to my father, at the end of a long, hot summer day steaming clothes in the sweatshops, the *Pavolye* was as luxurious as the *Twentieth Century Limited* would be in later times, so sometimes he splurged and invested a nickel in a *Pavolye* ride. More than once, it ended up costing him a hat.

In those days most men wore hats and all Jews who weren't wearing skullcaps (yarmulkes) wore the hard straw hats they called Katies in the summer, felt hats in the fall, winter, and spring. The changeover date was September 15. In the first half of September, the straw hats were inviting targets for the Italian and Irish kids whenever the *Pavolye* passed through their territory, moving so slowly that a boy could run alongside, reach in, grab the hat off your head, punch his hand through it, and throw it back on your head. We called this costly sport of theirs Italian basketball and they called it Jewish basketball. I could understand the early-September urgency with which the Italian kids felt time running out; soon there would be nothing but closed windows and felt hats on the *Pavolye* line. But I wonder if any one of them ever experienced or witnessed the grief and anger and wringing of hands in a Jewish home when the breadwinner brought home a ruined costly straw hat.

The Halloween Pogrom

Halloween was a big event on the Lower East Side. The parade celebrating the occasion was always routed along Madison Street. The marchers would follow the band, with flares blazing and black stockings, filled with ashes or flour, twirling. Every now and then, one or two of the marchers would flail at us bystanders—particularly the kids, who couldn't resist coming to a parade. Halloween to us and our elders had nothing to do with pumpkins and trick-or-treating; it had all the makings of a mini-pogrom.

Eventually some of the bigger Jewish boys got together and said, "We'll fix 'em. Next time they march through here, they won't know what hit them." The following Halloween they warned the rest of us to stay off the streets. Then they went up on the roofs.

When the parade came through, Madison Street was deserted. The marchers hardly had time to notice the small turnout, when down upon them came a rain of bags (and a few bottles) filled with water. Halloween that year was more trick than treat for the marchers. The next year the parade was routed away from Madison Street.

I was eight then, but I learned a lesson from it: You overcome might with might. And that's the lesson of Israel today. We Jews are only as strong as Israel, for the security of the Jewish people all over the world is in the strength of Israel. That's why our responsibility is to help our fellow Jew. Because in an economic crisis, he and then we or else we and then he will be the first sacrifices, the first scapegoats. It was ever thus. The world has pushed us into a corner and limited our rights and opportunities all the time. And pushed into corners, we acquired more knowledge, more education, more money, and now more strength—because we knew these were our only ways out.

King of the Sabbath, Queen of the House

My father was a religious man. He was a good husband. He was active in any community he lived in because he loved his G-d, loved his family, loved his neighbor—and these three qualities alone set him apart from many other men. In all the years I knew him—and he lived to be almost ninety—I never heard my father speak badly about anybody. All he would say was: "Well, he didn't do such a nice thing today; tomorrow maybe he'll do better." But my father wasn't a milquetoast. He was a man. He was also a Talmudic scholar who knew how to reason. When you talk about a great mathematician, you credit him with being a logician because he can figure out the highest equations—in other words, because he has a brain that he uses to think. A man who knows and understands the Talmud is a man of learning, too. In order to reason his way to certain conclusions just from reading the Talmud, he has to have a fine mind. My father was such a man.

There was always a great love affair between my mother and my father. I will tell you one secret of their successful marriage: Both worked so hard that they hadn't time to bicker. Even in her last years, my mother would sigh at how handsome my father was as well as how handsome he had been. He had a beautiful head of white hair to the end. He started out tall. He never shaved, but he never had a long beard—just a little whisker on the skin. It was against Jewish law to shave with a razor blade, so my father used barber's clippers. Other people used a strong-smelling sulfur cream (something like a depilatory). You'd take it off with a celluloid scraper and then you'd be beautifully clean-shaven. But oh, the smell!

In her final months, spent in and out of an oxygen tent, my mother would boast to us: "Look at your papa now. Such a beautiful man. Such a fine head of hair. And oh, Alice, if you had seen him when I first saw him, well, you'd have married him instead of Pinky."

I've said she was jealous of him; he did admire beauty in a woman. If he saw a particularly beautiful woman, he would stop and look her over. If I introduced him to one, he might take her hand in his, as any older gentleman would, and tell her, "You should be well and have good health because you are already so beautiful that is all I could wish you." On second or third meeting, he might place his hand on her arm and give her a kiss on the cheek.

"Papa!" I would exclaim. "Do you realize what you're doing?"

"What's wrong?" he would respond. "Isn't she beautiful?"

"Yes, Papa, she's beautiful. But don't you know what the Talmud says?

Thinking a misdeed is the same as committing it."

"No, my son. This only pertains to good deeds. If you *think* of doing a good deed, then, even if you forget to do it, you get a little credit. Anyway, now I'm doing a good deed."

After my mother died, I would tease him by saying, "Papa, you're cutting your beard thinner these days. You must be looking around for a girlfriend."

"No, no," he'd say. "It just looks more modern."

When I was a boy and my father was in his forties, I wounded him once by calling him an old man. Jokingly, he said, "My son, I can only hope that, G-d willing I'm alive when you are my age, I will remember to ask you what it is like to be an old man." And on my forty-second or forty-third birthday, he took me aside and said, "Tell me, how does it feel to be an old man?"

My father worked hard—leaving the house before six in the morning, Mondays through Fridays, never coming home before seven in the evening except on Fridays, and then often grabbing a bite to eat and running off to evening school for a class in English or Citizenship. He was just about the only man on the block who passed his U.S. Citizenship test on the first try. We had chicken twice that week.

Even after he was promoted to head presser at Schaff & Mandel, and given a five-dollar-a-week raise, our lot was not much easier. I shared in our money worries only when they affected me directly, such as: "How are we going to pay H. M. Shapiro three dollars a week for violin lessons?"

Only once did I get a glimpse of how hard my father worked uptown to pay our way into the New World. I had to deliver an urgent message from my mother about meeting a visiting relative who was sick, and was given directions to the shop, all the way up in the West Thirties. I will never forget how, when I walked in, I saw my father standing in his undershirt and an apron, lifting an eighteen-pound iron with flames shooting out of its big openings and running it across the cloth, taking care it wasn't cut or burned and worrying about each stitch as though it were a work of art, which it was for him. But what I saw was the man who was a king in my house toiling like a slave in hell.

I had to accept, as he accepted, that these were the two worlds he lived in, for when he finally came home each night and particularly on Friday afternoon, he took over from my mother as boss of the family to become king of the Sabbath. At the synagogue, his was an eloquent and influential voice that gave someone an honor at morning services or questioned why one man was sitting by the eastern wall and another wasn't.

In my childhood, I took lickings from my father that I felt were a little out of line, but I blamed them on my mother. By exercising her motherly and womanly powers, she could convince him I deserved punishment. Maybe she was right in many cases, but I felt there could have been less violent solutions.

She always picked the wrong time for these scenes: the Sabbath, his only day of rest. It would happen soon after the big Friday-night dinner of gefilte fish; noodle soup; sweet carrot *tsimmes* (a side dish of cooked vegetables and fruits); chicken; potato or noodle *kugel; kishke;* more challah than one should eat, and for dessert, cakes or *mandelbrot* with tea. After a strenuous week of work, at peace with the world and his family, with no boss breathing down his neck, feeling now like the Sabbath king, he would let my mother clear the table, sit down, and start telling him stories about me.

As truthful as the stories were ("He didn't want to go to *cheder,*" as Hebrew school was called), as justified as the stories were ("He didn't want to go to choir practice"), as exaggerated as some of the stories were ("He never practices the fiddle at all"), it was terrible for me to see her take this man on his day of rest and blow him up and make him angry because his wife, whom he loved, had complaints—which, once made, had to be acted upon. But when else could she do this? When he'd finally come home at night, he could only think about eating, relaxing a little, and going to bed. So the Sabbath was a day of judgment for me.

By the weekend I would have forgotten a little incident that happened on Tuesday. Not my mother. There would be big grievances ("I sent him out to buy a glass of sour cream and he ate it with a roll on the way home") and little grievances ("But when I asked him to go buy another he said he wasn't hungry") from the whole week. It was easy to be a prosecutor when you'd stored up grievances that long, but hard to be a defendant when you didn't even remember the alleged offenses.

My father would squirm a bit and say to her, "So what do you think?" Sometimes, if he found himself taking my side a little, he'd talk to her in Russian, which my brothers and I didn't understand, instead of our everyday Yiddish. He was a very just man, but he would never be so disloyal as to disagree with her in front of us. And once she had her grievances off her chest, this same steaming mother who insisted on justice being done would realize what a disturbance she had caused and try to find a way out for him and for us. Righteous though she felt, she really didn't want to see me take a licking. But my father was already committed to punishment. Sometimes, if I was lucky, he would just slap me across the bottom and that would be that.

More often, though, my mother had carried it so far that he'd start removing his belt. The punishment that followed was called *shmeisn* and my father would try to mitigate it by saying, "If you'll stretch out across my knees and pull down your trousers yourself, my son, then I'll only give you three *shmits*" (strokes of the strap; five if it was a major offense, such as yelling at my mother). My father was a powerful man and I know now that he went gently with me, but even the softest *shmeis* was a pain to bear when you had to pull down your pants and take it from your father.

Sometimes the punishment exceeded the crime—and once or twice I was absolutely innocent. But I never gave him trouble, and somehow never resented him—only my mother's role in stirring up a sour-cream storm.

When someone complains about you all the time, familiarity breeds familiarity. But she felt a great burden of moral responsibility, even about our wanting to skip Hebrew school. According to the Talmud, when things go wrong religiously with children, the mother is the most to blame, since she is responsible for their religious education. In fact, the mother is responsible for everything in the home, where the father is really the boss only on Sabbaths. My father gave her whatever he earned, first deducting his daily expenses. Mother ran the home. She was the force who brought everybody into line. It was one hell of an executive job.

Because of the job she did and the power she had, as well as the knowledge that her man loved and respected her, she was always able to get to him and tell him what he had to do to me. But once the object of her vengeance lay before her—with bottom bared—she would say to my father in Russian, "Go easy on him." My brothers and I resented these second interventions even more than the first. Children want a fair trial.

Sender and Mac didn't always take their punishment lying down, the way I did. Once some neighbors complained about their behavior. My father said, "I want to talk to both of you," but they ran away. We were in the dining room. My father made a grab at them, but missed. These little brothers of mine darted past me, around the dining table, over the black leather "lunge," turned left into the kitchen, and then ran out the door. With that, my mother hauled off at *me!* Her backhand swing knocked my glasses to the floor. Crying while I groped for them on my hands and knees, I said to her, "Why did you hit me?"

"You should have stopped them!" she shouted. "By not stopping them, you embarrassed Papa."

But I had been immobilized by my own astonishment at such injustice. And I felt she was wrong. I also knew that she had mistreated me because I was the only one in reach. Even if I hadn't been paralyzed by shock, however, I hope I wouldn't have grabbed my brothers and turned them in for the licking they eventually got when my father next laid hands on them (a dozen *shmits* apiece). If I had, we might never have stayed friends in later life.

I was very angry with my mother and though I did whatever she asked me to do, I didn't speak to her for a couple of days.

My mother was a wonderful woman with love in her heart, but she had a temper and a powerful way of telling you off; in other words, she was very much like me when something irks me. Once she'd told you off, though, she'd say, "And now that we've cleared this up, don't be angry. It's the truth and I had to tell you what I think. Now let's be friends."

I used to postpone practicing the violin as long as I could, but never beyond dusk, because then we would have to use the gas lights for me to see by. Like any pupil who had to practice half an hour, I was always very interested in the time. There was no clock in the "front" room, where I practiced, but there was a small alarm clock on the icebox in the adjacent dining room. Sometimes, in the interest of seeing how much time I had left, I would inch away from my music stand toward the dining room, improvising a melody as I went so my mother, working in the kitchen, wouldn't notice as long as she heard sound. One evening I was having trouble enough seeing the clock when suddenly there was a *crack!* and the bow broke in my hand. I had bumped into the icebox. Hearing the music stop, my mother came running—and found me holding the short end of a shattered stick.

"What happened?" she asked.

"I don't know," I said half-truthfully, for I was still figuring out what had happened. She figured it out, too, and for breaking a two-dollar bow I received three *shmits* from my father that same night and promised never to watch the clock again.

During my boyhood, the mantel (we pronounced it *mental*) came into fashion on the Lower East Side: a forerunner of fluorescent lighting for people like us, who didn't even have electricity. The mantel, which cost a dime, was a white fibrous cuplike shield that covered the gas jets, and it gave fancier and brighter illumination than the electric lights the rich folk up in Harlem were buying.

A time came when I was practicing my violin and wondering as usual how many more minutes I had. Despite my promise, I inched away from my music, flourishing bow and instrument aloft as a reminder not to bump into the icebox. I never got that far. As I squinted to see what time it was, everything went black. I didn't faint, but when I could see again, my bow was sticking through the shattered mantel and my mother was screaming with fright that turned to rage.

For breaking a ten-cent mantel: six *shmits.*

My mother's mother, Chashe Freda Posner, lived with us and had more
to do with my upbringing in some ways than my mother did. Chashe Freda
never lived to witness the fruition of her effort to promote me into manhood,
for my bar mitzvah was in June 1917, and she died on Election Day, 1916.

If I wanted something I was afraid to ask for or if I just needed to
confide, I would go first to my grandma. And there was a little rivalry
between my mother and Chashe Freda because of this closeness.

She was a little old lady, barely five feet tall, with no more than three
words of English in her vocabulary. Once she gave me an assignment to teach
her English. I sat down with her and tried to teach her the word for horse
(*ferd* in Yiddish). But I made the mistake of beginning: *"Bubbe* [Grandma],
do you know what a *ferd* is?"

She said, "Who doesn't know what a *ferd* is?"

And I said, "Well, in English—"

But she interrupted: "Don't go any further. If you start out by asking
me if I know what a *ferd* is, well, better you don't teach me."

That ended my career as an educator, although my children have had
occasional teachers who've made the same mistake I made with Chashe
Freda: I insulted her intelligence. What I should have said was: *"Bubbe, ferd*
in Yiddish is 'horse' in English." Instead I asked her if she knew something
I knew she knew.

She was a lovely, wonderful human being—the little light of my grandfather Berel's life. For each of her kids and her kids' kids, she always had
something special and personal to say. And she was addressed only as Chashe
Freda, not just Chashe or Freda. My older daughter, Joy, is named in her
memory. Jews name children only after departed relatives, not living ones
—which is why there are so few Jewish Jrs. My daughter Joy has one of those
rare names that mean what they say in several languages. For her Hebrew
name, Freda, is derived from *frayd,* the Yiddish word for "joy" (just as
Sigmund's last name came from *Freude,* the German word for "joy"). After
I met Alice and learned that one of her Hebrew names was Chashe, I knew
how right I had been to fall in love with her.

On Thanksgiving night, 1914, when I was eleven, I bumped into my
father on the street. He was coming back from *shul* and feeling pretty good
because he had the day off, so he handed me a nickel, thinking I would spend
it on a charlotte russe or some other sweet. Just in case, though, since it was
already dark, he said, "But don't go to the movies with it tonight."

This put into my head an idea that hadn't been there—particularly since
I'd already seen the silent film at our regular movie house on Rutgers Street.
But my friend Izzy Trakel had an idea: "Let's go to the movies on Grand

Street"—at the Windsor Theatre, outside our usual turf. They charged a nickel for adults and kids two for five.

In those days, if you went in after the picture had started, they gave you a "late check." When the movie was over, a man would walk up and down the aisles calling out, "All over! All over! Side way out! Only those having late checks may remain." Then he'd go around collecting the late checks.

We arrived five minutes after the movie started, so we got late checks. Then we saw the movie all the way through again—and liked it so much that toward the end, we moved off to a dark corner where we wouldn't be noticed. We saw the movie three times, and might have seen it four if he hadn't announced, "The last show is over. Side ways out."

"What time is it?" I asked Izzy.

"I don't know," he said, "but I think they finish at midnight."

When we rushed outside, Grand Street—which we knew in the evening hours as the brilliantly lit Great White Way of the Lower East Side—was dark, dark, dark. We ran all the way home, six or seven blocks, with me huffing and puffing as I screamed at Izzy that I'd never forgive him. On the last lap of our run, he went his way and I went mine.

Outside my house, people were standing around—which was not usual past midnight. One of them was my Uncle Abe Posner, who lived with us. As soon as he saw me, he rushed me upstairs to the second floor, saying, "Where were you? Oy, are they worried!"

The door of our apartment opened and there was my little grandmother, Chashe Freda, who embraced me and whispered in Yiddish, "What did you do?"

Before I could whisper the truth, my mother came out, whispering loudly, *"Where were you?"* dramatizing the situation even more than usual. My grandmother kept saying to her, *"Sha, sha.* Don't speak so loud. You can talk it over tomorrow." But my mother carried on and on until she woke my father, who came out in his flannel underwear. Despite his anxiety, he had gone to bed—because he had to be up at 5 A.M., and besides, he rather suspected I was out on some kind of spree with the five cents he'd given me. "Oh, you're here. Good," he said matter-of-factly, trying not to lose his fine edge of sleep.

But my mother put him on the spot: *"Give it to him!* Ask him where he was! What kind of a son keeps his father up to all hours of the night?" And so my father had to ask me.

Since he had said "No movies," I had what I thought was a better answer for him: "Nowheres."

"What kind of nowheres? You went somewheres! And you couldn't have been in the Rutgers movies because we went looking for you in the Rutgers movies. You weren't arrested in the police stations on Madison Street and Clinton Street because we went to both station houses to find out."

My mother said, "We thought you were lost! We thought you were kidnapped! G-d forbid!"

My father said, "Who knows what we thought? But you must have an answer!"

"Nowheres," I said.

My grandma tried to make us all go to bed, but my father said no—not with my mother standing there egging him on, warming things up. Finally, when I saw that none of us would get any sleep if I didn't own up, I confessed: "I went to the movies."

"You went to the movies? I told you not to go to the movies. Besides, you weren't at the movies."

"I wasn't at the Rutgers movies. I was at the Windsor on Grand Street."

"Grand Street!" my father exclaimed. *"Grand Street!"* my mother shouted. Even my grandma gasped, "Grand Street!" and covered her mouth at what she'd just heard herself say. For Grand Street was out of bounds, particularly for the oldest surviving son, who was watched like a diamond ever since the death of his big brother. My family didn't even like me to cross the street an extra time and here I'd gone seven blocks to Grand Street and seven blocks back in the middle of the night.

Then and there, my father held night court: "He's got to be punished now."

"Punish him tomorrow," my grandma suggested. "Go to bed now."

But my father said, "No! No!" and my mother said, "You've got to do it now! He's got to know!"

"He knows," my grandmother pleaded. "And if he doesn't, he can find out tomorrow. Please go to bed, everybody."

But my mother said, *"After you told him not to go to the movies, he goes all the way to Grand Street to see a movie!"* So my father went for the strap. As soon as my mother saw what she'd forced upon us, she began telling him in Russian to go easy on me, don't hurt me, try not to touch me. But by now he had to go through with his end of it—and I didn't want him to lose face either, so I quickly pulled down my pants and practically jumped across his knees so he could administer justice. I took five or six *shmits* from him and lost my movie-going privileges for six months. After that, I found I'd had enough of movies; I didn't see another one for two or three years. Even today I don't go much to the movies. But wouldn't you know that I'd have a son who's a successful movie director. And every time I go to see one of Larry's movies, I still remember where I sit.

People sometimes wonder at how many successes came out of the Lower East Side—and ask me why. I think the marvelous part of those years was the discipline we were taught. Our parents ruled with iron hands *and* velvet gloves. You knew the rules and you knew the penalties if you offended your parents or strangers or custom. And you were never promised a licking that you didn't get if you deserved it!

This kind of discipline helped the development of most of us. Of course, there were children brought up under the same circumstances on the Lower East Side who didn't profit as much. Perhaps their parents didn't earn their respect or didn't know how to reach their children. Even then, even there, yelling at a kid was not enough. Much of the time you have to be good to a child so that he or she will learn how to behave through goodness, not just from fear of punishment.

I Was in Love with Charlotte Russe

Charlotte russe is a sponge cake with thick whipped cream on top. She used to cost two cents, but Horton's charlotte russe cost three cents, then a nickel, and even later six cents. But Horton's was worth the difference. The cake stayed fresher for some reason and the cream seldom went sour. I bought mine at Kaplan's candy store, where I sometimes also stole an apple or a caramel when nobody was looking. *Carmels,* kids called them then, as now —*carmels* that could rip your teeth out or find your cavities faster than any dentist. And halvah—we called it *halavah*—that crumbled in your mouth. There were licorice sticks and chocolate-covered cherries, which were harder to steal, but it was impossible to steal a charlotte russe—and I loved charlotte russe.

I never got sick on candy, but once I got sick on charlotte russe. My mother arranged that. She got tired of hearing me say, "I wanna charlotte russe" and "Can I have another charlotte russe?" so she decided to cure me. Horton's was having a special sale and she bought me a half dozen. Then she tried to make me eat them all. When I was barely halfway through, I got good and sick and gave it all back in the toilet.

I didn't have charlotte russe again for at least a week. From then on I took her in moderation—and I'd love to do it again now, just once, for old time's sake. Not that I'd sell my own mother for it. But I've used my mother's psychology on my own kids: giving them an overdose of cake or candy or whatever else they craved too much. I wouldn't try it with sex, though.

I once almost had an argument with my father-in-law about how to

handle a child's demands. My son, Larry, was a fussy little kid. If we went
to a restaurant and he had to go to the bathroom, one of us would have to
take him somewhere else. He wouldn't use the johns in restaurants because
he couldn't stand the smell of disinfectant. Once in a restaurant on Fordham
Road in the Bronx, Larry had to go, but refused to. My father-in-law found
a cab, took him home (we lived six blocks away, on the Grand Concourse,
at the time), and came back in the same cab. I said to my father-in-law, "I
wouldn't have done that. I wouldn't have given in to the kid. I'd make him
use the rest room here and like it."

"That's why you're a father and I'm a grandfather."

Eventually, free from pressure, Larry learned to use, if not like, public
toilets. Recently he and I were having dinner in a California restaurant.
Larry, who's now in his forties, excused himself to go to the john. And I said
to him, "Don't you want me to call you a cab?"

Larceny in Our Hearts and Hub Caps

We're all born thieves. If we weren't born to steal and commit crimes, we
wouldn't need an Eighth Commandment. Not only did I steal from Kaplan's
candy store; I stole from my own father. At night he ran a cloakroom
concession at a banquet hall (as if he didn't have enough to do in the factory;
but he wanted better things) and he had a habit of hanging his vest on the
back of his bedroom door when he went to bed at midnight.

Once, passing by his vest in the grip of a need for an extra piece of candy
or a charlotte russe, I brushed up against it and heard a jingle of coins. Sure
enough, there was a little change in the pocket. And sure enough, I helped
myself to it. It amounted to a little more than a quarter, which in those days
was a big fortune for a boy of ten or eleven.

And a small fortune for my parents. With them, every cent counted—
and they must have compared notes and spotted a shortage. That evening my
father started out gently: "When I walk around, I feel as if I've lost weight.
I feel twenty-eight cents lighter."

I must have looked heavier from chocolate-covered cherries and charlotte russes, because he ignored my brothers and turned to me: "Did you or
did you not take money from my vest pocket?"

I was a thief, but I wouldn't lie to a man as good as my father—
particularly when cornered. So I said, "Yes."

Having confirmed his worst suspicion, I stood shamed and he stood
thunderstruck that a son of his should steal from *anybody*. I waited for the

heavens to drop on my head. A little lower down, however, I got the licking of my life: fifteen *shmits* and a reminder that a worse fate awaited me if I ever stole again because I had broken not only the Eighth ("Thou shalt not steal") but also the Fifth Commandment ("Honor thy father"). Those fifteen *shmits* must have hurt my father even more than they hurt me, for the idea of a son of his wanting something so badly he should break two Commandments went against his concept of the nature of human beings. It was worse than Original Sin, and the beast was in his own family!

The fear alone that this experience instilled in me was marvelous. I experienced crime and punishment at an early age and my crime wave ended before I was even bar mitzvahed.

Still, we all have larceny in our hearts—and what some men do for fifty cents only shows the mean and petty nature of their souls. I suspect they weren't lucky enough to have been caught and punished early.

On the other hand, as I've learned from experience, not only the earth is round. Life comes full circle—though never the same way, never too neatly. Unbeknown to me, when I was on tour trying to support my family, my son Larry as a teen-ager was stealing hub caps.

Alice Peerce: *In 1945, Larry was fourteen or fifteen and running around with some kids whose parents I knew. This was in New Rochelle and Jan was on tour. We couldn't afford to go on the road together in those days; somebody always had to be home with the kids.*

I was sitting home very calmly one night, with both our little girls sleeping and Larry out somewhere with one of his friends. The boy's father, a friend of Jan's, called me on the phone around nine o'clock and said, "Alice, I'm calling from the police station."

I figured the man was in some kind of trouble. "What's the matter?"

"Your son was arrested with my son."

"What are you talking about?"

"They were stealing hub caps. And they were with a girl." I didn't know what to say, but fortunately he had all the answers. "Don't panic, Alice. I'll take care of it; it won't even get on the blotter."

Half an hour later, this big six-foot bulk walked into the house and I did the first thing a mother does: I started to cry. After the first burst of tears was out, I asked him, "What have you done? Do you realize what you've done?" And when the bulk just hung his head down, I gave him a hard slap on the face.

His head hung lower—so low I couldn't see whether there were tears. Then I gave him a whole lecture on how awful and inconsiderate he was; how his father was working so long and hard and far away to look after us. Larry was contrite, miserable, unhappy—no doubt about it. Then my brothers, Walter and Sidney Kaye, arrived. I'd phoned them right after getting the news from the police station. Sidney walked in, making more noise than I do, which is plenty. "Keep calm! Keep calm!" he said. "Everybody steals a little bit. All kids do wrong when they're kids and they all get over it, Alice, they all get over it. He'll never do it again. Tell her you'll never do it again."

"I'll never do it again," Larry told me.

They were protecting Larry, of course, from me. Walter was only ten when he got to be Larry's uncle and Sidney had baby-sat Larry, too. And then I felt I had to protect Larry from Jan. I didn't tell Jan about it for another five or six years. By then Larry was at Chapel Hill and had been on the dean's list. But even then, bursting with pride, I hadn't told Jan about the hub caps. Now we were in Mexico for the first time. Jan and I were walking one night and having our usual discussion about whether he or I did this right or that right and I said, "Listen, Jan, you don't know what it means to bring up children."

Jan said, "I don't know how to bring up children? After bringing up three of them?"

I said, "You didn't bring them up. I brought them up all alone. What would you do if I told you your son stole hub caps?"

"You're out of your mind, Alice!"

"But he did, Jan." And I told him the whole story. The good thing that happened to Larry was that he was caught early and terrified and really smashed, not only by my hitting him, but from the way I crumpled and cried right before his eyes. And I'm glad I had the sense to hit him. Oh, boy, did I give him a sock!

I don't know whether Alice did the right thing by keeping it a secret from me for so many years. But I might not have understood then. I'm not absolutely sure I understand now. I mean, why steal hub caps? They were in vogue in suburbia among kids who could have afforded to buy not just the tires, but the cars that went with them. There was so much more reward in stealing a few coins. Twenty-eight cents, after all, was ready cash.

On Keeping Clean

I take pride in my people because we learned what we were taught. On the Lower East Side, the Jewish press educated us. We had five or six of our own daily newspapers in New York—the *Jewish Daily Forward*, the *Wahrheit, Tag, Jewish Morning Journal, Tageblatt.* Nowadays all New York doesn't have six dailies that I know of, Jewish, Spanish, English, or otherwise.

Our press took the lead in shaping our people's way of life here. But politely. They followed the Yiddish practice of "criticize the daughter when you mean the daughter-in-law." They wrote this way: "Not all of us have learned the first lesson of cleanliness—the bath is important. If you don't have a bathtub, here's how to use a washtub most efficiently. . . . If you don't have a washtub, here's how you can bathe all your body, a little at a time, with just a sink. . . . And if you don't even have that, here's a list of public baths."

Some of these baths are still in operation; at least, the last time I looked there was still one in business on Rutgers Place. The City of New York provided these buildings so that you wouldn't become (or feel like) a charity case. For a couple cents, you were given a towel and a little square of soap. You could stay in the shower as long as you wanted: the longer the better. And we were directed there, attracted there, educated there just by the emphasis in the press and by lecturers who told us to go once a week or once every two weeks—it's important!

I can't say that our parents and grandparents came to America well informed on the proper way to hold a knife and fork, or how to use a napkin, or even with views on which was better, knife in right or left hand. But the press taught our elders table manners. And we, as children, learned to imitate.

Years later, in Israel, I met a radio journalist named Chana Barli and I asked her what beat she covered. She replied a little sheepishly, "You may laugh, but I lecture on table manners, sanitation, how to set a table, how to prepare food, how to use a napkin instead of your sleeve to wipe gravy off your chin." She started to explain how refugees with different customs arrive from all over the world, how in those days almost all a Yemenite Jew knew about sanitation was that once a month a woman has to go to the *mikva* (ritual bath), but actual bathing was foreign to him.

Just as she feared, I began to laugh out loud. Then I explained I was laughing not because it sounded strange, but because it sounded so familiar.

The woman began to laugh, too. "Where do you think I learned what I'm teaching?" she asked me. "I came from Poland to America years before I went to Israel. I was young and I appreciated the guidance the newspapers and lecturers gave us. When I moved to Israel I felt the same need—but this time to teach, for the only way you can acquire habits is by exposure and teaching."

Back on the Lower East Side in my boyhood, the elders of my father's *shul* decided that to *chrrracke* (a succinctly guttural Yiddish word for hawking phlegm) on the floor was not in keeping with modern sanitation in the New World, so they installed spittoons. The first time one of the congregation's regular *chrrrackers* was confronted by the cuspidors, he cried out, "What are you trying to make of this place? A Reform synagogue?"

Moonlighting on Sunday Mornings

To help support his family, my father took on extra jobs. One of them, which lasted several years, was to sell women's blouses—of material called Georgette and crepe de Chine—which a jobber gave him "on memo." (This was how they said "on consignment" then; it meant Papa could return any he didn't sell.) There was an open-air market on Water Street. Every Sunday morning my father would awaken my brothers and myself around four-thirty so we could get there early and pick out a good spot. As Sender and Mac and I grew older and learned the blouse business, he would spread us around at different strategic spots. But he would check up on us from time to time.

My father believed experience was the best teacher. One cold Sunday (they always seemed cold on the Lower East Side), while I was trying to make my first sale of the day, a bunch of uptown women engaged me in conversation, haggling and bargaining, while one of them slipped a blouse out of its box and made off with it. My father happened to see her, but he let her get away with it.

"No sale," I said to him with a shrug when the ladies had left.

"But there's an empty box."

When I saw this, I said, "One of them must have stolen it!"

"Yes," he said. "I saw the one in green take it."

"You saw it? Why didn't you stop it?"

"Because you had to learn your lesson. *Always watch your stock.*" To this day, I choke up when I remember how this struggling, hard-pressed man was willing to take the loss so I should gain a little wisdom.

Only when the market was over, around 9:30 or 10 A.M., did we go home to eat our first food of the day: a big Sunday breakfast of pancake-like omelets called *feinkochen;* potatoes boiled in their jackets; and herring bought from the barrel. Today, in the fancy stores like Zabar's and Barney Greengrass, some of these things are called "Appetizing," which they certainly were when we brought our appetites back from a Sunday morning of work on Water Street.

Camp Felicia

Educational Alliance, University Settlement, Riis House, and, in my case, Madison House (an arm of the Ethical Culture movement) took us kids off the streets and gave us things to do: not just sports, but poetry sessions, playlets, and a chance to escape the city for a week or two in the summer. Madison House used to arrange two weeks every summer for me at their Camp Felicia in Mountainville, New York. And—as with the public baths— they charged a very nominal sum; paying was important, not only because you didn't feel you were on welfare, but also because then you could complain when you didn't feel you got your money's worth. Psychiatry today operates on the same premise; with some, it may be the only premise.

My two weeks at Camp Felicia cost my folks $1.25. This prodigious sum covered not only two weeks' food, but train fare, the ferryboat to and from the Jersey side of Manhattan, and even the trolley to and from the Jersey ferry: no hidden extras or service charges. But the time came when, suddenly one summer, they raised the price to $1.50. All of us boys in the neighborhood went on strike. We didn't sign up for summer camp. We didn't go to our daily activities in the neighborhood. And we won. Madison House backed down—and I think the man in charge, a great man named William Howard Bradstreet, even took pride in us for our spunk.

I won my first singing prize at Camp Felicia. I sang a ballad called "Underneath the Stars," with a catchy lyric that went: "Jack-o'-lantern in the lilac tree dances," which is not the easiest to sing. I won a box of candy. If you want to know why I was on the heavy side for a long time, it's because I started out singing not for my supper, but for my dessert.

I went to Camp Felicia until I was eleven. After that, I had to earn a living in the summer. My mother's favorite saying when we acted silly was: "Take off your baby shoes!" Now she addressed it to me as a way of life.

A cousin of ours was a partner in a metal-spinning factory that made brass and copper umbrella stands, ashtrays, and cigarette-and-cigar holders. I worked there as a nine-dollar-a-week errand boy and between deliveries I collected little pieces of tin and stuck them into a press in which, every time I stepped on the lever, a form came down and hammered the tin into the shape of a cigar holder for an ashtray. Later somebody would lacquer and polish it. I was no metal-pedal-pusher, so I sat there daydreaming or humming a song. Every now and then I'd forget to take my finger out of the machine, so it would get hammered a little—almost into a cigar holder. By the end of summer, I was running out of fingers and was literally all thumbs.

The following summer I lost three jobs. The first was for a tubby little guy on Seventeenth Street and Union Square named S. Klein. He gave me a wheelbarrow and I had to deliver cotton trimmings, canvas, and white binding tape for blouses. Every time I left with his wheelbarrow, S. Klein would wave a pudgy finger at me and say, "You be careful nothing is stolen." How could I? I had to leave the wheelbarrow, with the rest of the goods unwatched, outside any office building or factory I went into. Luckily, nothing was taken. But I did tend to come late and dawdle over candy on my errands, so after two weeks S. Klein fired me. He was very nice about it. (To this day, I've wondered whether he was connected with S. Klein on the Square, the big Fourteenth Street department store.)

I trudged homeward slowly and after an hour's walking found myself on Houston Street, looking at a sign: "BOY WANTED." It was a pants factory. The owner said, "You look like a nice boy," and introduced me to the presser, who was not a nice man. My job was to turn the trousers inside out for him. Life didn't depend on this for me and I could think of more pleasant places than a sweatshop in summer, so every now and then I handed him some pants right side up instead of inside out. Then I would catch hell from him and the owner. Or when I daydreamed and he had a backlog of *only* ten trousers, he would shout at me, "More! More! Faster! Faster! You'll never be anything. You've gotta work hard. Look at *me!*" It was a pretty small operation and I had already seen my father working harder and better with the same heavy iron at *his* sweatshop, so I looked and I laughed. For this and lateness, I was fired after four weeks.

I wandered aimlessly over to the West Side to the Breakstone Dairy Company, king of cottage cheese, sour cream, and butter. I was interviewed by a wicked witch who was called the head bookkeeper. Here I got my best-paying (twelve dollars) and best job yet: recording the gallons of milk delivered by farmers. It was indoor paper work, no lifting, with only the occasional strain of a trip to the bank. There was just one trouble: employees were expected to work a five-and-a-half-day week, but my family would never have allowed me to work on the Sabbath.

The first Saturday morning, I disguised my voice and called in to say, "Dis is Pinky Poilmoot's uncle. Pinky's sick wid a bad cold and can't go to woik today." When I arrived on Monday, even the wicked witch was solicitous. "I'm feeling much better," I told her. My pay was docked for having missed half a day.

The second Saturday, "my grandmother got sick," so I couldn't come in. The wicked witch didn't ask about her health on Monday, but docked me again.

The third Saturday, I had to "go to Long Branch with my father." Long Branch had a few Jewish hotels, which gave her a clue, because when I appeared on Monday, she said, "We know what you are!" She was Jewish, too, but I said nothing, so she went on: "You don't work on *Shabbas!* Why didn't you tell us? We never would have hired you."

"That's why I didn't tell you."

And that's also why I was fired.

I was booked a couple of winters ago with Dick Gregory for a performance in Lincoln Center to benefit the Neighborhood Settlement House. At the rehearsal, one of the society ladies running the show asked if I'd sing a number with a choir of kids. They trotted out a group of kids of all colors, neatly dressed. I admired the way they looked and behaved and the lady running the show told me the concert was to raise money to send these "underprivileged children from depressed neighborhoods for two or three weeks to a place you never heard of, Mr. Peerce."

"Try me," I said.

"Camp Felicia."

"Felicia? In Orange County? In Mountainville, New York?"

"Why, yes. Whom do you know there?"

"I used to know *me* there. That's where the Madison House used to send me." So first she had to tell the kids and then, at the show, I had to tell the audience. "Little did I know when I was nine, ten years old and singing in the Camp Felicia chorus that one day I'd be on the stage in a Lincoln Center telling you what Camp Felicia did for me and what you should do for Camp Felicia. Jan Peerce and a lot of others came from Felicia—and from this camp others will come." When those kids and I sang "You'll Never Walk Alone," the audience was very moved and Dick Gregory came over and embraced me.

I was never much of an athlete. I wasn't even good at chinning—and I had more than one chin. In the fifty-yard dash, I couldn't even make the distance, let alone time. But the Public School Athletic League (P.S.A.L.) used to have an annual fitness competition where your total points, if you passed, earned you a bronze or bronze-and-silver button. I was very envious of all my friends wearing those beautiful buttons. All the kids at Madison House wore them. So I approached Murray Berger, an athletic kid who lived on my block, and asked if he had any bronze buttons he could spare. He sneered, but he did have a bronze-and-silver button he was willing to sell for a dime.

The minute I wore it to Madison House, the other boys spotted it and nobody for a minute believed I'd won it. "Where'd you steal it?"

"How much did you pay for it?" I never wore it around the Lower East Side again.

The only place it was safe for me to wear my P.S.A.L. button was up in Harlem, where there was a substantial Jewish community between Fifth and Lenox Avenues, from 110th to 126th Streets. Music was the means that took me to Harlem several times a week. Even before I started fiddle lessons up there with H. M. Shapiro, I sang for seventy-five cents on the Sabbath in a synagogue on 118th Street. I loved to sing, but to me the voice, even more than the violin, was an instrument of pleasure.

First recognition as a singer came to me in my father's synagogue, the Horodetzer Shul (founded by people from my mother's *shtetl*), on Henry and Clinton Streets. Their very devout cantor used to hear me singing along with the congregation, and when I was nine, he invited me to sing with his choir of three: all members of his family. This in itself was an honor, but a greater honor was soon to come.

For the Jewish New Year, I was assigned a small but important alto solo —the part that says that from the earth we came and to the earth we return. When it was over, *the* elder of the synagogue, Reb Shebsl, left his seat of honor by the eastern wall and came to me where I was standing at the altar. He kissed me on both cheeks. This would be special on any day of the year, but on Rosh Hashonah, for an elder to kiss a choirboy! I still remember it, but it made an even greater impression on my father. At my debuts in Town Hall and the Met, upon any important triumph or honor, he always reminded me of "that Rosh Hashonah when Reb Shebsl kissed you on both cheeks in front of the entire congregation."

On the recommendation of our cantor, I was hired for the Harlem choir. The cantor there had a very good voice, but he wasn't what I would call a great musician. He was musical by instinct, wonderful at chanting, at express-ing emotions, at hitting and even milking every high note. But he couldn't really read music much—despite a key he wore that meant he had graduated from the St. Petersburg Conservatory.

One Saturday we were singing a duet, when he got lost, sang a wrong passage, and after a few bars of silence rejoined me. I'd plowed onward, but being a diligent, dedicated alto, I was as ashamed as if the heavens had fallen in on me. Later, when we went downstairs to the vestry rooms—to nibble on challah and cake my mother had sent with me—I was still mad. And fingering my unearned P.S.A.L. button, I actually had the nerve to say to that cantor, "This key that you're wearing—where did you buy it?"

The Cantorial Art

In Judaism, the possession of a sweet voice is regarded as a "heavenly gift" that belongs in the synagogue. And it was in the *shuls* of Eastern Europe that cantorial music—whose roots lie in both Oriental sound and Western harmony—flowered and flourished and spread the names of its singers far beyond the ghettos and *shtetls*. After Franz Liszt went to hear a famous cantor sing in Vienna, he wrote: "Seldom were we so deeply stirred by emotion as on that evening, so shaken that our soul entirely surrendered to . . . participation in the service."

Transplanted to America in the same wave of immigration that washed my parents and my wife's onto these shores, the cantorial art thrived here as never before. One of the great cantors of my time, Yossele Rosenblatt, was once offered one thousand dollars a performance to sing with the Chicago Opera Company, but he declined because he felt the life of an opera singer was not compatible with his role in the synagogue. On the Lower East Side, people argued with great intensity about the relative merits of Yossele Rosenblatt and the cantor Zawel Kwartin. (Evelyn Lear, who worked with me briefly in the Bach Aria Group and later became the great Lulu of our time to Alban Berg buffs, is Kwartin's granddaughter. So she comes by her musical career rightfully.)

My father himself had enough sweetness in his voice to emit a cantorial sound when he prayed. At our little synagogue, he officiated for seven or eight years after the cantor died. The congregation paid him a token sum, but he would then contribute double his fee to the synagogue's charitable or old-age funds. When I was eighteen, I joined my father's synagogue because he told me, "You're at the age when you ought to join," and I said, "If you say so, I'll do it." "It would please me if you'd stay with it," he added —so I have, by maintaining my membership, making an occasional contribution, and paying an occasional visit there. Now and then, someone comes backstage after a concert and says, "Your father and mine sat together there at the eastern wall. What a sweet voice your father had!"

A cantor doesn't necessarily have to be a tenor. In my boy-alto career, I once sang uptown with Cantor Kirchner, who had a beautiful bass-baritone. To my mind, he wasn't as great as Kwartin or Rosenblatt. The greatest were tenors, but Kirchner was certainly the Greatest Exception: that should be his title.

It's a question of taste, not religious decree, that almost all Orthodox cantors are tenors. The congregations are used to tenors, so now it's the custom. And if I may say so, as a rule, the most exciting voice in which to worship G-d is the tenor. It just seems to have something more to say to G-d.

Three of my best friends today are Moishe Ganchoff, one of the finest exponents of the cantorial art; Israel Alter, a masterful cantor, great musician and teacher with whom I once studied; and Kalmen Kalich, an equally fine cantor who goes back to the days of my childhood. He and I used to sing in a synagogue choir conducted by a fine musician named Shnipelinsky. Kalmen and I sang alto together and grew up there as singers. Our big battle was always over who would do the solos, so we were competitors.

Even as a child, though, I knew Kalmen Kalich's weakness. If he was mimicked, all the starch went out of him.

I am a Litvak (a Jew of Lithuanian or nearby descent) and he is a Galitzianer (a Jew of Galician descent), so all I had to do was mimic his singsong Yiddish dialect to win the battle. To this day, even on the phone, if I want something from Kalmen Kalich and he is reluctant, I have only to start mimicking his Yiddish and he'll say, "Awright awready! You win again!"

On Blind Faith

I never discovered my Jewish identity; I always had it. I can't think of a time when I wasn't going to synagogue. I must have started at the age of two.

It was only when I began going to school and moving around the Lower East Side as a kid that I discovered there were people in this world who weren't Jewish—or rather, weren't like us. There were churches in our neighborhood, kids in the class who were Catholic, and there were the Irish and the Italians and the Greeks—and they were all called Gentiles or *goyim*. But I was always a Jew and proud to be one.

To me, being a Jew or a Christian is just a mark of identification. I happen to be a religious Jew with more than an average amount of faith in a Superior Being or Power that helped create humanity.

I was asked recently, "What is G-d?"

And I said in all humility, "*I* am G-d."

While my listeners were getting their breath back, I added, "Don't get me wrong. I mean that if the way a man lives is in any way godly, then it's what has been dictated. I associate myself with this Power, this Goodness, whatever you want to call it. People can be godly by living a decent life. Some do it by going to church or synagogue three times a day. But that isn't enough. Just praying or falling to your knees and genuflecting isn't all of religion. But if you try to love the way the Good Book tells you, if you're good to people around you and help them find a little happiness, that's religion, that's being godly with a small *g.*"

The greatness of believing can be known only to one who believes. The important thing is to believe not only when life is good, but when it is at its darkest, at its worst. If you say, "How could G-d let this happen to me?" or "... to six million Jews?" or if you only think G-d is good when life is good, then you're not really a believer. One's belief must be an act of blindness— of blind faith, as I discovered at a stage in my life when I lived in great danger of blindness.

To some who heard me say "I am G-d" and to many who didn't, I must sound a little crazy. But I wouldn't think of sitting down to eat breakfast or start the day's work without first having put on my phylacteries and praying and chanting and praising the word of G-d. Between you and me, one certainly *can* start a day without this, if that's what you want or if you don't think you have the time for it. On the other hand, if it's what you believe in, it becomes such a part of you that you wouldn't do without it. Making my peace with G-d and doing my daily worship of His name is as natural and refreshing to me as breathing the morning air.

The High Holy Days

The morning service for Rosh Hashonah, the Jewish New Year, begins like any other—with thanking the Lord for, among many other things, not making you a *goy* (meaning, in this sense, not just a Christian, but an outsider, a stranger) and for making you a man. All this means is that according to our traditional teachings women have no place in the *minyan,* or quorum, of ten adult Jewish males required for religious services. If you don't have ten, it doesn't mean you don't pray—you pray individually—but a minimum of ten is the format for organized worship of the Lord. Women are not even required to say prayers. The woman's role in Jewish life is to keep a kosher home and look after the religious upbringing of the children.

The sexes are segregated in an Orthodox synagogue. In small ones like ours at Henry and Clinton streets, there was no balcony or no built-in line of demarcation, so they fenced off a little corner with a curtain, which could be lifted and looked through, and told the women to worship there in their own way. And their way was to read a special "pony" that had one line of each prayer in Hebrew and a summary in Yiddish explaining the rest of it.

Traditionally, the Levites were the great musicians and singers in the Temple. And the Cohens, who were descended from Aaron, brother of Moses, were the priests. They made the sacrifices and ran the Temple.

I am a Cohen. It came down to me from my father from generation to generation. When my father told me I was a Cohen, I took his word for it —just as I did about everything else. You don't have to prove your genealogy to the rabbi. When you go into another synagogue and they want to give you the honor of chanting a prayer at the Torah, they ask what you are: a Cohen, a Levite, or a Yisroel. The Yisroels are the rest of the Jews. My father used to say he was all three. And explain he was born a Cohen, his Hebrew first name was Levi, and he was a Jew.

There is much talk in the services about the fear of G-d, but the G-d I know is a merciful one. The fear of G-d they talk about is not meant to make you tremble every time someone talks of Him. By fear is meant respect, awe. When I was ten or eleven, I said to my father, "I don't fear G-d. I love G-d. I respect G-d. But I don't fear Him."

My father was a little shocked to hear his son talk this way. "What do you mean when you say you don't fear G-d?"

"Papa, the Torah teaches me to love G-d, to believe in Him, and put all my faith in Him. But not to fear Him." He was still a little shocked. Years later, when he had matured and I had matured, we still had the same kind of discussion and he would say to me that he used to be ashamed of what I said, but now he had caught the drift of my reason.

I myself never taught my kids to fear G-d. In the old days, Yom Kippur, the Day of Atonement, was looked upon as a day of dread. At Rosh Hashonah, the prayers involve who shall live and who shall die; what will be inscribed in the Book of Life at Rosh Hashonah and sealed at Yom Kippur. Some people act as though they're standing in a courtroom and their fate is being decided then and there. You do get those ten days from the start of Rosh Hashonah through the end of Yom Kippur to shape up, but the object of the High Holy Days is to expand those ten days into every day of the year. What the rabbis are saying in effect is behave yourself—and not just on these ten important days of penitence. You can't live fast and loose all year and then come in to be a good boy for a ten-day limited engagement only.

After the reading of the Torah comes the shofar, the ram's horn that is blown on the High Holy Days, except on the Sabbath, to recall the days of war and remind us that Abraham offered his son Isaac as sacrifice. Isaac was saved when G-d let Abraham sacrifice a ram instead.

The days between Rosh Hashonah and Yom Kippur should be the beginning of your reformation or, if you're too good to need reform, a reaffirmation of your faith, but not a time of dread. Nowadays I approach Yom Kippur—with its fasting and total abstinence—with a feeling of seriousness and sometimes I shed a tear to think of changes that have taken place in my life, of those who were here last year and are now gone, and of the fate of all the Jews—in Israel, in Russia, in our own country.

But the day *before* Yom Kippur was a day I always dreaded as a boy, for in our home we held a ceremony involving live chickens called *shlogn kapores,* which means "beating forgiveness."

My mother went to market and bought a hen and at least two roosters. The only place to keep them was in the bathtub. I love to eat chicken, but live fowl I can live without. I can't stand the smell of them. I'm not one for animals as pets. I've hardly ever fondled a cat or lifted a dog. So you can imagine my revulsion toward chickens in the bathtub.

At daybreak the cock would crow and we'd take the birds from the bathroom to the kitchen for the *shlogn kapores* ceremony. Each person had to take the chicken in his right hand and wave it three times in a circle over his head while reciting prayers. Then you had to squeeze its neck a little. I can still feel those necks. A lot of people don't eat the necks of chickens for one reason or another; that's my reason.

Just picture the damage the poor, frightened chicken might make when it was swinging over your head! After the chickens were slaughtered my mother had to salt them and soak them and pluck their feathers. We ate them for our last meal of the day before our twenty-six- or twenty-eight-hour fast began toward sundown.

Over the years, the *shlogn kapores* custom has changed—and we practice it the modern way in the Peerce home. You can use money instead of chickens. You go through the same ritual, using eighteen cents or eighteen dollars, because the word *chai,* meaning "life," is composed of the eighth plus the tenth letters of the Hebrew alphabet. Later you give the money to charity. It's much cleaner than chickens.

Nowadays, on the afternoon before Yom Kippur (which begins at sundown), I'll go to synagogue around three for the afternoon service, come back home, bathe, dress, and have dinner around four-thirty: a piece of boiled chicken, a little soup, a piece of fruit, and a cup of tea. If you stuff yourself, you only make more room that will feel empty a few hours later. Your atonement begins right after you finish eating. Even though the sun is not yet down, the women of the house will start lighting the candles. Just before sunset, the *Kol Nidre* ("All Vows") service begins. In the synagogue, the cantor chants the most sublime melody in the Jewish liturgy. Beethoven used a little of the *Kol Nidre* in his Quartet in C Sharp Minor and Tolstoy said it "echoes the story of the martyrdom of a grief-stricken nation." Sung by a good cantor just before sunset, it can move me as much as any great music can—and to sing it myself is, well, a story I will come to later. The text of the *Kol Nidre,* however—and this will come as a surprise to millions of Gentiles and quite a few Jews, who've heard it at Radio City Music Hall—is remarkably mundane:

> All vows, obligations, oaths, anathemas, be they called *konam* or *konas* or by any other name, which we may vow or swear or pledge . . . from this Day of Atonement until the next . . . we do repent. May they be deemed to be forgiven, absolved, annulled or void—and made of no effect. They shall not bind us nor have power over us [and] the vows shall not be considered vows nor the obligations obligatory, nor the oaths oaths.

In other words, it's a release, a waiver, an exemption, a way out—largely to protect our people who may be forced to swear other oaths to conquerors or oppressors. The cantor sings it three times—the first time softly, the second time louder, the third time majestically if he's any good—while the congregation recites the prayer responsively.

I started fasting when I was twelve. After the *Kol Nidre* service in the evening, it's early to bed, and you have four more services the next day—the most services of any Jewish Holy Day. In the morning I generally feel the first gnawing pang. Around 11 A.M., three or four hours of sitting alone doing nothing but praying gives me a feeling of emptiness. To avoid weakness I may go out for a breath of fresh air. Otherwise, if I feel strong enough, the emptiness passes. Your fast must be complete: no drinking water, no brushing your teeth. (In the old days, some worshipers didn't even go home during the night, but stayed in the synagogue to pray all night and all day.) You should suffer the full pangs of abstinence so that you leave the synagogue with a feeling that you'll be forgiven.

Thank You, Beckie Schiff!

Miss Beckie Schiff worked in my father's shop. She was a woman with a burning desire for beauty in her life—and by beauty, she didn't mean ladies' ready-to-wear, but the arts. For them she saved all her money; on them she spent all her money. What is more, she told my father, she believed children should be exposed to the arts early. And one Sunday night she invited me to go uptown with her to the Metropolitan Opera.

On Sunday nights in those days, the Met didn't give operas, but concerts at a reduced price. Admission was two dollars for the best seat downstairs; upstairs, you sat for less. We sat in the balcony and I can remember every detail of that program. The Metropolitan Orchestra was conducted by a fine musician named Richard Hageman, who later coached me in operatic singing and German lieder. Mischa Elman played the violin! A contralto named Sophie Breslau sang *Yohrzeit,* a concert setting of the Jewish prayer on the anniversary of a family member's death. The tenor soloist was Raffaelo Diaz, a handsome little fellow in his full-dress suit, but even then I could sense that a Caruso he wasn't. He was noted for one role that he'd made his own with his particular quality of voice, in Rimsky-Korsakov's *Coq d'Or.* When I met him years later, I told him he'd sung at "my debut at the Met" and he was pleased.

I remember that evening being enveloped with more beauty than I'd ever experienced in music, but I don't remember envying or dreaming I could be Raffaelo Diaz. Singing was something he did at the Met and I did in synagogues.

I have Beckie Schiff to thank, too, for introducing me to the ten-cent concerts at Educational Alliance and at De Witt Clinton High School, Fifty-ninth Street and Tenth Avenue. The *Evening Globe* had a music critic or editor named Charles D. Isaacson who ran the uptown series. Actually, this was a double luxury because in addition to the dime for the concert, it cost another dime in carfare to go and come back. The talent was always good, but by making us pay a little for it, just as the Rutgers Street baths and Camp Felicia did, they encouraged you to be not only grateful, but critical, too.

Since I was studying fiddle, I went mostly to instrumental concerts, but I did go to a few song recitals. Years later, I studied uptown with a voice teacher named Eleanor McClellan, who started reminiscing one day about a great singer, David Bispham. Then she corrected herself rather haughtily: "Of course, you wouldn't know him because you would have been a little boy not yet going to concerts."

But I told her, "Oh, yes, I do. I paid a dime to hear him when I was eleven years old."

Putting on the *Tefillin*

Tefillin (phylacteries) are a pair of thin leather straps with a little square leather box on each. One box goes on the inner side of your left arm just above the elbow (thus placing it next to your heart when you pray) and the other box high up on your forehead. In the boxes are little parchments containing, in Hebrew, four passages from Exodus and Deuteronomy.

The law says you start wearing the *tefillin* a month before you're ready for your bar mitzvah, at thirteen, so that by the time you're a man, you've mastered the complicated business of putting them on. You can't put them on and start praying in the morning until it is light enough to "recognize your neighbor, with whom you are slightly acquainted, at a distance of four cubits."

At the age of twelve years and eleven months, I put on the *tefillin* and felt very proud that I could start having my own adult relationship with G-d. The *tefillin* put me in touch with the unity of G-d, in touch with G-d Himself. And I've been putting them on every weekday of my life—except when I've been too sick and isolated to put them on or have someone put them on for me. The brand-new *tefillin* my father gave me then are still with me; every two years I have a rabbi inspect them for twisting and other defects.

Tears at My Bar Mitzvah

I had a spectacular bar mitzvah in June 1917, when I was thirteen. Instead of making the usual speech in the synagogue to all the assembled relatives and well-wishers bearing gifts—"Dear Mother and Father, dear friends and family, members of the congregation: Today I am a fountain pen"—I performed the morning service as the cantor. And behind me was Elias Shnipelinsky and the wonderful choir I used to sing with. It was a great honor. For bar mitzvah, most kids would do the *musaf* (additional) service or read part of the Torah, but I did both.

The bar mitzvah went on all weekend: a big party Saturday afternoon and evening and an open house all day Sunday. We even had a distinguished guest, who came on both days: Mr. Harry Esterman, the superintendent of my father's shop. Even *his* boss, Mr. Schaff of Schaff & Mandel, put in an appearance for an hour or so. All the people who worked with my father showed up. And they all brought presents.

The package that Beckie Schiff brought was the one that interested me most. It was heavier than the others. I kept trying to imagine what could be inside. And although the presents were put in the bedroom unopened, curiosity got the better of me. Toward nine o'clock Saturday evening, I quietly ducked into the bedroom and unwrapped Beckie's gift.

It was a complete set of Shakespeare in miniature volumes called the

Little Leather Library. They were the idea of Harry Scherman, who later said his Little Leather Library collapsed because it literally stank (especially in hot weather), but through it he discovered there was a deep and abiding thirst for culture in America and in 1926 Scherman started the Book-of-the-Month Club.

There couldn't have been a more elegant and exciting bar mitzvah present than a complete Little Leather Library. Even a rose by any other name would not have smelled so sweet.

I had my nose buried in *A Midsummer Night's Dream* when my mother came looking for me because she wanted to show me off to her guests by making me play the fiddle. She was shocked when she found me with an opened present. In those days, opening a gift while the giver was still there was considered the height of bad manners.

She started up softly: "What's this? You're supposed to be at your party. You're the guest of honor, the *bar mitzvah!*" (in Hebrew, "Son of the Commandment").

"I'll be there in a few minutes," I told her, without looking up.

Now she raised her voice: "Do you care more about presents than people?"

My father heard the argument and came inside. And right away he ordered me to go and play the fiddle.

Since today I was a man, I decided to assert myself: "I don't feel like it."

"What do you mean, you don't feel like it?" my father said.

"I'm tired. It's been a long day. I've done enough."

With that, I was yanked to my feet by both parents and told to go out there and play. Tears streaming down my face, I was pushed into the living room and handed my fiddle. I played "La Cinquantaine" madly and badly, but, lubricated by tears, very swiftly—and everybody applauded as if I were, for the moment, Mischa Elman, only more passionate.

Come Out of There, Michoil

My kid brother Mac, named after the angel Michoil, never was or will be an angel. He must have been born with a poker chip on his shoulder and all his life he's loved to gamble a little; but like the rest of us, he made himself respectable. Mac's last job before retiring to Florida with his wife, Irma (they were married in our garden in New Rochelle, by the way), was with the State of New York: Offtrack Betting.

The police who patrolled the Lower East Side on the lookout for crime seemed to take most seriously kids congregated in a backyard—or even in a little circle on the street—to shoot craps. Not that the stakes were high. In the whole circle there probably wasn't more than a couple of dollars. But even the Irish police, who thought they'd seen everything, were shocked when they caught a bunch of Jewish kids on Rutgers Street shooting craps on the Sabbath!

It so happened that my mother was taking her Saturday-afternoon stroll, for the Sabbath was a nice day when you didn't cook (puddings and other durables from Friday's dinner were left overnight in the pots to stay warm; other Saturday dishes were prepared in advance on Friday) and could even enjoy a little leisure time. The weather was nice and she was just thinking about going home when she was attracted by a crowd on Rutgers Street. The police had summoned a Black Maria and now a bunch of people were being loaded into it.

"What happened?" she asked somebody.

"Oh, they caught some nogoodniks gambling with dice."

My mother moved closer to see what kind of nogoodnik gambled on a Saturday—and who was the first to avoid her eye but her son Mac!

"Michoil!" she cried. "What are you doing there? Come out of there, Michoil! Don't you know you're not allowed to ride on the Sabbath?"

This upset her more than the gambling, the police, the Black Marias, and even her son's arrest. Mac was in enough trouble without disobeying his mother too. So he came bounding out of the Black Maria, only to be grabbed by a cop and flung back in. The policeman was very sympathetic, but he pointed out in a thick brogue that the first transgression was her son's and he was not the one who could grant absolution. As the Black Maria took Mac away, my mother covered her eyes so she would not see a son of hers riding on the Sabbath.

Then she marched to the home of our district's Tammany Hall leader, who took off on the run to the police station. My brother was out and the charge dismissed before he ever spent a minute in a cell. He insists that he was just playing the place's gum-ball machine for a cheap chew when the cops raided. It's still a family joke, though, and so is what we say to Mac at a party when we want him to leave: "Come out of there, Michoil!"

Charley the Stableman

While my mother had been running a private restaurant in our home and taking in boarders to pay for my violin lessons, my father had been making extra dollars with his cloakroom concession. It was from these earnings that I had taken twenty-eight cents out of his vest when I was ten or so. The cloakroom was at Applebaum & Smith's Kosher Wedding & Banquet Salon at 73 Ludlow Street. My father had the "hatcheck privilege." It meant paying a little to Applebaum & Smith for the right to work there all night, but you could keep whatever money you took in.

A hatcheck privilege was not the big deal it is today, when they ask you for fifty cents in advance. In those days there was no charge for checking a hat and coat, so my father (and the rest of us who helped out on busy nights and Sundays) had to rely on the customers' generosity. A dime was a lavish tip. The only time my father had any right to charge was when the customer said, "Please hang my coat up." Then it cost a quarter.

It couldn't have been the best feeling in the world, after a hard day at the garment factory, to stand from seven in the evening until one or two in the morning minding someone's coat and then find he didn't even give you a penny. There were nights when my father brought home only a couple of dollars. But other nights were better—and he managed to save a little money. Winters were always better than summers and the worse the weather, the better the cloakroom trade.

Not long after my bar mitzvah, Applebaum and his partner, Philip Smith, decided to try for bigger and better things: a place uptown, in Harlem, where the Jewish trade was (and a little Italian business, too). They bought a hall on 116th Street and before putting the old place up for sale, they offered it to their various employees and concessionaires.

My father wanted to buy Applebaum & Smith's downtown hall very badly and he had a little money put aside, but it wasn't enough. Philip Smith's brother Gershon, who worked as a waiter, was interested, too, so he put up the rest of the cash (after borrowing it from his brother) and went into partnership with Papa. They didn't call it Smith & Perelmuth, however, but Grand Mansion: "Weddings, Receptions, Bar Mitzvahs."

Such was my father's reputation that he was practically the only kosher caterer in New York who never had to hire an "overseer"—a learned man, chosen by rabbis, to make sure that everything was right. My father had the distinction of being his own overseer, for nobody was better qualified or more demandingly ethical. Even if he'd wanted to hire an overseer, he would have had a hard time. The rabbis knew my father and wouldn't have known whom to suggest.

My mother always believed that a woman was put on earth to help her husband, and the best way she knew to help him was by working like a slave. She really meant it when she said, "What else is a woman to do? She must be at her husband's side all through life." She had to participate. She had to do everything. Or as she put it when she took over the kitchen of Grand Mansion, "What else can I do? I'm not good at floral decorations."

My parents charged $2.25 to $2.75 per couple for banquets; $3.50 to $4.00 on weekends. For that price, each couple got two complete terrific meals—all custom-made, with my mother *flick*ing the chickens and chopping the gefilte fish herself, mixing the onions with pepper and salt, all by hand, with no grinders, no packages, no jars of Mother's or Manischewitz's gefilte fish. Even the noodles at Grand Mansion were made by hand. The meals included all the free punch you could drink and one free glass of wine apiece. Special dishes like sweet-and-sour tongue or sweetbreads in casserole cost fifty cents extra per couple.

I never worked there, except in the cloakroom and, later, as a musician. My youngest brother, Sender, was active in the business and for a long time made it his career.

Grand Mansion soon had a great reputation, but there were always two strikes against my father's business, particularly where wedding receptions were concerned. Across the street was the Ludlow Street Jail—*the* alimony jail for all Manhattan—not an auspicious landmark to begin married life across from. Far worse for atmosphere, though, was our next-door neighbor. Directly to our left, toward Broome Street, was a livery stable, where horses used for trucking were garaged. The smell on a hot day was bad enough when the wind was right, but the worst animal there was the owner: Charley the Stableman.

Charley was a horrible bastard: grotesque, stupid, arrogant, an ignoramus of the worst water. He couldn't speak a civil sentence in Yiddish, Hebrew, English, or horse talk. If you can picture a red-faced, bloated, swollen, brutish, hateful, lowly, insignificant baboon with a cigar in its mouth, that was Charley.

Charley's old workhorses had to be better human beings than he was. They were also romantics of a perverse sort, for they liked to drop dead on an occasional Grand Mansion wedding day. The bride and groom, in all their glory, all their splendor, accompanied by all their friends and relations, would draw up in limousines at the front door of Grand Mansion, to be greeted by a dead horse sprawled between the stable and the Mansion.

My mother would cry and wring her hands and my father would say in his quiet way, "Oh, G-d, but why should a man do this?"

If they tried to make Charley move his dead horse, or if we tried to move the horse ourselves, Charley wouldn't cooperate; in fact, he'd block the way, inviting a fight. He said it had to lie there until the city horse coroner came. Even after the city horse coroner established that the horse had died of natural causes, the corpse would have to stay where it was until the Sanitation Department came to remove it. The law was the law, Charley insisted, and nobody could move a dead horse until the coroner went and the Sanitation wagon came. If my folks pointed out that somebody must have moved the horse *to* the Grand Mansion, Charley would chew his cigar and say, "I dunno how't got over dere." Always, the coroner and Sanitation took hours.

One hot June day when I'd just turned fifteen, Charley sent over a dead horse for a Grand Mansion wedding, and I arrived to find my mother crying so hard that my father had his hands full comforting her. My parents were dedicated people in a business where any kind of stink could ruin you—let alone the stink of a dead horse. They were also people who wished everybody else well; was it wishing too much that a bride and groom should start out married life with some better omen? Why should a bride cry on her wedding day? She'll cry enough later. But never as much as my mother did that day.

Since I was now a man, my father sent me on a man's errand: "Pinyele, go and tell that Charley he should take away his dead horse."

I walked into the stable and tried to talk to Charley man to man. But that didn't work. I didn't get very far. He cut me off with language I was surprised I could understand. And I rose to the occasion by speaking the same language to this big smelly hunk of guy who stood a head above me and a waist beyond me. People who compliment my French and Italian diction don't know anything about the linguistic summit I achieved in that particular performance at Charley's Livery Stable.

When I went after him in his own filthy terms, I could see that it hurt him to have an equal in Yiddish abuse—which is the one area in which he must have considered himself superior to the advanced civilization that was everywhere around him. He thought he'd pacify or trick me with a relatively appeasing sentence like: "What do I care about your folks?"

When he said this, I told him that even his horses were ashamed to live with him. He said to watch my big mouth or I'd feel a hundred horses kicking me in the teeth. But I said to him, "Don't you ever talk about my parents again! These are people and you're nothing but a pig."

You can imagine what calling someone a pig meant in our community. But I've learned that when you argue with somebody—whether it's a taxi driver, a punk, or a cop—if you're right they'll know it, and if you use the language they deserve, they'll stand at attention. When you're right. And they'll know you're right if you're the kind of guy who doesn't often raise his voice or pick fights.

So I gave it to him and there he stood—clenched fists still at his sides *after* he'd threatened me. I told him that the next time a dead horse appeared in the street not far from the entrance of Grand Mansion, my brothers and I would see to it that a dead pig named Charley was lying alongside it by the time the coroner came.

I never had the opportunity to keep my promise, though Charley was our next-door neighbor for more than fifteen years after that—well into the 1930s. No dead horse came near Grand Mansion again. Charley kept his horses pulling ice wagons and milk trucks until a plumbing company—which later bought Grand Mansion, too—bought him out. In the 1930s, when I was starting to make a name for myself on the air and at Radio City Music Hall, he once or twice made so bold as to congratulate me: "Hearya did prity good up dere." I looked the other way, as if I didn't hear him.

"Maybe, Pinye, you should do what the Talmud teaches and preaches," my father would murmur. "Live and let live. Forgive and show a little compassion."

"No, Papa," I replied. "That's in the Talmud, but it's not in me. I don't want his blessings and I don't want his curses. I don't want his smells and I don't want his horses, dead or alive." And never did I look at him or speak to him again. If ever I despised anybody, it was Charley the Stableman.

With a Mouth Like That

When I sang in synagogues, I would be asked the same question by strangers, cantors, and choir members: "Are you studying singing?" I'd say no and then would come the next question: "Why not?" But when I began to consider taking singing lessons I was talked out of it by a well-meaning expert.

Joseph P. Katz had a music store on East Broadway next to the Forverts Building. All the musicians on the Lower East Side—professionals, prospectives, and dreamers—used to buy their music, strings, rosin, and other needs there. And Katz was a sort of Jewish father confessor: a little man with a deep bass voice who sang in choirs and quartets. When I confided in him that I might like to take lessons in voice, he asked, "Why do you want to study voice?"

"Because I want to learn to sing."

"Why should you want to learn how to sing?"

"Well, maybe I can make a go of it."

"What maybe? Why do you think you have that kind of voice?"

"Well, I want to find out if I do."

"You're just throwing out money. Who needs it? Play the fiddle. Go to school."

In retrospect, I am merely annoyed—not incensed. Katz knew already that I was singing in choirs, but he'd never heard me sing. I think he should at least have listened—and if he wouldn't listen to me sing, then he should have said, "Try it. If you make something of it, fine. If not, not. But at least you'll find out." I expected more from an intellectual.

In my own adult life, I have never said to others what Katz (and one of my uncles) said to me. I've never told anybody, "Forget it! Don't study! You're no good! You'll never make it!" Even when I've listened and come to this conclusion, I've sent them to or advised them to see a teacher. Let the teacher tell them.

Going to a teacher is like going to a doctor. There are times when a doctor can help you and times when he can't. But it never hurts to go see a doctor once or twice.

Somewhat discouraged by Katz, I suffered in silence through the musical menopause for a boy singer: the change-of-voice. Then, when I couldn't let go of the idea, I studied the ads in music journals for voice teachers. The one that caught my eye was for "Emilio Roxas, Coach to Giovanni Martinelli." I admired Martinelli, so I went to see Roxas. It turned out he was Martinelli's accompanist, not his mentor, but he listened to me and exclaimed, "With a voice like that, you should take lessons! I give them to you." He charged five dollars a lesson, but after two paid sessions, he put his money where my mouth was—by awarding me a scholarship that lasted almost five years.

Roxas gave me scales and exercises and a few good habits; I was too new at singing to have many bad habits. But I reached a point where I had learned all that he could teach me and I stopped going to him. He didn't seem to miss me until, a few years later, I was beginning to make a name for myself at Radio City and Samuel "Roxy" Rothafel had arranged a scholarship for me to study voice with Eleanor McClellan. Roxas came to my dressing room, congratulated me on my success, and asked me why I hadn't been coming to him.

I told him candidly that I had another teacher now.

"But you can't do that to me!" he protested. It turned out that he was dead set on advertising that he was teacher to me, too. The discussion ended, but he took me to court for $2,200 in back lessons.

The scholarship hadn't been in writing, so my lawyer advised me to "settle the case by paying him a couple of hundred bucks." Not I! It had become a matter of principle with me. The case went to trial.

After the first day of testimony the judge called me to his chamber. "Look," he said, "I happen to be an admirer of your singing, so I'd like to give you some advice. Your case is already more than halfway lost. Not only has the plaintiff presented himself as a poor, struggling teacher and you as a prosperous, ungrateful singer, but his lawyer is making a strong case on a principle no jury can resist: that a man is entitled to be compensated for his labor. I suggest you settle."

I drew myself up and said haughtily, "I want to thank you for your interest, Your Honor, but I'm accustomed to take advice only when I've asked for it."

"All right," he said, highly offended. "Good day, sir."

On my way out of the courtroom, Roxas's lawyer—Louis Lefkowitz, later the attorney general of New York State—told me that his client was willing to settle and I ought to be, too. I told Lefkowitz to talk to his own client, not to me.

When my own lawyer, Ben Levin, heard what I had said to the judge, he was furious: "The judge really gave you good advice and you could have been held in contempt of court for the way you behaved! I don't want to represent you in this stupid affair and if you don't do something about it first thing tomorrow morning, I think I'll call in sick."

The next day, my lawyer and I went before the judge. I apologized to him and Lefkowitz. And we settled for six hundred dollars in payment for my "scholarship." Nothing is free in this world.

McTiernan

De Witt Clinton High School, from which I never graduated, is way up in the Bronx now, but in my youth it was at Fifty-ninth Street and Tenth Avenue in Manhattan—which was so far uptown and crosstown from the Lower East Side that it seemed like a trip to the Bronx. In those days, if you were interested in mechanics and workshops, you went to Stuyvesant; if you wanted to be an accountant, you went to Commerce; and if you wanted a good general education, you went to Clinton. The Bronx High School of Science didn't exist then and I don't know whether the High School of Music and Art did, either. I never would have thought in terms of a musical education. My fiddle was something I studied outside school. Besides, my mother's ambition was for me to become a doctor—and while I didn't want to be one, what right did I have to believe I could make a living from music? I went along with my parents' plans. They knew what they wanted from me, while I looked at it all with curiosity, little knowing and little caring whether I would turn out to be Mrs. Perelmuth's son the doctor, lawyer, or Indian chief.

Two languages were required at De Witt Clinton. I studied Spanish and

Latin. Latin later proved to be a good foundation for me, since it was the root of the Romance languages I sing opera in. But at the time we found Spanish more useful. A bunch of boys had formed a group that spoke only Spanish and read *La Prensa* every day. Finding I had a flair for languages, I joined up and enjoyed it. But I didn't carry my linguistics to the point a shiny-faced kid two years ahead of me named Milton Steinberg did. Every year a Dr. Bryant offered a course in Greek. Milton Steinberg was his only student. He learned so fast that by his senior year, he was teaching Dr. Bryant advanced Greek.

One of everybody's favorite teachers was McTiernan, the elocution teacher. He would come in on Mondays bursting with enthusiasm over his weekend in Europe and would talk about what he did in Paris on Saturday and London on Sunday. This was almost ten years before Lindbergh and we used to look at him and wonder whether he was out of his mind. On the contrary, he was *living* in his mind, fantasizing a reality that was much more real than the jet-age Paris many tourists visit today. McTiernan was crazy with a vision that only a few men among us are capable of having.

I did well at De Witt Clinton, but I never took my final examinations and officially I did not graduate. I did take courses at Columbia University Extension Studies, but I didn't really want "higher education." Every degree, every credit, would lead me farther down the road to my mother's vision of her son Dr. Jacob Pincus Perelmuth, while I was beginning to have music in my heart, music in my soul, and a girl named Alice on my mind—and I didn't want to let go of any one of them.

2

Pinky Pearl

I'll Play at Your Wedding

Once my family owned the Grand Mansion catering hall on Ludlow Street,
I pretty much had the "music privilege" for wedding receptions. So I orga-
nized four neighborhood boys and myself into Pinky Pearl and His Society
Dance Band. Our fee (non-union) was four dollars a man plus tips.

Sephardic Jewish weddings were the most lucrative. They were usually
on weekdays, which helped my father fill in the slack periods. At a certain
point in a "Spanish wedding," as we called them, the guests would sit in a
circle and every man there would dance with the bride—dance, but not
touch. There was always at least a handkerchief between him and her. Pinky
Pearl's Band played the same tango melody over and over. The bride
blushed and tangoed and was adored and admired for dance after dance, by
relative after relative. And each man who danced threw a coin onto a plate.
Sometimes a rich relative would put down a dollar, but most gave a quarter
or fifty cents.

Fifty percent of these contributions went to the musicians. The other half
went to the bride and groom. She was paid for dancing at her wedding, but
believe me, she earned it. My feet used to ache for those poor girls. At one
Spanish wedding we each took twenty-six dollars home; we figured about

two hundred male relatives must have danced that night. There were other nights when we only made five dollars apiece—"working for pesos," we called it.

Rumanian and Bessarabian Jews are fun-loving people and their weddings were always gay. The Rumanians loved their wine. There was very little hard liquor; they sat in a circle like the Spaniards and passed around a jug of wine. But they didn't dance so much with the bride. So I'd play a *fraylech*—a happy tune—and announce that it was in the honor of the uncle of the bride who came all the way from Chicago for the wedding, or some such thing. And for that recognition he'd pay—not into a plate, but into a hat. Bessarabians also drank a quantity of wine and there was much cameraderie—less money, perhaps, but artistic compensation for a musician: our melodies were listened to and clapped along with—and the dancing was lovely to watch.

Polish-Jewish wedding guests concentrated on eating our food and drinking hard liquor. Those who could stand up liked to dance polkas and mazurkas. Lithuanian and Russian Jews were more fun-loving and danced not just the kazatske and the Bulgar but a kind of square dance in quartets: we called it the "Russian Sherr"—scissors.

Ninety-nine percent of the Jewish weddings ordered meals. Otherwise they had a sweet table and sacramental red wine. Italians as a rule didn't have food. They had wine and punch and Jordan almonds covered with sugared candy which I liked so much I used to sneak as many as I could. At Grand Mansion the Italians concentrated on waltzes and tarantellas. The amazing thing about Italian weddings was the number of people who showed up. When I saw *The Godfather*, it looked to me as if they had cast the extras on a shoestring.

As a result of my experience playing for tips, if I go to a restaurant and there's a guy on the cocktail piano, I always leave him some money, no matter how badly he plays. I can't pass him by. I know part of his income is tip money and my past comes back to greet me.

In the summers, when we moved up to the Catskills, Pinky Pearl and His Band became Jack "Pinky" Pearl and his Society Dance Orchestra, which despite the longer name was at first a trio (fiddle, piano, and drum). That was in our initial summer as a group, when I was fourteen; later we expanded to six. In that summer of 1918, the three of us were booked into the Breezy Hill Hotel in Fleischmanns, New York. My two musicians were paid fifteen dollars a week and I was paid twenty dollars because I was the leader and threw in a little singing. The cheapest and most scenic, but the slowest, way to get up to the mountains was to take the Hudson River Day Line to Kingston and the train the rest of the way to Fleischmanns. The boat ride went past Palisades and Westchester, Bear Mountain and West Point, and that first time, as I admired their majestic grandeur, I took up smoking—a vice that stayed with me for another thirty years. (Coughing in the morning and waking up in the middle of the night because I needed a cigarette didn't quite cure me, until my wife told me one night that I'd been "puffing in Maestro Toscanini's face.")

Back in 1918, I became addicted to the Catskills, too. From that summer on, I whiled away the winters and the school years as recesses while I waited to get back to the mountains and greenery and full-time music-making, around which my life came to revolve.

The Girl from Harlem

Harlem was a nice place to visit—for violin lessons and synagogue singing in the old days and, in my late teens, for weddings and other musical engagements—but scarcely a place I could aspire to without money, without higher education, without a professional title. Anyway, I didn't think in terms of upward or uptown mobility—or much about marriage, for that matter. Harlem was out of my league. People used to go to synagogue there in much the elegant way they still do in England or France today: wearing striped trousers, while high-hatted officials, called beadles, keep order in the aisles.

One of the boys in our neighborhood, however, had a pretty kid cousin from Harlem whose family would come visiting his family once or twice a month. They came riding down in her father's auto, which was a Flint. Nobody we knew had a car, let alone a Flint. It was a big car, but I don't think it ever compared to a Cadillac. Who could compare? A Flint was the biggest car I'd ever seen. All of us used to cluster around it, and if the Kalmanowitz family or any of the children were hanging around, we'd ask them a technical question or two. Alice Kalmanowitz appeared to be almost ashamed of her car and didn't seem to have any of the answers to our questions. Because of that and where she was from and how she came down from there, she became known in our circle as The Snob, through no fault of her own. Her cousin, Yaikey, said she wasn't one, but we wanted to think so. As she developed, I stopped noticing her background and started concentrating on her foreground, but our contact still was limited to a quick "Hello, how are you?" or maybe as much as a "Where've you been? I haven't seen you around lately."

Then one night I played a wedding uptown and a beautiful young lady in a yellow gown came over to me. I thought it was going to be a request, but it was something better, because she said, "Aren't you Pinky Pearl?"

My fame must be spreading uptown, I thought to myself, as I owned up aloud that I was indeed Pinky in person.

"And don't you recognize me?" she asked, deflating me only a little.

Gee, I thought to myself, she's beautiful enough for me to say "Yeah, sure" to, but I could not tell a lie—not to her. Before I could say anything as disgraceful as no, her father came up behind her. Him I recognized. He was Mr. Jacob Kalmanowitz from Harlem, Yaikey's uncle. And by the time she said, "Papa, I told you it was Pinky Pearl!" I was collected enough to say, "Good to see you, Mr. K., and I almost didn't recognize you, Alice, in that evening gown." It was a wonderful excuse to get a good look at her— but in the conversation that followed, I mentioned that I wouldn't have a chance to look anybody up because my band and I were leaving the very next day to play the summer at the Waldmere Hotel in the Catskills.

"Oh, we go up to the mountains, too, in a few weeks, but we go to the Flagler," Mr. K. said, brightening my summer no end, for the Flagler was very near, but then he added rather dubiously, "Is the Waldmere all right?"

"Oh," said Alice quickly, "if Pinky's playing there, it must be a very nice place."

I had never seen the Waldmere and I was grateful to have landed any kind of summer work anywhere in the mountains, but I played it big and said, "Why don't you come over and see for yourself?"

She said, "If my father lets me," looking at him in a way that would melt even a much sterner father than the kindly Mr. K.

"I'll tell you what," he said. "I'll let her go over there if you'll assure me you'll keep an eye on her"—a promise I was as eager to fulfill as I was to make.

Still, I didn't know if they took this plan as seriously as I did, and I was up at the Waldmere scheming for an excuse to drop over to the Flagler and remind them, when sure enough, a letter came saying that she and her kid sister Maye would like to drop over.

The arrangements took a little time, but meanwhile I went around telling everybody at the Waldmere, "My girl is coming up," and everybody wanted to know "Where'd you get a girl?" and when she walked into the Waldmere she was even more beautiful than the build-up I'd given her.

Having impressed all those eyes, I wanted to get her away from them. Someone else gladly squired Maye Kaye (all the Kalmanowitzes eventually changed their name to Kaye) while I took Alice rowing. Alice seemed just a little ill at ease in the boat, but I figured what girl wouldn't be, alone on Lake Shandelle with Pinky Pearl? Only later, much later, did I discover that it was her first boat outing in ten years. When she was five or six, a sailboat had overturned in a storm and she had nearly drowned. I found this out when I knew her much better and, having taken her swimming, I splashed her playfully in four feet of water; she shivered with fright.

At that time of my life, to impress people with what a serious young man I was, I used to carry a book with me at all times, even though I often didn't read it (I would switch from *War and Peace* to *Pride and Prejudice* anyway after a week). I don't remember which particular book I wasn't reading then, but Alice commented on it right away. I said quite honestly that I hadn't started it yet and she said too bad, because she was hoping to borrow it whenever I was done, and I said quickly please borrow it now, and she said no, I should read it first, and I said I prefer to read for pleasure rather than under pressure and I don't mind postponing a book I haven't yet started, and so she borrowed the book and I knew I'd have an excuse to call her up about returning it if she didn't call me.

She and her family went back to the city. They had moved from Harlem to Findlay Avenue in the Bronx. I had no trouble finding them, but when I did, I pretended I was after my book. Alice returned it, saying she now knew a little about my tastes in literature, and lent me a book she thought I might like to borrow from her. The exchange of books and other people's words became the love letters of our courtship.

Alice's Family's Restaurants

Alice's parents, like mine, had been born in Russia—but unlike mine, they hadn't met until they were in America. He came over with his parents in 1899, right after his bar mitzvah, while she arrived a few years later, met him, and married him. He made the money and she ran the house—with that Jewish mother's eagle eye on improving her children's culture and her own mind. She took lessons in reading and writing until she was sixty-five to improve her English because, as she put it profoundly, "In America, the ears and eyes of the world is in English." She was ambitious for her daughters as well as her sons. She wanted Alice to be a pianist or a lawyer. "In America," she told Alice, "you go to school, you graduate, you become a *mensch* [person], and when you can say, 'Today I am a *mensch*,' you can think about marrying well."

By the time I met Alice, her father had made a great success of Gottlieb Kosher Restaurant at 11 West 31st Street. With all due respect to the tailors and manufacturers who keep the kosher tradition alive and perhaps at its strongest in the garment district, the kosher restaurants of today are poor relations of what was there in the same neighborhood forty or fifty years ago. Instead of being a last bastion for the Orthodox cloak-and-suiters, Alice's father's restaurant was a place where you found Everybody Who Was Anybody. Judges, lawyers, rabbis came there not just to eat, not just to meet each other, but to talk with Mr. K. For in addition to being an outstanding restauranteur, he was a man who had been born knowing exactly how to talk to people. He would walk from table to table, talking about what interested his guests, not merely what interested him. He was a master diplomat and a very honest wise man, who offered his opinion quite frankly and candidly *if you wanted it.*

Among the many pearls of wisdom my father-in-law-to-be bestowed upon me was this one: "Wherever you go, tip generously—so you'll be remembered when you come back. If you think you can't afford it, stay a day less so you can pay for the tips." This particular advice always paid off. Even before I'd made it big, I was a long-time VIP at Lindy's Restaurant. Why? Because once upon a time, I had given a two-dollar tip to the big uniformed bear of a doorman who used to keep customers waiting on line outside—the colder the longer. Every time I went to Lindy's, I'd march up, without breaking step, to the refrain of "You gotta wait, you gotta wait, maybe an hour, maybe two, you gotta wait, *Oh, hello, Mr. Peerce! Your table's waiting. Just ask the headwaiter which one.* You gotta wait, lady, you gotta wait. . . ."

Mr. and Mrs. Jacob Kalmanowitz, alias Kaye, alias K., had two daughters and then two sons, Sidney and Walter. Sidney inherited his father's genius for running a restaurant—and took it a giant step farther into the most secular and glittering of all worlds when in 1945 he bought the Russian Tea Room, next to Carnegie Hall. He made it into the best Russian restaurant in the world. When Sid was alive I used to love the Russian Tea Room's blintzes, but what made me know I was in a great restaurant was that you could order a steak, which isn't a specialty there, and it would be at least as good as in the finest steakhouse. That's a sign of high standards.

I used to watch Sidney table-hopping in the Russian Tea Room and I would sometimes think: My G-d! There's the ghost of my father-in-law. But that was only the rear view. From the front, Sidney came on differently. He had more nerve than any other man I knew. He'd give you his opinion even if you didn't want it. Sidney was honest and even kind, but he was rough—and in a sea of sharks, he could tell the phony from the real faster than any of us. He was respected by both, because everything about him and his work was genuine quality.

Sidney Kaye was a genius who made the Russian Tea Room into an institution that endures beyond his lifetime as a worthy neighbor to Carnegie Hall. But when I first met him, he was just one of the two pesky kid brothers of the girl I was trying to court.

Two Weddings and an Elopement

Alice had been driven to school in a Flint automobile every day. I had had to fight my way. My parents were set on my being what I didn't want to be —a doctor—and marriage and children didn't figure in that uphill struggle. There were few Jewish medical students in those days—and no married ones. Her folks wanted her to marry someone with a future. Pinky Pearl scarcely had a present. But we loved each other and eventually we eloped.

Our courtship lasted several years, but nobody except us two took it seriously. My parents just weren't told much about Alice, because I was afraid my mother would end it as a distraction to my medical career. I was still living with my family on Madison Street, of course, the way all young men did until they married. And I couldn't have pleased the Kalmanowitzes even if I'd dedicated myself to becoming Dr. Perelmuth the physician and son-in-law. Once, when Alice discussed me in an abstract way at their dinner table, Mr. K. dismissed the idea: "If he should be a doctor, what will happen between you until he becomes a doctor and can marry you? What if you're too old for him by then?" Alice, who was younger than I, said this was nonsense, she'd still be a few years younger. But her father was a firm believer that if a girl waited too long to get married, she might "lose the little raisin on top of the cookie." By this he meant her youthful bloom.

So Alice and I decided to be sweethearts without telling anybody. Still, it couldn't go on forever—or even last long—because as she got close to twenty, the number of prospective suitors who marched into their Findlay Avenue house would fill all her time even if she rejected every one of them. Besides, her kid brothers were beginning to smell a rat—which is to say, they sensed my intentions were honorable.

[Interview with Alice Peerce and her brother Walter Kaye in the Catskill Mountains, September 1974. Walter—now a silver-haired executive—is perhaps Jan Peerce's closest friend and a trusted counselor.]

Walter: *Jan and I have been unbelievable friends—closer than two brothers could be. I have to admit that for most of my life I was closer to Jan than I was to my brother*

—and Jan says the same thing about his two brothers. Jan and I have a sort of father-son relationship, except I'm like a younger father to Jan and yet I respect him like he's my own father. It wasn't love at first sight, though. As a child I hated him. Alice was the woman in my life and now this guy was after her. I was six years old and I wanted to marry my sister! I spent an awful lot of time with her, because our mother worked in the restaurant.

Alice: *Our relationship was almost incestuous. I was ten years old when Walter was born. He was the baby, a toy come to life for me. I'd never even had a doll until I was five. Now, when I was ten, I had this real live baby boy. I loved him, I still love him—even now when I'm no longer the only woman in his life and he's not the only man. When he was three or four years old, we used to ask him who he'd marry and he'd say, "I gonna marry Alish." Soon he was bigger than I was. I mean, I was tiny and thin while he weighed ten pounds at birth.*

Walter: *To me, she was Goldilocks. When I broke my leg, Papa paid for a double room in the hospital and Alice stayed with me. So when Jan came into her life, I resented it so much that Papa used to have to carry me out of the house so that Alice could have a date with Pinky. But even before Jan, I didn't like any of her friends. When Pinky Pearl appeared, I knew my romance with Alice was in big trouble—and Sidney was worried, too. But our parents couldn't read the handwriting on the wall and they didn't take it seriously.*

The great thing about a friendship is that you can't really remember when it started. You may remember when you met, but was there a moment when you first began to like each other? I know that after a while there was a truce between Walter and me, and we were friends by the time I sang at his bar mitzvah. But Walter says that the closeness really came ten years later, when he was going off to the Navy and I was going off on a concert tour. I met him in front of Alexander's Restaurant on Sixth Avenue and Fifty-first Street. Walter was terribly touched that I would take time just to say goodbye to a kid-brother-in-law. But in any friendship, those little gestures mean as much to give as to receive.

In the beginning, though, I couldn't stand Walter. He was a brat who always got in my way. There I'd be, sitting and trying to put my arm around my girl, my intentions as honorable as the next fellow's, and just as I'd be about to give her a kiss, this brat would plunk himself down between us so I couldn't even move. And for this I had to take a bus and a subway all the way up to the Bronx!

Walter: *Cheap bastard wouldn't even gimme a nickel to go away!*

As with friendship, so with romance. I never proposed formally to Alice or got down on my knees. We just understood that we were both serious. In those days, to say "I love you" more than once was enough to start being engaged.

Alice: *I don't remember ever saying yes to Jan. I do remember saying no, I wouldn't marry him, after he flunked a couple of his extension courses at Columbia and gave up the ghost on Morningside Heights. He was up all night playing the fiddle and he had trouble waking for school. But I said to him, "I'm not going to marry you, because then your mother will throw it up to me all my life that I didn't let you become a doctor." Which is just what she did. But back in 1927, those fighting words actually led to our civil wedding and then our elopement. Because when I told him I wasn't going to marry him, he said:*

"If that's the case, then I'm going right to the 170th Street subway station and throw myself in front of the first train that comes in."

And I was dumb enough to believe him.

[As Alice reminisces after almost fifty years of wedlock, Jan heckles her:

"Whaddya mean? I just might have done it."

"You're not the type."

"Then tell me: Who is the type?"

"How can I? They're all dead."]

I don't know what I saw in Jan, except maybe three things. He was the first man who ever kissed me. Second, he had all the charm in the world. And the third factor —the strongest one—was that my parents said no.

I'd been a very obedient child all my life. When my parents said sit down, I sat down. When they said stand up, I stood up. They sent me to Hebrew school every day; I went. They gave me piano lessons; I took piano lessons. They told me to wash dishes, do this, do that; I did it all.

And now all of a sudden, I fell in love with a man they wouldn't even consider my marrying. This was my rebellion. I was hitting back at them in a way that even I couldn't fathom.

But the other two things—his sex appeal and his charm—must have come first, even if the third was strongest. Because if I'd married him just for spite, it never would have lasted.

Our first wedding was civil. A justice of the peace tied the knot for us on Tuesday, October 9, 1928, in upstate New York, not far from the city—we went by train— where we didn't have to post a notice and didn't have to spend the night. Jan and I were never together by ourselves between then and our elopement eight months later—

a month after our Jewish wedding. During those months of living at home—secretly married and scared to death because, since I was well under twenty-one and had lied about my age, they might have been able to annul it—I was a nervous wreck. My mother thought I was going crazy. When I broke out in a rash, the doctor took her aside and told her that if I had a boyfriend, she ought to see to it that I got married. Otherwise he was afraid I might be working on an incurable psychosomatic condition that could make me a spinster all my life.

It seems silly that when a nice boy marries a nice girl and they both have nice parents, all of them have to go through so much rigamarole and charade. But Jan and I were two scared kids who wanted to get married—particularly after Jan's suicide threat—and yet were afraid to face the music.

We decided to run off to Chicago. One of the guests at the Waldmere was Maury Schrager, a musician from Chicago, who said there would always be work for Jan as a fiddler out there. We forgot that before working, Jan would have to join the union and wait six months for his card. But we would have made it anyway, because I put together four thousand dollars to finance our first year on our own.

We both assumed that once we eloped, nobody in our families would ask us back, so I decided to shoot the works. My mother used to give each of her children five dollars a week allowance if we would put half of it into a school savings account. So I had five hundred dollars in the bank and so did my sister, Maye, who was in on the whole plot and volunteered to lend us her bank account, too. That made one thousand dollars. Then I went to my mother, who didn't disapprove of Pinky Pearl as much as my father did. But she had a couple of complaints: in addition to being a fiddler, he played cards. And preying on this second grievance, I conned her. I told her Pinky had lost three thousand dollars at cards and would have to go to jail. "Three thousand dollars!" "And if he doesn't get it," I said, "it'll be terrible." So believe it or not, my mother coughed up three thousand dollars she'd stashed away somewhere. Her only condition was: "Don't tell your father"—which, believe me, I had no intention of doing. With my mother's ransom and my sister's savings and mine, we had enough to elope on.

The forty-nine days that begin with the second day of Passover are a period of self-deprivation for the Jewish people. Haircuts, dancing, and marriages are not permitted, except on one festival day, Lag b'Omer, the thirty-third day Rosh Chodosh, and a couple of others, when the restrictions are lifted. Alice and I scheduled our religious wedding for Lag b'Omer, which fell on Friday, May 10, 1929.

I called up a very distinguished Orthodox rabbi, Herbert Goldstein. He was a friend of the Kalmanowitz family, so I didn't mention whom I was marrying because he surely would have called Mr. and Mrs. K. to congratulate them. I simply said on the phone that my name was Jacob

Perelmuth and that I'd like to get married on Lag b'Omer.

"Is she a Jewish girl?" was his first question.

"Of course!" I said.

"Well, I must warn you, Mr. Perelmuth, that right before I marry you two she'll have to go to the *mikva.*"

Alice: *I went to the* mikva *in our neighborhood that morning. A woman in a white dress told me to bathe myself in a shower first and sat there watching to make sure I cleaned myself thoroughly. Then we went into the* mikva, *which is like a small swimming pool the size of my kitchen, and I went down three steps and said a prayer. The matron in white said the prayer with me. Then I dunked three times—total immersion: my head, everything!—and now I had come clean. But the matron wasn't as happy as she should be. I was alone. A bride's mother should be with her at such a time. Nevertheless, she certified me—though Rabbi Goldstein didn't even have to ask whether I'd been to the* mikva *when I showed up with my hair uncoiffed for the wedding, just before noon.*

The rabbi, however, was even unhappier than the *mikva* matron when he saw who Perelmuth's bride was. "Where are your father and mother?" he asked. And Alice lied to the rabbi. "They're in Europe," she said. He believed her, even though he didn't like the looks of it or the civil wedding certificate from the year before. He went ahead with the ceremony, pronounced us man and wife, and then Alice went to the beauty parlor and I went downtown to see a man about a job. The way we were managing events, it was still too soon for a honeymoon or even a wedding night. In fact, that night we had a date: Alice was coming down for her first Friday-night dinner with my family. They had seen her two or three times and they knew her as Yaikey's cousin from uptown, but that's all they knew, so they were ready to make her welcome.

Alice: *After the beauty parlor, I got into my clothes for the big wedding banquet with my in-laws, who didn't even know it was a wedding banquet or that they were my in-laws. You can imagine how nervous I was. As I was putting on the finishing touches at our bathroom mirror, a bottle of iodine jumped out of the medicine chest and splattered me from shoulders to feet. I looked like a scarlet woman and could have used another* mikva. *Instead I settled for a shower and a complete change of clothes.*

We were a little late for dinner, but it was wonderful. My unknowing father-in-law made Kiddush *over the wine and Jan's mother made noodle soup with* mandlen, *and* kishke, *and her whole fabulous Friday-night menu, developed over the years at home and in Grand Mansion. I sat there eating and enjoying their dinner and all the time I was thinking how we were deceiving them.*

Jan and I didn't elope right away because I still had to shop for our trousseau. I say ours *because when the day came, Jan would leave 210 Madison Street carrying just one suit in a cardboard box so as not to arouse his family's suspicions. Actually, he hadn't much more to his name, but what he did have he couldn't take without risking a valise. So I went to my father's haberdasher, John Forsythe, bought everything Jan needed—shirts, ties, pajamas, underwear, socks—and charged them to my father's account. I went to Andrew Geller's, ordered fifteen pairs of shoes for me, and charged them to my mother's account. I went to the woman who made my mother's underwear. She already had heard (though not from my mother) that I was "keeping company," so she guessed that my big order was for a trousseau. But she kept saying, "Your mother should decide on this one," and I kept saying, "I'll decide. Just go ahead and order it." It amazes me to this day that none of these shopkeepers presented their bills the month before we eloped or mentioned my order to my mother or father, or that Rabbi Goldstein didn't call on them to congratulate them after their "return from Europe."*

The other big risk was where to store this lifetime supply of clothing. There was a big trunk in the cellar, so every time I came home with my bundles, I delivered them directly there before going upstairs. Thus I didn't have much packing to do when we eloped. But if one of my parents had gone down to the storeroom during that month, I might have had a terrible time explaining men's underwear in my trunk.

The day of our June elopement arrived. My mother and father went downtown to the restaurant. Walter wasn't around for once. But Sidney was a bigger boy and a big pest, a suspicious teen-ager if ever there was one, and like any boy of that age with an older sister, terribly curious about anything she did, the more intimate the better. I managed to pique his curiosity by asking him to buy something for me and I'd show him what I did with it when he brought it to me. It was a little white string with chalk that I'd pull under my nails to make them whiter—and I knew that nobody in our part of the Bronx carried this.

Once Sidney was out of sight, my sister Maye—crying something awful that I was doing this to our family—ran for a taxi. The driver loaded the big trunk onto his cab and Jan was waiting for us at Grand Central Station. We didn't want to dip into our capital for the extra fare they charged for the Twentieth Century Limited, *so we took the* Empire State Express, *I think it was, back in the days when you had your choice of overnight trains to Chicago. Just before we left, we sent a telegram from Grand Central to the Bronx:* "GOING WEST LOVE ALICE AND PINKY." *No details. No addresses. No way for them even to communicate that all was forgiven, come home. Jan had just turned twenty-five and I was under the legal age, but old enough to know better. Did you ever hear of such a pair of retards in your life?*

The telegram didn't arrive until the next morning. My father had what later turned out to have been a slight heart attack. He remained sitting in silence for the longest time at the round table in our—their—breakfast room off the kitchen. Then he accused everybody of knowing. Only Maye was guilty—and he might have killed her, except she denied everything and Sidney didn't squeal on her.

That night my mother and father went to see Jan's parents. Jan had been so afraid of his mother that he hadn't even notified them. As soon as they heard the news —and it was very little news, because the telegram certainly didn't say we'd been married, not even once, let alone twice—Mrs. Perelmuth started making terrible accusations. Right away, she implied that I might be pregnant.

My mother, who always spoke very softly, said, "I am sure, Mrs. Perelmuth, that if Alice is pregnant, it can only be from your son."

My mother, a very smart cookie, had already made up her mind to protect us. But my mother-in-law was not to be consoled that easily—and she was a shouter. I had ruined her son's life! Now he couldn't become a doctor!

Mr. Perelmuth was more philosophical. He kept saying, "She's a nice girl, from a nice family."

My father hired a private detective to track us down.

We checked into the Great Northern Hotel in Chicago and called our friend Maury Schrager. He took us into the warmth of his home and family as often or as little as we liked: invitations to lunch and dinner, even to breakfast if we wanted to get up early enough. But we were on our honeymoon, and besides, we slept a lot because we were living in limbo—waiting for our fate to be decided somehow at the other end of the bridges we'd burned behind us.

Ten days after we got to Chicago our phone rang. Mr. K.'s detective had found us and Alice's father was on the line.

There was no greeting, just a familiar voice asking one big question: "Tell me if you're married."

Flustered, I got on my high horse and said, "We can't tell you before we tell my mother and father."

Now the voice grew ominous: *"Tell me if you're married!"*

"I told you, sir, that first I—"

Alice pulled the phone away from me and said, "Papa, we're married, we're married, we're married!"

"By a rabbi?"

"By Rabbi Goldstein!"

"Then let me speak to your husband."

"Yes, sir," I said, taking the phone.

"If you are married, then I will send you money and you can take your honeymoon in California instead of hiding in a Chicago hotel."

Alice could hear every word. She was shaking her head. I said, "No, sir. We want to come home."

"I've seen your parents," he said. "They are well. Very worried about you, but well." This was a relief. I'd lived in fear of at least one death in my family. There had been tears, but nobody had jumped out of a window or committed hara-kiri. Mr. K. added, "I will tell them I've talked with you and that you're coming home soon. I'm sending you money for your trip home."

"Don't bother, sir," I said. "We have enough to get home on."

"Wait there for the money and then come right home."

The money arrived the next day with a salesman he knew. Even on the day he died, years later, my father-in-law never knew about the three thousand dollars his wife had given Alice to "keep Pinky out of jail."

The twelfth day after our elopement, we were back at Grand Central Station, where Alice's father was waiting for us. "While you're deciding what you do next," he said, "I've booked you into a hotel as my guest." Then he told us to enjoy ourselves: the honeymoon wasn't over yet.

The Paramount Hotel in Times Square was rather new in those days. And expensive. It was costing Mr. K. ninety or a hundred dollars a week for our stay there. But we decided to stay two weeks and then go directly to the mountains. In burning my bridges behind me, I hadn't even thought about the commitments I'd made in the Catskills that summer. I was a real Headless Horseman, but now that I remembered, we'd have another two months to make our plans.

There was, however, one dangerously overdue obligation that had to be fulfilled right away. I left Alice at the hotel and went downtown alone to see my folks. As soon as I walked in, my mother called a family conference, but she left most of the talking to my father.

"I want to say that we have no objection to your bride, only to the way you went and got married."

"You must be remarried—I mean, married," said my mother, who refused to recognize any wedding at which she wasn't present as official, "in the proper Jewish way by the rabbi of our synagogue."

I had brought along all our documents, including the papers from Rabbi Goldstein and the certification by the *mikva*. When I showed these to my father, he said, "Herbert Goldstein is a very distinguished name, an outstanding Orthodox rabbi. It would not be possible—or at the very least, it would be a grave insult—to try to improve upon a wedding he has performed." My mother couldn't argue with that.

Through the years, every time I met Rabbi Goldstein he would ask me, "Do you love me or hate me?" And I would say, "I'll always love you." "Well, I have to be careful when I meet people I've married."

It seemed that everybody agreed I should resume school immediately.

I hadn't even told them I'd quit Columbia. I just said I didn't see going back to school in my present position, but that with my fiddle and—

A moan went up from my mother. My father said scornfully, "You've got your fiddle? You're going to be a *klezmer?*" A *klezmer* in the old country was an itinerant musician who went from village to village, playing at weddings and festivals, achieving immortality only in the paintings of Marc Chagall, Chaim Gross and Manya Katz. *Klezmer* was a pretty accurate description of how I'd been making my living over the past few years. The union rate at the time was eight dollars for five hours. If you got the union price. If you took a job for less you said thanks, too.

I told my father I thought I could do better than that. A year or so earlier, while I was still taking courses at Columbia and trying to get Alice to marry me, I had gone over once to the Paramount Theatre (of blessed memory) in Times Square to audition for a singing job. Someone had told me that Paramount theatres was looking for a tenor to go on the road for forty weeks singing a number called "Laugh, Clown, Laugh" in various Paramount "presentation houses," which featured live entertainment along with movies. Since I had a special arrangement that I did in the Catskills with a couple of measures of "Ridi, Pagliaccio" in it, I went over there for a lark, taking Alice along. A hundred singers were trying out, but when my turn came and they heard me sing, they had me do it again—and then the auditioning stopped. "You're the fella we want," I was told. "You've got a forty-week contract at three hundred dollars a week."

I hadn't known there was so much money in the world waiting for me. I was about to faint from joy, when Alice's voice called out from the back: "I'm his manager. Go on with the auditions anyway. He'll let you know tomorrow."

"Uh-oh," the head man said. "We didn't know you had a manager. Maybe we can raise a little more to cover your commission."

"He'll let you know tomorrow," Alice repeated.

"What the hell are you doing?" I said when we got outside. "Trying to ruin my career? We could get married and live good on three hundred dollars a week."

"And save a lot of money," Alice agreed, "because there'd be no time or place to spend your money. The only thing is, you'd have to leave school. And go away from me for almost a year. It's good to know you can get such work, but you don't want to do this now. If it comes that easily once, it'll come again another time." So I turned down the offer, and even though I quit school anyway soon thereafter, I took from the experience a certain confidence that with proper handling and development, I might make a professional career—maybe even as a singing violinist.

And when I told all this to my family, my father said, "That's your outlook? Your future? If you're lucky, you'll be a *klezmer* at a Spanish wedding."

I Was a Gambling Man

My future was still in limbo when Alice and I moved up to the Catskills at the end of June 1929. It wasn't long before I succumbed to an old habit of mine: card-playing. You can't play the fiddle till two or three in the morning and then just pack up your case and go to bed. You're keyed up, ready for a little relaxation. I felt like playing poker till almost daybreak and then dropping into bed before the sun came up strong. But my losings kept me awake a lot longer. I was such a poor gambler, I'd play well into the morning, sometimes till almost noon, just trying to recoup. I came very close to losing much, much more than money.

For I was neglecting Alice. She tried to keep my hours while I played the fiddle—but not while I was playing cards. The other guys didn't want her around. By midsummer she had retreated to our room at the Waldmere and she warned me, "We're really not living together, Pinky, not the way you spend your time gambling. If it goes on like this, we are going to end up living apart." I knew she was right, but was convinced I'd quit cold the minute I got just a little ahead.

Alice went to both her mother and my family for help, but it wasn't until my mother and father confronted me with what I was doing that I gave it up—at least for that summer.

When we came back from the mountains, we went to live with Alice's parents on Findlay Avenue in the Bronx. That lasted barely three months and it's a way of life I don't recommend to anyone. You hear about how living with in-laws is bad for newlyweds' marriages. But you seldom hear about how hard it is for the in-laws. Alice and I fought like cat and dog. Nobody had any privacy when our battles raged through the house.

Alice: *We argued so much that Jan could just look at me and I would cry. We didn't have much of our own and if I asked him for something like a maternity dress, which cost about five dollars, he'd tell me I should get it from my rich father. Which I did. Every pair of shoes I wanted, what did I need it for? he'd ask. He'd never lived with any woman but his mother—and I just was not that frugal. For the first five years of our marriage I cried a private lake. Then I decided that I was going to learn from*

the one woman who had any power over him and do what his mother did: take a strong
position. And once I did, the tears stopped.

Alice got smart, I suppose, after five years, but my in-laws had trouble
surviving two months with the battling Pinky Pearls on their premises. And
I owe what happened next to my mother-in-law. She was a rare woman, who
probably saved our marriage more than once. I was so grateful that much
later, when she was ill and lingered on, not knowing anyone or anything for
several years before she died in the 1960s, I used to go visit her regularly.
Friends marveled at this thankless devotion and someone once said, "Either
you're the greatest son-in-law in the world or she was the greatest mother-in-
law ever."

"She is," I said. "But it isn't a question of how great anybody is. When
I was a nobody—even someone she had great cause to resent—and I needed
her and her husband, they helped us, often without even telling us and never,
never letting us feel we were taking charity from them."

Alice: *One day, when my mother had had enough of our fighting, she said to me,*
"Move out!"

I said, "How can we move out? Pinky's not making enough."

"Don't worry," she said. "You will have rent. You will have money. You will
have everything. But I don't want to see you two kiss and I don't want to hear you
two fight."

I didn't tell Jan about this conversation, but we started looking at apartments
for when the baby came: I didn't have to convince him that bad as it was for two of
us to live with my folks, three would have been impossible. I don't know how he would
have reacted to being told two was impossible for even the time being.

I was a pretty touchy, worried guy in those days, and at the very least,
I would have asked Alice to choose sides. But not knowing we *had* to get
out, I was willing to go apartment-hunting with her, though I had no idea
how we could afford even the cheapest apartment we saw.

The most important part to me was that we had to live in a building with
a big lobby, a showy, splashy, well-upholstered lobby. Alice, of course,
argued with me: "Why are you so interested in the lobby? We're not going
to live in the lobby." And she pointed out then what later became the motto
of lots of hotels I've stayed in: The bigger the lobby, the smaller the rooms.

Even though I wasn't making enough to support a wife, let alone a baby,
I felt I needed to impress people with my lobby and doorman and elevator
man. I was also victimized by the other young couples we knew. In certain

ways, there was more phoniness in those Depression days—a kind of reverse snobbishness in lying to one another—than there is today. As a rule, when somebody wants to impress you nowadays, he'll tell you how much more he's spending on air conditioning or his child's education than he really is. But then everybody wanted to show off what a bargain he got: "See this apartment? What do you think I paid for it? Fifty-three dollars a month—and I got two months concession." Concessions were free rent and you could get up to three months of them in the new apartment houses that had the bad luck to be born in the Depression.

What I thought I could afford, by stretching everything well past the breaking point, was fifty-five or sixty dollars a month. In those days you could figure one month's rent should equal one week's pay. Sometimes I made more than fifty or sixty dollars a week, but during Lent and between bookings I made nothing.

I was most impressed by the lobby of a brand-new apartment building at 2720 Grand Concourse, near 196th Street, in the Bronx. Alice liked one of the apartments we saw there—plus the idea that we'd be the first tenants to live in it. But the rent was ninety-six dollars a month, which was more than I could afford to budget even in a year of fifty-two good weeks.

Still, when Alice's mother asked her if she'd found anything, Alice said, well, yes, but it cost too much. Mrs. K. looked at the place and said ninety-six dollars a month was too much for it and didn't we realize we were paying for that fancy lobby, too? Alice explained how I needed not only the lobby, but a low rent so I could boast to my buddies that we got this real bargain for sixty dollars a month after concessions.

Mr. and Mrs. K. and Alice put their heads together. Then Mr. K. bargained the landlord into three months concession. That brought our rent down to seventy-two dollars a month over the year. Mr. K. wrote the landlord a check for $144 and told me he'd talked the man into four and a half months concession *if* I'd pay a straight sixty dollars for each of the twelve months of the first year. My friends, who'd never heard of half-month concessions, had trouble believing me, but I knew what I was paying, so my belief was contagious and they started bothering their landlords for my kind of deal.

Someone else had always paid the bills where I lived, so I didn't even think about electricity, gas, and telephone costs—the Kayes opened a special account in Alice's name to cover this and she pretended to me it was an account she'd had all her life. In the three weeks before we moved in, they spent ten thousand dollars on household furnishings for us. We're still using the silverware they bought us then. And do you know? I think this splurge was even more important to them than it was to us. They were buying us the trousseau we'd missed out on by eloping. They were beautiful to us. They gave Alice love and affection and they treated me like their oldest child—or rather, their biggest baby. Which I suppose I was.

Alice and I spent five glorious years at 2720 Grand Concourse. Years later, whenever we passed through that part of the Bronx on our way to or from New Rochelle, we would look at each other and smile. We had so many fond memories. But my first and fondest was the day I walked into that fully furnished apartment. My mother-in-law said half-jokingly, "Is there anything you think we left out?"

And I said, "Yes. Toothpicks."

She opened the kitchen closet and there were the toothpicks.

Alice: *We didn't have to buy so much as a toothpick for the apartment all those five years, but it wasn't all the feast Jan seems to remember. I spent some of my grimmest hours living and worrying in 2720 Grand Concourse.*

A few weeks into my pregnancy, I started to lose the use of my right leg. It just began to go out from under me, gradually but steadily. The doctors discovered that I had two tumors in my uterus, which were bringing pressure on the rest of me. One specialist said I should wait until the baby was born before having them removed. The other said the baby wouldn't survive if I wasn't operated on immediately.

I'm what you'd call a dynamic pessimist, so I accepted the second diagnosis and had the operation right away. I was in my fourth month. Both tumors were benign, but under local anesthetic I heard the surgeon telling the other doctors that one of the tumors was just about where the fetal head would have been, so there wasn't much chance of this baby making it into the world intact. They didn't know I heard him, and I didn't tell anybody what I'd heard, but I had to live with that remark for three weeks of absolute immobility in the hospital and then three months of brooding at home in that happy new apartment of ours.

In my eighth month, I gave birth. Larry was born weighing four pounds ten ounces at Beth Israel Hospital in the spring of 1930. To make matters worse, Jan wasn't there. He was in Lakewood, New Jersey, singing in a choir for Passover. My mother and father were on hand. They saw our baby boy brought out from the delivery room; his color was light green. Larry's lungs hadn't yet begun to function. A specialist appeared and said the baby was somewhat big for an incubator, and gave him a little oxygen apparatus that was more like a mask than a tent.

I knew something was wrong when instead of letting me breast-feed my baby, the nurses took the milk from me and gave it to Larry themselves. And when the mohel *(the man who circumcises boys) dropped by to arrange the* bris *(circumcision ceremony), the head nurse intercepted him at my door and I heard her tell him, "Don't bother going in there. The baby has very small chances of surviving."*

The mohel *came in anyway and pretended that because the baby was too small, they wouldn't have the* bris *as usual on the eighth day of his life, but sometime later, when he weighed more than six pounds. Again I pretended not to have overheard, but when the* mohel *was gone, I fell into the most terrible depression of my life. By the eighth day, Larry, who was sickly but sturdy, already weighed more than six pounds and was ready to go home, but they weren't sure I was.*

I was working the holidays at Laurel-in-the-Pines, which was *the* big hotel in Lakewood when the New Jersey resorts were in their heyday. All the affluent Jewish people who could get reservations spent their holidays at Laurel-in-the-Pines.

During the morning service, I got a call from my in-laws with the news that I was the father of a newborn son. Back in 1930, there was no Jersey Turnpike or Garden State Parkway, and besides, who drove? Right after morning services, I would take the Jersey Central Railroad, then a ferry to New York, and I'd have to be back that night. It was about a three-hour trip each way.

I was singing for the first time with Yossele Rosenblatt, the renowned cantor. This was the only engagement I ever had with him; he died a few years later, at fifty-one. Singing with Rosenblatt was a great honor for me. When he learned why I was hurrying to New York and back between services, Cantor Rosenblatt had me called up to the Torah for a special honor and blessing.

I made it to New York and stood, in all innocence, with my nose pressed to the maternity floor's showcase. I had just picked out a great big beautiful baby who looked exactly like the best of Alice and me, when the nurse pointed to the one next to him: the ugliest one in the whole hospital, all shriveled up, with some kind of mask to keep him from looking worse, I thought. Then my in-laws appeared and explained the difficulties to me. I visited Alice, pretended I was proud, and then, on my way out, I took another look at both babies side by side and asked aloud, "Why—*why*—couldn't I have had a baby like the other one?"

For me, the heavens had fallen in—and the trip back by subway, ferry, train, and taxi was part of the nightmare. All my connections went wrong and it was past midnight when I reached Laurel-in-the-Pines, to find Cantor Rosenblatt waiting up for me, not with reproach for missing evening services, but to hear all about the baby.

"Nu, nu, nu! *Mazel tov!*" he said. "Congratulations!" Then I told him how it was and how I felt and he said, "Nonsense! The boy is always different from the baby and sometimes the man is different from the baby, but you have nothing to worry about now." He talked with me into the night and really made me feel better, maybe even hopeful. Rosenblatt was truly a wise man, as much rabbi as cantor, certainly one of the greatest of the latter. After a few more days with him, I was inspired to consider a career as a cantor.

I dropped the first hint: "It would be wonderful, sir, if you could one day teach me your art."

Without a moment's hesitation, he responded, "No, I can't do it. It's impossible."

I flinched, but all I said was: "Why?"

"I think that I'm the greatest cantor," he began, truly in all modesty. "I also think that as you mature, you will be one of the great, maybe even one of the greatest, tenors of your time. If I teach you what I know, you're liable to become the greatest cantor, and what would happen to me?"

I've never felt that way about helping young talent, but I couldn't dispute his attitude because I might tarnish his compliment to me. So I put my cantorial aspirations aside. The few times I saw him during what was left of his life, he always was aware of the little smatterings of success I'd enjoyed and he would greet me: "Nu, didn't I tell you that you could have been the greatest cantor?"

Larry was circumcised at the age of seven weeks in our apartment, by the *mohel* who'd circumcised Alice's brothers. *Mohels* were just as competitive in those days, but in a lower key than today, when they flaunt the latest penis holders (one of them is called Circumflex) and travel with two-way radios in their cars for fear of losing an account.

Larry's *bris* marked the truce in a battle that had almost destroyed my marriage and my wife—with my mother loading the cannon on both sides.

Alice: *Larry's Hebrew name is Avraham Aryeh: Avraham after Jan's father's sister's husband, who had just died, and Aryeh after my father's father. The bride customarily names the first child. I wanted my grandfather's name to come first, but they picked Avraham and in our religion no name can precede Avraham. Mother Perelmuth argued and insisted and steamed up everything and everybody until, finally, my parents and I swallowed hard and let my first-born, our only son, be named their way.*

A week before the bris, *though, I had a screaming argument with my mother-in-law, who'd "dropped up" from the Lower East Side to the Grand Concourse just to ambush me with a few afterthoughts she'd had, and it was more than I could take. That was the era when Jan and I never had less than one fight a day—and now her, too! As soon as she left, I phoned my father at the restaurant. He said, "We're very busy, so I can't talk, but what can I do for you?"*

"Nothing," I said. "I just want you to know that I'm throwing the baby out the window first and then I'm going next."

"I'll be right up," he said. "Just control yourself until I can get to the Bronx."

He made it by taxi from Thirty-first Street and Fifth Avenue in forty minutes. I didn't even offer him coffee. He unclenched a little when he heard Larry cough in his sleep. I can see my father now, his elbows resting on the table, his head in his hands, as he said, "Now tell me what happened."

I told him all about Jan and all about his mother and all about how unfair this was to me and Larry and even to him and my mother.

My father just listened to me, which was maybe the most important thing he did, and then he said:

"I feel very sorry for you, Alice. But you know, Alice, you never asked me whether you should marry. In my way of thinking, every daughter should ask her father what a husband will expect from her. Because when your mother tells it to you, she tells you from a woman's point of view. But if you'd asked me, *I'd have told you from the man's side what your obligations were."*

When my father said this, I began to bawl. Not just because I realized again how much the way we'd married had hurt him, but because, as I told him when I found words again, "I didn't ask Mama either!"

His visit calmed me down, and after I'd unburdened all my grievances to him, I realized that my despair had been more a matter of life than death: I had merely been overwhelmed by an agonizing pregnancy and a perilous premature birth compounded by continuing domestic friction and a little in-law trouble. That was when we agreed to give Mrs. Perelmuth everything she wanted and concentrate on happy endings for the rest of my distress.

The biggest problem of 1930 between Jan and me, it turned out, was the same as the Pinky Pearl Follies of 1929: his gambling. I guessed he was playing cards at the union hall. He'd go down there in the middle of the afternoon to look for a job, and stay three, four, five hours. When I told him I knew he was playing cards, he didn't even try to deny it.

In the interest of saving my marriage, I tried to play cards. I never had the patience even for solitaire. I actively disliked my own cards, even when I had four aces. All they brought me were headaches. When I tried to play cards with Jan, we fought worse than ever.

I knew the problem would get worse when we went up to the Catskills that summer. In fact, our marriage was nearly destroyed by Jan's card-playing. One night at the Kiamesha Country Club, Larry ran a bad fever. I wasn't feeling well either. After Jan finished playing his music, he came up to our tiny room around midnight on his way to play poker. The room was so small we had to crawl over the footboard of the bed to get into it. I had a hot plate for heating up Larry's formula, and I asked Jan if he'd give Larry his two-o'clock bottle so I could get some sleep. He said he would.

At three-thirty Larry's crying woke me up, and I felt to see if Jan was there in bed. No one. The baby was feverish and hysterical and so was I. I looked out our window across to the cardroom, where I could see the game in progress, and flashed the light to attract Jan's attention. I saw him come to the window a couple of times and seem to look up, but he was totally unaware of us.

At 5 A.M. I got out of bed, packed all our things and dressed, then went back to bed to wait for Jan. At seven o'clock Pinky Pearl tiptoed into the room, got undressed, and crept into the bed. It was then he saw I was wide awake and fully dressed. "What's going on?" he asked.

"I'm leaving, and I'm never coming back. You broke your word to me. I can't stand the cards. Your mother always said when a man plays cards he can't even remember his mother's name. That's how it poisons you. You didn't know and didn't care whether we were dead or alive. I'm finished with you!"

Jan started to cry, really cry, and begged me not to leave him. He carried on until finally I said, "You can have me and Larry—or the ace, king, jack, and queen. But if you choose us, I absolutely will not tolerate them!"

He never played cards again—until years later, when I encouraged him to. That was when losing one hundred or even two hundred dollars didn't mean so much. And we weren't living off my parents.

Making Up with Lima Beans

A man and a woman live together as man and wife and most of the time they're happy. But they fight once in a while. Or one gets angry at the other and they stop talking.

As time goes on, if you don't speak to each other for a week, you begin to search your mind for what caused this terrible rift, why you're so angry. And you discover sometimes that you weren't so angry. Because if you really were angry, you wouldn't have forgotten *why*. Before you know it, you find a way of making up.

When we were young, Alice had her special way of making up. After two days of my silence, she made lima bean soup—which she knew I didn't like. In my boyhood I'd eaten more than my fill of cheap and filling lima beans.

So when the soup was put before me in all my sullen silent solitude, I would explode: "What's the big idea of lima beans? You know I don't like lima beans!"

"Oh," Alice would say ever so sweetly, "you *do* talk. I didn't think you talked at all."

I'd begin to sputter into my lima bean soup. When she took it away, she'd be shaking with so much mirth that she'd spill some of the soup. I'd get down on the floor, laughing all the way, to help her clean it up—but instead I'd take her hand and we'd be friends again. The war was over—until our next quarrel.

Fighting together is part of living together. And so is the making up, which is sometimes worth all the fighting. I don't mean to make us sound like Blondie and Dagwood, but that's part of what life's about.

There's no such thing as people sprouting wings. Such individuals you find only in heaven, where they're called angels.

I've never sprouted wings and I'm *not* the greatest and I'm certainly not the sweetest and I'm not the kindest and I'm not the best. I've got a temper and I don't mind letting people know I'm angry because that's the best way for me to get over my rage. If I didn't, I'd have had more ulcers than I've had.

The concept of turning the other cheek is not a Jewish one. Why go through life letting people step over you because they know you'll forgive them tomorrow? Let them know you have a temper if crossed. I want to be counted—and sometimes you have to fight for that.

My wife and I have had moments of anger and moments of love, our ups and our downs—and we haven't done so badly in nearly fifty years together. We think we're coming out all right and we're closer than ever. We're still together, and I don't think unhappily so.

Rules always change, but we have one rule that's worked. We made a pact a long time ago and we've kept it no matter how angry we've grown with each other: When one yells, the other should listen. For when two people yell, there's no communication, just noise and bad vibrations.

What a Pair of Pipes!

In the summer of 1932, I had a great job in the Catskills leading the dance band at the President Hotel in Swan Lake, New York. I was actually co-conductor. My partner was a wonderful composer, a fine musician and dear friend named Alexander Olshanetsky. I could lead the band while playing the fiddle, but when I sang, "Olshy" conducted. So I was getting more chances to sing. We had to work hard because in those days, guests came and stayed the whole summer, so you couldn't repeat the same show very often. Wednesday night was Cabaret Night, so I appeared as a soloist; Saturday night was Show Night, and I appeared in the show; Sunday night was Concert Night, so I appeared in the concert. The other nights, I played the fiddle and sang choruses for the dancing.

The best part of the job was that after paying off our musicians, "Olshy" and I were left with $130 a week to divide. From my sixty-five dollars I had to deduct the forty dollars a week they charged for bringing Alice and Larry along. Out of the twenty-five dollars or so left, there were tips to our waiter and busboys; cigarettes (I used to smoke two packs a day!); newspapers; and we still had to pay rent on our apartment in the Bronx. By the end of the summer we owed ourselves money, but at least I was giving my wife and son some good Catskill Mountain air.

One weekend, a man in the jewelry business heard me sing. He had once been married to a showgirl and told me he could arrange an audition for me with Earl Carroll.

Earl Carroll was then the King of Show Business and his *Vanities* were comparable to the *Ziegfeld Follies*. I was eager, but when the jeweler left on Sunday, I was sure that was the last I'd ever hear from him or Earl Carroll.

On Monday afternoon I got a long-distance call from New York, telling me to come in for my audition on Tuesday. Earl Carroll was rehearsing a new show at Fifty-third Street and Broadway in what's now the Ed Sullivan Theatre. The jeweler must have given me a fourteen-karat build-up and carried a lot of weight, because just as soon as I walked from the sunny street into that dark theatre, they called a break in the rehearsal so they could audition me.

Auditions are always awful. You can't see who you're talking to and you don't know who you're singing for. And it's particular hell to do an audition in front of show people. They're the worst audience in the world. If they're in the chorus, they do scales during your tryout; if they're dancers, they limber up; worst of all, if they're tap-dancers, all they do is stand in front of a mirror and practice. They ignore you. They interfere with you. You can sing your head off. Your life can depend upon it. You're looking for a break. You're dying to make good. And they know from nothing—just tap, tap, tap.

I handed a batch of my sheet music to the conductor Ray Cavanaugh, who was playing the piano.

On my way in, I had taken off my glasses. This was 1932, remember, when everybody had to be a matinee idol with twenty-twenty vision. Life was very stupid then; it was almost thirty years before Steve Allen walked onto the TV screen wearing a pair of specs. So I came onstage squinting and a voice hollered, *"Are you ready?"*

"Yes, sir. Mr. Cavanaugh has my music. What would you like, gentlemen? I can sing a ballad or an operatic aria or an Italian song."

"Sing a ballad!"

I sang "Song of Songs." When I started to sing it, I had piano and percussion, because the tap-dancers went on tapping, but after a few bars the tapping stopped. My voice took over their attention and they were vaguely interested in spite of themselves. They actually applauded when I finished the number. I had every right to be flattered.

"Just a minute!" the voice said. "You said something about doing an aria. What opera can you sing?"

I said, "Well, I have two or three, but how about *Pagliacci?*"

"You sing *Pagliacci?*"

To answer his question, Ray Cavanaugh began to play "Vesti la giubba" and I began to sing it—without a rehearsal, but we were both musicians. When we got through, I really won a round of applause.

"Thank you," said the voice. "Just wait outside. I'll be with you in a minute."

I found my way offstage without my glasses and onto the street with them. After a few minutes, a big guy, at least six feet tall, strode out. I knew he was Tom Rooney, Earl Carroll's chief talent booker.

The first thing he said to me was, "Gee, kid, you got a great pair of pipes! The boss thinks you're hot stuff. How would you like to be in a Broadway show?"

"Fabulous!" I said.

"How much would you want?"

"Well, I've never been offered a show and I don't know what they pay and . . ."

"Aw!" said Tom Rooney. "Figure it out and tell me what ya think you'd like to get."

This sounds like the Big-Break Write-Your-Own-Ticket Scene of so many backstage musicals, but it's the way such operators operated. Instead of saying what they could pay, they played it this way, just in case the talent was ready to work for peanuts. If not, they could always bargain down. There were probably people who would pay to work in Earl Carroll's *Vanities*.

Rooney kept pressing me, so I started figuring out loud: "Well, if I could get $125 a week, I could support my wife and myself and pay our rent and also have enough money left to study." All kinds of dreams seemed to be coming true, so why not a bunch of them at once?

Rooney began to laugh—a lilting baritone Irish laugh. When he stopped laughing, he said, "That's a lot of money."

"You asked me what I wanted and I tell you what I need to exist. I don't think I'm asking the moon." Even in those days, Broadway didn't pay as well as Hollywood, but if Paramount theatres could pay three hundred dollars a week, surely Earl Carroll could afford $125. And I was willing to negotiate.

"No harm asking," Rooney said to me, "but the boss would never go for a hundred twenty-five."

"All right," I said. "I think I could manage on a hundred dollars a week."

He started laughing four-fifths as hard. I came down to seventy-five dollars.

"Naw," he said. "You're way outta line, kid."

"Well, then, what would you offer me?"

Tom Rooney then started a speech that haunted me for many years. I can still hear him:

"Kid, if you were as tall as I am, if you looked more like me, if you had a good profile, and if you didn't have to wear those big thick eyeglasses, and if you were handsomer, instead of having that big chest and even bigger stomach, and if you weren't short and stocky, then you could name your price with Earl Carroll, because the boss is wild about your pipes."

By the time he was through, he had cut me up like a surgeon—from ear to ear, from nose to stomach, from head to toe. I'd come to see about a job, but what a job he'd done on me!

I was dying inside, but I retorted like a living man, fighting back the tears: "So tell me. If I were you, that would be one thing. But I am what I am. How much can you offer me?"

"Thirty dollars a week."

Even in the Depression, you couldn't live on thirty dollars a week. I said so.

"Well, that's what it is, kid, and if you were as tall as I and if you had a better . . ."

The tears were about to burst the dam. I also knew that he and I weren't going to do business. So without choking too much, I made a pretty prophetic speech of my own:

"You know something, Mr. Rooney? You keep harping on how handsome you are and how tall you are. But maybe there'll come a time when a little guy like me, with glasses and a stomach—small, stocky, overweight, with not such a great profile—could buy a cup of coffee for a big, handsome guy like you when you may need it."

With that, I turned and ran west on Fifty-fourth Street, with Rooney yelling after me. I ran down Tenth Avenue, cutting over to Forty-second and

Twelfth and the Weehawken Ferry to get the Ontario & Western Railroad, crying all the way back to the mountains, where I was making twice as much money as Earl Carroll was willing to offer me.

I fortunately didn't meet anybody I knew. I burst into our forty-dollar-a-week hotel bedroom and thank G-d Alice was there. When I was able to tell her what had happened, she said something that still rings in my ears:

"The hell with them. You'll see. Your day will come. You're good-looking. You're handsome. You're beautiful. Y'know, Pinky, I wouldn't have married you if you weren't plenty tall and handsome for me. If you're not as tall as Rooney, half would be tall enough."

She went on this way until I stopped crying, and I'll never forget how she summed it up:

"Don't worry about your nose, Pinky, there will come a time when *only* people with noses like yours will be great singers. Maybe your nose has something to do with the quality of your voice. Maybe even the shape of your face . . ."

This was ten years before Barbra Streisand was born! And Alice didn't really know anything, but in not knowing, she was right. The Lord and nature produce you in a certain way that your tones depend upon. Your resonance chambers, your whole making of a sound, all have to do with your physiological construction. Look at tenors! The greatest tenors were little squatty guys with short necks who ate too much. A bass is usually a big, tall fellow, slender, with a long neck; it's the length of the vocal cords that helps determine what kind of tones you produce. So when Rooney was telling me to look like he did, he was asking the impossible.

Everybody at the hotel wanted to know what had happened. Friends, cronies, colleagues all asked. And I told them. Olshanetsky and a couple of others held their heads because they ached or put their arms around me to comfort me.

I'd always had a complex about my appearance, but now it was becoming the Greatest Single Truth in my life—and only Alice's words kept me going.

The coda to this terrible chapter in my life is that without knowing it, I had jumped off a sinking ship before the journey began. Earl Carroll's wave had crested and he went from *Vanities* to nightclub revues to oblivion before petering out entirely. And Tom Rooney petered out with him. Sooner than anyone expected came the time when great big handsome Mr. Rooney could have used a cup of coffee. I hope somebody bought it for him, because I'm not sure I would have known how.

Roxy

Among the engagements I got on my return from Swan Lake to New York at the end of that summer was that of singing violinist at an Astor Hotel testimonial dinner for the vaudeville team of Weber and Fields. So many extra tables were booked that the Astor had to cover the dance floor with them and so they needed a performer instead of a dance band. The toughest kind of audience an artist can have is a fully professional crowd. And this one was mostly show people. Strike one: They're not interested in you, they're interested in talking shop—right through your act. Strike two: If you're good, they're better. Even if they're not, *particularly* if they're not, they'll give you the cold shoulder because they don't want to run into competition, especially not on a night off. Strike three: Even if you're great, you're not a name and they are—so there must be something wrong with you.

But I was determined to give these jaded ears my very best. After I did my first number, they gave me a lukewarm hand. Then I did another song. This time, the applause was up so strong that I milked a fast encore. And with that one the audience sat up and took notice. In fact, they yelled and screamed and made me do two more encores until the banquet manager started getting mad. I was only supposed to be a pause between the fruit salad and the chicken soup.

I saw a music publisher named Bobby Crawford at one of the tables. He knew me vaguely as a violinist who used to come in from time to time to pick up free orchestrations. A man sitting with Crawford sent his card to me. There was no message, no address, no phone number, just the name: S. L. Rothafel. But that was enough.

Samuel L. "Roxy" Rothafel was a pioneer in modern theatrical entertainment. He was the originator of "presentation houses"—combining stage and screen shows—like the ones on the Paramount circuit. He believed in thinking Big, building Big, and doing Big. He had decided that symphony orchestras didn't belong only in Carnegie Hall. Why not have them in a movie house, too? Why couldn't people come and buy a ticket to see a movie and be exposed to good music at the same time? Why not a chorus? Or a concert artist? Why couldn't a pianist like Mischa Levitski be brought up out of the bowels of the theatre on an elevator in full dress at night, striped trousers at matinees, and play a concerto? He didn't just pay lip service to bringing good music to the masses. He went ahead and did it. And the Roxy Theatre was his first monument.

When he sent me his card that night in 1932 at the Astor, I came home all excited. Alice had one very practical question: "What do you do next?"

I didn't know how to locate Roxy, but it was lucky I'd noticed he was sitting with Bobby Crawford. The next morning I called Bobby, who told me Roxy was operating out of a temporary office in the RKO Palace Theatre Building. He gave me the phone number. When I called, Roxy remembered me and invited me down to see him on Tuesday. I brought along my fiddle in case he wanted me to audition.

Roxy was a balding, aggressive ex-Marine with strong features. He pounded the table a lot. He was a small man, but he looked like Napoleon to me. And he had a heart bigger than himself—which I learned at that very first interview.

The first thing he said was: "What're you doing with a fiddle?"

"Trying to earn a living."

"Do you know what you have in your throat, son? My God!" Roxy exclaimed. *"That's* your career. Throw away your fiddle. You'll make millions on your voice. You can be a star!"

I started to laugh and he wanted to know what was so funny.

"I don't mean to be offensive, sir, but nobody can do this for me, not even you. Look at me! I'm short and fat and homely. And I'm the tenor—the guy who's supposed to win the girl. If I were six feet tall and had a profile like Lou Tellegen . . ." (Tellegen was an American actor with a Grecian profile, who was married to Geraldine Farrar. His profile was better than Barrymore's. I used to think the word "telegenic" came from his name.)

Roxy started pounding his desk, and before he was done I began to sense I had an ally second only to Alice.

"Whoever told you that?" he began. "You are the best-looking man I know. You are tall, you are handsome, you've got the most gorgeous profile, you are better-looking than Lou Tellegen even before you open your mouth. You're marvelous. You're beautiful."

"No, no, no, no, sir!" I argued back.

He got angrier. "What do you mean—you don't believe it? I've done it for others; why can't I do it for you? And look at me, son! Why can't you look me in the eye?"

"I *am* looking you in the eye."

"No, you're not. And I know why. Because you've given up on yourself. Now you look me in the eye and you listen to me and don't you *ever* let me hear you say you're ugly. You just sing, sing the best you can, and you'll be beautiful! You study and you sing and you'll be even taller and handsomer and more good-looking than you are now. Nobody'll be handsomer than you!"

Hearing this lecture from him after hearing it at home, I began to believe it for a couple of minutes at a time. But I stood there with my mouth open.

Roxy asked, "How much studying have you done?"

"Just enough lessons so I could sing a chorus with a band," I said.

"If you'll promise me you'll study, I'll promise to do something for you. And I know it'll work out. I think you have great talent. You'll hear from me."

I rushed home and whirled Alice around the room. But September went by and we didn't hear more from Roxy. In October I started reading that Radio City Music Hall would open in December. I told Alice, "I'll bet you that's what Roxy had in mind for me." But there was still no word from Roxy. Alice thought I should call him again. I thought maybe he was just giving me a run-around, but inside I knew he wasn't. So I called Bobby Crawford and told him Roxy had promised to call me, but hadn't.

"He's a busy man."

"So what should I do?"

"Do you know how to write a letter? Write him a letter. Remind him who you are."

I wrote a letter to Roxy. The next day his program director, Leo Russotto, called me up and said, "Roxy wants you to be on our radio program, *Radio City Music Hall of the Air,* next Sunday."

"No kidding? What should I sing?"

"Roxy would like you to sing a favorite number of his: 'Give Me One Hour' "—a ballad from *The White Eagle* by Rudolf Friml. I learned it and sang it at Rockefeller Center the following weekend. It didn't create a sensation, but it didn't do me any harm either.

The conductor was Erno Rapee and, for some reason, I wasn't his cup of tea at first. But he invited me back for the next week's program and asked me to prepare the "Berceuse" from *Jocelyn,* by Godard. Actually, he was setting a trap for me. He knew my voice wasn't trained and this particular number was a tricky one—all finesse and no high notes. For me today, it's as simple to go out onstage and sing it as it is to gargle with Listerine, but at that time it was difficult. And Rapee kept finding fault with me at rehearsals. I just wasn't prepared for the effects he wanted me to handle. He made a point of berating me loudly in front of the orchestra. Finally, rapping for everybody's attention, Rapee turned on me and said:

"Listen, I don't know what you're doing here. Roxy insists that you're good. I think you have a voice, but you don't have enough talent. You'll never fit in here. Why don't you go back and play your weddings with your fiddle? Go play bar mitzvahs and the Astor Hotel."

I walked out of the studio before I could cry and Leo Russotto, who was keeping an eye on me for Roxy, was right on top of me.

"Don't bother about that guy," Leo told me. "That's the way he acts to everybody. Don't feel bad. But listen. Is there anything else you know? Do you know any opera?"

Leo had a knack for taking my mind off my troubles. "Yeah," I told him. "I know a couple of arias."

"What do you know?"

"Oh, I know 'La donna è mobile.' "

Leo marched me into a little room, sat down at the piano, and played "La donna è mobile." He knew everything by heart; later, when he was my concert accompanist, it used to make everybody, including me, nervous when he showed up without any sheet music.

I sang my only Verdi for him and he stood up and announced I was going to sing it on the air, instead of Godard.

"Yeah? What about Rapee?" I said.

Leo pushed me back into the big studio, where Rapee was winding up his rehearsal. Leo said, "Erno, I want you to hear this boy sing something."

"This is no place for amateurs," Rapee snarled.

"Listen to him sing!" Leo shouted.

"I heard him already," Rapee replied, starting to leave.

Leo bounded in front of Rapee, sat down at the piano, played the introduction, and I began to sing "La donna è mobile."

Rapee listened to my high notes. Then he said, "Why in hell didn't you tell me you could sing this?"

"You didn't ask me."

"All right," he said. "Tomorrow we'll do this number." We did a quick rehearsal before we went on the air. I sang it, and I became a fixture of *Radio City Music Hall of the Air.*

Roxy knew I needed voice lessons and he sent me to see Eleanor McClellan. She offered me a scholarship which I learned much later hadn't been a scholarship at all: Roxy paid for all my lessons.

Mostly, Roxy stayed in the background, but on one significant aspect of my career he confronted me directly. "Pinky Pearl," he informed me, "is no name for someone who sings like you do."

"I agree," I said. "Anyway, my real name is Perelmuth."

"That's a nice name," he said, "but not for stage, screen, or radio. Let your mother call you Perelmuth. Let your wife call you Pinky. That's fine at home. But who wants to hear Pinky Perelmuth the tenor? You've gotta have something euphonious."

"So a phony name is more euphonious than Pinky Pearl?"

"Exactly!" he said. "Starting next Sunday, your name is John Pierce."

3

John and Jascha, Randolph and Paul

John Pierce and Jascha Pearl

"John Pierce!" I exclaimed. "That's a lovely name for a guy who's six feet two, blond, blue-eyed, with a straight nose, thin lips, fine profile . . . Mr. Rothafel, I don't look like John Pierce. John Pierce would be tall. John Pierce would be—"

There was an angry glint in Roxy's eye. "Well, you *are* John Pierce. Repeat after me: I *am* John Pierce, I *am* John Pierce. . . ."

"I am John Pierce? I am John Pierce. *I* am John Pierce. I *am* John Pierce. I *am* John Pierce?"

"I am John Pierce," I told my wife when I came home.

"Go on!" she said.

"That's what Roxy told me today."

"Well, he must know what he's doing," Alice decided, when I told her the details of our dialogue. "Besides, what difference does it make?"

"But I'm *not* John Pierce!"

"I thought you said you *are* John Pierce."

A few weeks before I started with *Radio City Music Hall of the Air,* Alex Olshanetsky had booked me to sing every Sunday morning with his orchestra on radio station WEVD's program sponsored by the *Jewish Daily Forward.*

The *Forverts* program paid ten dollars a broadcast and I sang Yiddish and Hebrew and cantorial music under the name of Jascha Pearl.

The manager of the *Forverts* was B. Charney Vladeck. He and Fiorello H. La Guardia were responsible for the first cooperative houses in New York City. They believed that a man who worked in a sweatshop or factory should have a decent place to live that wouldn't cost him a lot of money or make some landlord rich. Instead he would pay in a little money and buy an apartment.

Vladeck was a wise, fatherly man, so I went to see him about my John Pierce crisis: "This man Roxy wants me to change my name." Then I told him the whole story of how Pinky Pearl became John Pierce. When I finished, Vladeck said, "I will say this for your Mr. Roxy. He told you why. He told you it would be catchier. Maybe he is right. Now tell me something else. Does he object to your leading a Jewish life?"

"No, he didn't say that."

"Did he tell you not to bring up your children in a Jewish manner? Would he object if you went to synagogue?"

"No, no; all he wants me to do is change my name."

"So change your name," Vladeck concluded. "No one can condemn you. After all, to sing on WEVD for the Jewish people, you changed your name to Jascha Pearl. You couldn't call yourself Pinky Pearl or John Pierce or even Jehoshua or Jacob on the *Forverts* program. So if you changed your name for your people, you can change your name for this Mr. Roxy and the world, too."

So I was John Pierce. I gave the spelling of that name a six-month life expectancy. I certainly knew it wouldn't last forever.

Never Whistle in Your Dressing Room

In 1928, John D. Rockefeller, Jr., had leased some land in the center of Manhattan as the site for an opera house. But when the stock market crashed a year later, the opera patrons were among the first to bow out of the money scene. Rockefeller was left holding the plot and paying $3.8 million a year in taxes and rent to his landlord, Columbia University.

It was Roxy, a little man who thought big, who came to Rockefeller and sold him on building Radio City—not just the Music Hall, but a headquarters and nerve center for the whole communications complex of NBC, RCA, and RKO. Despite the Depression, Rockefeller gambled on expansion. In lieu of an opera house, he built Rockefeller Center. The Music Hall part of it cost some eight million dollars and was watched over by Rockefeller's wife and his son Nelson. The entertainment was entrusted to Roxy, who patterned it after an English music hall—all variety show, two shows a day, no movie in the format.

I had guessed right when I told Alice I'd bet Roxy had me in mind for the Music Hall. Sure enough, soon after I joined *Radio City Music Hall of the Air,* I was cast in the minstrel segment of the opening show.

The first show was planned as a blockbuster: sixteen Big Numbers that included Weber and Fields, Martha Graham, and a great new Roxy protégé, a fast-thinking young tap-dancer named Ray Bolger who could do anything —not just with his feet, but with his eyes, his hands, his personality. I was lucky enough to be featured in the finale, a minstrel show with Ray Bolger matching wits with DeWolf Hopper, a great actor in his late seventies, nearing the end of a distinguished career. For more than forty years, his annuity had been his famous recitation of the poem "Casey at the Bat." But strangely, there was no joy in Mudville when Hopper and Bolger played on the same team: It was like hit and run, with the wrong man on base.

We kept thinking everything would jell, but even before then, I knew *I* was in trouble. Two of the best songwriters around, Jimmy McHugh and Dorothy Fields (who'd already collaborated on "I Can't Give You Anything but Love, Baby" and "On the Sunny Side of the Street"), had been assigned to write me a tenor solo number—and I was very excited about this until I was shown what they produced: a dreadful song called "Journey's End."

I told Roxy what I thought of the song. For a minute I feared he was going to pound me instead of his desk. He exploded: "Since when do *you* choose songs for *me?* If I tell you Jimmy McHugh and Dorothy Fields wrote a hit song for you, you'll do it. And if it isn't a hit, it'll be your fault, not theirs, not mine. So you better do it right."

The finale was proving to be the very worst part of what was already shaping up as a pretty bad show. We all thought Roxy must know what he was doing, so we bore with him, waiting for him to work his magic. What we didn't know was that he was suffering from a painful prostate condition and had a date to go into the hospital for surgery on December 28, 1932, the morning after the premiere.

On the night of December 26, we had a rehearsal that dragged on into the early hours of the 27th. Everything else in the show went quickly and painlessly, if not well, but the minstrel finale was a mess. Bolger, whose big moments came elsewhere in the show, worked heroically to salvage our disaster.

I came to the rehearsal very cheerfully because this close to the opening, what could happen? In fact, I was so cheerful that I came into my dressing room whistling. The two tenors who shared the room with me were making up, but when they heard me whistle they dropped everything, knocking over a chair and a mirror, which shattered.

"Do you know what it means to whistle in a dressing room?" they shouted together.

"It means I'm happy," I said.

"It means the guy nearest the door will walk onstage and maybe sing off pitch or lose his job."

I was standing just inside the doorway, so all I could do was shrug and try to laugh it off. They insisted I try to break the spell I'd cast. How? By hopping around the room on one leg while both of them kicked me in the behind; by hitting my head against the wall until the wall hurt.

Ever since then, as a result of what happened next, I've been superstitious. I never put my hat on the bed. I don't walk under ladders and I avoid black cats. I won't move my apartment or office downstairs in the same building. And of course, I no longer whistle in dressing rooms.

As the rehearsal of the finale went into the wee hours of the morning, we could see that nothing was helping and that Roxy had had enough of it and us. Bolger was still saying, "Why don't we . . . ?" when Roxy stood up from his seat, lumbered (hard for a small, dynamic man to do) down the aisle, and climbed onto the stage, shaking his head.

Before Roxy could speak, DeWolf Hopper—a smart old codger who knew the score—drew himself up as if to do "Casey at the Bat," and said in his most commanding voice: *"Roxy!"*

Roxy stopped in his tracks, as though G-d were about to proclaim the Commandments. "Yeah? Yeah?" he said.

"Roxy!" repeated DeWolf Hopper. "We're all tired. We've been working hard for weeks."

"Yeah, yeah," Roxy agreed wearily, almost punchily.

"And *you*'re tired, Roxy. You've been working the hardest of all of us. So before you say anything, why don't we just recess? Let's all go home and get a couple of hours sleep. And then we'll all come back for a morning call, refreshed, and the whole finale will go differently."

"Yeah, yeah. You're right, DeWolf," Roxy said, shuffling toward the exit. If DeWolf Hopper had only brought that magnetism to the minstrel show, he could have held his own with Ray Bolger and the show would have played for years. All of us—Bolger and particularly myself and the rest of the performers who were in the finale—looked at Hopper with gratitude.

But he had bought us only a few hours time, not even a few hours sleep, for who could sleep? When I got home around 3 A.M., Alice woke up. I said, "Alice, we're in trouble," but I was too weary to try to tell her how bad.

That morning at ten, I was back at the Music Hall and went to the men's room before facing the music. One of my roommates was there, and he said, "Roxy's looking for you. I hear your number's out of the show. You shouldn't have whistled in the dressing room."

I found Roxy at the control board and I said, "Mr. Rothafel, are you looking for me?"

"Yes. Sit down," he said, very solemnly. Then he cleared his throat and said, "You know you're in show business. And in show business you've got to take the good with the bad. Now, it's not that you're not singing well. You're singing fine. But I'm taking out the whole finale, the whole minstrel show—and unfortunately, your number is in that part of the program and there isn't any other place in the show I can put you in. Therefore, you're out."

I exploded: "How can you do this to me? I didn't seek you out! You sent your card up to me. You promised me a role. You told me I'd be a smash. I asked you for nothing. You told me a song I didn't like would be a hit and I trusted you."

Roxy looked at me very coldly and said, "Look, I can't waste any more time talking." I tried to clutch at him, imploringly, beseechingly, and even without touching him I must have scared him, because he said, "Will you get away from me, please? I'm sorry. That's all I can tell you. I'm sorry."

I was close to tears, but the words still came: "People aren't going to believe I was ever in the show. What am I going to tell them? My wife's bought a new dress, a new hat, and a new coat for tonight."

"Look," Roxy said. "I'm in trouble, too. I don't even know what's gonna happen to me after tonight, so please go away."

At the time Roxy's daughter was being courted by a fellow named Bill Stern and Roxy had found Bill work as stage manager at the Music Hall.

When I blew up at Roxy, flooding the control board with my tears, Bill Stern was watching from a safe distance. After the torrent had slowed down to a drizzle, he said:

"Listen, kid, I know what's happened and I'm sorry about it. You're in a bad spot. But let me tell you something, because you don't know a thing about the theatre. Do you have a contract?"

"Yeah, and a lotta good it's done me!" I sobbed.

"How long?"

"F-four weeks, with an option to renew."

"So you've got a four-week contract. Good! Now let me teach you the

First Law of the Theatre. If you want to get paid, no matter what your contract says, no matter what's been done to you, you have to report to the stage manager's desk for every show—then we have to pay you. I know money won't make you feel any better about this, but at least you'll get paid. But you must come in, you must let me see you, so I can mark you present, otherwise you won't get your money. They're very strict about it and they'll dock your pay if you're a couple of minutes late. But once I've checked you off, you can leave until just before the next show."

Years later, when this same Bill Stern was the famous NBC sportscaster, I used to listen to his fifteen-minute program night after night even though I couldn't tell first base from the fifty yard line. I used to enjoy the inspirational sports sagas he told and particularly the way he told them. Bill Stern, the stranger-than-truth storyteller, made one believe—and he inspired me to go on. Going through the motions, even with your head dragging lower than your rump, you at least have a chance of picking up the pieces.

When I left the building, I wandered the streets. I needed a friend. I went to a phone booth and called my father at his catering hall. When he heard my voice he said: *"Mazel tov!* I know you want me to come to the show, but we have a wedding tonight at Grand Mansion. So I wish you luck, your mother and your brothers and your sister wish you luck, you should have a great success tonight." How could I spoil his good cheer? So I tried somewhere else: a more modern man than my father, who could react to the world as it seemed to me that day.

I phoned my father-in-law at his restaurant. He was in a very important meeting, but I needed him and he came right to the phone. I told him I had to talk to him immediately. All he said was, "Where?" I told him I was in a candy store at Sixth Avenue and Thirty-eighth Street. He said he'd meet me in the lobby of an adjacent office building. Five minutes later, he arrived by cab. Tears in my eyes, I told him my story, and as I did, I realized what griped me most: "Who will believe me? Nobody will believe me. Everybody will say I just didn't make it."

He consoled me in a very profound way: "Why are you worrying what anyone else will say? You know the truth. I believe you. Alice will believe you. You believe in yourself. So just don't go to pieces. The most important thing to remember is that you have talent and you're young. There's always someone who knew you'd never make it. There's always someone who knew all along that you'd make it. Sometimes he's the same person. He won't believe you this time. But the next time, when you're a hit, he'll be the first to take a bow for you."

There was one person I couldn't bring myself to tell. That was Alice. Maybe I was wrong, but I was scared. She was already so emotionally involved in my success that I wanted to protect her from the truth as long as I could. Misery may love company, but I was afraid Alice's misery on top of mine might wash us both away.

Mrs. First-Nighter

A re-creation of the opening night of Radio City Music Hall, December 27, 1932, was published in *Show* magazine in 1962. It went like this:

> A capacity audience of 6,200 showed up for the hall's grand opening. The first-nighters arrived unfashionably early to explore the Music Hall, which houses an imposing collection of privately commissioned art. They rode elevators lined with bird's-eye maple and decorated with hardwood inlays. Couples who rode downstairs parted in the Grand Lounge. The men went off to the men's lounge, where they studied an abstract mural by Stuart Davis appropriately titled "Men Without Women." The ladies adjourned to the ladies' lounge, which had white parchment walls, and a mural, "History of Cosmetics," by Witold Gordon. Men who rode the elevators going up could contemplate a black ceramic panther in the men's lounge on the first mezzanine; a wallpaper mural called "Nicotine," printed in tobacco brown on aluminum foil paper, in the second-mezzanine smoking room; or a "Wild West" mural in the third-mezzanine smoking room. All these and many other objects of art are still on display today in the rest rooms, making the Music Hall perhaps the world's only art collection whose viewers are segregated according to sex.
>
> After they had been shown to their seats, the first-nighters were serenaded by the Grand Organ—an awesome arsenal of pipes and hardware specially assembled by Wurlitzer. At the console, the organist can dial various musical instruments—including marimbas, tom-toms, chimes, a xylophone, snare drums, trap drums, bass drums, military drums, castanets, a grand piano, and a glockenspiel. The Music Hall claims that it would take at least three thousand musicians in an orchestra pit to duplicate the Grand Organ's sound effects.
>
> The first-nighters were enthralled by everything—until the world's largest curtain rose on a mammoth bore. . . . The show dragged on and on and on; although the huge auditorium was shaped like a sunrise, it seemed to impose a curtain of ice between spectators and performers. This was thawed only momentarily when Ray Bolger—standing alone on a stage 144 feet wide and 66½ feet deep beneath a proscenium sixty feet high—took a deep breath and ad-libbed: "You know, it's really wonderful what you can do with a few dimes."
>
> The drama critics wrote obituary notices. The public does not buy tickets to last rites. After two weeks of diminishing returns, the management

cut the show to fifty minutes (and doubled the number of shows to four a day) and added a movie, *The Bitter Tea of General Yen.* It took many months of the new policy, plus word-of-mouth enthusiasm for the Christmas and Easter spectacles, plus a management reorganization before the Music Hall was on its feet financially.

Alice Peerce: *Jan was too ashamed to tell me he was out of the show. So when I stopped by the stage door of the Music Hall, he handed me the ticket he'd managed to get for me in the uppermost balcony. He still didn't say anything.*
"Pinky!" I exclaimed when I saw him. "You're not shaved."
"Oh, I've got time," he said. "I've got plenty of time."
I knew he was in the last part of the show, so I didn't worry.

The show lasted till well past midnight. Everybody realized it was in big trouble when, long before midnight, John D. Rockefeller, Jr., stood up and walked out of his own monument. Faithful to Bill Stern's dictum, I had put in an appearance backstage at curtain time, and having nowhere else to go until the show was over, when I had to face my wife, I stood in the wings, watching and weeping. Bad as the show was, I would have given anything to have had the minor roles my two ex-roommate tenors were playing.

One of the actors, Taylor Holmes, tried to cheer me up. Ray Bolger took a different approach. Although he was my age, he talked to me like a brash young father and asked me what made me think I had earned the right to be onstage. "You ever play one-night stands?" he asked me.

"Hundreds," I said.

"Did you ever dance in saloons for pennies?"

"I've played my fiddle at Spanish weddings and brought home five and a half dollars."

"So you think you've suffered?"

"Yes."

"Well, you haven't until tonight. So the next chance you get, you'll *deserve* to be out there—and you'll get there. Just keep working and studying."

Ray and I still remind each other of this conversation when we bump into each other nowadays.

Alice: *When the show was over, there was so little applause I was sure it was an intermission. But at one o'clock in the morning? Still, Jan hadn't come on yet. . . . Then I heard people yawning and saying, "Thank G-d it's over!" and they were all claiming their coats and leaving for good. I knew something terrible had happened to Jan. I had to get to him fast.*

I could have been angry at him for not having told me he was out. All the way down, I was cursing and muttering, "What the hell is going on?" But I couldn't feel anything but pity and love when I found him, standing alone in the stage entrance, still unshaven and forlorn-looking. He was holding a box of flowers and there were fifty telegrams of congratulations in his mailbox. We crumpled them up without looking at them and stuck them in with the flowers.

We started crying together as we walked uptown and we walked crying along Central Park from Fifty-ninth Street to 110th Street, still carrying that stupid white box of flowers and telegrams. Then we took a cab up to the Bronx. And cried together all morning.

From Behind the Curtain

It seemed to bother Erno Rapee even more than it bothered me that I was being paid *not* to work. He used to see me reporting in to Bill Stern every day and it finally galled him enough that he said one afternoon:

"How do you feel about collecting so much money without working for it?"

This got me mad. "I'm not singing because they took my part out of the show. But I'd do anything—even sweep up the stage—just to be part of what's going on here."

"Calm down, kid. Nobody's gonna give you a broom. But would you be willing to sing with the organ without being announced?"

"I said *anything,* didn't I? Well, that's better than anything."

Dick Leibert, the organist, didn't like the idea and said so. This took me aback, but why *should* he have liked it? He'd had the audience and the whole theatre at several of its peak moments of excitement—when some twenty-five thousand people a day were coming or going—and now he had to share it with me. Still, I'm never offended by honesty and I quickly came to admire him for telling me the truth.

"One other thing," Leibert said. "You will never hit a high note at the end. This is an organ recital with an incidental song. If you try to make a big vocal concert out of it, I won't like you."

I respected his ego and musicianship and he and I got on fine. The first week, Leibert had me sing "Play, Fiddle, Play," and the second week, "Take Me in Your Arms," both of which showed my voice off to advantage, when he could have picked numbers that didn't. I was invisible, but there I stood, behind a curtain, singing into a microphone with everything I had in my heart and soul, hoping that Somebody Out There would hear me. After a day or two, when I got my bearings, people began to applaud the invisible man. And

I could peek through a split in the curtain while I sang. My sound would fill the giant golden theatre and people searching for seats would suddenly stop in the aisles and look for the source of that sound.

The Music Hall had its own spy system. Maybe it still has. Whatever remarks the ushers overhear, they must write down and enter in their reports: "I liked the picture." "I didn't like the picture." "I liked the show." "I didn't like the show." "He was good." "He was bad." In the early part of 1933, the reports on me began to flow in like a tidal wave: "Who is this singing with the organ? He's great!" They called me the Phantom Voice. Everybody was talking about it. The RKO man who assumed Roxy's executive responsibilities while he was in the hospital was H. B. Franklin. Looking over the ushers' reports, Franklin wondered who the Phantom Voice was that the audience raved about.

Franklin could press a button in his office and hear what was happening anywhere in the Music Hall. He took a listen and said he wanted to talk to me.

So Franklin met Pierce—which sounds like the making of one obscure President of the United States, but turned out to be an encounter between a couple of East Side New York boys. I don't know what RKO had changed *his* name from, but I could tell by the way he looked me over when I walked in that somebody must have given me the "fat little fella who's not the stage type at all" build-up.

"Sit down, Pierce!" Franklin said very warmly. "You know, I've just been listening to a beautiful voice. Let me ask you a question. Why are you singing behind the curtain?"

I could have poured out my misery then and there, but I thought a more businesslike answer would do more good. Besides, if you make yourself out to be a loser, you lose. So I simply said, "That's where they told me to sing."

"Well, how would you feel about singing in front of an audience? Are you nervous? Frightened? Ashamed?" Franklin ticked off a whole list of complexes I'd developed by then, so astutely that I knew I had run into one hell of a man. And I knew he knew he'd discovered a talented underdog, so I wound up telling him the whole awful story of how I started out to be the singing sensation of the first show and wound up in the wings and, only now, behind the curtain. He listened sympathetically and then interjected mildly, "But you should sing in front of an audience."

Franklin visited Roxy in the hospital. Roxy agreed with him, but asked him to wait until he came back. He told Franklin, "I like this boy. He's special. I want to do things for him my way."

When Roxy returned, he remembered. I was sent "downtown" to the

Center Theatre at Sixth Avenue and Forty-ninth Street, another part of the Radio City complex. It was to have been the presentation house down the block from the all-live Music Hall. Eventually, after the Music Hall succeeded at stage-and-screen shows, the Center evolved into an auditorium for ice shows and operettas (*White Horse Inn,* etc.), but at the time I moved over there in 1933, its way of life was five showings of a movie sandwiched around four stage shows a day. The picture I premiered with at the Center was *King Kong.*

The Center Theatre became my house of apprenticeship and I couldn't have acquired my stage legs under better auspices. In the pit, under the baton of Joseph Littau, were the team of Burt Shefter and Morton Gould at the piano, Jerry Colonna on the trombone, and Max Polikoff on the violin. And John Pierce! I still wasn't quite onstage. I was in the rising orchestra pit, which went up and down on an elevator, and I was dressed up like a musician in a black velvet monkey jacket with brass buttons. I looked just like a member of the band, except that my instrument was my voice. At a given moment in each show, I would stand up, sing a chorus and a half of a song that went "My darling, say you're mine tonight, my darling," and sit down. Every time, the applause was terrific.

After six weeks of "My darling" and *King Kong,* I was moved onstage in leather shorts and porkpie hat to sing a jolly Mitteleuropean farewell naturally called "Auf wiedersehen!" This was destined to be my farewell to the Center Theatre, where, unbeknown to me, I had been elected by Roxy to serve as a guinea pig. John D. Rockefeller, Jr., had not quite abandoned the idea of an opera house in Radio City. The Music Hall itself had no natural acoustics: it required heavy reinforcement of sound. But the Rockefellers and Sarnoff and Roxy had talked about converting the Center Theatre into the Center Opera at some future date and I had been sent over there to test the acoustics. Radio City's technicians had been acquainted with my voice, and knowing that it was of operatic quality, they wanted to see if the Center Theatre did it justice. Their answer was no. The next question was: With some adjustment or renovations, could it be made into a suitable opera house acoustically? Again the answer was no. And so my apprenticeship at the Center Theatre doomed a rival opera for the Met. In those Depression days, even a Rockefeller wouldn't build a Philharmonic Hall or a Center Opera without testing the acoustics first!

Once I had served my time and purpose at the Center, Roxy decided I was ready for my comeback a block "uptown" at the Music Hall.

"But not onstage for the moment," he said, handing me the Sicilian aria that Turiddu sings to Lola from offstage at the beginning of *Cavalleria Rus-*

ticana. Fortunately, Roxy's intentions were not the same as Mascagni's, so I would at least be visible—though only in my monkey jacket, going up and down on an elevator with the orchestra. But I had a bigger pit, a bigger spotlight, and sometimes a bigger audience.

After one round of rustic chivalry, Roxy told me, "All right, Pierce, the next time we change programs, you're going onstage."

"Ah! Moon of My Delight"

Less than a year after opening night at Radio City, when John D. Rockefeller, Jr., had walked out early, I stood on the stage of the Music Hall wearing a fez and sang a harem number called "Ah! Moon of My Delight," from a suite called *In a Persian Garden* by Liza Lehmann. John D. Rockefeller, Jr., had started dropping in on the theatre very often. Sometimes his son, Nelson, came along, too.

As John D. Rockefeller, Sr.'s, ninety-fourth birthday neared, I was called by W. G. Van Schmus, who was the Rockefellers' liaison man and managing director of the Music Hall. I couldn't believe my ears when he told me, "The Rockefeller family has asked me to extend an invitation to you to attend Mr. Rockefeller's birthday party."

"You must be kidding," I said. "Who else is invited?"

"Just twenty-six people—all members of the Rockefeller family—and Archer Gibson," he said. Archer Gibson was the Rockefellers' own organist, so I began to fathom what this might be about. I would be expected to perform. I asked what I should wear and Van Schmus said, "Evening clothes plus your Persian fez from the show." Now I knew *what* I was expected to perform.

"Where is the party going to be?"

"At their place up in Pocantico Hills," he replied.

"Hmm," I said. "I don't think I've ever been there. Which train do you recommend?"

"You'll be called for by a Rockefeller car. Please be ready on time."

"Don't worry," I said. "I'll be there with my fez on."

Even though 2720 Grand Concourse had a lobby to dazzle a Rockefeller chauffeur, our apartment there had one disadvantage: it faced the back, not the Concourse. So Alice went up on the roof to watch her husband being ushered into John D. Rockefeller's limousine by two men in livery.

The chauffeur drove and the footman or doorman or whatever he was, after making sure I was safely locked in, inquired about my welfare and comfort from time to time, but mostly they let me concentrate on my music and my surroundings. When we arrived, John D. Rockefeller, Jr., met me at the front door and said, "Here you are, Mr. Pierce. I'm so pleased to see you. Now that you're here we can begin the dinner."

"You mean you want me to sing now?"

"No, we want you to eat now. Later, if you'd like, we'd love to hear you sing."

A horrible thought occurred to me. Nobody had told the Rockefellers I followed the dietary laws! I hadn't mentioned it to Van Schmus and he certainly wouldn't have thought about my eating habits. Thinking fast, I begged off by saying, "I couldn't eat before singing."

"Oh!" he said. "Why didn't we think of that? Of course. Well, suppose we defer dinner and you sing first. Then you can enjoy your meal with us."

I knew this could never happen, so I said, "No, no, no, no! It's your father's birthday and *he*'s the guest of honor, not I. I insist that you proceed as scheduled and I'll sing after dinner."

"But I feel terrible," John D., Jr., said to me. "Promise us you'll eat *after* you sing."

At that point I was ready to promise him anything—so I said yes and they left me alone while they ate dinner. I was afraid to wander outside the house because I was sure I'd be mistaken for a trespasser. But after dinner my host asked if I'd like to walk in the formal gardens with him. John D., Jr., took my arm as we walked through his family's beautiful estate and asked about my boyhood and my career.

The one big thing that interested him was why I had had to wait until I was almost thirty, until I met a Roxy, before I could really get launched in show business. I explained, as best I could, some of the mysteries of managers and bookers, of people who judge and dictate, and, if you're any good, treat you as if you're taking something away from them. And this was as exotic to him as Pocantico Hills was to me.

"Let's go back a little further, Mr. Pierce," he said. "Where were you born?"

Now I was on home territory. "On Orchard Street," I began. "Now, you may not know where Orchard Street is—"

"Oh, I know where Orchard Street is," John D. Rockefeller, Jr., interrupted with a chuckle. "And Ludlow Street and Grand Street and East Broadway, all the way down." It took me a while to realize that he probably had at least a finger in all the real estate on those blocks.

When we returned to the house, all the Rockefellers and their relatives were seated on the veranda. The French doors from the living room were opened and from inside, Archer Gibson played a few selections on the organ. Then John D., Jr., asked me if I was ready and where did I want to stand. I said it was such a beautiful summer evening that I'd like to sing outside on the threshold, with Mr. Gibson accompanying me from just within the door. I did three or four standard numbers and then, as Archer Gibson started the introduction to "Ah! Moon of My Delight," everybody looked over at the ninety-four-year-old birthday boy and old John D. Rockefeller was twinkling like a star.

At the very moment I sang the title line of "Ah! Moon of My Delight," what do you think happened? As the luck of the rich would have it, the moon came out like a big hunk of green cheese: a full moon that just hung there as a beautiful spotlight. All the Rockefellers gasped and I couldn't help thinking of what the poor man in the park said when a bird flew over and crapped on his head: "And for the rich you sing!"

When the encores were over, John D., Sr., himself called me over, congratulated me, and gave me his usual trophy: a dime. That was his signature, his autograph, his reminder of the frugality that had brought him to where he was.

As I pocketed my dime, son Junior was waiting in ambush for me: "And now, Mr. Pierce, at last you can relax and eat!"

Eat? *Eat!* I had almost forgotten. I looked around, cornered, but there was no way out. "Er—er," I tried, "I'm so excited after a performance that I can't touch food for an hour or two."

"Of course, of course," Rockefeller assured Pierce. "You take your time and whenever you're ready, perhaps one or two of us will have a midnight snack with you."

"But shouldn't I be getting back to New York?" I begged.

"Take your time, Mr. Pierce. Wait until you have your appetite and then eat and relax, and *then* we can talk about saying goodbye. But not until you've eaten," said John D., Jr., and in the background, his father nodded. The Rockefeller patriarchs were really mothering me.

While we made small talk, I started to worry that they'd hold me prisoner there overnight until I ate. Twenty-six Rockefellers had come from all over the world just to hang around waiting to watch Pierce eat! My upbringing was experiencing its biggest test ever.

Then an idea occurred to me. "I get a violent craving for sweets after I sing," I said to my host. "I wonder if I could trouble you for some ice cream and a glass of milk and, what I came for above all, a big piece of your father's birthday cake"—all of which were safe for my religious diet.

He sent a servant on the run to the kitchen. There was some birthday cake left. It was brought out with a bowl of ice cream and a pitcher of milk from the Rockefellers' own cows, and I lapped it all up so happily, with all the Rockefellers watching so appreciatively, that I was afraid they were going to demand an eating encore—in which case, I suppose I would have obliged.

Cinderella time came, and I was chauffeured home from the culinary perils of Pocantico Hills to the middle-class comfort and security of the Grand Concourse, where Alice was sitting up, all smiles and tears of joy, waiting to hear all about my adulation, my adoration, and as it turned out, my abstinence.

A few years later, the Rockefeller family opened a rooftop gymnasium for all the employees of Radio City, including NBC and RCA as well as the Music Hall. For the dedication ceremony, the high-kicking Rockettes were a natural. When I was asked to appear, too, I knew it wasn't because of my athletic prowess. It was because of "Because," a song two years older than I which Mr. and Mrs. John D. Rockefeller, Jr., had requested I sing. Introduced to the Radio City Athletic Club, I glanced down at my audience—and there, in the first row, not five feet from me, sat Mr. and Mrs. John D. Rockefeller, Jr., their eyes agleam. When I sang "Because you come to me with naught save love/ And hold my hands and lift my eyes above," I saw him take her hand. They were still holding hands and crying a little together, this sixtyish couple, when I came to "Because G-d made thee mine, I'll cherish thee." Oh, yes, children, there was once a time when Rockefellers had loving and lasting first marriages.

The Yom Kippur War of 1933

Like any showman, Roxy always needed an audience. Even if it was only an audience of one, he had to have someone. So the composer Mana-Zucca was in his office the day Roxy summoned me and displayed a cruel side of his nature that I'd heard about, but seldom seen. This was an early afternoon in the summer of 1933.

"John," Roxy began, "I am going to build in this theatre, on this stage, the most beautiful temple you've ever seen. It will remind you of the Temple in Jerusalem. It will be ready for the Rosh Hashonah–Yom Kippur High Holy Days. And amidst all this beauty, in all its splendor, there you will stand on high, dressed in the pure white of a cantor. You will wear the whitest skullcap, the whitest robes, a beautiful prayer shawl, and you'll stand before a beautiful ark with the most beautiful scrolls you've ever seen. And you will have a chorus of one hundred and an orchestra of one hundred and you will sing the *Kol Nidre."*

"Gee!" I said. "That's marvelous! That's wonderful! When will it be?"

"For two weeks," he said, giving me some dates that spanned the High Holy Days.

"But you know I don't work on Rosh Hashonah and Yom Kippur," I pointed out.

Roxy not only pounded his desk, he rose from it and towered over it and me—no small feat for a rather small man. "Whaddya mean, you don't work!" he snarled. Then, trying to be reasonable, he said, "First of all, this is *more* than work. Second of all, you'll be creating something finer than any cantor in any synagogue can do. The people who don't go to the synagogue will come to the theatre and hear you sing the *Kol Nidre* and you'll reach them in a way the synagogue couldn't."

I said, "Look, I'm very sorry, but I'll be in the synagogue myself on those days, so it's impossible."

"Whaddya mean, it's impossible?" he roared. Saying "impossible" to Roxy was like waving a red flag in front of a bull. Roxy yelled louder and louder and the more I kept saying no, the more he kept insisting.

He paused for a moment and then said, "Now, what would you say if I told you that if you don't do this, you will never sing in this theatre again?"

I swallowed and then I said, "Do you know what I'd say, Mr. Rothafel? I would say that the same G-d who took care of me before I met you would take care of me after you threw me out."

My answer took his breath away. He still didn't have words when, after a couple of minutes of silence, I said, "May I leave?" Roxy just nodded. On my way out I glanced at Mana-Zucca, who looked away. Roxy could never back down now, with a witness to this scene.

All afternoon and all evening, I waited for the noose to fasten itself around my neck, but the show went on even though I was sure it would soon be curtains for me. And sure enough, after the fourth and final performance of the day, stage manager Bill Stern came over and told me Roxy was waiting for me. I knew this was it.

When I went upstairs and stood at attention before his desk, Roxy ignored me for two or three long minutes. Then he looked up and said, "Why don't you sit down?" And finally he said something I never dreamed I would hear from him: "Do you know something? I owe you an apology. I misbehaved. I said things I shouldn't have said. I threatened you when I shouldn't have."

I thought to myself that what I was hearing took a truly big man to say. But he was even more fascinated by me. "You really meant what you said? You really believe so faithfully and so ardently that you wouldn't sing on the High Holy Days even if I threw you out of this theatre? Right at the beginning of your career?" The more he talked, the harder it was for him to believe me, so he cocked an eye at me quizzically.

I said, "I'm afraid that's the way I was brought up to live and that's the way I'll die."

"Look at me," Roxy said. "I'm religious. True, I haven't been inside a synagogue for quite a while, but I keep a membership in a temple. I just prefer to do my praying by myself. I go to the forests and I commune with nature. I listen to the birds and I talk to the trees."

"That's fine," I said. "If that's what you believe in, I'm sure it's a great comfort. You have your way of showing your faith and I have mine, and I don't say mine is any better than yours."

Roxy stuck out his hand and shook mine, saying, "Well, I respect yours. Please forgive me. I didn't mean what I said to you this afternoon." Our late-evening reconciliation was one of my fondest memories of Roxy.

My father came to the Music Hall as often as he could. My mother, to her eternal regret, came only twice—and she never saw me at the Metropolitan Opera, even though I made my debut almost four years before she died. But she was already an invalid by then.

I remember both her visits to the Music Hall. It took a couple of years to coax her to come. I mean, how do you explain a Radio City Music Hall with dancing girls and fireworks to a mother who's never seen one before? Finally she came, she saw, but she wasn't exactly conquered, thrilled, or even fascinated.

A few years later she showed up backstage unexpectedly. A cousin of mine was getting married and had sent me an invitation to the wedding, which I'd declined. My mother wanted me to reconsider.

"Is that what you came all the way up here for?" I said to her. "Look, I hardly know him, but I'll send a nice present."

"He's your cousin," she insisted.

And when I realized that it meant enough to her to drag herself uptown and confront me backstage in that most alien of places, Rockefeller Center, I couldn't argue with her.

"All right. I'll go to the wedding if it'll make you happy," I said. "Now do you want to stay and see the show?"

"No," she said. "I saw it a couple of years ago." And she left.

Alas, Poor Jascha!

While Roxy had been lying in the hospital recovering from prostate surgery in 1933, he had not forgotten me. One of his Sunday visitors had been an RCA executive named John Royal. They had listened to the *Radio City Music Hall of the Air* broadcast together and when Royal admired my voice, Roxy had sold him on what eventually became a fifteen-minute Wednesday-night "sustaining" program on NBC, with Leo Russotto as pianist and Louis Katzman conducting. My fee was $25 a broadcast—$22.50 after commissions. This led to a regular stint in 1934 on *The A & P Gypsies* every Monday night on NBC. *Gypsies* paid $125 a show, but I was working without a contract.

After six months with *Gypsies,* I was invited to audition with a symphonic orchestra to do a new weekly show called *The Chevrolet Hour.* Having showed my stuff, I was offered $750 a week by Chevrolet, which I accepted.

When I broke the news to Harry Horlick, producer of *The A & P Gypsies,* he said, "You can't do this to us! We were just about to offer you a contract."

"But I have a contract," I told him, "with Chevrolet."

The Chevrolet Hour, which ran from 1935 to 1939 over CBS, Sunday nights seven to seven-thirty, was a great success. It featured myself and the singer Virginia Ray, and conductor Dave Rubinoff, alias "Rubinoff and His Violin." Rubinoff was also musical director for Eddie Cantor on the *Chase & Sanborn Coffee Hour,* so he was perhaps the most famous of the three of us.

Everything on *The Chevrolet Hour* ran like clockwork. You had to do a number in exactly two and a half or three minutes, whatever was specified. If you ran four seconds over at rehearsal, you'd have to call Detroit for permission to take four seconds longer—and the answer was usually no.

Even Chevrolet's clockwork, however, couldn't compare to my own calendar on my busiest day of the week, Sunday.

At ten in the morning, there was a rehearsal with Erno Rapee in Rockefeller Center for *Radio City Music Hall of the Air.*

Then I would race down to WEVD on Forty-sixth Street to do the *Forverts* program as Jascha Pearl.

In early afternoon, John Pierce would sing on the live broadcast of *Radio City Music Hall of the Air.*

And squeezed between four shows on the stage of the Music Hall, I would also rehearse and do *The Chevrolet Hour.*

Alas, poor Jascha! I enjoyed him, but he was the first to go. I'd gone on doing Jascha Pearl for ten dollars a broadcast, but eventually sharp-eared

Sunday listeners caught on to who he was. Someone told Rapee, who made me quit WEVD to avoid contractual conflicts.

I could afford to swallow my disappointment. Fortunately, *The Chevrolet Hour* was going great guns. Chevrolet paid Virginia Ray and Dave Rubinoff and me generous bonuses. Thus, one year Virginia and I decided it would be nice if we did something for the orchestra. How about gifts? Or a party for the musicians and their wives? We were both so grateful that anything would have been within bounds.

In early November we went to Maestro Rubinoff with our various ideas. He said, "Oh, yes. You're absolutely right that something is in order. In fact, I'm surprised *I* didn't think of it. But give me a little time to think over *what* we'll do for them."

Some weeks went by. We would remind Rubinoff from time to time, but he would say, "I haven't forgotten. I'm thinking about it. Don't worry. It's going to work out fine."

Thanksgiving came and went, with no progress toward the project, just reassurances from Rubinoff. But finally, when Christmas was just around the corner, he came to Virginia and me and told us, "I've not only made up my mind; I've gone ahead and done it!"

Wondering which hotel he had picked for the party, I said, "Where's it going to be?"

But Rubinoff said, "It's right here."

He reached into his briefcase and there, for each and every musician, was the same lavish Christmas present: an autographed picture of Rubinoff!

A Level or a Lover

Why do marriages end? One reason is that couples don't work at it. They just stay married and take each other for granted and aren't even particularly interested in each other's well-being or business or profession. Just being a housewife is not enough. Just being a breadwinner who brings home a pay check is not enough. There must be give-and-take in a marriage.

The weakness in childhood marriages—which ours was to some extent —is that the young boy, just married, starts out on some kind of career. He hardly knows who he is or what he wants, but as his career begins to shape him, his wife doesn't grow along with him, and that can spell the end.

In my case, Alice kept up with me. In fact, I'm not ashamed to say she's gone beyond me. She knows more about a lot of things than I do. She reads more than I do. I have to read music much of the day; she can concentrate more on what's in a book. I'll wake up in the middle of the night and her bed lamp will be on and I'll say, "What're you running, a bedroom or a library?"

Alice Peerce: *My mother said she'd never baby-sit for me if I played cards or did anything I shouldn't do. She didn't have to worry about my playing cards, G-d knows, but I resented being talked to like a little girl and I asked her what I was supposed to do.*

She naturally had an answer: "You're supposed to go back to school." And do you know what? She forced me to go back to school. I'd finished high school, but she made me take classes at Columbia Extension, NYU, CCNY—whatever was available afternoons. Education was the most important thing in life to her and it had to be for me. She laid down the law. "You must *go back to school!"*

But since my academic studies weren't being put to any creative use, I knew I had to find a level or else a lover. Either I would find a place to release all my energies and do something that would fulfill me or *I could consider the route one or two girls I knew were taking. They were having what the French call five-to-sevens; actually, I think there's more of this going on in America than in France these days. But for me, working for and with Jan was much healthier and much more creative. That's where I unleashed my imagination. I wasn't just there to stop him when he wanted to quit doing the NBC show after they cut him to fifteen dollars. I negotiated his prices, big and small, until—after he'd been singing at the Music Hall awhile—his price got up around three hundred dollars a booking. Then I began to look around for professional managers who might command bigger prices and see a bigger picture for him than a wife could.*

When I first started asking prices higher than three hundred dollars, there was some tension between us because Jan was convinced nobody would pay him more than that. He complained I was pushing him up into too high a bracket and worried that I'd price him right out of the market. It took a few years before I worked out all the management combinations with him and found the right people, but I knew he needed bigger operators than his faithful wife.

Still, I had my wifely worries. There was Jan spending the whole day with seventy-two young girls—the Rockettes and the Corps de Ballet. He might pat one on the behind and it was called "show-business cameraderie" or "good-luck gestures." It was part of why, in 1935, we moved from the Grand Concourse down to 400 West End Avenue, at Seventy-ninth Street, in Manhattan, so Jan would be closer to the Music Hall and be able to come home between shows whenever he could. I was at home expecting another baby—who turned out to be our Joy.

One day, a visitor let me know that Jan was dating one of the dancing girls at the Music Hall. This "news" came as the shock of my life. I was still at the stage of my marriage (though I was emerging from it) where I cried a lot and never raised my voice because I was so terrified of Jan I was afraid even to be jealous. Should I hire a private detective? Where would I get the money? Should I play it cool and say nothing to Jan? Or should I throw it up to him? Or maybe laugh it off to him as gossip I was hearing?

Not long after, Jan's brother Mac came to lunch with us at 400 West End. The boys got to talking about who was running around with whom, and as I waddled back and forth between them with my big belly, I said as casually as I could to Jan, "So what's new? I hear you're seeing So-and-so."

Well, you never saw anybody explode with indignation the way Jan did.

Not only because the report was false, but because whoever had brought it to Alice had picked out a girl who was not my type at all. So I really had every reason to be mad at Alice. "If I'm gonna pick somebody," I shouted at her, "I'm gonna pick somebody better than that!"

Alice: *I felt so relieved, yet so bitchy that I wanted to vomit. I knew right away the report was false because Jan wasn't that good an actor and there wasn't a glint of anything—just disgust—in the way he spoke of her. I'm glad I waited a month or so to bring it up. If I'd confronted him with it the first moment I heard it, I would have made a bigger fool of myself and might have provoked him into something.*

When our showdown was over and we were alone, I didn't apologize to Jan, but I did lay down this ground rule to him:

"If you ever play around, don't bring it to my doorstep."

I figured that whatever happened on the road I wouldn't know about anyway —and I didn't want to. Because if I knew, I would have to take a stand. And I wasn't ready to take a stand. I loved this crazy guy too much to risk losing him. I'd have killed him—even today I think I would. Certainly I'd have left him. I've told him, however, two or three times in our nearly fifty years together that I will never leave him because of another woman; but I will leave him if he disregards my advice and works with a bad manager or a bad teacher.

The Bluebird of Happiness

The beggar man
And the mighty king
Are only diff'rent in name,
For they are treated just the same
By Fate.

Today a smile
And tomorrow tears—
We're never sure what's in store,
So learn your lesson before too late.*

Sandor Harmati used to conduct the Omaha Symphony, but he was a serious composer and left conducting to devote himself full-time to composing. Unfortunately, hardly anybody was performing his original compositions and, in the Depression, he needed money to survive. He took a job as a fiddler and worked his way up to first violinist at Radio City Music Hall.

One day he was telling his troubles and ambitions to Erno Rapee, who interrupted him. "You tell me you need money and you don't want charity. Why don't you write a song for John Pierce? You know his voice. You like his voice. So write a melody that he'll be able to sing well."

Harmati sat down and wrote a simple, sentimental melody without words. Rapee found him a lyricist from Tin Pan Alley, Edward Heyman, who had written "Body and Soul." Right away there was an argument over the grammar of Eddie's lyric: "So be like I, /Hold your head up high." Both Rapee and Eddie's publisher, T. B. Harms, wanted it to be "like me," but Eddie insisted it should be "as I" because it meant "be as I am." Rapee compromised by giving Eddie his "I," but changing "as" to "like."

I started to sing it for the three of them, but Rapee cut me off. "It's very good," he said, "but there's something missing. We don't want to use it just as a song. We want to build a big production number around it. Not only will you sing with the chorus backing you up, but the Corps de Ballet and the Rockettes will come out and dance, all to this same melody in different rhythms. The great thing about this song is you can sing it and play it forty-eight different ways and then come back to finish up with the tenor singing: 'If you will be like I,/Hold your head up high. . . .' But what's missing is—I'll tell you what it needs. It needs a recitation."

We all looked at Rapee and somebody in the room said, "Aaah, those recitations are old hat already."

Rapee said, "So we'll write a recitation anyway. Something upbeat." He outlined a few ideas and Eddie Heyman went off and came back with: "The poet with his pen,/ The peasant with his plow,/It makes no difference who you are,/It's all the same somehow."

"Great!" said Rapee. "But you can't keep using the same melody underneath it. Keep reciting it." So we took turns reciting it over and over while

*From "The Bluebird of Happiness," lyrics by Edward Heyman, music by Sandor Harmati, published by T. B. Harms, Inc.

Rapee, sitting at the piano, began to pick out familiar melodies on the keyboard. "It has to be something in the public domain," he muttered once. After a while, almost without his realizing it, his fingers began to play "Chanson Bohémienne" by Boieldieu. And Rapee hissed at me, very tensely, "Start the recitation."

I did—and if you'll listen closely to my recordings of it, that's one of the hidden strengths of "The Bluebird of Happiness": the music Rapee put under the recitation.

It was a hit from the moment it was introduced around 1936. I ended up doing it at the Music Hall for two weeks of every year—always in a new staging, but as regularly and almost as popularly as the Christmas and Easter shows. Once I came out dressed up as an old Italian hurdy-gurdy man, the kind of organ grinder who was still making a living on the sidewalks of New York. Some of them had monkeys, but as a rule, the hurdy-gurdy men had little birds, and if you gave him a penny or two, the bird would pick out or peck out your fortune on a card. Nowadays, if you gave an organ grinder pennies—if you could find an organ grinder—he'd give you the bird and report you to the Antiquarian Society, but in those days it was a wonderful way to cue in "The Bluebird of Happiness." In another production, after my name was changed for the last time, the setting was a hobo jungle. First Buffalo Bill did his specialty. Then Raleigh Paulie. But even before I was introduced—heavily made up—as Jan from Spokane, someone in the audience would spot me and there would be a murmur of recognition and a few cries of "Bluebird!" For as inevitably as the Rockettes' toes would leave the ground, I was going to let fly with "The Bluebird of Happiness."

The success of "The Bluebird of Happiness" was almost enough to keep a songwriter comfortable for life. Eddie Heyman, who subsequently wrote "When I Fall in Love," and now lives in England, was in Belo Horizonte, Brazil, in 1948. He discovered that instead of Madonnas, the cabbies there dangled little wooden bluebirds, painted bluer than blue, from the windshields. He asked around and discovered that a whole bluebird cult had sprung up in Belo Horizonte around my recording. So he bought twenty-five bluebirds and brought them back. Just last year, Lawrence Welk, who now owns the rights to the song, stopped a movie company making Maurice Maeterlinck's *The Bluebird* in Leningrad from calling their movie *The Bluebird of Happiness*. But this didn't prevent the movie's star, Elizabeth Taylor, from sending the Apollo astronauts and Soyuz cosmonauts, somewhere out in space together, a congratulatory message "from our little bluebird of happiness."

Eddie Heyman was living up in Maine a few years ago when I gave a concert at the University of Maine. At intermission, I learned he was in the audience. He came backstage and said, "I hope you're going to sing *our* song."

"Well, you asked for it," I said.

But I kept Eddie biting his nails because "Bluebird" wasn't on the program and I didn't make any additions. At the end, though, when the crowd was clamoring for encores, I said, "What would you like to hear?" and as usual, a few voices said "Because" and a lot of voices cried "Bluebird!"

"All right," I said. " 'Bluebird' it is." When the applause which followed that announcement had died down, I didn't sing it right away. Instead I said, "Not only are you going to get this treat, but I want you to meet a celebrity in your own midst: the man who wrote the lyric for 'The Bluebird of Happiness,' Mr. Eddie Heyman!"

Eddie stood up—and with that one little speech, I had introduced him to the friends and neighbors he'd lived among for ten years (not many of whom knew he'd written "Bluebird") and ruined whatever anonymity he may have sought up there. Maybe that's why he moved to Europe.

> And so remember this:
> Life is no abyss.
> Somewhere there's a bluebird
> Of happiness.

The fate of the composer of "Bluebird" is a different story. Sandor Harmati committed suicide a few years later. But what he really died of was a broken heart, for his serious compositions never achieved any success, while "The Bluebird of Happiness," which he did not hold in such high esteem, made him a mint.

"I owe you my life," the letter from a Philadelphia woman began in 1970. With a first line like that, you have to read on. The woman had just been dealt a terrible blow: she had divorced a good and faithful husband to marry another man, who then jilted her. All of a sudden life had become worse than meaningless. She had driven her car up to the edge of a river and had just started to walk into the rushing water. Her car radio was on, the door open, when some disk jockey announced he was going to play Jan Peerce's record of "The Bluebird of Happiness." Tune and voice were familiar, but suddenly she was riveted by the words. "If things don't look so cheerful,/Just show a little fight,/For every bit of darkness,/There's a little bit of light" had a stronger hold than the water. She looked up toward heaven, she wrote, decided she was making a mistake, and went home to write me her letter.

Now, *you* may laugh at "The Bluebird of Happiness." The lyric may not be the greatest poetry since Omar Khayyám, but because of the simplicity of the song, I can sing it every day and find something new in it. It still has something to say to me. Must every idea be revolutionary or even new? It's not Goethe, it's not Wagner, but it's damn good Heyman and Harmati.

Musically, I never thought of the song as more than a stage vehicle: a production number. I never guessed it would have the appeal it did on record and radio. I think it's a wonderful song for what it is: an unpretentious, lovely ballad. If I had to choose between it and a Mozart aria, I'd probably choose the Mozart—though there are some bad Mozart arias!

"The Bluebird of Happiness" has a simple philosophy that you can feel in your daily life. It's so simple, in fact, you don't have to be a philosopher to understand or practice it. I've received more than five hundred letters and telegrams from people whose lives have been changed by that one song.

In Ramsey, New Jersey, a man's wife died, leaving him with three daughters to rear. One day he called a disk jockey and requested "The Bluebird of Happiness." So did a woman who had lost her husband and three daughters in a fire. The disk jockey didn't need a computerized matchmaking service to bring them together. They're married now and the man credits "The Bluebird" with bringing him back his happiness.

Sure, the song is corny. Why? Because it talks about common sense, and in today's world, common sense is corny, if not crazy. Because loving your wife is corny. Because being a good friend is corny. Because showing kindness to a stranger is corny. The best things in life are corny. So call the song corny if you must. Call my own philosophy of life old-fashioned or corny if you will. But I say to you: it suits me fine!

In the 1950s, I did a concert performance of *La Bohème* with Erich Leinsdorf and the Robin Hood Dell Orchestra in Philadelphia's Fairmount Park. Pretty good opera. Pretty good composer. Good cast and good conductor. The performance went extremely well and you'd think that after yelling "Bravo!" for a quarter of an hour, those twenty-six thousand people would pack up and go home. But what do you think happened? A group of young people unfurled a huge homemade banner—yellow with black letters—reading "WE WANT BLUEBIRD! BLUEBIRD! BLUEBIRD!" And they started chanting, *"We Want Bluebird!"* and the crowd took it up.

Imagine my embarrassment, with Erich Leinsdorf and my co-stars smiling wanly at the audience and glaring at me, while I could hear Puccini turning in his grave. Then Fredric Mann, the Mann in charge of the Robin Hood Dell, came over to me and said, "I hope you've got the music with you, because if you want to leave this park alive tonight, you'd better do 'Bluebird'!"

I never go anywhere without my "Bluebird" music. So I told Fred where to find it backstage and he gave it to William Smith, the assistant conductor of the Philadelphia Orchestra, now also conductor of the Trenton Symphony. With Smith accompanying on the piano, that was how "The Bluebird of Happiness" became an encore to *La Bohème.*

Although "The Bluebird of Happiness" was born in Radio City, New York, it took on its impact and momentum in Philadelphia—not just in Fairmount Park and the Robin Hood Dell, but as a recording in the 1930s, when it enjoyed a very special kind of life there.

Soon after its Music Hall debut, I recorded "Bluebird" for an outfit called World Broadcasting, which was like a lending library for radio stations. The record was not for public consumption, but only for rental by individual stations. For "Bluebird" and five other songs, I was paid $250, plus another $150 for waxing remakes of four of the songs. When they play the record on the air today, I get no royalty for it. So I was, in effect, paid sixty-six dollars for recording "Bluebird." But at the time, with two kids, Alice and I needed that four hundred dollars for the six songs—four hundred dollars extra to us then was like four thousand dollars now.

It was tempting to make money we could use, but World Broadcasting's rates were familiar to the trade, so recording "Bluebird" under my own name would detract from my market value as a serious singer. I couldn't expect to ask for larger fees if it became known I'd made a cheap recording. A bunch of names for me were kicked around at World Broadcasting and we finally settled on two of them: Paul Robinson and Randolph Joyce. I think Paul Robinson was picked because the name sounded a little like Paul Robeson. And Randolph Joyce seemed like just the right name for a tenor who'd tell you that a beggar man and a mighty king are different only in name.

In Philadelphia, there was an auto accessories firm called the Pep Boys (they're still there), and they believed in advertising in a very positive and prolific manner. So World Broadcasting enjoyed its best rentals of "Bluebird" in Philadelphia, where the Pep Boys used to bring you "The Bluebird of Happiness," sung by Philadelphia's own Paul Robinson, at 1 A.M., 3 A.M. and 5 A.M. on radio station WIP. Paul Robinson had a following in Philadelphia second to none among milkmen and other night owls like medical students and college kids who would tell me they could time their late-night work by my singing.

Since the record wasn't for sale in the stores, a black market in "Bluebird" developed in Philadelphia. Bootleg copies—shellac on top and aluminum underneath—were selling for ten or fifteen dollars apiece, whatever the traffic would bear. Even now, there is still some trade in the 78 RPM Paul Robinson or Randolph Joyce "Bluebird". And if you walk into radio studios today, you'll find that four out of five are still using my Randolph Joyce and Paul Robinson recordings.

Henry Pleasants is an author and the London-based music critic of the *International Herald Tribune*. But he used to be a critic for the *Philadelphia Evening Bulletin*. He was a tall, skinny, kind of agitated WASPish guy, who'd earned my respect from the start because he's one of the very few critics who've studied voice. So Henry Pleasants tends to know what he's talking about when he praises vocal qualities.

Being a serious music critic, Henry wasn't very much in touch with popular tastes—so it took him longer than most Philadelphians to find "The Bluebird of Happiness." But this mystic experience happened to Henry Pleasants in the early 1940s, when I was already making a name for myself as Jan Peerce, the opera and concert singer.

I was doing a summer concert in Philadelphia when Henry met my wife in the audience. He took her aside and said, "Alice, I have something to tell Jan and I don't know how to go about it."

"Well, try it out on me first, Henry," Alice suggested.

"Jan has said to me at least once that if he ever heard of a young tenor with a good voice, Jan would be interested in helping him along so he wouldn't have to endure the struggles Jan had."

"Oh, yes," Alice agreed. "He's said that to me often."

"Well, I have found that voice, I have found a new Jan Peerce!"

"Really?" said Alice. "Who is it?"

"A Philadelphia boy named Paul Robinson."

Alice began giggling, to Henry's annoyance. "Why don't you discuss it with Jan?" she said, inviting Henry to come backstage after my performance.

When Henry told me about Paul Robinson, I shocked him by saying, "I know him Henry, and I don't think he's so good. You may think I'm jealous, but here you're praising this guy as a young Jan Peerce and hinting I'd better look to my laurels because after a while he may go beyond me. I'm only saying I don't think he's so good."

"What's wrong with his voice, Jan?"

"It's not a great voice—not very musical. . . ." With that, I proceeded to tear down Paul Robinson like a professional critic.

The more I spoke, the hotter Henry grew. Finally he couldn't stand it any longer, and burst out at me.

"I'm disgusted with you, Jan. I always thought you were different, and I believed you when you said you'd help a new Jan Peerce. Now I know you have the same hatred in you as everybody else in your profession. Why, you're jealous of Paul Robinson!"

With that, Henry Pleasants stormed out, slamming the door so hard I thought my whole dressing room was going to cave in. I opened it again and called after him:

"Wait a minute, you bum, don't be so stupid!"

Henry turned around to shake a fist at me.

"You know who this Paul Robinson you've been talking about is? It's *me*. When I talk about myself, why can't I tell you what I think?"

Henry was struck dumb.

"That young Jan Peerce you've been praising is I. Singing under a different name."

I have to give Henry credit for a quick recovery. He staggered back in, clutching his stomach, and sat down hard in an empty chair. "All right," he said, "but I have a good ear, don't I?"*

When I started recording on a regular basis for RCA Victor in the 1940s, the letters were still coming in, addressed to Paul Robinson or Randolph Joyce or even to Jan Peerce (sharp-eared listeners were clued in by the song's recurrence at the Music Hall) and postmarked Seattle or Squeedunk or points north, south, east, and west—telling how "The Bluebird of Happi-

*This mistaken-identity incident with Henry Pleasants strained even the credulity of Peerce's trusting biographer. After all, a knowledgeable critic's failure to recognize a voice he knew well —particularly the "signature song" of an artist he knew personally—was hard to swallow. Interviewed in Vienna in September 1975, however, Pleasants confirmed virtually every detail, starting with "Why does Jan call me WASPish when I'm a self-styled WASP?" The rest, he said, was "a basically true story, except where Jan may have embroidered my tantrum: I don't remember behaving quite that violently." Pleasants's explanation of not recognizing Jan Peerce's voice: "I had more than the usual critical ignorance about pop singing: a deficiency I hope I rectified when I wrote a book called *The Great American Popular Singers*. But I was sitting home one night having dinner when I heard this tenor singing this song I'd never heard before. I turned to my wife and said, 'This bastard can sing! The only tenor I know who can sing like that is Jan Peerce. I'll have to tell him about it.' I didn't make the connection at all between Paul Robinson and this great young tenor who was singing *Traviata* and *Rigoletto* with Robert Weede in the Philadelphia Grand Opera Company. Jan was young and strong and everything came easily to him. Once, in the first act of *Traviata,* at a point in Violetta's aria 'Sempre libera,' where the tenor's voice flows through from offstage, repeating the theme of the love duet, Jan interpolated as beautiful a high C as I've ever heard from any soprano. I knew Jan in Philadelphia; he still had a tendency to sing a little too openly and brightly—with a little bit of the cantorial influence—but he was working with Philadelphia's own Giuseppe Boghetti to put the finishing touches of style and taste on what was already a very good singer. . . . The last time I heard Jan was five or six years ago, but he remains an unceasing delight to the ear." —A.L.

ness" changed a life here and saved a life there.

Alice rang up RCA and asked why I shouldn't record "Bluebird" for commercial sale. They weren't interested because John Charles Thomas had made a record of it that had failed in the shops. So Alice sent RCA our backlog of more than a hundred letters. As each new letter came in, she would answer it and forward the correspondence to RCA. Within a year, the RCA people realized we were on to something. They calculated that each letter written must represent at least a hundred letters that people meant to write and maybe a thousand sales to people who wouldn't write letters.

My RCA record of "The Bluebird of Happiness" has sold well over a million copies to date, has been reissued several times, and is second-ranked among all-time best-selling recordings by opera or concert singers. It is still gaining ground on number one, which is Enrico Caruso's recording of "Over There," released during World War I. I do earn royalties from store sales, so please remember this when next you visit your friendly record shop. Forgive my directness. But when I'm number two, I have to try harder.

After I'd recorded "Bluebird" for RCA, I listened to John Charles Thomas's version. What was wrong with it was the recitation. Thomas didn't know how to speak to the man in the street. He did "Bluebird" as though he were playing Hamlet: "The po-*ett* with his pe*nn,* the peasa*ntt* with his pl-*ow!*" You don't talk that way to the man in the street. Him you've got to talk to the way he's accustomed to. The way I'm talking to you now.

Jan Peerce Is Born

I never did think of myself as John Pierce, even months after Roxy renamed me that in 1932. We put the name on our door and mailbox, but whenever I came home, I almost felt that I was in the wrong apartment. But I accepted John Pierce as an unhappy necessity of my career.

Roxy had a radio program of lighter music on Monday nights and I became a regular on that, too. He was the master of ceremonies, and while he never used a script, the show was very carefully planned. He cultivated a manner of talking to an unseen audience of millions through a microphone just as if he were chatting with four people in a living room. Actually, none of it was improvised.

Still, Roxy took this member of the cast by surprise on the air on a certain Monday night when he began his fireside chat with:

"Our friend John Pierce here has been a little unhappy ever since we gave him his name." Then he told the nation the whole history of Jacob

Pincus Perelmuth. "Now, I know John here would still like to have his name changed to something else, but we can't change it much. You've all been listening to him, you've all been admiring him, you've all learned to love him as John Pierce."

He paused, pretending to think aloud on the air, and then said:

"I'll tell you what, ladies and gentlemen. We can change the spelling of his name and it'll still be the same name. Why, we could take the name of John, and if we wanted to give it a French touch, we'd make it Jean. Or it could be J-o-n. You know, the Bohemians and the Polish spell it J-a-n, which they pronounce *Yon,* but here we can pronounce it *Dzhayun* or any way we please. So in order to keep it within the frame of his name, we'll call him Jan. Those of you who want to be Bohemian can call him Yon. Those who want to Americanize his name can call him Jan with a *J.* And those of you who want to can go on calling him John." Then, turning to me, he asked, "Which do you prefer?"

"Jan with a *J,*" I said, speaking the only truly improvised line on the whole show.

"Then Jan it is," Roxy resumed. "Now about the name Pierce. P-i-e-r-c-e can also be spelled P-e-a-r-c-e or P-e-i-r-c-e or P-i-e-r-s or P-e-i-r-s or even P-e-e-r-s, but how about P-e-e-r-c-e? I think that would go best with a name like Jan. So we retain the flavor and most of the sound of his name by changing the spelling just a little. It's a euphonious name, an easily remembered name. So from now on, I want you all to know that our John Pierce is going to be Jan Peerce and don't forget to spell it with two *e*'s when you write us about him."

I'd been so absorbed in what was happening to my name that I'd whipped out my notebook, written down all the possibilities, crossed out all but Peerce, and underlined the two *e*'s so I wouldn't forget how to spell our name when I told Alice about it later. But Alice had been listening to the radio, and when I came home that night I found that the name on our door had already been changed to "JAN PEERCE." Alice had continued to call me Pinky during the John Pierce era, but she started calling me Jan that very night. A few days later we went to court and legally changed my first name and our last name. It was like getting a divorce from myself. For a little while, Larry had problems with his school records, and I sometimes had trouble cashing a check that came in payable to my old name, but the changeover was remarkably easy.

Only a few times in the last forty years has Alice called me Pinky: the last time I can remember was in an argument over when the last time was she'd called me Pinky. Jan Peerce meant a new life in art for us; Pinky Pearl was left behind in another lifetime.

Roxy always used to say to me: "Jacob Perelmuth was a wonderful name, too; no matter how often I changed it, I always respected it by never changing your initials. They were always J.P."

4

Jan Peerce

No Second Caruso

Roxy & His Gang was a show my boss used to take on cross-country tours, with himself as MC. He always had something to say about each artist and, again, he pretended to improvise even though he might say the same thing at each show.

On one such tour, when he came to me, he would put his arm around my shoulders and tell the audience, "And now, ladies and gentlemen, I'd like you to close your eyes and just relax. In a few seconds, you will hear a voice that I can only describe as a second Caruso."

Caruso had been dead barely a dozen years. There must have been people in the audience who had heard his voice and I didn't want to risk comparison. Besides, I was superstitious. If you give a guy such a glorious build-up, you can never tell what will happen next. He's likely to sing badly; it happens to too many.

I put up with it for a while, but I felt self-conscious about the introduction and one day I begged Roxy:

"Look, whatever you say when you introduce me, please, Roxy, none of the 'second Caruso,' either before or after. I want to be the first Jan Peerce."

I could tell he was hurt. After all, he had invented the first Jan Peerce and it pleased him to think of me as the second Caruso. But he went along and I'm glad. As young and unprofessional as I was where opera singing was concerned, I was on the right track. To this day, whenever I hear someone described as "a second Caruso" or "the second Gigli," I think to myself: Maybe second fiddle?

Audition at the Astor

Oddly enough, it was not as an Italian opera singer that I attracted the attention of Arturo Toscanini at the beginning of 1938, but as a Wagnerian tenor:

> For persons who suffer from influenza hangovers the radio this past week-
> end has been both a cultural force and a musical delight. There was, for
> example, the Radio City Music Hall broadcast of the first act of *Die Walküre*
> by Mr. Rapee and his accustomed forces. Mr. Jan Peerce, familiar to Music
> Hall patrons as a purveyor of popular ballads, sang the role of Siegmund,
> and it seemed to me that I had never heard the part sung so beautifully, so
> easily and so intelligently. If Mr. Peerce's voice is ample enough to fill the
> great spaces of the Metropolitan—and perhaps it is—there should be gold
> for that institution, in this amazing young tenor's throat.
>
> —Samuel Chotzinoff, *New York Post*

Toscanini heard that broadcast, too. He told me later that what appealed to him was hearing a Siegmund who sang the part with the proper lyricism. After reading the review, he asked Chotzinoff—who was a consultant to NBC—if he knew me. Chotzinoff said yes, but he never would have dared propose a Music Hall singer to Toscanini.

"I'd like to hear this boy," Toscanini told him. He was looking for a tenor for a broadcast of Beethoven's Ninth Symphony.

Chotzinoff phoned me and asked if I'd like to audition for Toscanini. After I'd almost fainted and got up from the floor, I said, "Of course!" Not just at NBC, but in the newspapers, I had been following every detail of the great maestro's career; his creation of the greatest orchestra America has ever known; his escape from Italy by seaplane to Switzerland and then on to America just a few weeks earlier, when Mussolini took away his passport. I also knew about his reputation as an autocrat and I'd heard the joke around Radio City that "either Mussolini or Toscanini had to go, because Italy wasn't big enough for both of them."

Now, the tenor part of Beethoven's Ninth is not exactly a showcase for the soloist. It's no aria. You sing sixteen bars and then the tenors of the chorus join you. You're inundated. You're a thwarted man. To sing with Toscanini, however, I would have prepared "Home on the Range."

Chotzinoff was to accompany me on the piano for my audition and we agreed to meet in the lobby of the Astor Hotel, where Toscanini was staying. I waited and waited, but there was no Chotzinoff. Later he told me he was scared of how I would do. Knowing him better by then, I think he didn't want his presence—to which Toscanini always lent great weight—to influence the maestro's opinion of my singing.

After a quarter of an hour, I decided Chotzinoff must have gone upstairs, so I rang Toscanini's suite to ask if he was there. When I mentioned my name, a rather gravelly voice said with an Italian accent that I should come right up. I figured that whether or not Chotzinoff was already there, I was off to a bad start—but on the way up in the elevator, I reminded myself that the Astor was my lucky hotel, where Roxy had discovered me, so I shouldn't worry too much.

I rang the buzzer of Toscanini's suite and the maestro himself answered. He was dressed like a picture of himself: formally, in a dark suit, with a bow tie. I noted he was half an inch smaller than I. He was seventy-one years old at the time.

He greeted me very cordially, shook hands, and told me that Chotzinoff hadn't shown up—which didn't seem to surprise or distress him too much. He had been a cellist, I knew, but he said he would accompany me on the piano himself. He asked if I had brought any music with me.

"Only the tenor part of the Ninth Symphony," I replied.

Toscanini laughed and said, "Oh, I wanted to hear you sing something more . . . more . . ."

The word he was groping for was "singable," but I wasn't there to teach Toscanini English, so I simply said, "I'm sorry, but I don't have anything else with me." It was really going badly, I thought, Astor or no Astor.

"Do you *know* anything else?" he asked.

I said I knew some arias and he asked which ones. The first that came to mind was "Una furtiva lagrima," from *L'Elisir d'Amore.*

"Oh," he said happily. "You know 'Una furtiva lagrima'! Come, I play for you."

He sat down at the piano—without music—and began to play. Now, Toscanini was not a very good pianist, but he prided himself on being a precise one. That day, however, he made a mistake.

The two stanzas of "Una furtiva lagrima" begin the same way, but continue differently. In the first stanza, Toscanini played the continuation of the second. It was enough to ruin any tenor's audition and any music-minded judge in the world would have understood if he clobbered the accompanist. When Toscanini realized what he'd done, he stopped playing. He was totally immobilized by rage at himself.

Five years of singing over crackling candy wrappers and missed cues at the Music Hall had taught me never to stop, but to plow forward. Unfalteringly, I went on singing "Una furtiva lagrima" without accompaniment. It had begun to snow—and a Times Square snowfall is always very beautiful, until it hits the pavement. So I concentrated on Donizetti and the snowflakes I could see through the Astor Hotel window. Somehow Toscanini didn't matter much at the moment, even though I could hear him swearing at himself in Italian.

Then I could feel him admiring my poise and my voice, and somewhere in the second stanza, he rejoined me and we finished together. Whereupon he exclaimed, *"Bella voce!"* and came right to the point: "Would you like to sing the Ninth Symphony with me?"

"It would be the greatest moment of my life!" I replied.

"All right. You sing with me," he said, giving me the date: February 6, 1938. And that was how my association with Toscanini began.

Fifteen Years with Toscanini

Erich Leinsdorf prepared the singers. He had just come to America and was working as an assistant to Toscanini and in some minor capacity at the Metropolitan Opera. Constance Hope, the publicist, had found him a room with an upright piano in her mother's boardinghouse in the West Eighties. Leinsdorf was very self-effacing and easy to get along with in those early times.

One day while we were rehearsing at his place, a phone call came for him and he had to run downstairs to take it. He came back up walking on air toward seventh heaven. He was aglow. "The Metropolitan Opera just called," he told me. "In six weeks I am going to conduct a performance of *Die Walküre* with Flagstad and Melchior."

"Congratulations, Maestro!" I exclaimed.

"Only in America!" Leinsdorf went on. "Only in America could this happen. If I lived in Vienna for the rest of my life, nothing like this could ever happen to me. Thank G-d I came here! How wonderful this world is!" I let him enjoy this moment and I was honored to share it with him as he went on and on. "Everything is rosy! America! America! I love everybody in this country!"

When he began to run out of steam, I remarked, "You know, Maestro, it's really great to see a man react this way to something good that's happened to him. I mean, you're so thankful. But listen, I hope that as you make a bigger and bigger success, you'll still be the same grateful, thankful, humble guy you are now."

He made a great success of himself with the Met and later with the Boston Symphony—and I leave it to others to decide whether he is still the same humble, grateful guy he was then.

As I've said, for the tenor, Beethoven's Ninth is not the most demanding part, although it's a trying experience to sit silently for three whole movements knowing that when the time comes, you have to open your mouth to sing sixteen beautiful bars. The bass for my first performance with Toscanini was Ezio Pinza and he had the same complaint: "You sit for forty-five minutes and then you have to start with 'O Freunde'!" Pinza kept clearing his throat and finally he muttered to me, "I always promise myself I will never sing with that man the Ninth Symphony. But when he calls me I can't resist him." Pinza worried about "O Freunde" popping out as a big frog in his throat; it never happened.

By the time I came to the first piano rehearsal with Toscanini, I knew my part pretty well. What struck me right off was Toscanini's concentration and self-discipline. When he sat at the piano, the most important thing in the world for him was what was happening at that moment. If you pleased him by just doing the music—no matter what it was—*as written;* if you gave the notes the right values and the words their right pronunciation and flavor, he was the happiest man in the world. Every time you sang a phrase he liked, he acted as if he had found a thousand dollars.

With Toscanini, it wasn't just a piano rehearsal or two and then the performance. You saw him for weeks—three times, four times a week, as often as he felt was needed. At rehearsals he was the professor, a teacher of musicians; that was where you really learned. Any day you had a rehearsal with him, that was it for the day. You made no other appointments. If he called you for a three-o'clock rehearsal, you had to be rested and prepared, and then he might keep you until six or seven at night, maybe later; there was no telling. When he was happy after a good rehearsal, he would offer a cup of coffee or tea and a piece of cake and sit around, reminiscing about other performances, other singers, other conductors—tossing out opinions like: "Coloratura sopranos! If I had a daughter who wanted to be a coloratura soprano I would cut her throat!"

At the NBC Symphony Orchestra rehearsals, Toscanini was so dynamic, so forceful, so fiery that I couldn't take my eyes off him—which was true for all the fifteen years I worked with him. I *had to* watch the expression on his face as he conducted, for it conveyed his innermost feeling. And because of his drive, I responded as if I knew exactly what he wanted. He had this power not only over his singers, but over the instrumentalists in his orchestra. They were all great musicians to begin with—they had played with all the major conductors and they knew everything backward and forward—yet the way they responded to this man was a surprise even to them. They *wanted* to please him. He was so sincere in what he asked for, they were anxious to do the right thing.

It's been said that musicians played or sang over their heads for him, but I don't think he ever made me do the impossible. What I would say is that he got as much out of you as he could—and as much as you *should have given.* But he never asked for anything that wasn't in the score. In fact, I'm sure that if you had tried to *overdo* something, he would have objected strongly. He wanted passion, but passion from within. He wanted warmth, but not manufactured warmth. And he wanted you to know what you were singing. He always said, "Say the words correctly. The tone will come." He was right. If you know what you're saying, the meaning of the words will bring out the quality of the tone—provided you have the tone in your voice.

People often ask me about the theatrics associated with a Toscanini performance: "Was he acting or was he sincere?" And my answer is: "He was *he.*" Once he was on the podium, he was a different man—he was pure musician. He was an actor, too, but he acted only what he truly felt. When we did the broadcast performance of *La Bohème,* tears streamed down his face. They weren't put on. Nobody saw them except us singers. In this we were more fortunate than the audience, for all they could see was his back and his arms waving. We could see the man and what the music meant to him—whether it was a Beethoven symphony or a Puccini opera.

After the Ninth Symphony went well, I was "Toscanini's tenor." What he came to like especially when we did Verdi and Puccini was my pronunciation of Italian. In fact, when he found fault with some of his Italian singers' pronunciation, he would say to me, "Peerce, you show them." I used to feel terrible when this happened, and of course the Italians felt worse.

Toscanini used to insist that I must have Italian blood in me to speak his language so well. I said I knew that, at least as far back as my great-great-grandparents, my origins were Russian. "And before them?" Toscanini asked. "Before that," I said, "who knows anything?" And Toscanini exclaimed: "Ah, I knew it! Before them, they must have traveled through Italy."

He himself once told me he thought he had Jewish origins. In Italy, he said, Jews very often bear names of places: Giuseppe Siena, Giorgio Firenze. And the root of his name was, of course, Toscana. With that, Toscanini paused, looked at his wrists, and said: "So, you see, Peerce, I may have Jewish blood running through these veins—and I feel good!"

Toscanini's tirades and temper tantrums were legendary and some that I witnessed were indeed savage, but I prided myself that in my decade and a half with him, I was never on the receiving end of one of his attacks. Once, though, I thought my time had come.

We were rehearsing *La Traviata* and I sang the wrong article: *un* instead of *la.* Toscanini, who was playing the piano, looked up at me incredulously and shook his head. All he said, however, was: *"Andiamo. Un'altra volta.* Again."

So I relaxed, which is always dangerous, and began to sing it again. And I made the same mistake.

This time his hands dropped from the keyboard. I braced myself for the storm, murmured my prayers and farewells, and I said to myself, "If there's got to be a first time, let's hope it's the last." But Toscanini looked at me with those bright, dark eyes and uttered just three little words: "Peerce! You, too?"

I was mortal now. What everybody else was guilty of, I was guilty of, too. But his three words broke the tension one could practically see in the air. Everyone laughed, I smiled, and I did it right the next time.

Once Toscanini engaged a friend of mine for an opera in German. When I called the singer up to congratulate him, I added some advice: "Now listen. In order to make good with Toscanini, you must know your part better than you know your own name or your ten fingers. You must be sure of every word, every phrase, every sound, every nuance. Therefore, as a friend, I would advise you to go to the most proper expert who can help you prepare for this: an authentic German professor of music. I can give you a couple of names."

"Don't bother," he said. "You know I can speak German."

"I didn't ask you whether you spoke it. The question is whether you can sing it to satisfy Toscanini. I suggest you go to the best man money can buy."

He didn't—and it was the only time he ever sang with Toscanini. He was a big man and Toscanini taunted him for his every mistake to the point that, in retrospect, it's amazing one of them didn't attack the other. The showdown between them came at a rehearsal for which I was a few minutes late. Why? Because I had just bought a new hat. Ever since the Lower East

Side and my father's straw-hat disaster on the *Pavolye* line, buying a hat had been a very special occasion: You bought one only when you could afford it. I had reached the station in life where I didn't just go and buy a Truly Warner for $3.85. It was a twenty-five-dollar Cavanaugh, and perhaps because I was proud or else because I was late, I didn't hang it up on a hook, but laid it on an empty chair near where I was sitting and Toscanini was berating my friend. He had made several mistakes already. As I came in he made another mistake and Toscanini hit the ceiling, yelling aloud in Italian, asking why he had ever engaged him, denouncing him as an *assassino* and a general nogoodnik. Tears started running down the big man's face and the rest of us turned away. But Toscanini wasn't done with him yet! Still in a rage, the maestro lifted the heavy score from the piano. I was sure he was going to hit the singer with it. Instead he slammed it down on the nearest inanimate object. Wham! My brand-new hat was now a twenty-five-dollar beret from Cavanaugh's. So absorbed was he in what he was doing, Toscanini never even noticed what he had done to me.

When Robert Merrill, Licia Albanese, and I did *La Traviata* with Toscanini, Bob was still a young man and he sang Papa Germont's aria "Di Provenza" too romantically for the maestro's liking. "Mayrrill," he said. "You have a beautiful voice, Mayrrill . . . You're a great baritone. But *don't* be a baritone, be a *faather."* And this is still an occasional greeting I give my New Rochelle neighbor: "Be a *faather, Mayrrill!"*

During my first few years with Toscanini, Alice kept complaining that I never invited her to a rehearsal, even when I told her that they were better than the performances. To come to a rehearsal, however, you had to know the right person. This was Chotzinoff, so when Alice persisted, I asked him.

"Of course!" Chotzinoff said. "For Alice, anything! Ask her which day she wants to come next week."

"Would you like to come Monday?" I asked Alice.

"Monday I can't. I've got a meeting."

"Then Tuesday."

"Tuesday I have to go to Brooklyn."

"How about Wednesday?"

"No. And Thursday's the maid's day off, so I've got to stay home and look after the kids. Friday's the best day."

"No," I said. "Friday's the worst. It's the final rehearsal, a general run-through. Come any other day of the week and I can guarantee you that with Toscanini you'll see fireworks."

"Well, I can always come and just listen to the music, Jan. That's what it's about, isn't it?"

"Music you can hear at the performance on the weekend. I promise you that every day before Friday, he'll raise holy hell with the musicians."

Which he did—with the musicians and with just about everybody else. And every day that week I would turn to Licia Albanese and say, "Oh, boy, I wish Alice were here." Alice didn't come until Friday, however.

Toscanini always made a dramatic entrance, even at rehearsals. The musicians would be tuning up until, all of a sudden, the manager of the orchestra would come out and clap his hands twice. This was the signal that the Great Man was coming.

In would walk Toscanini, to an outburst of silence. He would play with his mustache, pushing it up, stretching it a little, and otherwise just stand there, thinking and thinking.

On this particular Friday he said, "All right. Start with the prelude to Act Three."

The orchestra played only five notes before he stopped them with a shout of: *"Piano!* [Softer!]"

They started again. Ten notes this time, before he rapped and said, "Basses! *Piano!!!"*

The third time, he had a tantrum the likes of which I'd never seen—even from him. Shouting *"Voglio PIANO! PIANO!!"* he broke his stick, stamped his feet, slammed the score to the floor, and threw the stand to the side. Everything within reach flew, while we all ducked. He cursed in the lowest Italian dialect. Albanese said to me, "Sometimes I'm sorry for you, Jan, that you don't understand all his Italian."

"Sometimes I'm glad," I said, particularly when I glanced through the glass and saw Alice mouthing my own words at me: *"Don't come on Friday. Nothing ever happens."*

The violence had gone out of Toscanini, but not the anger. Playing with his mustache, he addressed the orchestra: "Next season, anybody in this orchestra who wants to play with me must have an audition. Nobody can play next year without audition." He glanced down to see the effect of this announcement and, naturally, the first face he saw was that of his concertmaster, Mischa Mischakoff, a cherubic little violinist who had been through a dozen-odd years and many sieges with Toscanini and always came up smiling. This was what he was doing now. Looking straight at Mischakoff, Toscanini growled, "You, too!"

Part of the greatness of Toscanini was that no matter how inexcusable his outburst, no matter what he said or did, he never meant it personally and never bore a grudge. If, in a fit of anger, he told you off one day, the next day it was old business forgotten; new business, please!

Once he insulted a flute player so much that the man decided he'd had enough and would risk telling him off. At the next break, puffed up with anger, the flutist rose from his chair and stormed over to Toscanini, saying, "Listen, Maestro—"

That was as far as he got. Toscanini glanced at him and said, "Don't apologize!"

Toscanini was very near-sighted but very vain, and he wouldn't wear glasses. Or maybe they wouldn't have helped; I never discussed it with him. He used his ears to see as well as hear everything he needed to know. When somebody hit a wrong note, he could pick out a guy sitting way at the end of the middle section—and he always pointed to the right guy, even though he couldn't possibly have seen him.

Whenever I mention Toscanini in this book, even incidentally, you'll find I do so with reverence. Where conductors are concerned, he was my man. I don't have to think twice about anything I tell you about him. I lived with him in music and loved living with him, even at moments when he may have misconducted himself—though, thank G-d, never toward me and never toward music. If, in fifteen years, Toscanini never raised his voice toward me, perhaps it was because my respect for the man was such that if he thought enough of me to give me an assignment, I came prepared for it.

Not that we didn't have our disagreements. I turned him down twice, once for *Aïda,* once for *Die Walküre,* both for the same reason: in my opinion, the part wasn't for me.

About *Aïda:* He wanted me to be Radames on his first TV program. I said no. He said, "Why?" I said, "I'm not an *Aïda* type. I'm not a Radames."

Toscanini knew what I was getting at. "Who told you that a Radames has to make a lot of noise?"

"That's the custom, Maestro," I replied, "and I don't want to have to force."

"But with me, Peerce, you won't have to."

"If I don't," I said, "I'll be criticized, and I don't want to be criticized. I just feel that it's not the right part for me." The big tenor aria, "Celeste Aïda," is all right; in fact, everything in the first act is all right. But when you get to the Triumphal Scene, you have to fight orchestra, chorus, onstage band, and five soloists. I'd have to push and it could hurt my voice. Some people have the voice for *Aïda,* but I'm a sentimentalist, my voice is sentimental; I'm a lover. I love to sing of love. I'm not a warrior, a Radames or a Siegfried. Sure, I did both on the air with Erno Rapee long ago. But at any stage of my career, I'd have looked ridiculous wearing a leopard skin. I didn't want to sing Radames with Toscanini and I never did. The same goes for

Wagner, although Toscanini once asked me to record some excerpts. But I'm no Wagnerian. And when I explained why not, Toscanini wrote me a letter beginning: "Who told you that in order to sing Wagner you don't need to know how to sing?" Years later, he would still say to me, "Peerce, you should have sung Wagner with me." But I'm glad I didn't.

From the very beginning, I was careful about my choice of repertoire, because I hoped to be able to sing for a long time, and if you give too much —especially in your early years, when you don't know as much about vocal technique as you learn later—your voice may not last as long as you'd like. By the time the technique is part of you, you may wonder: "But where's the voice?"

The biggest mistake young singers make is to step more than a very tentative toe beyond their immediate powers. When you're young, you think you can do everything. You're told you can, too. Particularly in opera, if you're young and if you learn two roles and sing a high B flat and hold it till you get green in the face, especially if you accompany it with grand theatrical gestures, why, you're great, you're fantastic, you can have a career. Young singers think that's what it's all about. They forget that from one gesture to another, there's some music to be sung. Between high notes, there's something to be said in the middle of the aria. The valleys are sometimes more important than the peaks; if you nurse the valleys, the peaks will be more impressive. Most sensational new singers, though, keep punching away up on top, overdoing everything—and they have nowhere to go but down.

A long, hard climb to the top doesn't always work to an artist's advantage, but maybe I was lucky I was in my thirties before I made my way into serious music. I knew how to protect myself by then—even from Toscanini. Which is why I refused Radames and Siegmund.

Early in my concert career, I remember listening to a Toscanini broadcast of an opera while I was getting dressed for a concert in Cleveland. I said to my accompanist about two of the singers: "They never sang like this before. And I predict they'll never sing like this again." They were fantastic, but they gave too much too often in their careers and got into vocal trouble afterward. Singing is like charity: You give—but you don't give everything so that you have nothing left for yourself. You have to be a little selfish.

Toscanini never carried on about my two refusals, but we did have one serious estrangement in the 1950s, toward the end of his life. I had been promised the role of Riccardo in Verdi's *A Masked Ball (Un Ballo in Maschera)* when Toscanini did it on NBC radio. I had been singing with Toscanini for fourteen years by then and I might have assumed the role was mine. In any event, I was assured of this by Chotzinoff and by George Marek of RCA. It was a live performance at Carnegie Hall, to be broadcast by NBC and recorded by RCA. For its own contractual, political, and recording reasons, however, RCA wanted my friend Jussi Bjoerling to sing the part; they persuaded Toscanini, too. That was bad enough. To make matters worse, nobody notified me that Bjoerling was singing *my* part until I read about it in the papers.

"Oh, yes, there was a change," Chotzinoff told me, when I phoned about it.

"What do you mean, there was a change? I was *promised* this thing!"

"Well, he had a change of mind."

"Who had a change of mind?" I asked. Right away, the people around Toscanini began to guard him so I couldn't get to him and change his mind back. Before then I'd had access to him any time of day. Alice and I had had a wonderful relationship with the Toscaninis and their son, Walter, and their daughter-in-law. Now I was heartbroken, because I worshiped this man. For me, he was someone on a pedestal who could do no wrong. When this happened, however, I said, "I don't ever want to see this guy again or even talk to him, great as he is."

[This memory is so painful to Jan that Alice Peerce tells what happened next.]

Alice: *Jan took it very, very badly. Naturally, I wasn't exactly overjoyed either. Though he hadn't practiced, he'd been preparing mentally from the moment he was promised* Ballo. *Ten days before the performance Bjoerling had to withdraw and they came begging for Jan to step into the breach. Walter Toscanini called on the phone, as if they'd just begun casting. Jan said no; absolutely not. Then Bob Merrill, who was the Renato in it, called to tell us the maestro was so contrite and Jan couldn't do this to the maestro and ruin the project. Jan said he could. Then Chotzinoff called me up and pleaded with me to intervene with Jan. I told Jan he'd be cutting off his nose to spite his face if he turned it down. Jan said to me that he wouldn't do it nohow. He didn't care if the world turned upside down. They'd insulted him. He didn't care to listen to any story that RCA pressured Toscanini to take Bjoerling. By then the performance was only a week off.*

I said to Jan, "You must realize that the morning after someone else sings this concert instead of you, you will be smashed. If Bjoerling did it, that would be one thing. You'd be hurt, but you didn't have any choice. But if now they pick someone else to do it instead of you . . ."

"Well," Jan said, "if you think you're so smart and you know everything, you should realize that I haven't looked at the score of Ballo *in five or six years. How could I do it on one week's notice?"*

I said, "Jan, don't give me that bunk. Knowing what you know, you could read through it and pick it up right away."

The fighting over this was terrible—not just in our house, but it spread to others. Some friends gave a dinner party in our honor that they'd been planning for months. Jan told me at the last minute that he wasn't going. He just stayed home and sulked. Well, to save the friendship, I went to the party alone. When I got there, our hosts and their guests all acted as if I were the villain of the piece. "To leave your husband alone at a time like this!" "How can you eat dinner, thinking maybe you'll find him dead when you get back?" "Go home to your husband, Alice, where you belong!"

So I drove home. Along the way, I threw a nickel instead of a dime into the exact-change collection at a toll booth. The cops came chasing after me. I got home in a rotten mood. When Jan told me that he'd hung up on both Chotzinoff and Walter Toscanini after I'd been saying to them "Give him time," we had one of our worst fights ever. I told him he was a fool for passing up a lost opportunity that he'd regained. He told me to leave him alone.

The next day, both Chotzinoff and Walter called me to say that the old man himself was going to call Jan. And Jan said that if Toscanini did phone, he wasn't going to speak to him. I told Jan that would be the worst offense in the world. The maestro had given so much to Jan that he was entitled to this much consideration. When Jan just shook his head no, I packed a bag.

"Where you going?" he asked me as I started toward the door.

"Out!" I said. "I don't want to be around to hear you say no to Toscanini."

Our youngest child, Susan, had just come home with her governess at the height of this argument. She began to cry. The governess pleaded with me: "Mrs. Peerce, don't go!"

Jan said, "I want you to know that if you walk through that door, you don't ever have to come back." This was his way of asserting himself. I don't really blame him, because I was shoving, hitting, banging, and pressuring him all the time on this, not physically, but emotionally. He told me, "You're doing this yourself, Alice. I'm not the one who's sending you out of the house. It's your responsibility. You're doing it and you're wrong."

"No, you're wrong!" I kept saying—and poor little Susan began to scream. Anyway, I went right through the front door and Jan ran after me. He caught up with me on the lawn, saying, "All right, I'll talk to him!" Then he brought me back in—and everything was all right.

An hour later, the phone rang. I picked it up and I heard Toscanini's voice saying, "Peerce—Peerce—believe me, it is not my fault." He started to explain about RCA and Bjoerling. I felt miserable—not only because he'd hurt me and he'd been victimized, but because I hated to hear a man like that, whom I loved so, apologizing. We were both moved to tears and I found myself saying, "But, Maestro, I haven't done *Ballo* in six or seven years, and I don't remember it."

Now *he* was all business, too. "Peerce, you will know it. You will know it."

The broadcast was on Saturday. I had a concert the Sunday before it and a performance of *Lucia di Lammermoor* at the Met on Tuesday, so we couldn't start rehearsing until Wednesday—with the orchestra; there was no time for piano rehearsals. This worried me, but Toscanini said, "You don't have to memorize it. You can hold the book." I wanted to do it right, however, so I squeezed in a little time with my accompanist and my coach, Dick Marzollo, and got *Ballo* back into my system.

On Wednesday, when I came into Carnegie Hall for the rehearsal, the air was electric. People who knew about all the backstage difficulties were wondering what was going to happen. Toscanini was still contrite. He took me around, introducing me to everybody—all of them people I'd known for years—and saying, "This is the person we should have had all along." When we got onstage to rehearse, he said to me, "Just sing. I follow."

"I'll follow *you,* Maestro," I insisted.

"No, no. You sing, I follow."

We went through the first act without a mistake. Before calling an intermission, he jumped off the podium and threw his arms around me and kissed me. This was the side of Toscanini that seldom came out. I felt just like a kid, not a man getting near fifty.

Upstairs, Toscanini said to me, "You afraid? You afraid? I told you: you just sing."

"But, Maestro," I said, "I was worried about not satisfying you."

He said, "Don't worry. Just sing." He was right. *Ballo* was a fabulous success. The notices we got were unreal. The fire he gave to it!

Arturo Toscanini, in the 87th year of his life and the 68th year of his career as a conductor, led a performance . . . in Carnegie Hall that was conspicuous above all for its virility, dramatic fire, and glowing impetuosity.

Supreme among the solo accomplishments of the occasion was Jan Peerce's Riccardo, sung with surpassing beauty of tone, technical finish, warmth and variety of color and last but not least, superb musicianship.

Mr. Peerce substituted for the suddenly indisposed Jussi Bjoerling only last Wednesday, and he was equal to every demand of the score and of Toscanini! Whatever the passage, whether of dramatic declamation, or lightness and gaiety, or the molding of a lyrical phrase, Mr. Peerce was the master of his means.

We know of no finer tenor voice now accessible to the American public. When the possessor of such a voice adds to that possession the high intelligence and the beautiful Italian diction that Mr. Peerce accomplished, the art of singing is vastly the gainer.

—Olin Downes, *New York Times,* January 18, 1954

When Toscanini died in 1957, I was interviewed on the air by Tex McCrary about the world's loss and my own. Tex said, "Your association with Toscanini was marvelous, of course. But who do you think, at this time, is rising to his place?"

I said, "No one!"

"You mean to say that of all the people . . . ?"

I said, "No! No one!" I was so vehement that I made a number of enemies, even among conductors whose friendship I cherished. I stuck to my guns, though. Toscanini was a genius.

Before I tell you about a number of other conductors who weren't Toscaninis, let me end this tribute with a few words of his own that I like to remember him by. During one of his gargantuan rages at his musicians, he practically spat out this declaration:

"You know, we all must die! I shall be reincarnated as the keeper of a brothel. And I will not let any of you in."

Of Florestan and Knappertsbusch

I sang Beethoven's only opera, *Fidelio,* for Toscanini in 1944, during the war, when its message of freedom in German was especially timely. Toscanini worked us particularly hard for this broadcast. He didn't speak German fluently, but he knew every word and corrected our German and made us enunciate it clearly. His tempos were fast, but he could justify every one of them.

I've never sung *Fidelio* on the stage. Some of the other singers had done it at the Met. It's an opera about which everybody has ideas and feelings. You could always talk to Toscanini about interpretation: "Maestro, is there any special reason for this? Don't you think we could do it a little slower?" He'd tell you why you couldn't—what would happen if you did: "If you sing it slowly, you will lose the intensity." But he listened to you; he wasn't the ogre he was painted. The only time he was a tough guy was when he got angry. When would he get angry? When he thought you were betraying the composer's wishes.

Toscanini made me learn the part of Florestan in *Fidelio.* I was willing to sing it, but why should I learn a whole role that I'd never do again? He said, "You learn the part. You please me." This time I did.

Toscanini's *Fidelio* was much more fiery than the *Fidelio* of Hans Knappertsbusch, with whom I sang it years later for a recording in Munich. Now, Knappertsbusch was a wonderful musician and conductor, but he did a slower, heavier *Fidelio*.

When my name was first mentioned to him, he hadn't heard of me. Kurt List, the record executive, persuaded him I was a good tenor whose name would help sell platters. When I reported to him for the first time, Knappertsbusch said, "Mr. Peerce, you come here with a great reputation. I am told you are a very good tenor and a fine musician." I beamed, until Knappertsbusch added, "And now that you are here, you will have to prove it to me."

With that, the smile fell off my face and I straightened up to my full five feet six. "Maestro," I began, "I've heard about you, too. And people who ought to know say you're a very fine conductor, a great musician. But now that we're both here, you will have to prove it to me too."

Knappertsbusch bristled. Then he rapped for us to start work right away. To my amazement, he was making the recording without so much as a piano rehearsal first. There wasn't even the usual talk-through for the engineers. After all, this was the Munich orchestra, which was his very own. He gave me no cues. There I stood, thirty feet away from him, and I never knew what his tempo was. We started the aria. I did it.

When it was over, we went into the control room and listened to the playback. There, Knappertsbusch hit me playfully on the back and said, "You know, Mr. Peerce, you have a surprising voice and I like your interpretation. But if I may make a suggestion, it's a little too fast."

I wasn't going to let this man get the better of me if I could help it, so I said, "You know something, Maestro, I like your interpretation, too. But if I may make a suggestion, it's a little too slow."

Even the engineers looked up at this. But Knappertsbusch slapped me on the back again and said, "So now let's try to strike a happy medium."

Which we did, now that we understood each other. In fact, we started with the recitative "G-tt! welch Dunkel hier!" and went right through the aria "In des Lebens Frühlingstagen" in one take. What you hear on the record is what we did right after leaving the control room: no splicing, no *schmeiss*ing, no fixing, no dropping in of just one note. Nowadays, there's so much engineering that you can sing half a note at a time. When you hear such a recording, you're not hearing real singing, you're hearing a feat of engineering.

Knappertsbusch and I became great friends in that control room, but I have Toscanini to thank for teaching me Florestan so I could carry it off years later without even a rehearsal. As the recording progressed, Knappertsbusch said he wanted me to do the dialogue in German. I said I didn't speak German well. But he said he liked the German he'd heard me speak to the musicians and engineers, which I adapted to easily from my Yiddish background. So against my better judgment, I said I'd do it. I reminded Knappertsbusch that in my contract, I had the right to veto anything I didn't like. In this case, it meant that he could hire a German actor to read my lines if he and I weren't satisfied.

Thanks to Toscanini's groundwork and Knappertsbusch's encouragement, I did the dialogue and we both liked it. The German critics loved it; one of them mistakenly paid me one of the finest compliments of my life by adding to an otherwise glowing notice: "What a pity that Jan Peerce doesn't speak German, so a professional actor had to be found to speak his dialogue for him."

Milton Steinberg, Rabbi

After a year and a half at 400 West End Avenue, beginning when I'd started working steadily at the Music Hall, we had moved nine blocks uptown to 580 West End Avenue, at Eighty-eighth Street. Back in 1936, this was one of the grandest buildings in New York. There was one tenant on each floor. Every apartment had nine or ten rooms and four or five baths. Even in Europe, you never saw such big, gorgeous, spacious, high-ceilinged rooms. You had all the privacy you could ask for. And for the first year or two, our rent was only $200 a month, even though such an apartment had rented for $750 earlier. As the Depression took hold, such luxury apartments were a drug on the market. The management was more than willing to make concessions to an up-and-coming young family man who worked for the Rockefellers.

My most vivid memories of 580 West End Avenue are of my friendship with Rabbi Milton Steinberg, no relation to the conductor William Steinberg. Milton Steinberg was the boy, a couple of years ahead of me at De Witt Clinton High, with such a passion for dead languages that he'd wound up teaching the Greek teacher Greek. He had also won first prize in the De Witt Clinton poetry contest, although his runner-up was Countee Cullen, later an eminent black poet.

I'd lost track of Milton after high school and figured he was teaching Latin or Greek in some school somewhere. My lawyer, Ben Levin, had been in his class and kept closer touch. One day in the mid-thirties, he said to me,

"You know what I read in the *New York Times?* There's a new rabbi coming to Park Avenue Synagogue from Indianapolis. His name is Milton Steinberg. Wouldn't it be funny if that's *our* Milton Steinberg?"

The Park Avenue Synagogue at the time was "Progressive Conservative." Ben and I went over to East Eighty-seventh Street to check out the new rabbi. We didn't have to hear this ruddy, jovial young man more than a few minutes to know that he was not only the same brilliant Milton Steinberg we'd known in high school, but a great rabbi. He preached that faith and reason need not be enemies in religion. He espoused, in the worst of times all over the world, the compatibility of Judaism with joy and Judaism as a corrective to the spiritually unhealthy modern theologies of gloom and despair. Pugnacious kids as young as sixteen used to come to the Park Avenue Synagogue to argue with him: rebels who found fault with G-d, the Bible, and organized religion, and who didn't want to be Jews. Milton Steinberg —always laughing and twinkling—talked to them not like a rabbi, but like a big brother with two small *b*'s—and brought them around by reasoning. From Riverside Drive to the borders of Yorkville in Manhattan, many young people's idea of a Friday-night date was to go over to the Park Avenue Synagogue to hear Steinberg. Not just kids looking for a cheap date, but married couples like Mr. and Mrs. Jan Peerce—who, to our own amazement, joined the Park Avenue Synagogue. For Milton Steinberg knew whereof he spoke—and the depth and sincerity with which he said it was a revelation in itself.

At that first session, Ben and I went up and reintroduced ourselves to our old high-school friend. He invited us over to his house on Ninety-second Street for a cup of tea. We met his wife, Edith, an intellectual who was ultra-frank. If Edith had an opinion, she told it to you—even if it was unflattering to you and you were the president of the synagogue.

Alice hit it off well with the Steinbergs and soon there were three couples going steady on most Saturday nights: the Peerces, the Steinbergs, and the Al Ostrikers. Al was in textiles and the Ostrikers lived in the Beresford on Eighty-first and Central Park West, where Isaac Stern, Abe Burrows, Beverly Sills, and Leonard Lyons have lived. We would take turns hosting dinner for six. Toward the end of the evening, we'd have a little drink of champagne or sweet wine. If Milton Steinberg took an extra drink or felt a little bouncier than usual, he would sit on the floor, reclining on a pillow, and recite Shelley or Keats, for an hour or two of listening as beautiful as any music I've heard. Or I would ask him a casual question and sit for hours as he'd expound. It could be about anything in the world: What was wrong with society? What were the best books of our time and all time?

Often on those Saturday nights with the Steinbergs and the Ostrikers, we talked of Torah and music. Sometimes I sang. For that last drink was a send-off to my crowded Sunday of radio broadcasts interspersed with Music Hall stage shows. Milton would ask what I was singing the next day on the radio. If he didn't know the piece, I'd say, "Well, it goes something like this," and end up holding a midnight rehearsal. Or giving my chamber audience of five the whole tabloid opera we were going to do the next day—complete with my own commentary, sometimes a denunciation. Milton's favorite was *Madame Butterfly,* which was my least favorite of the operas I do (in one period I did it four times a day in a capsule version at the Music Hall with Earl Wrightson and Anne Roselle, but I did it only twice at the Met and only a few times with the San Francisco Opera Company).

Milton used to love to hear me, Jack "Pinky" Pinkerton, condemn Puccini because in the first act, the tenor does only difficult singing, and when he starts to sing some beautiful phrases, the soprano takes them away before he's even warmed up. In the second act, Pinkerton can play cards backstage if he wants to. In the third act, he comes on, sings a page of music, and by the final high B flat, he's through for the night. Its being a one-act opera for the tenor (with a little encore in the last act) is why I never did many *Butterflys.* My price became too high to justify so little work in an evening.

Milton Steinberg would cheer and applaud my midnight *Butterflys*—and I'd go to sleep laughing so hard I never had to worry about stomach butter-flies for Sunday, my busiest day of the week. Milton was an opera lover and a Peerce fan, too—one of my first loyalists. When I did my first full-length opera—in Baltimore in 1938—Milton and Edith traveled two hundred miles to root for me. When I made my Metropolitan Opera debut on the last Saturday matinee in November 1941, the Steinbergs were there—and it wasn't easy for them to go. For despite the Progressive Conservatism of his synagogue, Milton Steinberg was traditional and so was his wife. When their sons, Jonathan and David, were born, they would arrange for someone else to wheel the baby carriage on Saturday. So for my Saturday-afternoon debut at the Met, they ordered *three* tickets and picked them up well in advance. On the appointed afternoon, they walked the three miles from East Ninety-second to West Thirty-ninth Street in cold, windy weather. At the Met, a non-Orthodox friend was waiting. He did the giving in of the tickets and the taking back of the stubs.

Milton Steinberg died from his dedication to Judaism. Even though he was overage, he tried to become a military chaplain in World War II, but the doctors diagnosed a slight heart impairment. Instead he became a civilian troubleshooter and traveling inspector of Jewish chaplains.

Even on this side of the ocean, those were difficult days for the Jewish religion and Milton Steinberg's devotion to keeping the faith with younger people. At various boot camps, young draftees were going for advice, passes, and favors to chaplains outside their faith. There were some Jewish chaplains who didn't behave well. The boys were literally drifting away.

On the first anniversary of Pearl Harbor—December 7, 1942—while en route from Brownsville, Texas, on a strenuous tour of Army bases, Milton Steinberg suffered a near-fatal heart attack. He had just turned thirty-nine. Although he tried to remain active, he was an invalid from then until he died in early 1950, at the young age of forty-six.

Rigoletto in Tights

Robert Weede was a big, strapping six-foot baritone with whom, appearances to the contrary, I had a lot in common. Born of German-Irish descent with the name of Wiedefeld, he, too, was discovered and renamed by Roxy. Over the years, starting at the Music Hall and continuing into opera and show business (he was *The Most Happy Fella* on Broadway while I was playing nightclubs), he and I were not only great friends, we were the Damon and Pythias of the music world. Bob Weede, three parts Irish, one part German, and a devout Catholic, would remind me, who was Orthodox, whenever a holiday was coming up, or on Friday, what time was sunset—"just in case you forgot." And I'd remind him whenever I thought he ought to go to church, though it invariably turned out that he'd already been. Many a time, going down Fifth Avenue after rehearsals or between shows, we'd pass by St. Patrick's and he'd say, "You wanna come in for a minute?" and I'd say, "Why not?" He wasn't proselytizing me; he wanted to share what he loved with somebody he liked. So I would go stand at attention while he knelt. After he'd made his prayers, he'd show me around the cathedral and introduce me to some of the big shots there.

He and I were very close from the day Roxy introduced us in 1933 to the time he finished his mission on this side of the world. In fact, I spoke to him just a week before he died. I knew he was sick, but I didn't know how sick. It turned out he had a heart condition and knew about it, but the most he ever said was "having a little trouble with a disc." I'll always think of him as being so big and strong that with one hand he could turn this room I'm sitting in around.

It was Bob Weede who, with the Columbia Opera Company in his home town, Baltimore, applied the first makeup I ever wore for an opera.

The Columbia Opera was a traveling company founded by Armand Bagarozzi, the son of an impresario. Whenever he could engage somebody whose name would sell tickets—James Melton, Frank Parker, Bob Weede—he put together a cast and an orchestra, rented some costumes, hired a hall in New York for a couple of rehearsals, and then his troupe would make a tour: Baltimore, Washington, Buffalo, and Syracuse, as a rule. He had a young conductor named Emerson Buckley and an eighteen-piece orchestra —some of whom played the whole tour (without music, since they were Bagarozzi regulars who knew the scores by heart—or thought they did) and others of whom were picked up and discarded on the road from city to city, but all of whom managed to play out of tune at one time or another. Still, there was a need for such outfits as the Columbia Opera Company then just as there is now. Back in 1938, I think there was only one full-time traveling company: the Fortune Gallo San Carlo Opera, which played New York a little but spent most of the year touring the U.S. and Canada, particularly college towns, and bringing opera to places that had never had opera.

The Music Hall was a natural source of talent for Bagarozzi because the most any soloist worked there during the year was thirty-six weeks. Of course, I had to be available for the Easter and Christmas shows (yes, it was the voice of Jacob Pincus Perelmuth you heard warbling "O Holy Night"!) as well as the annual "Bluebird of Happiness" presentation—but I was otherwise fairly available, though I did have to go to New York, even while touring, almost every Sunday to do *Radio City Music Hall of the Air.* Nevertheless, after my friend and personal representative, Mike De Pace, introduced me to Bagarozzi, we did *Rigoletto* together, with Bob Weede in the title part and me as the Duke of Mantua. Bagarozzi organized a tour when I learned *Traviata,* too.

This was another *raison d'être* for the Columbia Opera Company: by the time a young singer had played four weeks in four different cities, he felt he had the role down well. The local critics would come to cover us and it was more likely someone from the Metropolitan Opera would go all the way to Baltimore to catch Weede's performance or mine than from the Met at Thirty-ninth to Fiftieth Street to hear us at the Music Hall. At least, we always sang as if this were the case.

No makeup man traveled with the Columbia Opera Company, so Bob Weede put on my grease paint for me at first and then taught me how to do it myself. He watched me like a hawk, correcting my moves. He taught me where to go, where not to go: he knew all the standard positions in opera, which is important when you have little or no direction. I was like his kid brother in opera and I knew then that he had the makings of a great teacher.

Years later, in the one period when I had vocal trouble, Bob came to the rescue in this capacity.

In describing my evolution into opera, I've made it sound effortless—particularly with a friend like De Pace to introduce me to Bagarozzi and smooth the way. It wasn't that easy, though, for my biggest obstacle in those days was still myself. The first time Bagarozzi made an offer, of the part in *Rigoletto,* I turned it down. Why? Because I was ashamed of how I imagined I would look in tights.

When Alice argued with me, all I could remember was Tom Rooney and me behind-the-curtain all over again. Roxy wasn't around to help when I wailed, "Look at me!" But Alice said it: "Jan, you're great, you're handsome. How could I love anyone who looks the way you say you look?"

"But I in tights?"

"Jan, you'll have them fitted on."

"Fitted, shmitted! How do you think I look in tights? You must be crazy. I'll look like a fat sissy, not a playboy duke."

"Not with a beard, you won't."

"Beard? What do I need a beard for? Nothing will help!"

Bob Weede tried to convince me, but I wouldn't listen even to him. In spite of my doubts, Alice and Mike De Pace contacted Bagarozzi and sold me to him. They signed an airtight contract. The next I knew, I had six weeks in which to learn the part of the Duke.

The first time I saw myself in tights, it was a revelation. I looked in the mirror and—do you know what?—I appealed to myself. My first words, in fact, were: "Yeah yeah! Hear hear! I should dress up this way more often." There I was in red tights, a Sir Francis Drake collar up against a pointy little dark beard, a mustache, and marceled hair instead of a wig. I said to myself in the mirror, "Hey, you know, you got possibilities, kid!"

The me in the mirror said back, "Thank you, sir."

Alice added, "What did I tell you?"

"You know," I said, "I wouldn't have minded living in those days and dressing this way—particularly if I had a good tailor."

At that time, I was getting $150 a performance from the Columbia Opera Company. Out of that, I had to pay De Pace's ten percent commission, my hotel, a little for publicity, and the salary of my substitute at the Music Hall. Bagarozzi paid for my travel and costume rental. The first time I bought my own costume was when I was booked for *Rigoletto* at the Chicago Opera for the princely fee of four hundred dollars. My room and board, travel and costumes for that engagement set me back six hundred dollars. The Duke has to wear three costumes in *Rigoletto:* the Sir Francis Drake in red tights get-up for Acts One and Three; a black-and-white student disguise for Act Two; and a rather flattering cavalry officer's greenish garb for Act Four. In that splurge, I also spent fifty dollars on a pair of suede boots; they would cost three hundred dollars now. The costumes I bought stood me in good stead when I came to the Metropolitan Opera in 1941, for in those days you furnished your own wardrobe. In the 1950s, the Met got generous and used its own tailors and designers and costumes, which is easier on the singers' pocketbooks and better for the unity of the production, but it's led me into a number of arguments, which I've won every time. For no matter what the designer's concept is, I insist upon the collar—even a Sir Francis Drake turtleneck—being loose. For drakes and turtles, like tenors, need freedom to sing.

On Psyching Myself

My early insecurities concerned my appearance and getting started. Once I was launched, I gained all the confidence that success breeds. I never professed to be the best; I just worked at getting better. The greatest insecurity is when you think you're the best, because then you've stopped growing and you have nothing to strive for. My philosophy has been to aim for the perfection I can never achieve.

There isn't an artist in the world, no matter how modest he appears, who isn't an egomaniac. Some of us are fortunate enough to control it or channel it—or at least not flaunt it in public to the point of arrogance. But when you walk out onstage, what is it you are saying without quite saying it? "Ladies and gentlemen, here I am. This is the way it's done. And I'm the one to show you how." You wouldn't dare say it, but you have to think that way.

Laurence Wasserman, who managed a European tour of mine in the 1960s, once was waiting in the wings of a German opera house when I was about to go onstage in *La Forza del Destino*. He overheard me, as I passed a mirror, say to myself, "You look good, you feel good, so now *make* it good!"

Larry burst out laughing and said to me, "What on earth are you doing, Jan?"

I told him, "I'm psyching myself up." That's all I had time to say, but it's not just that you are a guy in his sixties playing a dashing, impetuous young lover. If you don't psych yourself into a certain swagger, you have no right to walk out on that stage. If you walk out there like a blushing rose and, in effect, beg for the audience's support, you won't make it.

You have neither the power nor the will to win the crowd.

Certain artists—conductors, singers, pianists, violinists—annoy the audience the minute they strut out because arrogance is written all over them. This isn't what I'm advocating. But if you walk out with a positive air about yourself, you'll have them with you from the start, and they will know you mean to give the best you have.

There is a built-in hostility in any audience, even if they're your friends. By friends, I don't mean intimates: just people who've been buying tickets on your name. I mean, after thirty or forty years, I'm no longer a curiosity to them. Sometimes your friends don't seem to be your friends when they come to hear you. If you give a great performance, they'll be the first to stand up and cheer and yell, relishing that moment when you please them intensely. But they also come like *aficionados* to a bullfight: to see the giant fall, the matador gored. If, G-d forbid, you give a bad performance—or what they think is bad—they are the first to walk out, to criticize, to say, "You know, he's been slipping for a long time already." Friends!

No man is a machine or an automaton, but you must have standards. Perhaps there's no limit to the heights you may scale in a performance, but there must be a minimum that you won't go below. If your voice is bad, don't go. Just stay home and lock yourself into a room and read the newspaper or a book. Or think about pleasant things and hope that tomorrow will be a better day. If tomorrow and tomorrow and tomorrow creep past with no improvement, you should seek help.

When you walk out on that stage, though, there's no help. You're on your own, no matter who is in the audience and how much faith you have in the Lord. And to the people out front, even if they're all long-time admirers, you're only as good as you are tonight. If you don't prove it now, you haven't got a case.

Hurok and His Children

To be the greatest impresario of our time, he had to possess a great ego. Every printed piece of paper pertaining to any one of his artists had to bear his name: either "S. Hurok Presents" or "Appears by arrangement with S. Hurok, Inc."

And for all this printing he charged his artists.

I used to wonder: Now why should I, Jan Peerce, pay for printing that bears his name? I pay him his commissions; that's one thing. He gets the bookings; that's another thing. But why should I pay to publicize *him?*

I came to realize that, foolish and unfair though it may sound, his name helped sell my name, as well as other ones on his list.

To prospective buyers, if S. Hurok put his imprint on an artist, then that artist was acceptable. By the time I came along, they all knew the name S. Hurok.

In my case, there were people who weren't sure about me because I came from the Music Hall, not from the concert stage or grand opera. For a while, in the flesh-peddling league, I was too light for heavy work and too heavy for light work. The Broadway people said I belonged in opera; the opera people said I belonged in shows. It took a Hurok to say, "Look, your concert house is where a Jan Peerce belongs." Of course, by the time he took me on in 1939, I was helped by the imprint of another man, named Toscanini. But Hurok's name carried its own weight. He was my manager for thirty-five years, until he died in 1974.

For a year or so before we hooked up, I used to bump into Hurok at the barbershop in the RCA Building. I would be having my hair cut and he would be getting boiled and basted under hot towels and he would ask how I was doing at Radio City Music Hall and I would say fine and he would say I should do concerts and why didn't I call him up?

I did, but he had a secretary, Mae Frohman, who was his right hand and terribly protective. I could read between the lines of the run-around she gave me: "I'll look [across my desk] and see if he's here. No, [he says] he's not in." Sometimes Hurok was "too busy to talk" and other times he would "call right back," but never did. Finally, when I met him in the barbershop another time, I leveled with him when he asked, "Listen, Pirs, why don't you call me?"

"I *am* calling you," I told him, "but your secretary is protecting you. I guess we'll never see each other, except here."

"No, no, no! I tell her next time to put you through."

I gave him time to go back and deliver the message. Then I rang up and told Mae, "This is Jan Peerce and your boss says he's in to me today."

"Yes, yes," she said, handing the phone to him.

He told me, "Pirs, I'd like to hear you privately." He knew I was studying with Giuseppe Boghetti and made a date to meet me at my teacher's studio. I sang a couple of numbers for him and Hurok said, "All right, Pirs, you'll be my artist."

"Is that all there is to it?" I asked. "Shouldn't there be a contract between us?"

"We shake hands," he said, "but all right, I'll send you a contract in the mail." Which he did. It was a standard contract—twenty percent for concerts and ten percent for records and radio—which we didn't change over four decades.

(Years later, I tried to ease the way for another who was experiencing similar difficulty trying to see Hurok. An unknown out of Israel and South America was still looking for a big break as a pianist. He couldn't get in to see any manager, let alone Hurok. Finally the pianist's uncle in New York, a friend of mine named Alberto Boyne, asked me to intervene. After much persuasion, Hurok reluctantly agreed to an appointment with the young man. Hurok met with Daniel Barenboim, heard him play, took him under his wing, and helped him develop into a great pianist and now a conductor.

Another fine pianist I gave a hand to, though not through Hurok, was Byron Janis. He was studying in New York with a friend of ours named Adele Marcus. When Adele moved to Dallas to teach at The Hockaday School, Byron didn't have the resources to follow her. Adele asked our assistance. Alice and I had a friend in the oil business there, and when we inquired on Byron's behalf, he was taken into the family and fed and kept like one of their own talented children so he could continue his studies without interruption. The rest is musical history.)

Hurok sometimes made you feel he did everything for you—including the singing, the playing, the applauding, and the reviewing. He would refer to "our success," or say, "John, we did a wonderful *Rigoletto*," or "Oy, were we ever in our best voice at Carnegie Hall!" When he was actually present at Carnegie or Town Hall, he would stand in the wings complaining about the encores the public made me sing: "Give them what they pay for, John; save your voice for the next time they pay to come."

"Stop it already!" I'd tell him, and go back out.

And he would protest, "But we'll get tired!"

Even in the wings, Hurok the impresario was always onstage. No actor ever looked as theatrical as Hurok in his black fedora, with his black cane and pink cheeks, his cape over his shoulders. John Barrymore couldn't have looked more grand. Certainly, Hurok looked more artistic than most of his artists. He was a major figure and that's the name he was selling: "S. Hurok Presents."

His beginnings were humble. Born in 1888 near Kharkov, he arrived at Ellis Island in 1906 with $1.50 in his pocket. He was a streetcar conductor in Philadelphia and a porter at the Brownsville Labor Lyceum in Brooklyn. He booked his first concert there when he began to feel the need for music for the masses, so he persuaded Efrem Zimbalist to come out to Brownsville and perform for a low fee. From there he grew to booking attractions for the Educational Alliance and the old Hippodrome on Forty-third Street and Sixth

Avenue. He was always willing to lose money for the sake of quality. He lost money on Pavlova, on Isadora Duncan (when she bared one breast in Boston), on Chaliapin in the beginning—and didn't get rich on Peerce for the first three years. He went bankrupt any number of times. He and Michael Todd were people who went broke with a flair. Whenever they crashed, they landed on their bottoms higher than most people ever rose.

When I first came under Hurok's management in 1939, he asked me, "What kind of a career do you want? A fast career or a slow career? If fast, I'll give you a big build-up and you'll make a lot of money in a short time. But a slow career is one where you keep growing from year to year; it will go on for many years if you are lucky. So you have the choice: make money fast or make progress slow?"

I didn't hesitate to say, "I'll take the long way."

"Good!" said Hurok. "So then you must be told that to be any kind of success, you must keep the local manager happy. He's the man who books you for the concerts. Now, John, do you know how to keep a local manager happy?"

In those days, there was no wash-and-wear. I'd heard managers griping about touring artists whose shirts were on their third day or whose bra straps were dirty. So I started to guess an answer: "Be punctual. Stay sober. Be in good voice. Wear clean clothes and well-pressed suits—"

Hurok, who always called me "John," thinking he was saying "Jan," interrupted me: "Good, John, but you're still not making the local manager happy. The only way to make him happy is to let him make a dollar. In other words, if you don't price yourself out of the profit range for him and if you deliver, then he's your friend."

Over the years, I've experienced the wisdom of Hurok's words. There are singers who are hot that everybody *has* to have. To keep his constituency happy, a manager may pay through the nose because his clients demand *that* artist. But if the manager can't make a profit on that singer, he won't sing for him when newer stars appear on the horizon, no matter how good he is.

If an American manager makes money on a concert of yours, he'll say, "Great. You must come again next year"—which usually means the year after. But if you gave the greatest concert in history and it didn't make as much money as he thought it was going to make for him, he'll call up the Hurok office and say, "Hey, he wasn't so good last night," or "Oh, he was adequate."

Of course, if any manager ever told me I was adequate, I certainly wouldn't like it. "Adequate" is the worst word in the language to an artist. Even if the manager had a music degree, he'd experience the other side of Peerce's temper.

Like every manager, Hurok had his special pets, his lambs, certain artists he called his "children." These were Artur Rubinstein, Andrés Segovia, Marian Anderson, Isaac Stern, myself, and, a little later on, Roberta Peters. All his artists were important to him, but of his "children" he spoke in a special, fatherly tone.

Of course, like most children, we had fights with father. He wasn't feeding us enough engagements! Or he was feeding us the wrong kind of engagements! Still, in the showdown, he produced for us—and sometimes he even yielded. With Toscanini, I was paid three or four hundred dollars per performance. Hurok hated it when I turned him down because of a prior commitment to Toscanini. "John, why do you do this for so little? To pass up a lucrative engagement to appear with this man for almost nothing is terrible." But he always let me, even when he had contractual priority. Later on, when I joined the Bach Aria Group, he settled for a ten percent commission.

Sol Hurok was a warm person, funny, a great storyteller, but I never really got close to him—nobody did—even though we spoke the same language and shared many things. There was a certain reserve to him, although we had beautiful rapport. To put icing on the cake, he loved Alice, too. This was rare; many of the wives of his other artists he wouldn't even talk to. He would always grant Alice an audience, and he listened to her. But in the early years, whenever she urged him to promote bigger audiences for me, he would quiet her with one of his more celebrated Hurokisms: "When people don't want to come, nothing will stop them."

The Hunchback of the Opera

Mike De Pace got better results for me than Hurok in my early years with the great impresario. In 1939 Mike made a date for me to meet Edward Johnson, the general manager of the Metropolitan Opera. Johnson had expressed interest in and appreciation of my work and Mike had followed up on it. Though Johnson had nothing for me at the time, he agreed to an appointment in his office.

I should have been grateful because in 1935, when RCA and NBC had been unhappy with the commercial possibilities of my Wednesday-night sustaining program, I had received a telegram saying, in effect, "YOU'RE OFF THE AIR." Six hours later I received a second telegram saying, "DISREGARD PREVIOUS WIRE. YOU'RE ON THE AIR." When I asked around to find out what had earned me my reprieve, I was told, "There was some kind of inquiry from the Metropolitan Opera about you." The Met, I guessed, meant

Johnson himself. (I confirmed this a few years after our meeting.)

I also knew something else, however. Mike De Pace told me that though Johnson had been following my voice on the air, someone had told him, "Oh, Peerce has a great voice, all right, but have you ever seen him? . . . Well, he's short, he's so blind you have to lead him around, he's hunchbacked, and he has a clubfoot." It was enough to scare Johnson into five years of second thoughts about me.

Thus I arrived for the interview with a chip on my shoulder. As soon as we shook hands, I said, "Mr. Johnson, I'd like to clear up a few matters. It's true I'm not the tallest man in the world, but I'm not the shortest. I'm nearsighted and I have to wear contact lenses, but I'm not blind, I don't have to be led around." Next, I took off my jacket. Johnson must have thought I wanted to fight, but I just wanted to show him I didn't have a hump. Then I lifted my trousers above the ankles to show him I had no clubfoot.

As I did all this, Johnson—a tall, silver-haired, ruddy-faced gentleman to begin with—blushed red to the roots. All he could say was: "Well, Mr. Peerce, you can see I haven't lent much credence to what I've been told." Then he went on to tell me to keep up my good work and he made it clear —though he didn't say so and I knew enough not to trust such promises anyway—that I'd be hearing from him again, sooner or later. Despite this first encounter, Edward Johnson was my friend from that day on.

Accompanists I Have Supported

When I gave my first New York concert at Town Hall on November 7, 1939, the critic the *New York Times* sent over to cover my "debut" was a converted sportswriter named Howard Taubman. The gist of his notice was that Mr. Jan Peerce, who belts them out big at Radio City Music Hall, had the *chutzpa* to come downtown from Fiftieth to Forty-third Street to try to sing Brahms, Handel, Schubert, and other songs. I was a lowbrow trespassing on highbrow turf. Taubman had a few good things to say about me, but was compelled to add: "There are times when he strains to reach high fortes. . . . One would think that his method might affect his durability."

Twenty-five years later, in November 1964, when I gave a recital at Carnegie Hall, Theodore Strongin wrote in the *New York Times:* "Judging by the quality of his voice at 60, he will still be giving successful recitals in the year 2000. There's not a mark of age on his voice."

A year or two after that, Dan Sullivan, a young reporter on the *New York Times* (now drama critic for the *Los Angeles Times*), interviewed me. He showed me both clippings. I glanced from one to the other, looked at Dan, and said, "Well, *one* of them was wrong."

Actually, my most vivid memory of my Town Hall debut is not of how well I sang or of Howard Taubman sitting on his hands or even of Mr. and Mrs. John D. Rockefeller, Jr., applauding me from a box. It is of my accompanist and old friend from my earliest days with Roxy, Leo Russotto. When I think back to November 7, 1939, I see Leo playing the piano without any music before him. He did indeed have the photographic memory he claimed to have. But on November 7, 1939, I made a vow: Never again will a pianist sit on a stage with me without music. For no matter how well he knows the music, I have to stand up there for two hours worrying whether he's going to make a mistake. In Leo's case, it was academic, because we split after that first concert.

His wife, Eda, was our undoing. She felt that in the program, ads, and publicity, Leo's name wasn't big enough. One day not long after the Town Hall concert, he called me up and said he wanted to see me. "I wanna have it out with you once and for all! I gotta tell it to you because I'm a very honest man."

When he came over to our place on West End Avenue, I could see he was breathing enough fire to burn down the Woolworth Building. So I tried to cool him off: "Look, Leo, before we talk, let's have a cup of coffee. I can see you're hot and bothered."

"No, no, Jan! I'm gonna tell you right out. You took advantage of me. You underpaid me. You—"

I protested that I had paid him whatever he had asked.

"Yeah, but you didn't give me big enough publicity."

"Hurok didn't want to advertise your name at all," I told Leo. "As a rule, they don't."

Nevertheless, Leo insisted, I could have done this and I could have done that—and besides, I should have paid him more for a Town Hall concert. (I think I'd paid him $150.)

"Look," I repeated, "whatever you asked for, you got."

"But you should have offered me more!"

"Why should I? Am I rich? But I don't want you to be unhappy. You tell me how much you think I owe you and I'll pay it." Do you know how much his own estimate of his grievances amounted to? Fifty dollars. I wrote him a check and said, "Leo, are you satisfied now?"

"Yeah, except you should have done it sooner, without my asking."

"Well, here it is. And, Leo, this is the last check you'll ever get from me. You will never play a concert with me again."

He left, pocketing the check and calling me a sorehead.

Leo Russotto and I stayed good friends and we are to this day—even though we haven't worked together since 1939. As it turned out, he wouldn't have been able to travel with me because he took sick with phlebitis. When I heard he was in the hospital, I called up and was told he was too sick to have visitors; he was awaiting blood transfusions. So I came down and offered my blood, but it wasn't the right type. Later Leo worked with Broadway shows as an assistant conductor; he lives in California now, and we keep in touch. Of course, he and I never forgot the day I wrote him that check. But he also remembers how I was still willing to help him when he was sick.

After my break with Leo, I called Warner Bass. Warner was a counselor at the summer camp where Larry went. On a visit to my kids, someone had said to me, "The music counselor here is a German refugee and he'd love to meet you." Warner told me he'd been involved in opera in Kassel and Berlin before fleeing Hitler. Warner knew opera and lieder, and the next time I came up to the camp we made music together. He was good and I took his phone number and told him if I ever needed him, I'd call. Then Leo came storming in.

Warner Bass worked with me for more than twenty years. He almost gave his life for me in Japan when he came down with diverticulitis and wouldn't seek medical attention, until a doctor in the audience saw how ill he looked and came backstage to see him. He sat up in coaches on the two- and three-day train journeys through the U.S. that were our lot in the 1940s, sometimes insisting that I use a little of our hard-earned take to buy myself an upper berth because *I* needed my rest to be good the next day, while he was young and rugged and resilient. He wouldn't even consider my offer to take shifts of sleeping in the upper.

The first concert tour that Hurok booked for me lasted almost three weeks and took Warner and me to three cities: Janesville, Wisconsin; Salt Lake City, Utah; La Grande, Oregon. My total fee was $1,550, out of which came Hurok's $227.50 commission (he took only fifteen percent on civic concerts), Warner's fee of $105 for the three concerts, and both our train fares, room and board. Plus (or rather, minus) paying a replacement at the Music Hall. I came back from that triumphal tour owing myself money. Aside from a few new friends and some nice clippings and a hopeful career as a recitalist, I had little to show for it except a bit of a tan—our railroad ticket had included a bonus outing to Sun Valley during our four-day wait in Salt Lake.

The life of an accompanist was a thankless one in those days. Unlike a singer, or a solo instrumentalist, there was a very low limit to what an accompanist could make financially. As for recognition, generally there wasn't much, especially when you consider how important the accompanist is. You took a bow (when you worked with a nice guy like me!), but you lived in the shadow of the artist you traveled with. Unfortunately, even nowadays critics often don't mention the accompanist—which is a terrible sin of omission. All too often, critics blame him for the artist's inadequacies.

Warner Bass had the ambition to be a conductor, and this was where we started coming apart after more than two decades together. He wanted me to launch him. He suggested more than once that when I was booked to appear with an orchestra, I recommend him as conductor.

"You mean I'm to tell them yes, but not with their own conductor?"

No, he meant that *their* conductor should conduct until *I* came out onstage. Then *my* conductor would conduct.

I told Warner I couldn't do this. It would be insulting to them and ruinous to me. The conductor is the one who decides to ask for an artist to sing with an orchestra. What I would be saying, in effect, was: "You're good enough to ask for me, but not good enough to play with me."

I did get Warner some bookings to conduct for me on certain records. He did excellent work, and he was a very good arranger, too. But recording companies have their own contracts, their own stable of people, and I could push Warner only so far. Then he came and wanted me to make certain appearances that it seemed to me he'd been promised only if he could bring me in. One day he suggested that I do something else for him. When I refused, he said our collaboration would have to end.

Instead of pleading with him and saying, "Hey, don't do this to me!" I just didn't reply. In my silence he found his answer. That was how, after twenty-one years, I was fired by my accompanist.

At first I worried about how Warner would fare on his own. I was genuinely concerned about him. But he did very well from the start. He gave lessons, which he'd been doing on a smaller scale for years, and he worked in the universities. He got a teaching job at NYU and then moved on into the City University of New York system.

My accompanist for the last dozen years has been Allen Rogers, a native of Kansas. Allen had the makings of a fine concert pianist. After studying in Kansas, he came east to study with Carl Friedberg, who had just left Juilliard. But Allen decided early that instead of struggling and fighting for a solo career, he would concentrate on being an accompanist, coach, and teacher. He is a Professor now at Boston University, commuting once a week to and from Brooklyn Heights, and doing almost all my concert dates. It's worked out very well. He's one of the greatest accompanists in the world today. But he's a very self-effacing chap and totally concentrates on the music itself.

Allen Rogers: *Jan was near sixty when I started with him. One day he asked me how many years I thought his voice had left. Knowing his age, I gave what I thought to be an optimistic estimate: "Oh, with a little luck, five more years." Jan said, very disappointedly, "Are you kidding?" He expected, rightfully, a lot more.*

The Sex Life of a Singer

Shortly after I started singing with Toscanini, Sergei Rachmaninoff heard me and decided mine was the right tenor voice for his musical setting for chorus and orchestra of Edgar Allan Poe's poem "The Bells," which he'd written in 1913. It was done in Philadelphia at the Academy of Music. With all its clamor and clangor and tintinnabulation, *The Bells* didn't impress me as the greatest piece of music I'd ever participated in, but it was good enough. The great thing about it was not just that the composer had selected me, but that he himself was to conduct it—not an everyday affair, since Rachmaninoff's forte was as a pianist. He was a tall, somber, serious man who was sitting rigid at the piano one day when I arrived a little late for rehearsal. "I'm sorry, Maestro. I'm five minutes late."

Rachmaninoff took his gold-chained watch out of his vest and said, "You are six minutes late, Mr. Pirs, but let us go to work." I know it dates me when I boast that I sang with Rachmaninoff. A lot of people think he's been dead a hundred years, though he actually survived my rendition of *The Bells* by several years, before his death in 1943. But I'm as proud now as I was then —because for an artist in his thirties hoping and praying and looking for recognition as a serious musician, being chosen by Toscanini and Rachmaninoff was a great honor.

One day around 1940, I was sitting home listening to the Pepsodent-smiling voice of the tenor Lanny Ross singing "Moonlight and Roses" on the radio. My cousin Yaiky was listening with me and he said, "Why don't you get yourself a program like that?"

I said, "It's not that easy. Lanny Ross is lucky."

Well, the Lord must have said, "If Lanny Ross is lucky, I'll make you lucky, too," because the next day, Squibb toothpaste's ad agency called me up and said they wanted somebody to sing five fifteen-minute radio programs a week on CBS. They offered me a contract starting at seven hundred dollars a week, rising to two thousand dollars eventually. I knew I would be needing lots of money soon, because I was starting to cut loose from the Music Hall to devote myself to lesser-paying serious music, so I okayed the Squibb contract without telling Alice.

Pinye, age 3, all
dressed up, but look
at the holes in my
shoes!

Here I sit in my
father's lap. Standing
by are my mother and
my big brother Mot'l,
who died in an
accident when he
was six.

My mother, the
former Anna Posner,
and my father, Louis
Perelmuth, around
1940.

I was a 9-year-old
choir boy: lower
right-hand corner.

Samuel L. Rothafel, alias "Roxy,"
who gave me two names of my own:
first, John Pierce; then, Jan Peerce.

Music Hall days: three Radio City roles:
(top) Be a clown. (middle) "Jan from
Spokane" in a "Bluebird of Happiness"
production number set in a hobo jungle.
(Barrett Gallagher) (bottom) As organ
grinder in another "Bluebird" number,
1935. *(Courtesy Radio City Music Hall)*

It's the *Chevrolet Hour* on CBS in the 1930s, co-starring with Virginia Ray and Dave "Rubinoff and His Violin." Sorry Dave never autographed this picture for Christmas.

A rehearsal with Toscanini—plus Nicola Moscona (far left) and Claramae Turner and the NBC Symphony—at Carnegie Hall.

Sol Hurok, left, and
Edward Johnson,
general manager of
the Metropolitan
Opera, flank me at the
Waldorf party
following my Met
debut in 1941.
(*Drucker–Hilbert Co., Inc.*)

With my wife, Alice,
at my Met debut
party. (*Drucker–
Hilbert Co., Inc.*)

Looks like a *Rigoletto* in San Francisco with me on the left,
Armando Agnini, director of the Opera Company, and Robert Weede.

Passover in New Rochelle: a Seder at our home. Alice is standing at left;
her mother is sitting to my left; and our younger daughter Susan is at
the head of table in foreground.

This picture looks phony to me. I mean, Alice has accompanied me during most of my journey through life, but not at the piano! *(Ernest M. Silva)*

Presenting Pope Pius XII with Toscanini's recording of Beethoven's *Missa Solemnis.* Licia Albanese is kneeling to kiss the ring and Alice is at right.

At a dinner honoring Harry S. Truman in the 1950s. *(Max Bengis)*

Why? To surprise her? Well, not quite. I was afraid she'd veto it—because she was dead set on my reserving time on my calendar for that "inevitable" offer from the Met, which I had long ago decided was never going to come. In not consulting Alice, I landed myself in one of the worst messes of my career. For what I didn't reckon on was something I remembered a little later. In signing with Squibb and CBS, I was violating three other contracts: one with Hurok, one with Mark Hanna, my personal representative in the pop music field—both of them had to give their approval of any other contract I made—and one with the Music Hall.

In our compartment on the overnight train back from Chicago where I had just sung *Rigoletto,* I had the upper berth and Alice the lower. Instead of basking in my Chicago success, I was tossing and turning and disturbing Alice's sleep, so she said to me, "Jan, why don't you go to sleep?"

I said, "I can't."

"Something is bothering you."

"Well, not exactly," I said. Then I told her. I thought Alice was going to be angry at me, but the first words she spoke were:

"You signed those papers? The first thing we're going to do in New York is go and unsign them."

With that, I rested a little less uneasily, while Alice lay awake wondering what to do next.

Alice went to Hurok. Hurok was furious. She went to Mark Hanna. Mark Hanna showed her the door. She went to CBS. CBS said it was sorry, but a contract was a contract. She went to the Geyer-Cornell advertising agency and they said sorry, but the deal is all set. So she went to see the president of Squibb, one Lowell P. Weicker, Sr., the father of the present U.S. senator from Connecticut. Mr. Weicker must have stood a good six feet six inches tall—about the height of two or three Alices as she pleaded with him to release me from the contract. Mr. Weicker said no.

"But Jan's violated all these contracts and he has Mr. Hurok terribly upset," Alice said, almost in tears, "because he's spent all this money to build Jan up as a concert artist. Mr. Hurok won't budge."

Mr. Weicker chuckled at the thought of such a minor matter upsetting an operator like Hurok. "Well, let's see how upset and inflexible Mr. Hurok is," Weicker said. "I will telephone Mr. Hurok and you, Mrs. Peerce, will please lift the extension and listen to our conversation."

To Alice's amazement, Hurok was very obliging. Instead of being the immovable stone in the way of a deal with Squibb, Hurok told Weicker he wouldn't stand in the way. He, Hurok, was perfectly willing to sell "Pirs's contract for $25,000." What a windfall for Hurok! It would have taken a lot of years' commissions on my earnings to get him that kind of money.

It certainly wasn't what Alice and I wanted, and it taught us very early an important lesson about Hurok—he was a businessman, and his friendship or love was something else. Hurok never learned that Alice had overheard his offer to Weicker.

Now Alice had the gall to try another tactic on Weicker. She told him that she feared for her marriage because with all the added work I'd taken on for Squibb, it could ruin our sex life. "You have to understand, Mr. Weicker, that a singer—especially a tenor—can't have sex with his wife very often because it would affect his singing. And if he has to sing every day, where will that leave me?" Can you imagine little Alice Kalmanowitz saying such a thing to *the* Mr. Clean from Squibb almost forty years ago? It shocked *me* when I heard of it and it must have shocked Mr. Weicker, but he didn't relent.

I do believe that high notes can be temporarily affected by sexual intercourse a night or even two or three nights before a performance. Singers can't afford to overdo sex.

Maybe basses can get away with more than higher voices can. After intercourse the voice settles and that's okay for the bass sound. The more his voice is down in his shoes, the better a bass sings. Whenever I hear a bass hitting lots of rolling low notes, I'll say to him, "Hey, last night must have been a good one!"—anything not to credit him with being a great singer! Overdoing sex is risky for a baritone and very dangerous for a tenor who needs his high notes that evening. Maybe my conservation—call it conservativeness, if you will—is part of the secret of my longevity. All I know is that if I'm in my seventies now and still sing like a young man, maybe I'm some sort of ad for the discipline I preach.

Another singer I knew felt the way I did and his wife used to complain aloud and in public: "You can't do it before, certainly not during, and afterward you're too tired. When can you do it?" Later she found out he was having a backstage romance *during* his performances. I'll say this for him: even his mistress had to wait until his big arias were done. But people began to notice he was a little stooped when he took his bows.

How much must a tenor limit his sex life? I believe in moderation, as in everything I do. My rule has been no sex for three or four days before a performance; thus, a busy season at the Met was off season for the Peerces. But I want to make one thing perfectly clear: *Denying sex does not make you sing well.*

What happens if a tenor has sex the night before a performance or even on the same day? There's no set rule, but a man about to perform a professional act of singing must train like an athlete. Sex the night before won't kill you and it may even help you to sleep better, but it can also weaken your general condition and depress you. You'll still have the high notes, but you may have to work to reawaken them. Done properly, the sexual act settles and relaxes you—too much so for the singer who's got to be up for another kind of performance. With a tenor, it may not tell on the first or second or third high note, but eventually there will come a moment of reckoning onstage.

Drinking should not tempt the tenor before a performance. I may take tea or Sanka or a soda before a performance if I feel dry, but never wine or beer or booze, which may relax me too much. You can't tell how any of these things will affect you: some people get weepy drunk, others get happy drunk. But alcohol tends to be a depressant. The best thing for a tenor to do is to steel himself against any temptation that might blunt the sharpness of his mood.

Onstage, the Lord helps only those who help themselves. Onstage, I look for no outside help and no outside interference. So it's nice if I can come to the dressing room around 6 P.M. to put on my makeup and vocalize at leisure, fresh from a couple of nice days in which I slept and ate well, but didn't overindulge. Around four o'clock, I will have eaten a small piece of boiled chicken or steak or, if I wasn't that hungry, cottage cheese and a couple of canned peaches. All I need is the sugar of the peaches, the protein of the cheese, and maybe the starch of a piece of toast. After the show, my desire is for sweets. This can be candy or ice cream or cake or anything else sweet. Even sex.

Some singers, including women, feel that they must eat a huge slab of steak at four o'clock and another one after the performance. Some get a kick from champagne. I sang once in Philadelphia with Frieda Hempel. She sipped champagne from a little glass throughout the evening. "Take some," she said to me.

"Oh, no, Madame Hempel," I said. "I'll fall asleep."

"No, no," she insisted. "Your performance will only be better."

I declined. She went on sipping and singing—and it seemed to work for her at a time when she wasn't a young woman anymore. Her performance that night was, in fact, sparkling.

When even Alice's plea to save her sex life didn't work on Mr. Weicker, she went to the union (American Federation of Radio Artists) and told them what *they* wanted to hear: that her husband was crazy, like most tenors. A nice young man named Heller tried to extricate me from all those moguls. When he failed, we got our lawyer, Ben Levin, on the case. Ben said I was in the wrong, but he'd do what he could.

The night before the big meeting with all the parties concerned—one of which was going to sue me for $85,000 and another for $33,000—I mentioned in passing that the head of the CBS legal department had asked to see my existing contract with Hurok.

Ben Levin got very excited. "Why didn't you tell me that before? Did you show it to him?"

"Yeah, and when I did, he said, 'We'll get rid of that contract.' "

"Wow!" said Ben. "I think we may have them."

The next day I went in, with Ben's instructions to keep quiet in mind. "Don't even open your mouth," he had said, which is a terrible thing to tell any tenor. Eventually Alice took the floor and began, "What do you gentlemen want? Yes, Jan signed four contracts. Do you want to cut him into four pieces and throw them in the air? The part that comes down singing, you can have."

"Now, now, Mrs. Peerce," said the head of the CBS legal department, a Harvard gentleman. "Aren't we being a little melodramatic?"

Alice whirled on him, saying, "Don't you remember telling Jan, 'We'll get rid of that Hurok contract'?" It was more than a little melodramatic. Although we were very much on the defensive, she attacked like a prosecutor on cross-examination. The CBS man looked at her and everybody in the room could see, in that instant, that Alice had him.

The man from Geyer-Cornell advertising, who looked whiter than Squibb toothpaste, said to the CBS lawyer, "Why didn't I know this before?"

We knew we'd won, but it took another ten weeks—and even then we weren't home free. I had to do two penances; one of them lasted five years. After Frank Parker took over the show, I had to work four weeks for each of five summers as his vacation replacement—not at two thousand dollars a week, but for the union minimum of forty-nine dollars a broadcast.

The other penance was quicker, though even more severe. The day we signed the settlement, I came home and bent down to take a clean shirt out of my bottom drawer—and I couldn't straighten up. The doctor diagnosed it as a sacroiliac condition, which I never had before or since, so I knew it was part of my punishment.

Since then I've never signed a piece of paper without telling Alice.

Medical History

Like her brother, Larry, our youngest child, Susan Barbara, was born prematurely. Susan's Hebrew name is Sara Bracha: Sara for my paternal grandma and Bracha for my maternal grandpa Berel. Bracha also means blessing. Susan has been a blessing to us and to the world: a lovely wholesome girl who now makes her living teaching the deaf and handicapped. But her early years were not blessed.

On the fourth day of Susan's life, at Doctors Hospital on East End Avenue, a nurse with a staphylococcus infection gave it to Sue. For eight months we didn't know whether she would survive. She had to have three blood transfusions a week during that time.

At the age of three months, she had no shoulder; the staphylococcus had eaten it away. The doctors rebuilt her shoulder. Even after eight months, when Dr. George Ginandes and the other doctors said she would live, plastic and other surgery had to go on. In all, she had some fifty operations. This took all our savings and we went into hock borrowing on our insurance, but it was worth anything and everything to save first her life and then her looks.

Our Sue *was* a victim of careless nursing, but she *is* a triumph of modern medicine. And to see her now, you would never suspect any of this ever happened to her. She's beautiful!

[Dark and petite, Susan Peerce is also articulate when asked, as she often is, how special it felt to be the daughter of Jan Peerce.]

Susan: *I'm the last person you should ask that. I have no experience with any other parents, so how can I make a comparison? The other day, though, I was introduced to someone as "Miss Perez, the singer Jan Merrill's daughter." I let it pass because I never was a Jewish princess and I never went around telling people who my father was.*

Alice Peerce: *Sue got the worst of our married life. All Jan's success happened during her lifetime. Larry and Joy had a little childhood as individuals, but Susan was always in Jan's shadow. Besides, he was away on tour during much of her childhood. Susan told us one day: "Until I was six, I didn't know I had a father."*

Susan: *Joy's birthday was in the summer and our folks would always come up to camp to celebrate it. Mine was in November and Dad was always away on tour, sometimes with Mom, too. So my uncles and aunts would give me a party. It was always the* *same. They'd bring a cake and I'd lock myself in the bathroom, having hysterics, and shouting, "Get out of my house!"*

We were always told to walk around my father: never go to him, but walk around him. Joy was the only one who did walk around him. He and she got along. I didn't walk around him—because I wanted his affection and if I couldn't get it by asking, then it was the next best thing to get him yelling and take his anger as a kind of affection.

During the terrible time we were having with doctors and bills after Susan was born, my mother had the first in a series of heart attacks. At least, it was the first we knew about. She had neglected her health for a long time and never told the truth, even to herself, about her physical condition. When even she was convinced she needed medical attention, she called in an old family doctor and swore him to secrecy. The first thing people used to say to doctors in those days was: "Don't tell my husband. Don't tell my children." And the stupid old man didn't.

There came a time, however, when she knew she needed more help than a family doctor could offer. And to whom did she turn in the crisis of her life? To her daughter-in-law, Alice, whom she never stopped blaming for keeping her oldest son from becoming a doctor. "Alice, I'm sick," she said. "You'll have to take me to your doctor because I think I'm sicker than I thought."

Alice took her to our doctor, Louis Soffer. The first question he asked was: "Why didn't you ask Alice to bring you here six months ago?"

"Well, I didn't want to annoy anybody, worry anybody," my mother replied.

Later Alice asked him if six months would have made any difference and he said, "Yes, we'd have had a much better chance."

For more than four years, though, with the help of the Lord, he kept her alive. She wouldn't go to a hospital. Mothers in general, especially Jewish mothers then, didn't think they belonged in hospitals. They considered their presence there a disgrace and insisted on dying in their own bed. So Dr. Soffer installed a hospital bed at 210 Madison Street, plus cans of oxygen, an oxygen tent for emergencies, and a practical nurse. By giving up his catering business, my father could be there, too, on twenty-four-hour-a-day duty. He learned to work with oxygen, and several times on the nurse's days off, he saved my mother's life.

The doctor visited her four or five times a week. He charged for the trip down from Park Avenue to the Lower East Side in his chauffeured car—but no matter what he had charged for a house call, we would have paid. More than once, he actually brought her back from the dead.

At that time, my brother Sender and I were having a feud and hadn't spoken to each other for three or four years. We'd meet at our mother's bedside and ignore each other. The time Dr. Soffer brought her back from the dead—with oxygen and a heart massage—he exclaimed, "She's alive!" which we found hard to believe until, a couple of minutes later, she opened her eyes and said in Yiddish, "Did Sender and Pinky make up while I was gone?"

I said, "No."

She said, "How long is this going to go on?" as if to say: "I don't have much time to wait around." Then she shut her eyes, and fearing she was resigning herself to death, I answered very quickly, "If it'll make you happy, Mama . . ."

She said, "Never mind making me happy. Do yourselves a favor." Sender and I made it up then and there.

From West End Avenue to Westchester

The rent at 580 West End Avenue was going up, up, up! Even in our financial straits, we decided the solution was to move to Westchester. And Westchester meant New Rochelle, where a Jew didn't need a passport in those days as he did in, say, Bronxville. (A frequent definition in those days of the Yiddish word *farblondjet*—meaning "lost" or "truly mislaid"—was "a kosher butcher in Bronxville.") Alice and I checked out New Rochelle and it looked good. There were three temples: Orthodox, Conservative, Reform. We checked out the Hebrew school. There was a good public school system, with excellent teachers and a sound modern teaching system. We thought we could have the private, religious life we needed.

To make sure we would like it, we rented a house at 44 Rose Hill Avenue. New Rochelle was about a thirty-eight-minute drive when we moved there. Today, thanks to traffic and other "improvements," the drive takes Alice almost an hour. The New York, New Haven & Hartford Railroad is now the Penn Central and it takes only thirty-three minutes if the train's on time, which it seldom is. Not that the railroad service back then was anything to write home about. The service *was* pretty good in the mornings. They'd make sure to get you *in* to work on time. Coming home, though, they didn't care what happened.

In those days, there weren't bar cars or club cars on the New Rochelle locals; even on the through expresses, bar cars struck me as a *farblondjet* institution. Most of us married men used to bring home dessert from a bakery in Grand Central. During our first winter in New Rochelle, I was stuck for a couple of hours on a commuter train marooned in the snow. After an hour or two, we opened up our little packages and started eating our cake. It was a regular party. Some of the pastries were still warm, but that was the only warmth we got: the train's heat had failed, too.

That first winter had its rewards, however. In the beginning, New Rochelle was so quiet we could hardly stand it. We stayed up late watching our first snowstorm in the suburbs, which was even more beautiful than the one I watched from high up in the Astor Hotel when I was auditioning for Toscanini. Once, an hour or two after midnight, there was a shuddering noise, as if the New York City subway had just passed through. We jumped out of bed. Hunting high and low, Alice discovered what had happened: the snow had accumulated on our roof and then a big mound of it had dropped with a thud to the side of our house.

When we realized this, we laughed and I said, "Can you imagine? Who in New York would have thought snow can make a noise?"

And Alice said, "In New York you can't even hear each other. How can you hear the snow?"

So we stayed, looked around, and liked it in New Rochelle. While we were shopping for permanent quarters, we saw a cozy turreted twelve-year-old two-story Tudor house on Beechmont Drive that was available for twenty-five thousand dollars. Even then the wisdom in suburbia was that New Is Better, so a lot of people told us we were crazy to spend twenty-five thousand dollars on something a dozen years old, when for that money we could build our own. But Alice's father, who was in real estate himself, told us, "It's sound. It's built to last. And if you tried to build it yourself today, it would cost you twice as much and it wouldn't be as good."

(When Hurok heard we were thinking of buying the house, he advised, sight unseen, "Buy it!" When I asked him how I could afford to, he said, "So we'll get you more concerts." And when we considered buying the adjoining lot, which we eventually did, Hurok again said, "Buy it!" Thus Hurok used to claim, whenever he came to dinner, that he was the one who inspired us to buy what he called "our house." Sometimes he would say, "But for my twisting your arm, John, you would still be living on West End Avenue paying that enormous rent." As he grew older, he started to remember that he, personally, had forced us to move "from the Lower East Side to Westchester, thank G-d!" Such is the managerial ego.)

I love our part of New Rochelle. From the back, we look out over Beechmont Lake, where ducks swim and boys skate and fish through the ice in winter. The lake is now too polluted for people to swim in, so I hope they don't eat the fish. Still, whenever we turn into Beechmont Drive from North Avenue, there is a certain quiet and serenity and a special beauty that I feel nowhere else in the world. Leaving North Avenue, we're leaving the buses and trucks behind. It used to be that we could sit home for a whole day without seeing or hearing a car pass except for those belonging to people who lived on Beechmont Drive. Now it's different, but the changes have been small and it's always with fresh wonder that I enjoy the thrill of coming home: from a tour, from the city, from a hospital, from synagogue, or from a stroll. I feel this is where I live and this is where I want to be; if I'm going to be sick, this is where I want to be sick and this is where I want to get well. That must be my heritage from my mother. I'll know I'm dying when I stop marveling at just the joy of coming home to Beechmont Drive.

After thirty-two years, we haven't outgrown the place and—though all three of our children are grown and living away from us—we never will. I've always called it our "big small house" or "small big house" on Beechmont Drive.

As you come into our foyer, the dining room is to the right and behind it is our kitchen, with separate dish cabinets and separate refrigerators for meat and dairy. There's nothing especially luxurious or ultramodern about the kitchen, except that Alice likes her instant coffee to be hot *and* instant, so we have an extra faucet that dispenses boiling water. This is especially appreciated on the Sabbath, when heating up water is proscribed.

To the left of the foyer is the living room, with a two-story-high ceiling and, of course, no rooms above it—a marvelous place for rehearsing and vocalizing at the piano, for entertaining or just living. Behind the living room, looking out over the lake, is my "library." It's the kind of room for showing off trophies and collections, and I've decorated one wall of it with human and not-so-human heads. I collect conductors—autographed photos of them. Toscanini. Rachmaninoff. Bruno Walter. Leonard Bernstein. William Steinberg. Fritz Reiner. George Szell. Virtually every conductor I've ever sung with, loved, hated, or in between. Some of the inscriptions are glowing (James Levine in 1973: "To Jan Peerce, an incredible phenomenon") and some are funny (a John Groth sketch of Leopold Stokowski, after we recorded *Samson and Delilah,* autographed by the maestro with "Bravo, Samson!"). In most singers' homes you'll find nothing but their own faces on the walls. To me, though, all these conductors' faces bring back memories, both happy and unhappy. I feel perfectly safe with them pinned to the wall where I can talk back to them.

Coming back to the foyer and before I take you up the staircase, there's a bathroom and also a maid's room, which was occupied by one lady for more than twenty years: Mary Brown, who became such a loyal and devoted member of our family that *we* wanted better things for her. With our encouragement, she studied and became a practical nurse, but we still see Mary socially two or three times a month.

Upstairs, when we moved in, there were four good-sized bedrooms and a bathroom. The room in which Alice and I've always slept isn't one of those Westchester Massive master bedrooms where I'd have to chase after my wife if I wanted to give her a kiss or phone her if I wanted to say hello. Each of the kids had his or her own room, but all the rooms were in a cluster at the top of the staircase, so we were literally a close family. Everybody had privacy, but everybody was within reach. Now that the kids have moved out, our four bedrooms at the top of the stairs have become master bedroom, guest room, dressing room, and office for our part-time secretary, Jo Quain. Jo—who is older than I am, though I won't say by how much—has been with us for eight years now, long enough to become the only Irish Catholic member of our family. She makes my appointments, copes with my mail, pays my bills, and pretty much runs this house I'm describing. But I know we're in good hands: Jo Quain is not only a fan of mine, but she roots for all the Peerces.

The house is decorated with at least two hundred china, marble, jade and plastic bluebirds. Alice buys them as souvenirs everywhere I sing. In New Zealand, they took the national bird, the kiwi, and made up a blue one for her. So I collect conductors and she collects bluebirds and you don't have to be Dr. Freud to interpret the symbolism.

What might take Alice a good ten years on the couch to fathom is why she has adorned our house with more than one hundred mahogany, walnut, even leather hippopotami, with their great big fat mahogany, walnut, and leather asses.

Alice Peerce: *My hippopotamus fetish began in South Africa. I'd seen these big ugly creatures in the water and then, in Johannesburg, I met a ceramist who made all kinds of animals, but the most beautiful was this green ceramic hippo with one gold tooth and, in the back of its open mouth, a uvula—the part of the throat that vibrates when you sing or talk. That uvula is what made me flip out. It reminded me so much of some singers I've seen, which is why and how I began my collection.*

The Profligate Duke in *Rigoletto*

"Don't make too many commitments," Alice kept telling me from the late 1930s onward. "We must leave time open for the Metropolitan."

"How can you say that?" I asked her.

"It's natural. It's inevitable. If G-d gave one human being such a voice and such musicality and linguistic ability and intelligence, it's hard to believe it won't be heard by the Met."

Perhaps I was destined for the Met, but I didn't feel any forward motion along a fast track until Mike De Pace booked me for an August 1941 outdoor performance in the Hollywood Bowl doing *La Traviata* with Jarmila Novotna, Richard Bonelli, and George Burnson (now George London). The conductor was Gaetano Merola, general director of the San Francisco Opera, who had taken me on Mike's say-so. In the audience of more than twenty thousand was Sol Hurok, who apparently opened his ears to me for the first time. The next day the *Los Angeles Times* declared I had "one of the finest tenor voices in the country." Even before the reviews, Merola had booked me for October in San Francisco to do *Rigoletto* with Lily Pons and Lawrence Tibbett.

Since I made my debuts with the Columbia and San Francisco opera companies in *Rigoletto,* I have a special affection for it, even though the title role is sung by a baritone! I've sung with some of the greatest, including Tibbett, Weede, Cornell MacNeil, Leonard Warren, and Robert Merrill. Warren may be the most fabulous Rigoletto I ever had the joy to work with.

Rigoletto is the tragic jester and the tenor is the Duke of Mantua, the "profligate duke." When I first studied the role I had to look up the meaning of "profligate," and that's when I started worrying about looking sexy in tights. At any rate, the Duke is a rakish fellow who likes girls. Verdi gave him quite a good aria in the first act, "Questa o quella" ("This girl or that one"), in which his character is immediately delineated—any girl will do for him.

"Questa o quella" comes right at the beginning, so you'd better be warmed up when the curtain rises. After you finish it, no matter how well you sing it only a few people will appreciate it that early in the opera. It takes the *audience* a little time to warm up. I myself never have trouble warming up. I vocalize every day so I can stay fresh. On days when I'm singing a performance, I vocalize and then come to my dressing room early: at least an hour before a concert, two hours before an opera. I sing some scales and use my voice. When I walk out on the stage, I'm ready. A singer should never warm up at the expense of his audience.

Toward the middle of the second act, the Duke zeroes in on Rigoletto's daughter, Gilda—he sneaks into their house while Rigoletto is warning Gilda to be careful of strangers. Disguised as a student, the Duke waits until the father goes, and then comes out and kneels at her feet, singing "T'amo!" ("I love you!"). Now, this is an important moment, in which a lot depends upon the interpretation. Some tenors walk out as if they're going to swallow the whole stage or kill Gilda and the audience in one swoop. But this guy is *surprising* the girl he's on the make for. He wouldn't come out roaring like a cannon. The fact that you cut in on her while she's singing is enough to frighten any soprano.

Gilda is easily convinced and you go into the love duet, which has a couple of high B flats where Verdi really tests his tenors. If you sing this badly, you're in dreadful trouble because you're singing with a soprano and not only is she going to sound better in the duet, but as soon as you exit she sings "Caro nome," and you'll leave nothing but a bad taste in the audience's mouth. When you're singing duets, you'd better be up to each other and not try to compete. If one singer is no good, the whole duet is ruined. If one is much better than the other, the duet isn't much good. Ideally, one helps the other and then both shine as one: Bidú Sayão was especially effective in drawing the best out of both of us in this duet, as were Lily Pons and Roberta Peters.

When the duet is finished, you let the applause wash over you both, while you kiss her. The maid enters, you grab your hat and coat, and sing "Addio!" with Gilda for several minutes. This amuses a good many opera nonlovers, but it shouldn't. A person who buys a ticket to an opera should know he or she is going to a make-believe event. When you begin to reason it out, then nothing works. If I hear someone complaining it took forever for them to say goodbye, I don't blame Verdi; I blame the soprano and the tenor (even myself).

In the third act of *Rigoletto,* the Duke comes into his palace and sings a splendidly agitated recitative, "Ella mi fu rapita." Then he goes right into the aria "Parmi veder le lagrime." Now, this is a perfectly lovely aria, but the kind you can break your neck doing. You must sound like an instrument. Verdi also put a cadenza in there, which few tenors sing, but I always do it because I pride myself on being able to execute a cadenza. The aria ends in the middle part of the tenor voice, so it's a little anticlimactic. People wait for the big ending in an aria. But either Verdi didn't have a way out or else that's what he wanted. Maybe he was mad at some tenor. It doesn't have an ending that brings the audience to its feet. Only the connoisseur appreciates it—which is why I led off with it, a little later in 1941, at the most crucial audition of my life.

Although the fourth act—with "La donna è mobile" plus a great slice of the quartet—is the tenor's act to shine in, Verdi set one last trap for him. While Rigoletto is dragging away the sack that he thinks contains the assassinated Duke but actually holds his murdered daughter, he hears the Duke singing, in the distance, a reprise of "La donna è mobile." It's a big dramatic moment, but everything depends upon the tenor, seen walking in the distance, while hitting and holding that last high B natural, "E di pensier," by which time he is offstage. And, G-d forbid, if that last stinking note, sung backstage, is no good, then the whole performance was no good. No matter how well you've done everything else all evening, your reputation will ride on that last sound you leave in people's ears.

I remember well a certain Saturday matinee of *Rigoletto* in Dallas when I was touring with the Met—I'll return shortly to my story of how I made it there—and I caught a cold. I started to feel bad Friday night. When I woke up the next morning, I was hoarse and my temperature was 102. This was before modern medicine could give you a shot and a pill to keep you afloat for two or three hours. So I called in sick. I was told: "We'll try to find a replacement, but come to the theatre just in case."

When I staggered in, they did have a tenor standing by: Armand Tokatyan, a very good Armenian singer. But Edward Johnson pleaded with me: "Jan, we've got a sold-out house that came to see *you*. You can get through it. We'll do things to help you. We'll transpose this and cut that."

I agreed to go on, saying, "So they'll *see* me, but they may not hear me."

I got out on the stage to sing "Questa o quella" and as soon as I opened my mouth, the courtier I sing it to, Borsa, gave me a look as if to say: "What the hell are you doing on this stage?" He'd heard me many times. A lot of people in Dallas hadn't ever heard me, so I got by—though I must have been a little disappointing to them. I went from bad to worse. In the third act they cut out the aria. By the end of the act, though, I said I'd had it.

Johnson said, "If you can't, you can't. At least you've tried and you've done very well. We'll have Tokatyan do the fourth act."

Then Tokatyan came to my dressing room and said, "Look, Jan, I'm sicker than you are." I realized that sending in a sick him to replace a sick me would really wreck the show—and ruin Tokatyan with the public and with the Met.

I caught up with Johnson just as he was about to make the announcement. "I'll tell you what," I said. "If you transpose 'La donna è mobile' so

I can do it half a tone lower, then maybe I can make it to the quartet."

"We'll do anything you want, Jan," said Johnson—and on I went.

I sang a pretty good "La donna è mobile," hoarse though I was. One or two of the highest notes, I sang an octave lower. Only the professional ear caught what I was doing. John Rosenfield wrote in the *Dallas Morning News* that "Jan Peerce could easily have left his colleagues holding the bag, but only a musician like Jan Peerce could have gotten around it the way he did."

Even a knowledgeable critic like Rosenfield apparently missed what happened with that final offstage high B natural in the reprise of "La donna è mobile." But a few trained ears in the house recognized that I delivered the last high note in stereophonic sound.

By that point in the fourth act, I was actually beginning to feel better. The more I sang, the better I sang. So I knew I could make the high note fine and only wished I could have sung that well earlier in the afternoon.

I was gaining confidence, but the stage manager, Désiré Defrère, wasn't. He used to be an opera singer himself and although he was nearing seventy, he still had a few high notes in him. Knowing that the whole performance depended on the final offstage B natural, he stationed himself backstage— and when I hit and held that high note, he sang it, too!

Backstage, I stormed over, almost ready to strangle him. When I finally caught up with him, he said, "I did it for you, Jan. I didn't think you could possibly make that high note and if you'd missed it, it would have been curtains for you in Dallas."

"And what would it have been if you'd missed it?"

"Never happen," he said. "I may not have much left as a singer, but I've still got my B natural."

And I said, "Well, let me tell you something. So do I."

Enter Zitomirsky

Lawrence Tibbett, Lily Pons, and I sang *Rigoletto* on the road—Portland, Seattle, and Sacramento—with the San Francisco Opera in early October 1941 before we opened in San Francisco. Tibbett had just begun to suffer from throat trouble.

Traveling with Tibbett was a little man named Zitomirsky, whom people identified to me as "Tibbett's teacher." Now, this was quite a status symbol: to have a teacher who would give up his other pupils to travel with you on the road.

One day I struck up a conversation with Zitomirsky and he told me, "I'm not just a teacher, you know. I restructure voices for people in trouble."

Out of insecurity (and with Alice a couple of thousand miles away looking after the kids), I said to him, "You know, you interest me. I'd like to study with you a little."

"No, no, no!" said Zitomirsky. "You don't need me, Peerce. You sing beautifully." I thanked him, but asked why I should wait until I might need him.

"Peerce," he said, "you're a very smart boy. And I'll tell you what I'm going to do for you. I will teach you. When we get to San Francisco, you come to see me at the Fairmont Hotel."

There was almost a week between the opening night of the season and the first *Rigoletto,* so I had quite a bit of free time on my hands in San Francisco. I visited Zitomirsky at the Fairmont and saw another status symbol: a piano in his hotel room. Now he had me hooked, because I hadn't rated one at my hotel, the Whitcomb, where I had trouble getting into the ballroom to rehearse.

We talked, and he told me how Tibbett was improving under his tutelage. He also told me that he charged fifteen dollars a lesson, which was a lot in those days. I said fine. He said, "Would you like to pay me for ten lessons in advance?" I said I'd like to. I wrote him a check for $150.

We had two lessons at the Fairmont before my debut. They were nothing exciting and nothing new—just scales and vowels, capably administered. But I told myself that I was doing preventive maintenance that would spare my voice a stint with a rebuilder years later.

My San Francisco debut was on a Sunday afternoon, October 19, 1941. That morning I awoke early, prayed to the Lord, took a light breakfast, did my vocalizing, and walked over to the opera house. It was a gorgeous day out—and inside, on that stage, I hit the jackpot. Such was my ovation that Tibbett made me take an extra solo bow—something to which, as a newcomer, I had no right. A few hours later, without consulting each other, or telling me, Tibbett and Lily Pons each sent a telegram to Johnson at the Met saying I was sensational and he should grab me. (The conductor, Gennaro Papi, also sent Johnson a letter, saying he'd love to work with me at the Met.) Even before then, as the curtain calls finally trickled out, I thanked Tibbett for "being so wonderful to me and letting me have all the glory."

"Listen, kid," he said in his deep baritone, "why shouldn't I? First of all, you deserve it. Second of all, didn't somebody do the same for me?" I knew how, when Tibbett sang his first Ford in *Falstaff* at the Met in 1925, the other baritone, Antonio Scotti, pushed him onstage for a solo bow and people went wild, for Tibbett was good-looking, tall, slender, and American! Many an established singer I know would have pulled rank on a Tibbett or me. But Tibbett kept his greatness as a man long after his voice began to fade.

One or two critics came backstage to congratulate and interview me before rushing off to write their glowing notices.

"Hats off, ladies and gentlemen, to a great new tenor!" Alexander Fried began his review in the next day's *San Francisco Examiner.* "Jan Peerce is his name. He is a New Yorker, still in his thirties. In the San Francisco Opera's matinee *Rigoletto* yesterday at The Memorial Opera House he was the finest sounding Duke (not barring memory of Gigli, Schipa, or anyone else) whom this city has heard in decades." John Mason wrote in the *Oakland Tribune* that "Jan Peerce . . . acquitted himself gloriously. . . . He took his high Cs with an ease that defies comparison." Alfred Frankenstein wrote in the *San Francisco Chronicle:* "Peerce made one of the most startling successes achieved by any of the new singers Maestro Merola has brought here in recent years. He belongs to a rare breed, for he is a tenor who does not sing as if it hurt. His voice is tremendously powerful, and likewise amazingly free and effortless. It is devoid of holes or worn spots, and is beyond reproach both in tone quality and musical handling. Peerce, one suspects, is a newcomer who is going to stay."

The first man into my dressing room, however, was Zitomirsky—and as the others assembled there to open the champagne, Zitomirsky said to me, "Nu? So you were great!"

I said, "The Lord was good to me."

Seeing the others crowd around and knowing we had an audience, Zitomirsky raised his voice on high to exclaim, "Two lessons! Two lessons and look what I did for him!"

An Audition for the Met

Two weeks after my West Coast debut, I received calls first from Mike De Pace and then from Hurok and Frank St. Leger of the Metropolitan Opera to audition for Edward Johnson. I replied that I was beyond the phase of my career in which I did auditions, since I was a known quantity. Hurok and Alice, however, convinced me to swallow my pride and to audition. Hurok said, "It's not really an audition, John. They just want to hear you in the house once."

On Friday, November 7, 1941, at two o'clock in the afternoon, Hurok, De Pace, Warner Bass, and I went over to the Metropolitan Opera House at Thirty-ninth Street and Broadway.

No matter how good you are, most auditions are ghastly. You walk into an empty theatre. Everything is dead. On stage, just one forty-watt work light illuminating a battered old upright piano, out of tune from whatever pounding it took in the ballet rehearsals. It has all the show-business, grand-opera atmosphere of a haunted house.

You don't know and you can't see who's out front. I had decided to begin with that most difficult and thankless of arias, "Parmi veder le lagrime," from the third act of *Rigoletto.* If the invisible beings out there knew what they were supposed to know about music, they would know that this is one number where Verdi tests *all* the singer's resources. You can't get away with singing this one loudly or hitting spectacular high notes. It requires an artist. You must phrase. You must know the value of the words. You must enunciate. At an audition, you can't cover anything up. The operatic stage can be a great coverall: if you're not singing well, you can throw your sword for emphasis or stamp your foot to distract from the high note that isn't there.

In all humility, I've never sung that aria better. I could hear an intake of breath, no applause, when I finished—and I knew that there was at least one knowledgeable music lover in our midst. Then, with total confidence and complete ease, I did four other arias from *Rigoletto* and followed them with "Una furtiva lagrima" from *L'Elisir d'Amore,* the same piece with which I'd auditioned for Toscanini.

When I was done, I addressed my unseen audience: "Gentlemen, may I leave?"

"Just a minute!" a voice called out. "If you're not too tired, would you repeat that last number?"

I turned to Warner Bass and said, "This is the first time I've been asked to do an encore at an audition."

The people out front laughed at this, but when I sang "Una furtiva lagrima" once more, I was distracted by voices talking in the audience. One of them sounded like Hurok's. This can be annoying, but being a pro, I finished up with a flourish.

The voice that had addressed me before said curtly, "Thank you very much, Mr. Peerce."

I walked off, wondering why they seemed to have lost interest and how long I would have to wait for word. But there was Hurok standing in the wings and throwing kisses at me. When I drew closer, still ready to berate him for talking during my encore, he said to me:

"Mazel tov! Very good, very good! Now go home, make *Kiddush* over your sweet red wine, eat some good gefilte fish with horseradish, some fresh challah with a little salt, and kiss Alice. You are a member of the Metropolitan Opera Company!"

5

Peerce of
the Metropolitan

METROPOLITAN OPERA ASSOCIATION, INC.

NEW YORK

PRESS BUREAU

Please print Tuesday, November 11, 1941

Edward Johnson, General Manager of Metropolitan Opera Association, Inc., announced yesterday the engagement of JAN PEERCE, the American tenor of international fame.

This nationally known tenor is a native New Yorker, who began his musical life by playing the violin to work his way through medical school. He also sang in an alto voice which matured into a tenor and as such he was engaged to sing at the opening of Radio City Music Hall. Something happened to deprive him of this debut, but eventually he did make his first appearance there but sang first behind a curtain and later with the spotlight on him in which position he has sung for six years. In addition he has given concerts throughout the United States and has sung on the air in a number of important radio hours. He was chosen by Toscanini to sing the tenor part in Beethoven's Ninth Symphony, and he was also soloist in Rachmaninoff's "The Bells."

—Metropolitan Opera Archives

Debut at the Met

The following Monday, I gave my notice at the Music Hall. I was still excited, and a little nervous, when I called to tell W. G. Van Schmus I wished to be released from my Music Hall contract, which had another two years to run.

As soon as I told him I had "this other contract to sign," and even before I could tell him what it was, Van Schmus interrupted me to say, "Whatever it is, you sound so happy about it, John, you have my blessing."

At the Met, they were discussing which opera I would make my debut in. The reason I'd been asked to sing "Una furtiva lagrima" twice at my audition was that the various officials had *L'Elisir d'Amore* in mind for me. This is an opera I've never done. It's a good one, but aside from that one great aria, the tenor part of a country bumpkin has never been one I've burned to do.

Mike De Pace told me, "They want you to learn *Elixir of Love* in three weeks. Do you think you can?"

"I guess I can," I said, "but do you think I should?"

Edward Johnson answered the question for us by intervening with his underlings: "Why do you ask him to learn an opera he's never done in three weeks when we can give him something he already knows and show him off at his best? He can do Donizetti next season."

They gave me *La Traviata* with a bunch of old friends from my Coast appearances: Novotna (my Hollywood Bowl Violetta), Tibbett, and Papi in the pit. And to top it off, a Saturday matinee—which meant a nationwide radio broadcast with Milton Cross intoning: "Texaco presents . . . the Metropolitan Opera!"

The rehearsals went well. At 10 A.M. on Thursday, November 27, 1941, two days before the performance, Johnson was sitting with Alice when I came out to begin the rehearsal by singing the second-act aria in full voice. Johnson, as a former Met tenor himself, marveled to Alice, "How can he do this at ten o'clock in the morning?"

Alice replied, "He's been doing it for eight years at the Music Hall, where rehearsals start at *eight* in the morning."

I woke up in New Rochelle on Saturday, November 29, feeling good. As soon as I'd sung a couple of scales, I knew it was going to be my day.

I had reached the pinnacle of a singer's dreams. I felt everybody backstage—including the stagehands and the kids in the chorus—was rooting for me. So were the people out front and listening at home. I wasn't an unknown quantity to them. They could share the thrill that a fellow born and raised in New York, who'd studied his music in New York, and *whom they had discovered for themselves,* was asking for the ultimate stamp of approval.

For me, making the Met was a logical culmination, but I had no feeling it was overdue. Instead I was glad it had taken a little longer, for I had acquired experience at the Music Hall and with different opera companies. I knew my stuff. I knew my way around a stage. I knew how to sing with a hundred-piece orchestra.

I had no time for nerves. Just in case it would scare me, though, nobody told me that Maestro Papi had dropped dead in his bathroom a little more than an hour before curtain time. Tibbett, Novotna, and Johnson talked it over and decided not to tell me because the shock might upset me, to say the least. Frank St. Leger conducted the national anthem while Ettore Panizza got ready to replace Papi. I knew none of this. Thus if Alfredo Germont looked a trifle flustered right after he made his entrance that afternoon, it wasn't debut nerves. It was surprise at perceiving, as soon as I sang my first word ("Marchese!"), that Papi was not conducting. I had met Panizza, but never worked with him before. Well, this was the Met, I decided, telling myself to look forward to a long career of many surprises. There have been quite a few, but none ever came close to that first one.

Once I had sung the sparkling drinking song, "Libiamo," a few minutes later, I was over my shock, for I knew that Panizza and I could work together. What's more, the ovation and bravos that followed "Libiamo" told me I was "in."

Just before I came out for the second act, I met Norman Cordon, the bass, who told me he was sorry he couldn't come to my party afterward, but he was "all broken up by Papi's death." That's how I found out—less than a minute before my entrance. At such a moment, you have to be the most selfish guy in the world. You've got a mark to make. You can't allow emotions to play a part. It's a terrible thing to do, but you close your eyes and forget it. Not only the show must go on: *you* must go on!

I sang *Traviata* sixty-seven more times for the Met and two or three dozen times elsewhere—with Licia Albanese, Bidú Sayão, Dorothy Kirsten, Eleanor Steber, and Helen Jepson, among others—but the one I think of as Violetta is Novotna that afternoon. Whether or not she was a greater singer than the others, I wouldn't say, but I think she may have been one of the better actresses who ever played the part. When Alfredo had to get angry at her in the third act, I found myself hating him—that is, hating myself.

Novotna was so good that she made everybody around her look good.

And she was a blessing to me, for I lacked experience as a stage lover and she guided me until I felt secure enough to assert myself.

PEERCE HEARD IN OPERA DEBUT AT METROPOLITAN

Tenor Sings Alfredo Role In "La Traviata"; Panizza Takes Baton as Papi Dies

BY JEROME D. BOHM

. . . The performance was a stirring one and some of its emotional impact was indubitably brought about by the knowledge on the part of those concerned that Gennaro Papi, who was to have directed it, had died only shortly before it commenced. I have seldom heard a presentation of this opera of Verdi's in which every member of the cast was so submerged in the music and action of his role.

Since it was Mr. Peerce's first appearance here in opera, his delineation of Alfredo will be discussed first. It may be said at once that this New York–born tenor, whose work has been familiar to radio listeners and concert goers for some time, proved a genuine acquisition to the Metropolitan's forces. His singing throughout the afternoon was of a high order. His naturally persuasive voice was projected with consistent artistry throughout its range. His top tones emerged with resonance and in unforced fashion. Especially impressive were his deliveries of his second-act aria, "Dei miei bollenti spiriti" and of his part of the duet with Violetta in the last act.

Not only did Mr. Peerce sing well but, more surprising, he acted well, too. Although he had appeared previously in Hollywood and in San Francisco in "Traviata," his operatic experience has been limited and it would not have been astonishing had Mr. Peerce seemed less at home as an actor than as a singer. But he disclosed a genuine histrionic talent which enabled him to impart a touch of ardor and reality to his impersonation. . . .

—*New York Herald Tribune,*
Sunday, November 30, 1941

THE OPERA IN REVIEW

BY OLIN DOWNES

. . . Then there was the new Alfredo. Mr. Peerce's audience, whether present on the other side of the footlights, or in coast-to-coast places over the land, was delighted, and with good reason, by the appealing quality of his voice and his manner of using it. He had his full meed of applause.

Little more than this is customarily asked of the man who sings the lover's music. . . . Probably on the occasion of his Metropolitan debut Mr. Peerce thought about two things: the conductor, and his duty as a singer. Yet he appeared confident, cool, an Alfredo by no means as green or excited as the ardent young man of the beau monde of the Paris of the Fifties. . . .

—*New York Times,*
Sunday, November 30, 1941

The John D. Rockefellers, the Milton Steinbergs, and most of the Kalmanowitz-Kayes and Perelmuth-Peerces attended my debut. So did my son

Larry, at eleven our only child old enough for the occasion. But the loudest and most prominent figure in my dressing room after the performance was Tibbett's voice-rebuilder, Zitomirsky, telling the world that it was he who made me what I was—even though I hadn't even had time to take my third lesson from him.

Alice was furious. "Get rid of him," she muttered to me—and she meant as teacher as well as backstage visitor. But I couldn't, particularly since I'd paid him for eight more lessons. We made a date and, at that third lesson, I mentioned that my wife was skeptical.

"We'll fix that," he said. "Please invite her to our next lesson."

For our fourth lesson, Alice came along and Zitomirsky was delighted to see her. He and I did a couple of scales when suddenly he stopped as if he'd heard a burglar or, in those days right after Pearl Harbor, an air-raid siren. "Do you hear that, Mrs. Peerce?" he asked.

Alice said: "Do I hear what?"

"Do you hear how your husband is singing the scales? Isn't it better than ever before?"

"No, I wouldn't say so. Jan always sings his scales well."

"No, no, no!" Zitomirsky insisted. "I tell you it's better. Listen again!"

I sang again and, when he pressed her to say I'd improved, Alice drew herself up to her full six-foot-four and said: "Listen, Maestro! You're setting yourself up as the great *I Am!* Well, I want you to know that my husband sang well before he ever heard of you and he made his success without you. So don't you play Creator to me! Or to him!" Then, turning to me, she said: "I don't want you to study with this man! I'm going—and, if you don't come with me I'm leaving anyway. Have I made myself clear?" With that, Alice left. I ran right after her, saying "Wait a minute! Wait a minute!" By the time I'd caught up with her and patched it up, we were home in New Rochelle —and I never went back to Zitomirsky.

I learned a lot more from a very fine radio conductor who had come to the Met, Cesare Sodero, when he and I were preparing for a subsequent *Traviata* there. Right before the first-act aria, "Un dí felice," when Alfredo confesses his love to Violetta and she asks if he has loved her a long time, he says, "Ah, yes: a year now" (in Italian, "Ah, si, da un anno"). At a rehearsal, Sodero seemed startled by this phrase. He stopped the rehearsal and had me repeat it. "Ah, si, da un ano," I sang. I had fallen into a bad habit of overlooking the double consonant. Sodero explained to me that with one *n, anno* (year) becomes *ano* (ass), so what I was telling Violetta was that I was loving her like an ass already.

To this day, whenever I have the chance to sing *Traviata,* you will hear me emphasizing the double *n* in *an-no* for all I'm worth. I don't want to make an ass of myself on stage.

Rigoletto for the Record

Rigoletto was my second opera for the Metropolitan, exactly a month after *Traviata*. I sang the profligate duke fifty-six times with the Met in New York and on tour. But the most awesome *Rigoletto* I ever sang in was in San Francisco in the 1940s.

In the middle of "Parmi veder le lagrime" at the San Francisco Opera House, I felt a little tremor underfoot. I could also just see the huge chandelier swaying. It was distracting, to say the least, and when I came to a high B flat in the aria, for once I didn't hold it. I sang it and went right away from it to finish the aria. There was a smattering of applause, but I could see people heading for the aisles. All because Jan Peerce, for once in his life, hadn't held on to a high B flat?

As I came offstage, expecting my comeuppance, I ran into Lorenzo Alvary, the bass who was playing Sparafucile. "Why didn't you hold that B flat?" he began, then he went on: "You know why you didn't hold that B flat? I'll tell you why. There was an earthquake!"

I said, "Thank G-d it was only because of an earthquake!"

Lily Pons, who was standing there waiting for her cue, laughed and said, "Tonight Jan Peerce really rocked the house."

With the coming of the long-playing record, RCA Victor decided in 1950 to make the first American recording of a complete opera: *Rigoletto*, starring Erna Berger, Leonard Warren, and myself in the three main roles, with Italo Tajo as Sparafucile and Nan Merriman as Maddalena. To this day, I think there is no better recording of *Rigoletto*.

The making of *Rigoletto* cost sixty thousand dollars, an astronomical sum in those days. Today's costs, however, are so high that American companies can hardly afford to record whole operas—even abroad, now that the dollar has been devalued.

Recording *Rigoletto* for RCA in the late spring of 1950, we had to watch the budget—and the clock, too. Each session was three hours long, with ten minutes off per hour. If you went one minute past three hours, you'd have to pay seventy or eighty musicians fifteen minutes of overtime. If you went under three hours, you were wasting RCA's money, too.

One day we had seven minutes left and everybody was running around asking, "What're we gonna do?" The conductor, Renato Cellini, said, "Jan,

do you think you could do the aria from the third act in those seven minutes?"

Actually, the singing time of "Parmi veder le lagrime" is about three
and a half minutes, which didn't leave me any chance for retakes or even for
thinking it over. "What're you wasting time for?" I said. "Let's try it! We
either make it or we don't."

With that, we went into the aria. What you hear on the record today was
made in the last seven minutes of that session. We even had a minute or two
—no, just *one* minute—left over!

Today, if you're a singer, you come into a recording studio and you can
do one note twenty times until you get the B flat or high C that you want
or the conductor wants or the engineers want. You put on the earphones and
when you come to a certain mark in the music, you bleep in whatever is
lacking. By the time you get done with it, the note is distorted from all that
work. That's not making music! That's leaving a message with a telephone-
answering device.

Many artists suffer from a certain sickness that results. They sound so
good on a record that they can't duplicate it on the opera stage or in a concert
hall. They sit and revel in *their* sound, forgetting that they didn't sing it in
one take. What happens when a singer engineers a beautiful record and
people come to hear him because of it? The disappointment is keener. An
adequate performance becomes a bomb. He is forgotten fast.

I have no patience with the hi-fi stereo buff who boasts that the finest
concert in the world is not such good listening as a perfect recording, with all
the distractions engineered out. The record may be fine, but it lacks the life
that music should have. Music must live—not be planned at every note with
everything measured out. I shouldn't sound the way the technician in the
control booth thinks I should sound; I must sound the way *I* sound.

The greatness of Toscanini was that whatever we did with him was
performance, not just broadcast or recording. We always worked with an
audience, whether we originated from Carnegie Hall or from Studio 8H in
Radio City. That's why a Toscanini recording lives today. That's why it
breathes. That's why you feel the burning of the music and the passion he
poured into it. Today, when I listen to WQXR and hear a recording of
Toscanini's that I was on—*La Bohème, Traviata, Masked Ball,* the Ninth
Symphony, Verdi's *Hymn of the Nations,* or the last act of *Rigoletto*—I can say
to myself: "This is really the way I sang on that day."

I Love *Lucia*

Bel canto means beautiful, fine, flowing singing—and I know of no opera that gives the tenor more of a chance than *Lucia di Lammermoor.* I did *Lucia* twenty-one times on tour and forty-one times at the Metropolitan Opera House, making it the opera I sang the most at the Met, and second only to *Traviata* (thirty-four plus thirty-four) for total performances with the company.

Lucia is a lyrical opera. When Edgardo enters and sings his first sentence of recitative, begging Lucia's pardon that he has to go away, he is agitated, but he should give it a lyrical flow.

Edgardo grows more ardent, and when he sings "Verranno a te sull' aure," it has to be sung with *legato,* and be well sustained, not punched out. Verdi, Puccini and Donizetti knew the voice and never asked the singer to go beyond its range or force his way beyond its extreme natural quality. Hammering your voice into a trombone sound can be done very easily. For a month or two, you can wham away and bellow at will. I'm a lyric tenor, not a heldentenor like Lauritz Melchior and maybe not even a dramatic tenor like Kurt Baum. If I had done *Il Trovatore* or *Aïda* or Wagner, I am sure I would have managed, but I would have been doing repertoire that didn't belong to me. And I've seen what can happen: a wobble can develop in the voice, and all of a sudden you can't sing a lyric phrase.

If you stay within your range and do your work properly, you have a chance of singing for a long time with the bloom still on your voice. If, within your repertoire, you're always improving, well, that's what the great art of *bel canto* is all about. If you don't stay within the realm of your natural voice, you begin to force—and you may be in trouble.

The toughest spot for the tenor in *Lucia* is at the end—after the soprano does the Mad Scene, which is always a show-stopper. As soon as the soprano has finished, some of the audience gets up and exits, leaving the tenor to sing to an almost empty house.

This is folly, because the Tomb Scene that follows the Mad Scene is one of the greatest pieces of music ever written in any operatic score. It takes approximately eighteen or twenty minutes for Edgardo to die. You have a great time dying, singing beautiful melodies with long breaths. But which of us likes anybody to walk out on our own funeral?

I have to admit that after I began singing Edgardo in 1942, the audience stayed for the Tomb Scene. I'm glad I helped arrest this condition before it became an American reflex.

Once in Chicago, I was on tour with the Met and Olin Downes of the *New York Times* dropped in on a busman's holiday. When Downes came backstage, his congratulations were tinged with surprise. "Haven't you heard me do the Tomb Scene before?" I asked him. "I've done it so many times at the Met."

"I know," said Downes, "but I've always had to leave after the Mad Scene to meet my deadline."

My Lucias have included a number of good-looking girls: Roberta Peters, Anna Moffo, and Lily Pons. Even though *Lucia* was the opera in which Lily made her debut at the Met way back in 1931 (she took sixteen curtain calls) and which she had subsequently made her own, she had a nervous stomach and tended to get sick before it or any other opera. Many times I'd make my entrance in *Lucia,* grab Lily, who'd just finished her aria, and feel her shaking; a few times I'd catch her just as she began to swoon and then, as the applause went on, I'd whisper to her, "You're doing great, you're fine, you're wonderful, I'm here, don't worry." In one *Lucia,* though, she sang the last high note in the Mad Scene and fainted dead away. The audience saw it. The curtain came down. There were gasps and murmurs and a few screams. Two minutes later, there she was—out in front of the curtain, taking her bows. I was backstage, waiting to go on in the Tomb Scene. One of the other singers asked me, "How're you gonna top that, Jan? Faint, too?"

"I'm not the fainting type," I said. "I'm the singing type."

Around Yom Kippur, though, I'm the fasting type. Once in San Francisco, Merola had to have me for a performance that began the night Yom Kippur ended. This meant I'd have fasted twenty-six hours and then would do a performance of *Lucia,* beginning at eight o'clock.

I said I could do it, but it took some planning. I staked out a Compton's cafeteria on Geary and Van Ness, three or four blocks from the synagogue, and made sure they'd be open. When the services at the Geary Street temple ended, a little before 7 P.M., a friend was waiting with a car. He drove me to Compton's, where I shoved an orange juice and a roll and coffee into my system. Then we drove six blocks in the other direction to the opera house. We were there at seven twenty-five. This left thirty-five minutes for me to shave, freshen up, dress up, make up, and tune up. Actually, I had a bigger margin than that, for a couple of scenes precede Edgardo's entrance, but I was ready to go at eight o'clock.

I gave one of my better performances that night. The fact is that after a rigorous day of fasting and worshiping followed by breaking the fast in a moderate way, I found myself onstage trying even harder than usual and not at all overconfident. When you make such a special effort, the result is good —that is, if you have everything else that goes with it, including, in this case, a slightly empty stomach.

The Rise of Roberta Peters

In 1942, I was singing at Grossinger's in the Catskills one weekend when the maître d' told me he had a grandchild with "a real voice on her." I said, very casually, that I'd like to hear her sometime, and a few months later a girl named Roberta Peterman came down from the Bronx with her mother to see me at my accompanist's studio on West Seventy-second Street. To my amazement, she was only about thirteen. To my further astonishment, her grandfather had been absolutely right.

Paul Althouse (a fine tenor and well-known teacher) concurred that she had a most interesting, extremely high voice (she could go up to A above high C). He added that Roberta had "a wonderful neck, a real singer's neck."

I took Roberta and her mother out for a snack and told the girl, "Look, you have the makings of something more than just a singing swan. So get the right teacher. Don't sing anywhere in public. Don't be just a child prodigy who'll make a career on kiddie shows and be finished when you're sixteen." I sent her to a teacher named William Herman, who was starting to do great things with an unknown young girl named Patrice Munsel. Herman took over Roberta's learning and her whole life—to such an extent that she never went to high school or college, just to the William Herman School of Music for almost eight years. Every couple of months, I would drop in to observe her progress.

By the time Roberta was sixteen, she was singing Handel and Bach. At that time she was offered the role of the ingenue in Kurt Weill's musical *Street Scene* on Broadway, singing a great song called "Moon Faced, Starry Eyed." I told her, "Look, Roberta, I know it's very tempting, but you can be smarter than that." She had a repertoire of several operas and I knew she was destined for the Met at an early age. Wonder of wonder, miracle of miracles, that talented teen-ager not only asked my advice, she took it! She turned down *Street Scene,* which is a classic now, but was a quick flop then.

A couple of years later, I arranged for Roberta to audition for Sol Hurok in Bill Herman's studio on East Ninety-fourth Street. Warner Bass accompanied her on the piano. When we left, Hurok, Bass, and I were caught in a downpour. We stood under the awning of Cantor's drugstore at Ninety-sixth and Madison. Hurok kept saying, "She's got time, John, she's got time. She is not ready yet." I kept elbowing him, saying, "You've got to take her. You *must* put her under your management. This is *your* girl. You are going to be so proud of her that you're not leaving here until you say yes." I didn't mean to jostle Hurok, but my elbowing was pushing him out into the rain. Finally, just to stay dry, I think, he agreed to audition her again for his people the following month: "But if she makes a fool of me, it's on your head, John."

At Town Hall in December 1949, Roberta sang for Hurok's staff and they were sufficiently impressed to urge him to give her a contract. The following month he had her sing for Rudolf Bing, who had just come over to head the Met. Bing took her on, but put her way down on the roster. The rest is history. That November, Nadine Connor took sick and Roberta Peters, as she was now called, literally stepped into the part—wearing Nadine's shoes—of Zerlina in *Don Giovanni* on just a couple of hours notice. Before the night was out, Roberta was a star—not just with the critics, but with her conductor, Fritz Reiner, who said, "Her fine preparation should be a lesson to other young American singers. When the chance came, she was qualified."

To this day Roberta Peters says that she was "Jan Peerce's protégée." Just lately, I said to her, "Don't you have anything else to talk about? In radio interviews, television interviews, newspaper interviews, magazine interviews, you're always bragging about our association. What else is new?"

"But I love you," Roberta replied, "and I'll never forget you. You did so much for me that whenever anyone asks for the secret of my success, you're the answer."

Tosca: "They've Shot Daddy!"

Mario Cavaradossi, the Italian patriot and liberal, is the most appealing of all the operatic characters I've played—twenty-one times with the Met, starting on January 29, 1943. Yet the first act of *Tosca* brought me into conflict with two fine conductors, Dimitri Mitropoulos and Fausto Cleva.

Mitropoulos was a marvelous old man, a very religious Orthodox Greek, whose room in the Great Northern Hotel on Fifty-seventh Street was a museum of icons and relics. The trouble in *Tosca* was that, in his first aria, Mario, an artist, is standing up on a high scaffolding, painting a fresco on the wall of a church, while the conductor is way, way down below in the pit. Perhaps because of this, Mitropoulos and I didn't see eye to eye. So when the sacristan of the church was talking with Mario and I'd have to sing "E vero. E tanto ell'era infervorata nella sua preghiera," all on one note, Mitropoulos and I were often not together. We would finish together, we were together on all other things in the opera, but that one little part frequently gave us some trouble.

One day I said to him, "Something seems to be wrong. If *I'm* wrong, tell me and I'll do it the way you want me to do it, but we ought to straighten it out."

He tried to tell me I was too fast while I refrained from saying he was too slow, but we had difficulty uniting with any consistency. Sometimes I'd slow down, at which point he'd speed up to make me look good. Whenever I did *Tosca* with Mitropoulos, some of my fellow singers would stand in the wings betting on which of the two of us was going to run a better race that night.

Fausto Cleva was very different from Mitropoulos. When I coached with him, I learned a great deal. Physically, Cleva was short—and if you think *I* had had complexes about *my* height, well, Cleva had a Napoleon complex.

Whenever we did *Tosca,* he would warn me about the duet in the first act: "Don't hold that B flat!" He was referring to the note in the middle of the line "Occhio all'amor soave." This was a simple, but very passionate phrase with a typical Puccini way of spilling forth.

One of my trademarks, if I may say so, is that I rarely overheld high notes; I was never trying out for the show-off Olympics. Once, however, in San Francisco, I was swept away by my own feeling for the role and quite without thinking, I held the high note for an extra second.

There was a snort from the pit. Cleva's teeth were grinding. His eyes were blazing. If he could have immolated me from the pit, he would have. I couldn't believe that this kindly fellow had suddenly become a dragon breathing hate.

When the act was over, he summoned me to his dressing room and began his denunciation even before I entered the door. "Why did you do that? How could you insult me like that? Who do you think you are?"

"Maestro, what did I do? What crime have I committed?"

"You held that high note!"

"Ohhh, Maestro, if I held it, it was just for a second. It was really nothing, just the feeling of the moment. I'm sorry if I upset you like this; I really didn't mean to do it."

I was truthfully apologetic, but Cleva had to have what he thought would be the last word: "And if you *were* going to hold it, Peerce, why didn't you warn me? Why didn't you at least tell me what you were planning to do?"

I had to say it: "Y'know, Maestro, I didn't know it was going to be so good!"

Cleva put on a show of fury, shouting, "Oh, go to hell, Peerce! Get the hell out of my room!" I knew, however, that he wanted me out of there fast for the same reason I wanted out: to keep from laughing.

If I say Fausto Cleva had a Napoleon complex, I'm not necessarily knocking him. Cleva was a very fine gentleman, at least when he didn't have the stick in his hand. But as soon as he did, he used to get in his own way —antagonizing people and, worse still from the musical standpoint, insisting that everything had to be measured and exact. Nothing could flow extemporaneously—which is a hell of a way to do Puccini!

In 1956, just before I went to Russia for the first time, I took stock of my finances. Going behind the iron curtain during the cold war was so new and adventurous then that it was natural to want to put your affairs in order. Who knew what would befall me? Maybe they'd keep me there because one of my ancestors owed the czar some money or some time. Even if I survived my Russian trip, what if anything bad happened to me or if I had to retire? It was time to take inventory.

I went to see my new lawyer, Felix Langer, who asked a number of questions about our way of life and the future we hoped for. Then Felix spent three or four weeks evaluating our income and holdings, papers and possessions—and asking more questions. Finally he called Alice and me into his office and said, "You're in a very good position. If, G-d forbid, anything should happen to you tomorrow, you're taken care of to the point that you could at least continue living the way you do—that is to say, in the same category or standard without endangering your principal." This was good news indeed.

The next day I went to rehearsals at the Met with Cleva. Cleva and I respected each other, but it was his way to pick on one person: a different one each day. That day it happened to be my turn. He stopped me early. Then he started me and stopped me again. Not only did he get into my hair, but he split hairs right and left and kept snipping away until he was under my skin. At last I exclaimed, "For crying out loud, why don't you cut this out?"

This was the tone Cleva sometimes took with artists, but not the way anybody dared talk to him. It was not a way I used to speak to very many people at the Met. There was a hush in the room, for everyone was shocked to hear anyone talking back to Cleva. But I really went after him: "For Chrissakes! I'm tired of your damn nonsense!"

Cleva was struck speechless and signaled a break with his hands. Roberta Peters and Robert Merrill were rehearsing, too, and they came over to me. Bob said, "What's the matter, Jan?" Roberta said, "What did he do to make you explode like that?"

"First of all," I said, "I am genuinely tired of his baloney. And second, I just found out yesterday I could retire this minute and go on living the way I'm living now without ever doing another day's work. I don't want to retire, but I've got this new feeling of independence and I guess I had to try it out."

The gist of my explanation must have been conveyed to him, for he resumed without a word and wasn't in particularly bad humor after that. I had made him the butt of my anger, and realizing that, I was able to go back to work for him and take whatever he might have in store for me.

The moral of this story is: Save your money. That way, you can afford not just to tell people off now and then, but to be secure in what you're doing without having to take a lot of nonsense. You'll still have to take orders— but if you're given orders that you think are wrong or if you think you're being mistreated, you'll have enough of a feeling of independence to speak up and say what you think. Once you know you can retire anytime, you never have to act retiring.

Toward the end of Act Three in *Tosca,* Mario is executed. *Tosca* is such a realistic opera that I always reminded the firing squad to point their weapons over my head—just in case somebody followed the script too literally or some rival tenor or other enemy might have sneaked in live ammunition. I took this precaution even before Rudolf Bing appeared on the scene.

I was doing *Tosca* at the Met on a Saturday afternoon and our custom was that the Peerce children came to matinees I was in. Susan must have been nine or ten around then and it was her first *Tosca.* The big moment came in Act Three. There was a hush. Then the command to shoot me was given. *Boom!* A volley of shots rang out and I fell to the stage. There is always a reaction—a gasp!—from the audience. This once, however, as I fell, I heard Susan's voice ring out loud and clear: "Oh, my G-d, they've shot Daddy!"

Her projection was marvelous and so were the acoustics, for she brought down the house. Lying there dead, I could have died.

Some of the Best People

[Alice Peerce recalls an embarrassing experience in Skokie, Illinois.]

Alice: *Jan gave a concert in Skokie, and in those early years I didn't applaud. Why? There were several wives of singers at the Met who, whenever their husbands sang, were the most dreadful cheerleaders. They would sit in one part of the house, applaud their husband, and then, for the next act, they'd go to another part of the house and shout "Bravo!" I resented this and didn't try to compete. Instead I played it very cool* *and never applauded Jan or anyone else. I just sat there like a* klutz. *A* klutz? *That's Yiddish for dummy.*

In Skokie, I was sitting in the third or fourth row, with everybody around me applauding after the first group of songs. Then, after the second group, the audience went out of its mind. Just before intermission, Jan did an eight- or ten-minute aria. The house literally shook with applause and stamping of feet.

I said "Excuse me" to the people in my row and made my way backstage, where I told Jan how great it was going and how all the people around me were loving it. Back in my seat, though, somebody tapped me on the shoulder. "Excuse me," she said. "Don't you like Mr. Peerce?"

"Of course I do!" I said. "I'm enjoying him very much."

"But you haven't applauded once."

All I could think to say was: "I never clap."

"Then you shouldn't go to concerts," she said.

Someone sitting near us knew who I was and said, "Listen, lady, this is Mrs. Peerce."

"I don't care who she is! If she goes to a concert and the concert is good, she should applaud."

I took her advice. Ever after, I've applauded good and loud. But only from one seat.

I sing many parts of a concert with my eyes closed. That way, I meet some of the best people. Besides, have you ever looked at the faces in an audience? For me, when I close my eyes, I have nothing to concentrate on except what I'm doing. I'm not distracted that way. Marian Anderson used to keep her eyes closed *most* of the time. In opera, of course, you have to look at your partner, though sometimes you wish you could shut your eyes. With Roberta Peters, I keep my eyes open.

As a rule, I don't always see my audience even when my eyes *are* open; spotlights and footlights are pretty good blinders. But in concert situations, I can see the people in the first few rows, so I frequently shut my eyes and close myself out. After a song, I'll see fifty or a hundred people yelling and screaming "Bravo! Bravo!" and one *klutz*—not Alice, but some real *klutz*—sitting absolutely rigid in the front row. Him I didn't move. Only an undertaker could move him. For he's the big connoisseur. He's going to wait until everybody else gets tired and then maybe he'll begin to react. After I've taken ten or eleven bows, he's convinced he can commit himself. Then he starts up like a claque.

One guy who did this came backstage to congratulate me in Chicago in 1973. I couldn't forget his great stone face. He began, "Mr. Peerce, you are fantastic. I always sit in the front row when you sing, so I can watch your phrasing, your breathing—and I'm always in rapture."

I let him finish his gushing. Then I said, "Now let me tell you something. You shouldn't sit in the front. You're the most annoying person in the whole audience."

This staggered him. "Who? Me? How can you say that? I love you!"

"Well, the way you showed your love was torture to me. You tortured me for more than an hour and *then* you began to applaud!"

Whereupon he said, "Look, Mr. Peerce, I'm not the average listener. I have to be convinced."

"After all these years of coming to see me and ruining my concerts for me," I shouted, *"you* had to be convinced? And it took you more than an hour!"

Still, as Alice keeps reminding me, he bought his ticket and I should be grateful.

Ballo

In Verdi's *Un Ballo in Maschera (A Masked Ball),* as soon as the tenor, Riccardo, sees Amelia's name on the guest list, he sings an arietta about his ecstatic desire for her, the wife of his best friend, the baritone, Renato. The stage directions specify "Aside," but many a tenor goes out there and sings it in full voice when he should be confiding it to himself—particularly with Renato making his entrance. Fortunately, I coached *Ballo* with Bruno Walter. I coached with others, too, but I learned most about the role in the 1940s from Walter at the Met (where I did it twenty-six times starting in 1943) and in the 1950s during my cram course to replace Bjoerling for Toscanini.

Soon after Riccardo sings about Amelia, someone suggests that they all go to see a fortune-teller. In the second scene, they go to her, with Riccardo, the king, disguised as a fisherman. The fortune-teller tells him that he is going to run into trouble that will cost him his life: "You will die at the hand of the man who is next to shake hands with you." Nowadays everybody laughs a little at the idea of going to a fortune-teller. But I remember how once, at the Waldmere Hotel in the Catskills, the wife of my trumpet player read my tea leaves and said, "You are giving your girl a ring." It was Alice's and my secret that I was indeed planning to buy her a ring, but this woman either knew or guessed the inevitable. Right away I said, "Awwww"—and that "Awwww" of insincere denial is the quality I try to give Riccardo at this point: to impart the ring of truth, as it were.

Riccardo doesn't take the fortune-teller seriously. He walks around trying to shake hands with his companions, but they all shy away. Now his best friend, Renato, enters. Riccardo sticks out his hand and Renato takes it.

Riccardo laughs it off, however, by singing that marvelous laughing song "È scherzo od è follia" ("It's all a joke"). He's laughing throughout, but he's laughing with tears in his eyes and a knife through his heart and it hurts when he laughs. By then Verdi and his librettist, Somma, and the fortune-teller have you believing.

In the next act, after his supposedly happy experience, Riccardo meets Amelia and declares his love for her. As they finish their tremendous duet "O qual soave brivido," in which both pour forth all their love and passion, Bruno Walter never used to let me kiss her. He told me to kiss the hem of her skirt.

I objected to this. "In the greatest moment of passion, he kisses the hem of her skirt?"

Bruno Walter pointed out that in the finale, after Renato has stabbed Riccardo at the ball, Riccardo sings a beautiful melody swearing that Amelia is pure, swearing to his best friend, even as he's in the arms of death, that he never touched his wife. "Well," said Walter, "kissing is touching and I don't want the audience disbelieving with its own eyes." Thus, instead of getting a good kiss from a nice healthy soprano, I wound up with dust and thread in my mouth. With every other conductor or director, I try to do it Walter's way until and unless I'm ordered to kiss Amelia, which happens most of the time. As stagecraft, however, Walter's way works very well. (Walter had the nickname "Bravo Bruno" among a few of us, though he was not a man any of us would ever dare address by his first name. He had a one-man claque so that whenever he so much as conducted an overture, there would be the usual applause and this one ringing voice from the standees shouting out, "Bravo, Bruno!")

"Ma se m'è forza perderti" is an aria Verdi just couldn't find a suitable way out of. There's a certain pattern ordinarily followed in a song, but here Verdi wrote the climax before the end. He had nowhere to go but to end the aria down, in the middle of the tenor's voice. It thus is one of the more difficult arias to do, technically. It's not that it has very many high notes. But the aria takes the tenor voice and works with it from the middle up. The difficult part of the tenor voice—the most dangerous part—is in the beginning of the upper register: where the break in the voice is and you go from F to B flat. Verdi keeps going—F,G,A,F,G,A—and the tenor has to sustain it, has to be under it, has to *sing* it. High notes you can push a little; these you can't—particularly if you're going to stay in character. That aria reminds me of going up and down a staircase gracefully: not four steps at a time or with a running high jump.

Some time after doing *Ballo* with Toscanini, I had a *Ballo* with Dimitri Mitropoulos. Once again I experienced difficulty with that perfectly nice man. "Non sai tu che se l'anima mia," in the second-act duet, is written in six-eighths. But if you try to sing it in six-eighths, it gets jumpy. Instead of having me sing it six to a bar, Toscanini did it two to a bar. Otherwise you miss the *legato,* the smoothness of it, the singable part.

At the piano rehearsal, Mitropoulos did it in six-eighths time and I kept turning away. Finally he said, "What's the matter, Peerce? Is something making you uncomfortable?"

"I'll tell you the truth, Maestro. I'm not accustomed to doing it this way. I feel it in two instead of six."

"But it's written in six."

"I know it's written in six, but I can't find the *legato* that goes with it," I said, making a violin motion, because I look upon my voice as an instrument.

"But, Peerce!" Mitropoulos said. "I heard you do it with Toscanini. I was there!"

This was what I was waiting for. "Then you should know," I said succinctly. After that, he counted two to a bar.

Hymn of the Nations

One day in 1943, I was mad at everybody—including Alice, Toscanini, and Hurok. Alice was still managing some of my career and so, when Samuel Chotzinoff called up to invite me to sing with Toscanini on a national radio hookup at 5 P.M. on a particular day, she said yes without consulting me or the Hurok office. As it turned out, Hurok had booked me that night for a formal concert at the New York Young Men's and Young Women's Hebrew Association, Ninety-second Street and Lexington Avenue.

Everybody, including myself, was hysterical. I raged at Alice. I denounced the maestro to Chotzinoff. "I've sung four Ninth Symphonies!" I told him. "That's enough!"

"Who told you it was Beethoven?" Chotzinoff said, looking perplexed.

"Well, I presumed—"

"You presumed wrong," he told me. "You'll be doing Verdi's *Hymn of the Nations.*"

Now, that was much more interesting and exciting! But Mae Frohman at the Hurok office wouldn't let us out of the booking at the Y. Alice, however, had a solution: "Jan can do both concerts." Even I was dubious about that, but Alice insisted: "I want you to know that Jan could shake both those programs out of his left sleeve, and that isn't even his good sleeve. And it's important to me that we honor our obligation to Toscanini."

"All right," said Mae Frohman. "But remember, Alice, if anything happens, it's your responsibility."

What happened was one of the high spots of my life. Here was Toscanini —the son of a soldier of Garibaldi; a musician who had escaped into exile rather than let his baton become the tool of a tyrant—playing a piece that Verdi had written for a Garibaldi Day celebration honoring Italy's struggle to free itself from foreign domination. Toscanini actually changed the wording of the hymn from "Italy, my beautiful country" to "my betrayed country": "mia patria tradita." And he made sure that when "tradita" came along, I said it and meant it.

The date of the concert happened to be the day Mussolini fell as dictator of Italy. The announcement was made over NBC during the first half of the performance and Toscanini led a concert that was absolutely earth-shaking. Thanks to the broadcast and the film that was made of it and shown in fifty countries around the world, *Hymn of the Nations* became a universal ode to liberation—particularly the way Toscanini had my difficult tenor part end up with *The Star-Spangled Banner* and the *Marseillaise* and *God Save the Queen,* sung with the two hundred voices of the Westminster College Choir. Years later, at Toscanini's funeral service at La Scala in Milan, that's the recording they played. The day after Mussolini fell, La Scala had been plastered with posters saying: "Return, Toscanini!"

The impact in New York was even more immediate than that. By the time we had driven by taxi from the RCA studios at Radio City to the Ninety-second Street Y, I had trouble getting into my own concert. The place was mobbed by radio listeners storming the box office for tickets. I sang the concert without any hesitation or strain, and when it was over, Hurok was there to take the credit.

"Look what we did!" he said. "And I was the only one who knew we could." From that moment on, selling me for concerts was a cinch for Hurok because everybody in North America knew me.

My Bohemian Life with Grace Moore and Toscanini

I first did *La Bohème* at the Met on December 1, 1944. During the next couple of years, before her untimely death at the beginning of 1947, when she was forty-five, I sang Rodolfo several times with Grace Moore. She was a lovely person, with whom I also did *Tosca,* but I had to put her in her place at our first *Bohème.* As soon as I began to sing "Che gelida manina" to her, this Great Lady began to primp, fix her hair, and straighten her apron. Looking out of the corner of my eye while pouring forth my great love, I could see she was running her own beauty parlor as she readied herself for her aria, and in the process upstaging me.

Acting on anger and impulse, I walked away from her, off to the right a little and then closer to the footlights, where I sang my aria directly to the audience. Since I was supposed to be telling her the story of my life up to the moment I met her, I figured that if she wouldn't pay attention, the audience would. I guessed right. Toward the end of the aria, she'd stopped primping. In fact, she was altogether paralyzed with amazement. Seeing this, I finished the aria walking slowly back to her.

We never said a word to each other about this little duel of ours. But she never tried to upstage me again. From then on, we got along famously —so famously, in fact, that when Alice and I met the Polish tenor and European hero Jan Kiepura, who used to be carried by his admirers through the streets of Vienna and Cracow, singing all the way, his first words to me were: "Ohoho! Yon Peerce? So happy to see you. You must be living with Grace Moore." This, in a room full of people eager to hear how tenor greets tenor! I blushed and must have looked guilty. I know it took me a few seconds before I could say, "That's a nice idea, but what makes you say it in front of my wife and all these people? And what the hell are you talking about?"

"You must be lovers," he said loudly. "I hear when you finish an act you kiss each other. I fight with her, and you she kisses! There must be a romance."

"No, no. No romance; we're just good friends." But the truth sounded hollow even to me, so I added, "I do my job and she does hers; we don't move the chairs around." For when Kiepura and Grace Moore sang their first-act duet in *Bohème,* they would disagree over where the chair should be. During his part she shoved it forward scratchingly, and during her part he pushed it back scrapingly. Finally the management intervened, picked out a proper place for the chair, and nailed it in.

A lot of tenors doing *Bohème* worry about the high note in that first-act aria. Once you're over that one, you're on your way to glory. In the second act, though, Rodolfo doesn't have too much to do, except establish that he can be a very jealous lover. When Mimi looks at someone else, he steps in front of her to block her view.

In the third act, Rodolfo and Mimi have quarreled. Rodolfo complains to the painter Marcello that Mimi flirts with everybody and he imitates how she makes her eyes flutter. Mimi, who is hiding behind a tree, starts to cough. Rodolfo discovers her and they patch up their differences in each other's arms. The quartet that ends Act Three—with Marcello and his on-again, off-again sweetheart Musetta battling in contrast to Mimi and Rodolfo, who are all sweetness and light at this point—is one of the greatest ensembles in all opera, full of beauty and fun.

The last act begins with Rodolfo and Marcello at work in their attic. Musetta appears to announce that Mimi is outside, exhausted from climbing the stairs. Rodolfo and Marcello help her into the room. She knows she's dying and she wants to see Rodolfo once more. He tries to make her comfortable in the bed and tells her she's still as beautiful as a sunrise. "No," she sings, "as a sunset." While Musetta is bringing some medicine, Mimi dies— and when Rodolfo discovers this, he sings her name, "Mimi. Mimi," desperately and falls sobbing by the bed.

When you sing those last notes, you shouldn't try to blow the roof off the opera house. If you sing, people will hear it—whether you sound like a trumpet or a violin or a flute. Mob psychology and the critics, however, dictate bravos only when Rodolfo yells his brains out at the end of *Bohème.*

A conductor can give you his concept of a role, but the singing must come from within and express the way *you* feel the character. How do you make love to a girl on the stage? The answer to that riddle is in another question: how do you love naturally, in real life? When you see a man playing a love scene onstage, you can probably figure out his own love life. If he behaves like a boor or a pig, then that's probably the story of his real life, too. Some Rodolfos don't know where to begin and some don't know where to end, but you can be pretty sure that their wives or girlfriends are experiencing the same problem with them. You express *yourself.*

Bohème is thickly orchestrated, yet it's a very lyrical opera. Puccini put a wall of strings against the voice, which the singer must cut through. So there's always the danger of either the musicians or the singers performing too loudly.

You could take the score of *Bohème* and play it without singers. As far as the melodies are concerned, it's all in the orchestra. With Verdi, you couldn't do this. With Puccini's mass of music, however, conductors sometimes forget that if the score says one *f (forte),* and two *f*'s, which mean a little more *forte,* everything depends on where the *forte* starts. If the orchestra starts way on top with just one *f,* as though it's four *f*'s, where can they go from there? And the same with *piano/pianissimo* notations: they mustn't be so soft that you can't go any softer, for there are phrases written with two, three, four, even five *pianos*. Some conductors, however, fall in love with Puccini's melodies so much that they milk the *pianos* and *fortes*.

Toscanini was criticized for playing some of *Bohème* too fast, but whatever he played fast should have been played fast. Some conductors who do it too slow tell me I sing it too fast. Well, those are the guys I don't even say "Thank you and good night" to. And once, just once, at the Met, I was told to forget some of the things I had done with Toscanini. I made a point of forgetting *that* conductor fast.

When we did *La Bohème* for Toscanini, Licia Albanese, Francesco Valentino, Salvatore Baccaloni, George Cehanovsky, and I had to forget a lot of things we'd learned from others. Toscanini spent hours with the baritone Cehanovsky, who, as Schaunard the musician, tells Marcello Mimi has died: "Marcello, è spirata." He was trying to get Cehanovsky, a marvelous artist and actor, to speak those words the particular way he wanted: with a breathless quality that Cehanovsky just didn't catch at first. "Marcello . . ." Toscanini would whisper, "Marcello . . ." over and over until he had Cehanovsky doing exactly what he wanted.

Toscanini had something to say to each of us to impart the feel of the part. "The notes!" he would say. "Everybody knows the notes! The thing is to make the notes mean something." Even when he didn't say a word, when you just listened to an orchestral passage as he zipped into it, there was only one way to answer it when your cue came. Or right before I'd sing "Mimi è tanta malata!" just the expression on Toscanini's face told me how to sing the phrase.

During the broadcast of *La Bohème,* which was recorded by RCA, he sang along with me, in the first-act aria especially, and in the third act you can hear him helping me cry. Some people say, "It spoils the record." But I tell them that for me it makes the record. Imagine hearing Toscanini—not planning it, just naturally singing hoarsely in the background—and knowing this great man's heart is in that record!

At the end of the opera, after Mimi's death, there is one beat of rest. It's a tradition that the conductor doesn't beat that rest. Toscanini had explained to the orchestra that he wouldn't. At the broadcast, however, he was affected by the drama of the moment. He was crying. His hand made some sort of movement. Some of the brass thought he was giving them their first beat and came in, but others didn't. There was bedlam. It took Toscanini only three beats to straighten them out, but it was the end of the world for him. Everything went black before his eyes. He wouldn't take a bow. He cried. He carried on. He bawled out the brass section and I remember him saying pathetically:

"What did you do? What did you do? You're sorry! What, sorry! *You* go home now with your wife and have dinner. What do *I* do?"

Bohème ends sadly enough. To end this account with Toscanini in mourning would be too sad entirely, so let me switch back to Grace Moore. She was the first lady of claquery. She recruited her claques three ways: for good projection of *bravas*, for thick palms to applaud with, and for good aim. At the end of each act and on all her bows, she would have people planted to throw little bouquets of violets. Always, very gallantly, I'd bend down, pick up a few, and hand them to her. She always smiled and said the same thing to me: "I wish I knew who's doing that." Every time in every city, she would say that—and I would refrain from saying I knew damn well I was giving those flowers back to her unknown admirer every time I handed them to her. Once, though, I answered her very good-naturedly, "Just take a look at your payroll the end of this month."

A Lesson at the Met

Riccardo Dellera was a coach at the Met, a fine musician and gentleman who spoke very little English, but didn't need to, since he was strictly business. If he gave you an assignment, he wanted you to come prepared and know your stuff.

One day during the zenith of my career at the Met, I came for a lesson, put the score on the piano, stood behind him, and began to read while he played.

"No, no, no!" he said. "Get away from here. Stand over there."

"Oh," I said. "I can't do that."

"Why not?"

"Because I didn't study what you told me to study for today, so I have to read it."

Dellera was incredulous. "You didn't study? You didn't prepare?"

"No," I said blandly, like the fair-haired boy I was at the time.

Dellera took the score, closed it, handed it to me, and said, "I don't need money so badly I have to teach you when you're so unprepared."

I made my excuses, but the lesson was over. I had learned a bigger lesson, though. Dellera embarrassed me so thoroughly that never again in all my years with the Met did I ever show up, even for a lesson, the least bit unprepared.

When My Mother Died

My mother died on Saturday, April 7, 1945. She was sixty-four, by her count, though I think she might have been four or five years older than that. Like many other women in those days, she tried to make herself younger—not for vanity, but for insurance purposes: the rates were lower.

Five days later we were mourning my mother's death in my father's house on Madison Street.

When you sit *shivah* in an Orthodox home, the door is open so that people don't have to be invited to come in. You don't say hello and you don't say goodbye and you certainly don't say "So glad you could come" or even tell the visitor to sit down. Nor do you offer a glass of water; if the visitor wants some, let him go get it. You're in mourning. Your visitors come to console, to share your grief. The conversation also includes discussions of the Talmud. Of course, more and more, people tend to drop in and talk about baseball or the stock market or whatever else is on their minds. But in my family we observed mourning according to the book—with decorum.

Thus it came as a shock when a neighbor we hardly knew barged in, saying at the top of his voice in Yiddish, *"He is dead! He is dead!* This horrible man! He should have died a long time ago!"

I thought he was a madman. "Who are you talking about?" I asked.

"That rotten Roosevelt!" he replied, telling me that F.D.R. had dropped dead from a stroke in Georgia.

In my grief and horror, I started to scream, "My mother is dead! Roosevelt is dead! And get this man out of here or he'll be dead, too! I'll murder him!"

In those days I loved Roosevelt. Years later, though, I read how Roosevelt and Cordell Hull had, just before the war, kept a ship full of Jewish refugees from landing its human cargo on our shores, and sent them back to Europe and death. All he had to do was lift his pen, but only Eleanor Roosevelt fought for our people at the time.

My father outlived my mother by seventeen years. He died in 1962, just six months before his ninetieth birthday. Over those years of widowerhood, he seemed to grow as a man at least as fast as I was growing in my profession. We were both proud of each other.

When he was eighty years old, we gave him a family party. This was a sad occasion for my wife and me, as we had just learned the day before that he was sick with prostate cancer. Dr. Louis Soffer said, "You don't operate on a man eighty years old because it would kill him. But don't be too upset; he'll have no pain." Seeing that this was very little immediate consolation to me, the doctor went on: "Let me ask you a question. Your father is eighty years old. What would you, as a religious man, pray for? How long would you ask the Lord to let your father live, knowing he can't live forever?"

I said, "If my father lived another ten years, I would consider that a great, great gift."

"Well, what if I told you that in his case, if the Lord wills it and we watch him and give him the proper attention, he may even live to be ninety?"

"You're just trying to comfort me."

"No," he said, "I'm talking to you as friend to friend and man to man." And he was 95 percent right. My father lived nine and a half more years.

At his eightieth birthday party, only Alice, my brother, Mac, and I knew. One of the others complained later, "Why didn't you tell me?"

"What good would it have done?" I said.

"I would have had a chance to—"

"To what?" I said. "You didn't do anything to hurt him, anything to offend him. You just would have cried at the party."

My son, Larry, brought a wire recorder to the party and decided everybody should make a little speech. I, as the oldest child, went first. I knew how I felt, but I had to say something too. So without thinking about it, I simply said what came to mind:

"First of all, I want to thank the Lord for giving you eighty good years. With all your ups and downs, you've had a good life and you're having a good life. But more than anyone else, I want to thank you for being the man you are, so I could love you even if you were somebody else's father."

Everybody applauded, except my father. He didn't get it. He just shook his head sadly. Other people spoke. I thought my little speech was forgotten by the one person to whom I wanted it to matter.

A couple of days later, Larry sent him the recording. This gave my father a chance to listen over and over and analyze it in his Talmudic way. It was only then that he truly understood what his son had said about him. He called me up and asked, "Do you really think I'm that kind of a man?"

I said, "Yes. I love you not because the Bible says I have to love you, but because I regard you and respect you as a great man who happens to be my father: not just a great man, but a good man."

I love to say kind things about people when they can hear them, just as I love to send flowers to people while they can still smell them. Sometimes the people who say the nicest words at funerals are the ones who didn't return the dead man's calls.

One of my fondest memories of my father in his years as a widower will show you what a distinguished-looking man he was. As you must know, press agents and public relations men often concoct stories and statistics to get their clients' names into the gossip columns. I've seen nonsense about people breaking records when the truth was they were dying at the box office. One of the nicest and most receptive columnists was Leonard Lyons, now retired, whose "Lyons Den" column in the *Post* was a New York institution for forty years. Once, though, Maurice Feldman, my friend and press agent, gave Lyons a story about my father and me that Lyons was convinced Feldman had concocted. He wouldn't run it. But I was there and I *know* it happened to us. So here is a real Leonard Lyons column (written by Feldman) you never saw in Leonard Lyons's column!

> Jan Peerce invited his elderly father to watch him rehearse for the Workmen's Circle 50th anniversary gala at Madison Square Garden. Upon arrival at the 49th Street stage door, where they were to meet, the father wasn't there and Peerce himself had great difficulty getting past a belligerent stage doorman, who refused to admit anybody without a ticket or a badge—not even the headliner.
>
> Committeemen and management intervened on Peerce's behalf, but by this time he was ten minutes late and worried that his father, showing up without any credentials or acquaintances, would be similarly abused. When Peerce went upstairs to the auditorium, however, there was Papa Perelmuth sitting in the first row watching the orchestra rehearse. "Papa!" Peerce exclaimed. "I thought I told you to meet me downstairs."
>
> "I waited for you a couple of minutes, Pinyele," his father told him, "and when you didn't come, I went over to that nice doorman, and when he asked me who I was, I told him I was Jan Peerce's father, and he let me in."

For the first twelve years, parents worry whether their children are going to shame them. For the rest of their lives, the *children* fear that their parents will shame *them*. My father used to love to hold forth about the Torah —not just at home or in his own synagogue, but among the great and important rabbis he knew. I was worried he might embarrass himself and me by choosing the wrong subject or saying the wrong thing. Once I shared this anxiety with Rabbi Moshe Feinstein, one of the deans of Orthodox Judaism in the world. Rabbi Feinstein put my mind at rest: "Jan, don't you worry about your father. He has nothing to be ashamed of and neither have you. Your father is a learned man. Be proud of your father and let him hold forth."

Grandma's Legacy

Larry Peerce: *Even before she died, we inherited from my grandmother the black porter of her Lower East Side catering establishment, a fellow called Ruby. His real name was Grover Hall, but Grandma could never say "Grover" so she called him "Ruby." He called himself "Ruby the Butler."*

Ruby was extraordinarily bright. He was the black sheep of a family of ministers and Harvard graduates. He spoke Yiddish and looked like Uncle Ben on a box of rice. But the most remarkable thing about Ruby was the quantity of booze he absorbed.

My folks regarded Ruby as a legacy and they would never go against Grandma Perelmuth's wishes. When it was time for my bar mitzvah, my grandmother was too sick to go to synagogue and a reception, so we held my bar mitzvah and the celebration right in the house in New Rochelle. This was in wartime, when good liquor was so scarce that for every bottle of Scotch you bought, you had to take seven bottles of rum, too. My folks had been laying in the liquor for weeks. The morning of my bar mitzvah, Mom went down to the cellar to check the supplies. She discovered to her shock that Ruby had drunk almost everything—Scotch, rum, champagne, wine. There was panic, but my folks finally found a relative in the business who brought over enough to make it a festive occasion.

In a funny way, Ruby was a blessing for us kids. He was the first black servant we had who didn't call me "Mister Larry" as if he were auditioning for Gone with the Wind. *I was always wary of that. Ruby was a wonderful storyteller, a baseball nut, and the children's link with the real world.*

What I'm getting at when I say this is that it's very bizarre to know you've been raised by people like my parents. In a funny way, it's almost like being a Kennedy. You feel awfully special. Above and beyond all else, the strangest part of being this man's child was the revelation that came to me very young, and that I kept to myself —that I was the son of the King of the Jews of the United States of America!

I remember being dizzy in synagogue one Yom Kippur from no water all day and saying, "I've gotta go to the bathroom." And just as if he knew, he turned to me and said, "Not one sip of water, do you hear me?" This was before closed-circuit television, but I was sure he was watching me in that john.

I broke away from active religion when I was fifteen and he never pushed at me about it. I've never really understood his faith, but I've known and sensed that it was very important to his survival as an artist and as a human being. His faith and his voice are the most genuine things about him.

Susan Peerce: *A man like Ruby around the house became my father. Ruby was a very stabilizing person. If I had an argument with one of my parents, Ruby would* *say, "Don't be so upset, Sue. They mean well." I'd say, "But I'm so mad, Ruby!" and he'd say, "Don't be." He was always like that.*

Believe it or not, Ruby had a girlfriend named Topsy. He was still living at home with us and I was very little when I had a traumatic experience. One morning I wandered into Ruby's room and then ran to my parents and woke them up with: "Somebody's in Ruby's room with him and it looks like Topsy." My mother said to stay with my father while she went and looked. I heard a lot of commotion near the back stairs and I thought I heard a car in the driveway, but then my mother came back and said, "You must have been dreaming, Sue. Look, there's no one in Ruby's room but Ruby." I went and looked and she was right!

The Golden Boy

If I was Edward Johnson's fair-haired boy at the Met, Giuseppe di Stefano was everybody's golden boy: particularly at the Hurok office in the late 1940s. This boy, seventeen years my junior, had a beautiful voice. I don't know whether Hurok ever asked di Stefano if he wanted a fast or a slow career, but the answer seemed to be "a quick killing." Rolling in money and glory, he had no use for any advice anyone tried to give or tried to share. One day he interrupted me to say, "But I can't be like you. I'm not like you."

I said, "Why would you ever want to be like me?"

"I couldn't be. You're too old-fashioned, too serious. You're always studying, rehearsing, looking to improve. Me, I just go out there and do it right—just like that!" he concluded with a snap of his fingers.

I took his "criticism" in my stride, saying, "You know something, Giuseppe? You don't have to emulate *me*, but if I were you, I would look at anyone who's serious and try to follow his example."

"And if I don't?"

The words just jumped out of my mouth. I bit my tongue hard as soon as I'd said them: "Then you'll wind up in the gutter."

We were sitting in a room with six people at the Hurok office. When I said it, I could have died. In the room, one could hear a chorus of bated breath and communal sigh. We all tried to go on with the meeting, but after a few minutes Giuseppe excused himself. When he was out the door, the whole group turned on me, asking how I could have done such a thing.

"I'm very sorry. I'm a bastard," I said. "I shouldn't have said it, even when he asked for it. But now that I've said I'm sorry, I want to tell you guys something. You all know that what I said was true. Unless some one of you brings him into line, what I predicted is just what's going to happen to him."

I've always regretted having made that prophecy aloud. Even more, I've regretted that nobody managed to get the message across to him. He was and is an intelligent man. A lot of singers have egos that would have blotted out my remark. Not di Stefano. We are friends today and he still remembers it ruefully. But he continued to do things his way.

He thought he could sing everything. He never directed his talent. He never said, "This I can do, this I can't do." He sang every opera under the sun. He sang *Otello* in Pasadena. He sang everything everywhere. If you drive a car, it doesn't mean you can drive a taxi, let alone a big Mack truck. It's a smart man who can drive his own car properly and the same is true of singers. You can challenge yourself and broaden yourself, but if you go too far beyond your natural capacity, then you may be in trouble. You have to stay where you can still feel comfortable enough to make it right by working at it, not by forcing it.

Giuseppe di Stefano had a big following. At one period he'd been living in Westchester and the Hurok office had booked him into Carnegie Hall. But on the day of his sold-out concert, he canceled—and left the country the next morning for Italy. His career was in a shambles.

A few months later, I was making a recording in Vienna when di Stefano rang me up. He and Alice and I had lunch together. He was unhappy, bemoaning the fact that he had ignored friends' advice.

"Don't go on like that," I said. But he told me something that made me feel worse than ever:

"You know, Jan, the night before that concert I canceled, I watched you on the Johnny Carson show. You were on TV at midnight and you were singing the aria from *Pagliacci* and you sounded gorgeous and as fresh as a daisy—"

I tried to head off what was coming: "Thanks, but the program was prerecorded. I did my singing at six-thirty that night and I wouldn't have sounded as good at midnight."

"Doesn't matter when you sang it," Giuseppe said. "It was a beautiful performance. It was on my program and I suddenly realized I could never sing it that well."

By the end of the meal, all three of us were sobbing into our Sacher torte. I felt miserable for what had happened to my friend. Giuseppe was one of the finest tenors of his time or any other. He's still performing and has a large and faithful following.

Some singers have wonderful excuses for awful performances. A baritone I know once explained away a bad job in Vienna by saying he'd had trouble parking his car before the performance and he'd worried throughout the evening whether it would be stolen—in Vienna yet! So I said, "Next time take a cab."

"You're right," he said. "The trouble tonight was that my car was five blocks away."

But the trouble wasn't where his car was; it was where his voice wasn't.

Finding the Handel

What a wonderful thing is improvisation! When I make a mistake and use a wrong lyric, I keep going with the melody, without a break or stop, until it is virtually indiscernible that I made a mistake.

This happened once in Vancouver. I was singing Handel's "Waft Her, Angels," from the oratorio *Jeptha,* when I had a total lapse of memory. It lasted two seconds, which can feel like two hours. But I kept going with the names of a few of my friends that fit the music, and hoped nobody noticed. What if Handel's Messiah had heard?

After the concert, people came backstage to congratulate me or get my autograph. One unobtrusive, rather dapper little fellow waited and waited, however, until everyone was gone. At this point, I said to him, "Excuse me, sir, is there anything I can do for you?"

"Yes," he said. "First I would like to greet you and say what a beautiful concert you gave. . . . Then I have a question to ask you, which I hope you won't mind. You changed the lyric in your second number tonight, 'Waft Her, Angels.' Now, did you change it because you didn't like the original, or was there some other reason?"

"I cannot tell a lie," I replied, "at least not to someone who sat through a concert listening so closely to all kinds of music I sang and who still remembers something that happened two hours ago. To be honest, I had a lapse in memory."

"Ohhh!" he exclaimed. "I'm so relieved. I know Handel very well and I didn't know whether to be shocked or just surprised when you sang those strange words!"

We laughed about it then and we laugh about it now, for every time I go to Vancouver, the same man attends my concert and comes back afterward. Each time, he tells me I haven't made a single mistake with my Handel and I say, "Not in Vancouver anyway, because I know you're there to keep me on my toes." I don't know his name or what else he does, but I always greet him with a hearty "Hello, Mr. Handel!" Back in 1966, when Mayor

John V. Lindsay awarded me New York City's highest cultural award, the Handel Medallion, and I received a wire from Vancouver saying "BRAVO" and signed "HANDEL," I knew who it was from.

Alice vs. the Shrink

The longer I sang, the more I had to fight going stale and falling into certain isms: mannerism, good-enoughism, looking-backism. I would be in big trouble if I didn't have somebody around to tap me on the shoulder and say, "Hey! Be careful. You're living off the past instead of building your future." For two years, this is what happened to me—and I was in the worst trouble of my singing career. Fortunately, though, I have Alice.

In the late 1940s and early 1950s, she would come into my dressing room after a performance. Everybody else would be milling around, complimenting me. Alice would say nothing until we were in the car and she was driving me home. There, she didn't have to look me in the eye and see the hurt she was inflicting upon me. In fact, we generally did our fighting in the car—it was our closed-off capsule, our wrestling arena, where we could thrash it out without the kids or anybody else for an audience. Living with a strong, famous man and a strong woman was a chore in itself for our kids without making the home a battlefield, too. Besides, I think Alice felt she retained a certain element of control of the situation by being behind the wheel.

"I hope you don't mind my telling you," she'd begin, "but you're not singing well."

"What're you talking about?" I'd say.

"It's not good," she'd say.

"Everybody tells me I was great. Only *you* tell me I stink."

"Jan, I only know one thing. If I'm in the tenth or twelfth row, I don't hear you. And I know you have a voice that could blow a building apart. What're you saving it for? The senior prom?"

"How is it possible that everybody thought it was good—and I also felt it went well—but you sit here giving me a lecture on how bad I am?"

"How bad *it is,* Jan," she'd correct primly, like a diction teacher, which would only infuriate me more.

We had many such arguments. I remember one particularly terrible one. The minute after we drove away from the Met, she started offering her opinion: "Your projection was bad. Your intonation has been better. Your phrasing wasn't what it could be or should be. Your intensity tonight wasn't what it was a year ago. . . ."

Only the fact that she was driving kept me from hitting her on the head in traffic and killing us both. Instead I just yelled and screamed and called her names.

She pulled up opposite the Plaza Hotel and stopped the car. "If I'm what you say I am, I wouldn't be telling you anything," she pointed out. "If you're so annoyed at what I *am* telling you, why don't you just take the car and drive home alone?"

"You know damn well I can't drive," I said. "Is this your idea of a fair choice? Don't be so sure of yourself. I can pay some taxi driver to take me home."

I didn't budge, however, and she began to cry. I sat rigid until she stopped crying, and we didn't speak a word all the way home.

Alice Peerce: *Jan once threw a chair about this—and I almost deserved it. I came into his dressing room at the Met between acts of a performance. Mike De Pace was there. Jan said to me, "Well?"*

I said, "Jan, I can't hear *you."*

"What do you mean, you can't hear me?" he yelled.

"You're not projecting. I can't hear you."

In its dressing rooms the Met had those old ice cream parlor chairs made of wood. One of them went flying through the air. It didn't come anywhere near me, but he had every right to bust my head. That wasn't a propitious moment to tell the truth. I should have waited for that capsule period in the car.

Everyone else around him was flattering Jan until I began to wonder whether I was crazy. Nobody knew what I was thinking except Jan and Mike De Pace, who told me I shouldn't worry. Then one day, my kid brother Walter, who'd had a box at the Met ever since the year after Jan's debut, said to me out of the blue: "Alice, do you think I'm going deaf? Or is it the acoustics?"

I burst into tears and then I poured my heart out to Walter. He was a great consolation. He warned me against humiliating Jan in front of people or even in private. I used to rehearse with my brother what I was going to say to Jan. "I don't know how I'm going to begin," I'd say, "but I've got to, I've got to." I had to work up a will of steel to be strong enough to say to a man the world recognized as a great singer that he was falling apart. It was particularly hard because I was married to him.

Around that time, I had to have an operation. My sister, Maye, drove me to the hospital on Rosh Hashonah. After the operation I was still quite drugged, but even so, I couldn't help noticing how Jan kept popping in and popping out. Instead of staying by my bed, he would stay for an hour and disappear. He seemed very distracted. Something was wrong. I thought he might be angry at me for criticizing his singing and I was almost glad to be unable to attend his performances for a while. When I'd ask where he was going, he would mumble something about "going to see Roberta." He was preparing to do Don Giovanni *for the first time.*

I came home from the hospital. My father died ten days later and I couldn't pay much attention to what was going on with Jan. But when I'd recovered sufficiently to drive him into town, he'd say, "Y'know, I think I'll go in by train today." I began to feel pretty sure he was mad at me and wondered whether he was seeing another woman.

Then one day when I was almost fully recovered and Jan was down in bed fighting a cold—with the vaporizer going and the hot tea running and everything else being done to make a performance possible that night—the phone rang. I picked up my extension at the same moment Jan picked up his. I heard a man's voice say, "I don't think you should do the performance tonight."

Ordinarily, I hang up right away if the call's not for me. This time, however, I listened. I heard Jan say, "All right, I'll cancel."

Hearing this, I ran up the stairs to ask, "Who is that?"

Jan hung up the phone fast and said, "Nobody."

"Don't tell me it's Nobody!" I cried. "Did Nobody tell you to cancel tonight? You're listening to Mr. Nobody and you're not listening to me!"

I hadn't expected my rival to be a man. And the more I let his voice echo in my mind, the more I suspected who Mr. Nobody was: Bill Herman, the mentor of Patrice Munsel and Roberta Peters, for whom he may have been just fine, but I didn't think he was the best for Jan. Jan was concerned about doing his first Mozart at the Met. He felt he couldn't diminish his voice from forte *to* piano *as easily as he thought he should. Today you can hear him do it at a concert with no effort at all. Back then, however, instead of developing Jan's voice for Mozart, Herman's method was somehow thinning it for everything.*

Singers are insecure. They block off their abilities with their insecurities. When I saw this happening to Jan, I became a wild animal about it.

Singers aren't equipped to hear how they're projecting, so they have to depend on others. My argument to Jan went: "When you had none of these teachers, you were producing the most magnificent, exciting tones. Why should it stop now?"

The horrible thing was that there had been almost nothing wrong with Jan vocally before he went to Herman. By nature, he was a saver. He wouldn't expend his voice all at one time. Me, I thought all along that the voice was a muscle, and the more you exercised it, the stronger it grew. Jan has come around to this view, too.

At the time, though, Herman picked up Jan's insecurity about spending his voice and made him into a miser who couldn't be heard beyond the tenth row. Have you ever heard a Joseph Schmidt recording? Absolutely beautiful voice! But in a large auditorium, Schmidt's voice didn't project terribly well. Nonprojection may have been Joseph Schmidt's misfortune, but I didn't want it to be Jan's.

I carried on like a betrayed wife. Now I knew why Jan never went with me in the car. He wanted to get off the train at 125th Street and Park Avenue because Herman's place was in the East Nineties. If he had driven in with me, I would have taken him down to West Fifty-sixth Street, where our garage was. For Jan, this would have meant going downtown and then backtracking. I might even find out where he was going. After my attitude toward Tibbett's "voice rebuilder," Zitomirsky, Jan could guess how I would feel about Herman. I called Herman "the shrink."

I told Jan he would have to choose between Herman and me. Now, you may wonder how I could carry on like that after more than twenty years of marriage. I believe that after a certain point, a singer can still go for coaching or expression or histrionics or learning how a part he's studied should be projected, but vocally, Jan knew what to do. Here Herman had taken a voice like Jan's, which had its own natural placement—something many other singers would envy—and now Mother Nature was being undone.

"I'm no voice teacher," I'd say to Jan, "but I know when you're hitting it right and I know when you're hitting it wrong. I can't tell you how to do it, but I know what my own ears hear."

My children were taking piano lessons from a man who also taught Jascha Heifetz's children. One day I said to this teacher, "Tell me. You go to the Heifetz house. Does Heifetz still take music lessons?"

"Mrs. Peerce! What are you talking about?"

"Does Heifetz go to a teacher who tells him how to do the scales?"

"Of course not!" He was so shocked he didn't know what I was getting at.

I said, "Would you believe that this is what my husband does?"

When Jan wouldn't listen, I used my brother Walter and his wife, Selma, as my sounding board.

"How do you know he's bad for Jan?" Walter asked.

"I know because the quality of Jan's singing has changed," I insisted.

It was a terrible position for a singer to be in. Jan, in all honesty, wouldn't accept my judgment. Instinctively he ran to his teacher. And then Jan came back to me, looking more benign and conciliatory than I'd seen him in a long time. "You must make a concession," he said. "You must come and watch a lesson with Bill Herman and you must listen as objectively as you can."

I accepted the invitation. Herman was a small, light, very elegant-looking man. His town house was furnished beautifully: Oriental rugs, antique chairs, sarcophagi carved in wood—a regular museum. He sat me down in a chair that was like a throne. And he told me to listen.

In that setting, at his mercy, I listened.

When it was over, Jan said, "Well?"

This time I knew to say nothing. Herman showed me the Oriental hangings behind the piano. We chatted about everything but Jan's singing. But he was civil and so was I.

After we'd said goodbye and Jan and I were back in the car, Jan said again, "Well?"

"Do you want to have a fight now or when we get home?" I asked.

"Might as well have it now," he said.

"He's ruining you," I said. "I don't like what he's doing with you—it's not helping you at all."

We had a big blowup even before we were out of Manhattan. Jan said he might "consider" giving up Herman, but I insisted on an absolute yes or no.

By then other people were mentioning to me, but not to him, that something seemed to be happening to Jan's voice. The same people would then come backstage and congratulate Jan while sneaking a wink at me.

One day, though, Olga Troughton, an associate of Mike De Pace, said to me, "Alice, it's terrible. Everybody's talking about how Jan can't be heard."

"Olga," I said, "would you come back and say the same thing to Jan?"

"I couldn't," she said, "but I will tell him what Bill Herman is saying. . . . He's standing in the back of the Met when Jan's singing and telling everybody in earshot: 'Poor Peerce! He's not projecting. He's not singing well. But now that he's studying with me, I'm sure it will improve!' "

When Jan heard this it was the beginning of the end for him and Herman. Poor guy! He talked himself out of a good thing with Jan—and that was a good thing for Jan.

Alice was a nervy little bitch. She had to be—to reach me, to face up to me, to tell me what some manager might say to her that he wouldn't say to me. She was the go-between, the buffer. While the others were patting me on the back, telling me I was the greatest, she had to be the one to say, "Jan, remember, if you go on singing like this much longer, there won't be anyone around to pat you on the back."

After a while, I had to take stock of myself. Here I had a woman whom I loved so dearly. I knew that she loved me. We were sharing a life together, one of understanding and mostly peaceful coexistence. I knew that nobody rooted harder for me or helped me more. Why, then, must she harp consistently on my inadequacies and what people were saying behind my back? Eventually the answer began to dawn on me. It must be serious. It must be so!

This happens every now and then in life. By instinct or innermost feeling, you divide the good from the bad, the men from the boys, the honest from the dishonest—until one day you are convinced there must be something to it. Alice certainly had nothing to gain from saying my voice wasn't as good as it should be, or by starting ferocious arguments, if it weren't so.

Weede and Lorber to the Rescue

If someone asked you how to walk, and you tried to explain the process, the first question might well be: "Which leg do you put out—the left or the right?" You might say, "The left." "Well, when you put out your left foot, what do you do with your right arm? Is it in front or behind?" Before you know it, you'll be so tied up in the theory of walking that you'll have trouble walking straight.

Walking should be automatic. Once you're a year or two of age, you just stand up and you walk. Singing technique should be even more automatic. A baby who cries in her crib doesn't have to learn about projection; she knows how to make herself heard in the next room. By the time she's ready to study singing, no matter how early she starts, her vocal technique has begun to wander. The whole essence of teaching is to bring the voice back to where nature wants it.

Until that time of trouble with my voice, I never overprotected it, but just sang automatically and quite properly. All theory of singing is much that way. To make you do what Mother Nature dictates, however, to show you how to do it—that's the hardest part. The rest must be the teacher's honesty and his ear for detection: to know what the singer is doing wrong.

My old Radio City Music Hall and Columbia Opera chum Robert Weede had begun teaching privately. Mario Lanza was one of his pupils and used his apartment in New York when Bob was away. In my vocal crisis Alice eventually suggested I go to Bob. "I think the basics that Bob uses to produce his sound are what you need now."

I rang Bob's number in Manhattan. "I think you can help me with a problem I'm having," I said.

"With pleasure," he said. "Come right down."

A few sessions with Bob convinced him and me that my instincts were still good. The voice didn't have far to come back because it was never out of my body.

After Bob Weede had helped put me back on the right track, he had to go on a tour, but he felt I needed someone to redevelop good habits in me. Both Bob and Alice agreed upon Alexander Lorber. Alice said, "Alex Lorber was born with a special something. He is a gifted teacher and knows just about everything about the voice."

I had met Alex in the early 1930s, when he had just come over from Hungary. He had a lovely singing voice, but was not as aggressive as an artist needs to be. He loved to sing. When he sang, he worked hard and did everything right. If that were all it took, his would be a famous name today.

Having a career, however, meant that you had to knock on doors, knock yourself out, and absorb many hard knocks. You had to charm flesh peddlers and managerial monsters who claimed that G-d had given them the right to decide who would have a career and who wouldn't. They could make you or break you. To face that kind of effrontery, to be insulted several times a day, to keep from becoming hopelessly discouraged, you had to be as brazen as they were. Alex Lorber wasn't. I hate to say it, but I guess I was.

Alice Peerce: *Jan was always aggressive with me and the people he's close to, but not with the world. That's what makes him such a nice personality to the public. His public humility helped make him what he is. He's genuinely interested in other people and he sees them as individuals, not just as the public.*

Don Ottavio Is a Don, Too

I don't mind telling you that my role in *Don Giovanni* was the one that scared me the most. I did not feel equipped to handle Mozart, which was what brought me under Bill Herman's influence in the late 1940s. As a younger man, I had sung the tenor role of Don Ottavio on *Radio City Music Hall of the Air,* but I hadn't been satisfied with either my singing or the role itself. Only in the 1950s, as I neared fifty myself, did I begin to mature in the part.

Don Ottavio is the guy who never gets the girl. He's in love with Donna Anna; he gets very near to her; they sing their duet, he's moving even closer to her; she's about to say yes—but then she puts her hand up and says, "Wait! Hold off!" Another stage wait comes for him and for the rest of the opera he never quite gets the girl.

I don't play Don Ottavio the way many others play him. Some see him as a gutless Milquetoast. But Don Ottavio is as much of a don as Don Giovanni. True, Don Giovanni is bolder, more daring—going after all the women and getting them even if he has to rape them. But Don Ottavio is a nobleman, too, full of vim and vigor. Right at the beginning, he hears a noise and comes rushing out. Donna Anna tells him how she was attacked and her father killed. He swears vengeance. Milquetoasts don't go around swearing vengeance. He'll avenge Donna Anna's loss and he vows it with force and intensity: "Lo giuro."

In opera, as I've said before, a tenor can get away with murder. You can throw a sword when you feel a piece of phlegm coming on. You can kick up your heels and stamp your foot. You can drag certain light-weight sopranos halfway across the stage to show jealousy or disgust. You can use any kind of emotional outburst to make it look real. But in *Rigoletto*, no facade in the world will help the tenor with "Ella mi fu rapita." He must just stand and sing, because Verdi said: In this moment, I want him to sing.

Don Ottavio in *Don Giovanni* is that way throughout. It's an artistic singing role with two outstanding numbers that you'd better know how to sing right: "Dalla sua pace" and "Il mio tesoro." Both were conceived by Mozart as virtuoso displays of *bel canto*. The emotion in them is involved in the singing of what Mozart has written in his most beautiful form. Those two arias call for the most fluid *legato*. The tenor must show off his breath control, support, flexibility, and prowess in singing a scale of utter clarity without any slurring. The voice more than ever becomes an instrument and the tenor must sing each note the way a good fiddle or flute would play it. I had to work on Don Ottavio for many years before I felt it was *my* role.

For my Met debut as Don Ottavio on February 3, 1950, my Donna Anna was the Bulgarian bombshell, Ljuba Welitsch, at the peak of her brief glory. Welitsch was gorgeous to look at and a very nice girl, too—to men, that is; she was very bitchy to her female colleagues.

Such was her schedule that she could spare only one day to rehearse at the Met for the very meticulous Fritz Reiner, who had the rest of us rehearsing for six weeks with no soprano. Finally, two days before the performance, this very busy lady flew in from Europe. There were two general rehearsals. She missed the first one. Before the second, Reiner called an extra morning rehearsal so that the rest of us—Paul Schoeffler and Salvatore Baccaloni and Regina Resnik and myself—could get together with Welitsch and she could get together with the opera.

Regina and Schoeffler and I began to sing the way we'd been taught, corrected, drilled, and rehearsed by Reiner. Welitsch, however, sang Mozart *her* way. Hers was an entirely different conception from Reiner's. She never cared to get her voice down soft enough for the first-act quartet. Instead she sang the music with full throat. I'm not criticizing—she did it very well and this was what everyone was coming to hear—but it wasn't our way and it certainly wasn't what Reiner had been teaching us. Reiner, however, didn't have a harsh word to say to her.

At intermission, Regina Resnik said to Reiner, "Fritzl, this is what you rehearsed us for five or six weeks? For this you filed us down to our finest edge and now you let the lady come and do whatever she wants?''

Reiner answered very truthfully: "If you want to have a performance of *Don Giovanni* tomorrow night, you have to let the lady do what she does." He was perturbed and annoyed, but she was the prima donna and he knew the score—musically and realistically.

Still, the anger Reiner suppressed had to come out somewhere. On the night of the performance, it came out at me.

In the second act, Welitsch sang "Or sai chi l'onore," a big aria for which her management had hired an even bigger claque. The tenor comes on next. I waited in the wings with Herbert Graf, the director, until the applause began to die down. Graf told me to get ready to go on. The signal for my entrance was a chord from the harpsichord in the pit, which Reiner was playing himself.

The chord sounded. I stepped out onstage. But the claque got its second wind and new shouts of "Brava, Ljuba!" filled the air. Graf grabbed my hand and dragged me back, leaving Reiner with a lost chord. He had played his chord and received no answer—just Welitsch taking her umpteenth bow. When Graf sent me out again, I glanced down toward the pit. I could see fire pouring out of Reiner's nostrils and hear him snorting like a dragon. Worst of all, his glasses were down at the tip of his nose, a sure sign he was sore at someone.

I checked all my buttons and took stock of my voice while I sang "Dalla sua pace" and I knew I was doing okay. So I figured Reiner was mad at Welitsch or her claque or possibly at Graf, although the director had done right to yank me back. I finished my aria, drew a big hand, let the opera work into the finale of the act, took a few curtain calls with Welitsch and the others, and headed upstairs.

Reiner's dressing room was right opposite mine. As I reached the top of the stairs, this great maestro snorted at me, "Peerce! *Komm hier!*"

In Reiner's room were a number of people I knew. Mae Frohman and Walter Prude of the Hurok office, and Martin Feinstein, the publicity man. I was glad to see friends there, because with Reiner on that night, I knew I was not at the mercy of a friend. "How dare you?" Reiner began. "How dare you?"

"Dare what?" I said. Mae Frohman flashed me a signal to hold my tongue, but I was genuinely perplexed. "What's the matter, Maestro?"

"Don't you realize you insulted me? You offended me. And before an audience!" He was doing quite a job on *me* before an audience, but I let him rage on. "Don't you have any respect? If you ever dare to do such a thing again, I'll—I'll— In all my years of experience, *nobody—*"

"What are you talking about, Maestro?"

"You heard my chord—you stepped out—your business was to start singing no matter what!"

"Now wait a minute, Maestro. The claque was working and Welitsch took another bow and Graf pulled me back and I gotta take orders—"

"That's the trouble with you! You take orders from anybody! But around here, you'll take orders only from me! I am the boss! I am the man who gives the orders." Fritzl was waxing more autocratic than usual.

"But the director onstage pulled me back physically," was all I could say and all I should have needed to say.

"He is under me!" Reiner insisted, going right back to yelling at me and going on and on about it. I had to get dressed for the second act, so I looked at my watch and when I decided I had just enough time to do my job, I used a little Perelmuth psychology from the Lower East Side and my Charley the Stableman days. When you keep quiet for a long time and *then* yell back at someone who's yelling at you, he either kills you on the spot or shuts up. So when I caught Reiner between breaths, I bellowed, *"Are you through?"*

He stopped dead. There was a very long second or two of silence. Then he said meekly, "Yes."

So I said, *"Excuse me!"* and went to my dressing room.

I didn't talk to Fritz Reiner for almost a year. We would work together from time to time, but I had nothing to say to him, just "Yes, sir." He and his wife, Carlotta, started inviting me to their home. I would decline curtly.

Finally Hurok and Mae Frohman started working on me. "Reiner loves you," she said. "And I was there, but after all, what did he do?"

"Look!" I said. "I don't have to take any guff from him. He's a great conductor, but there was no reason for him to insult me—let alone in front of a roomful of people. Why didn't he go and insult Graf? Why does he have to tell *me* how important he is?"

I took her and Hurok's advice, however, and accepted the Reiners' next invitation. Everything was fine and affable after that, and we were great friends by 1951 when Reiner and Risë Stevens, Licia Albanese, Bob Merrill, and I made an outstanding recording of *Carmen* for RCA—an album of such impact that a lot of people remember "seeing" me in *Carmen,* even though I've never done it on the stage.

The Bach Aria Group

If I walked through the glories of the 1930s and 1940s with any chips on my shoulders, they were Bach and Mozart. About these two giants I had

complexes—feelings of inadequacy that drove me to voice teachers, to bully-
ing strangers, and even to changing some of Bach's Lutheran lyrics because
they accused my people wrongly.

One Sunday in the thirties after a *Radio City Music Hall of the Air* broadcast in which I'd sung some Mozart and Handel, Alice and I went to a party.
This was back in the days when nobody we knew drank much. It was just cake
or candy and coffee or tea and maybe you exchanged a few stories and left.
As I walked into this party, however, a woman jumped me with: "Ohhh, Mr.
Peerce, I heard you on the radio today and you were *mahhhvelous!* The way
you did Handel, with your gorgeous *legato* and phrasing, and the way you
did that Mozart aria—ohhh! Would I love to hear you sing more Mozart!
And some Bach!"

I turned on this poor woman. "You and your damn Mozart and Bach!
What do *you* know about anything? I'd rather sing anything Handel ever
wrote than the best Bach, the best Mozart." On and on I went, like Fritz
Reiner in his dressing room, until I had reduced the woman to tears and our
hosts were angry at *her* because she must have said something terrible to
offend me so.

On the way home, Alice started in on me:

"Why don't you attack a strong person? You always pick out the weakest
one in the room because you're afraid of the strong people. Why did you
attack this woman? Because she said she'd like to hear you sing more Mozart?
Well, you know and I know you didn't do 'Il mio tesoro' as well as you'd
have liked today. Maybe you're afraid you can't do justice to Mozart. And
what's wrong with singing Bach? You know why you went after her that
way? Because you're afraid you can't do it! You attacked her because she
stepped on your Achilles heel. Well, you better settle down and learn to sing
Bach."

Alice needled me into rising to the challenge. It took more than a
decade. But she's always had the best needle: the truth.

William Scheide's grandfather was running a refinery in Titusville,
Pennsylvania, in the nineteenth century when John D. Rockefeller, Sr.,
bought him out. William Scheide's father also retired early—to devote himself to the arts. William Scheide himself taught music at Cornell and then
settled in Princeton, where there's a family archive of artistic and musical
treasures. Finding that half of Bach's 650 cantata arias could be performed
by various combinations of five instruments and four voices, Scheide dedicated his life to bringing Bach to the public—properly done and within the
concertgoer's economic reach. Scheide's emphasis was on the original, natu-

ral form: no deletions, no changes, except that he uses a piano instead of a harpsichord. For his Bach Aria Group, founded in 1946, he eventually assembled the finest conglomeration of people imaginable: Eileen Farrell, a great soprano who became a good friend of ours; Carol Smith, a big, tall, lovely contralto; Norman Farrow, the bass; Julius Baker, flutist; Robert Bloom, oboist; Maurice Wilk, violinist, replaced after his death by Oscar Shumsky; Bernard Greenhouse, cellist; and Paul Ulanowsky, pianist.

It was a great group and he paid us not just with the opportunity to do justice to Bach in an ensemble, but with good annual salaries for three concerts in New York and two short tours. He financed all this, but he was no dilettante. He didn't want to sing or conduct or splash his name all over the place. Other people give money and endow scholarships and chairs and put their names on buildings and foundations and underwrite undertakings that will never mean a thing. Scheide, however, didn't just love Bach; he knew every word, every note—the whole Bach works. Sometimes he'd play at rehearsals if Ulanowsky came late. He was a lousy pianist, but he'd laugh at himself. If, however, I mispronounced a syllable or gave the wrong value to a note, he would correct me firmly. I learned how to handle him by shushing him right away, before he could get worked up at the affront to Bach. "Don't get upset," I'd say. "Just tell me what's wrong."

Then he'd reply, very sheepishly, "Well, I don't like your F sharp. Please do it this way."

When he first approached me, I told him Bach wasn't my métier. He insisted he knew better. When he couldn't interest *me*, he and Herbert Barrett, the group's manager, went and sold Alice on the idea. She negotiated a contract with him six months before I found out about it. Then I had to do it.

When the news was announced, there was a whole chorus of doubting Thomases, but I was the biggest doubter of them all. "What? Jan Peerce do Bach?" they said. "I'd like to hear *that!*" Which they did. And which they liked.

Up until then I had sung just one Bach number, "Bist du bei mir?" at my Town Hall debut in 1939. So I didn't know much about Bach. Scheide swore I could do it. He booked me for just one concert in 1951—in case he or I wanted to back out. Alice practically had to drag me there. My concert was a revelation—not just to the audience, but to me. When I felt I could master Bach, I knew I not only had something—I had more than I knew about. For even more than being Mozart's Don Ottavio, singing Bach in concert means standing and singing, not waving your arms or strutting around in high-heeled boots and cape. You just sing—and you'd better stay within the pattern and format of this great music. Bach wrote some terrible things for the tenor. The tuning pitch was much lower in his day than it is today. You don't sing like a castrato, but you sometimes sing as if you're fighting castration.

By the following season I was a full member of the group. That was the beginning of thirteen wonderful years: 1951 to 1964.

Of course, there have to be jealousies, particularly on the road, when you have a group of nine people. Eileen Farrell and I were the so-called headliners, because people knew our "names." Local managers sometimes gave the two of us bigger billing, which used to kill some of the others. In Bach, sometimes it's the oboe that has the star part and sets the pace. But Eileen and I brought in people who never would have been caught dead at a Bach concert. Some of them even clamored for "The Bluebird of Happiness" as an encore and were disappointed not to get it, but others came storming backstage (and back to future performances of the group) to thank us for discovering Bach for them.

Even with the billing, for thirteen years I managed to submerge myself into the group, which is an important asset, too. Onstage, I'd sit with my hands clasped and I'd walk off. Then I'd come back to sing a solo with the oboe or the flute or all the instruments or a duet with the soprano. In between, I'd sit and listen. I found it easy. Bach is the star. It was very good to know that I was not the kingpin, but part of a great musical ensemble.

Somehow, my warmest memories of the Bach Aria Group go back to our three European tours. I remember a side trip to Toledo, Spain, where we visited a synagogue that had been changed into a church, but where the Hebrew words were still carved into the molding. Seeing this, without a word to each other, Alice and I both began to cry.

"What're you crying about?" said Maurice Wilk, who was an athiest.

I said, "I can only think of all the Jewish blood that was spilled in this room—just because these people wanted to be Jewish and practice their religion without committing themselves to something else."

With the Bach Aria Group, I was introduced to the only queen I've ever met, Elizabeth of Belgium, a great music enthusiast who helped artists and festivals. She came to the Casals Festival in Prades, Southern France, in 1955. There we performed in a church with beautiful acoustics and atmosphere. Nobody applauded. Instead people rose in your honor after you finished a selection. Or there would be a shuffling of feet on the floor of the church to make you know you have thrilled their owners. Of course, if they shuffled their feet *during* the number, it meant something else.

The Queen of Belgium met us after a performance. In her very quiet

manner, she complimented my singing and asked if I missed my usual outburst of applause.

"No, Your Majesty," I told her. "On the contrary, I welcomed this
outburst of silence."

Pablo Casals was there, too, for this was before he moved his place of
exile and the Casals Festival to Puerto Rico. He was a great man: musically,
humanly, politically, and personally. If he wasn't performing with you, this
vibrant man would perch on a chair between the vestry room and the altar
to watch. As you walked off, he would jump to his feet, embrace you, and
kiss you on both cheeks to thank you for your efforts.

Running the Bach Aria Group cost Scheide a lot of money every year.
Every concert we did meant a loss to him. Even if he negotiated a top price
for the group, like $3,500 an evening, he had to pay our salaries. We all got
good ones: annual retainers plus fixed amounts for each performance. He
even added a pension plan. Eileen Farrell and I actually drew small pensions
when we left the group.

As I've said, I never minded submerging myself in the group—but
Hurok did. "John," he would say, "you are getting more than five thousand
dollars a concert. Now you go and do a concert with eight other people for
only $3,500. Tell me. Why should a manager buy just you or Eileen Farrell
when he can buy you in a whole group at discount?"

Hurok had a point. Scheide paid me well so that if ever a conflict of dates
arose, he had priority. Sometimes, on an open date during a Bach Aria Group
tour, Hurok would book me a solo concert engagement. At first Scheide used
to let me fly to do a date somewhere and then fly back to join the tour. Later,
though, he tightened up and forbade it—and he was right. He wanted me
there on the tour so we could all rehearse, rehearse, rehearse together. He
sought perfection and I was all for it, but eventually I figured it was Hurok's
turn. I was thinking about this when, in 1964 in Portugal with the Bach Aria
Group, I had a freak accident—and I took that as a sign it was time to go.

We were staying at the Ritz in Lisbon, one of the great hotels in the
world, with marvelous furnishings and great food. We'd all had a lovely
dinner the night before and we'd laughed a lot; whenever I think of the Bach
Aria Group, I don't hear only music, I hear laughter. I went to bed early,
vocalized the next morning, and joined the others just as they'd decided to
eat somewhere else in town.

I would have preferred to eat at the Ritz. Even without knowing the
other restaurant, I knew my luncheon egg would taste no better and probably
be worse there. But I went along with the group. The girls went in one taxi
and the boys in a couple of others. Julius Baker and I were delivered across

the street from the restaurant. On a round curb with an incline from the sidewalk to the gutter, I slipped and almost fell. Julie Baker grabbed me, saying, "Don't worry, Jan. I got you." He was a friend I would have trusted with my life. I tried my utmost not to fall. As a result, the weight of my body all shifted to the left side and, though I never fell, my left knee buckled under me and the pressure and weight of my body ripped out the tendon from the kneecap. It felt all right when I stood with my left foot stuck out, but when I straightened the foot, there was nothing underneath. "I'm in trouble," I said.

Alice came out of the restaurant and took me back to the hotel, where they found us a good young doctor who had done his residency in Houston. While he wasn't an orthopedic man, he diagnosed my case absolutely accurately as a torn tendon and placed a great premium on speed in repairing it. He started talking to me about going to the hospital. I figured he was referring to a cast, but when it turned out he was talking surgery, I said, "I don't want to have surgery here. I want to be with my family."

"But your wife can be with you," he assured me.

"I know," I said, "but to tell the truth—and I hope you don't mind—I come from America and I'd like to go back to America when I'm in trouble."

"And be with your own doctor," he said, laughing. "I understand. But you must move fast, because otherwise the veins and arteries atrophy and then, at the very least, they'll have to graft tissue from one leg to the other."

He put me in a temporary cast. The next morning we went by ambulance instead of limousine to the airport and by plane to New York, where another ambulance was waiting to take me to Mount Sinai Hospital for five hours of surgery once the doctors had quickly confirmed the Portuguese doctor's diagnosis. And that was how I made my break with the Bach Aria Group.

A Visit to Casals

I met Casals in Prades with the Bach Aria Group, and after he relocated to Puerto Rico, we did two concerts at the Casals Festival in San Juan.

After one of these performances, there was a party. Casals came with his very young wife, Marta, sixty years his junior. He was a very light eater. So was I. I helped myself to cottage cheese and fruit from the buffet. Casals glanced at my plate and said, "Peerce, do you always eat like thees after a concert? No steak? Your appetite should be voracious enough to eat a cow."

"No, Maestro," I said. "This is the food I like to eat."

"Ohhh! You will live long. You will live to a great old age."

Since Casals, of all people, was an expert on that, I asked, "How do you know that?"

"First of all," he replied, "you're an artist. You have a soul. You are blessed with a beautiful voice. You are a musician. You live in beauty—but not only that, you eat the way a human being should eat."

A man who lived to be ninety-six should be listened to. To the end, his memory was great. You never had to be reintroduced if he met you once. I've met diplomats who forgot your identity at a cocktail party they gave in your honor.

A year later, Alice and I were in San Juan on vacation with her brother Walter Kaye and his wife, Selma. Alice suggested I call up Casals to say hello.

"This is his rest period after the festival. He doesn't want to hear from people. He wants to be alone."

"This is *your* vacation," Alice pointed out. "Do *you* want to be alone? . . . Then why is he so different from you? He's human, too. I'm sure he'd love to hear from you and if he invites you, fine! If not, not. Don't make him feel obliged, but I think he'd be hurt if he found out you'd been here and didn't call him."

When I called, he exclaimed, "Juan! You are here in Puerto Rico? You *must* come to the house." It was a command, but I said I had to check our itinerary with my brother- and sister-in-law. "Breeng them! Breeng them! But come right away!"

Now, my brother-in-law Walter knows fairly little about music and he had never heard Casals play. But he was thrilled! Walter is a great human being whose life is a concert and whose heart is a symphony, so I didn't hesitate to bring him and Casals together. We took a taxi and Casals met us at the front door. He showed us around his house and garden, which, even in those exotic surroundings, were, like the man himself, simple rather than lush. We stayed two and a half hours, and as we finished our coffee, the moment came when I started to say goodbye. "Y'know, Maestro, we've taken up so much of your time that we must leave so you can get your rest. Thank you for a wonder—"

"No, no, no!" said Casals. "Just a minute! You have honored me by coming to my home. Now what can I do for you?"

"Nothing," I insisted. "Your friendship is my honor."

"No, no, no! That's not enough. Would you allow me to play something for you?"

"Would I *allow* you to play? Whenever you're in the mood to play, Maestro, that's the greatest thing that can happen to any creature with ears."

His wife brought out the cello. Sitting on a straight chair in his living room, he played some Bach with the greatest intensity—as though he were playing before the Queen of England and a full house at the Festival Hall.

When he was through, he dropped his bow arm, looked up at us, and said, "Thank you for honoring my home. And thank you for allowing me to play for you."

If that wasn't greatness and humility put together, you tell me what is.

To Israel with Love

In 1950, just the thought of visiting the Jewish homeland was a thrill. On the plane from New York to Paris to Tel Aviv, I said to Alice, "Can you imagine? Everybody in our audience, practically, will be Jewish. Just about everyone who will come to our concerts will be a Jew." I kept saying "Jew this" and "Jew that" so much that Alice remarked, "And you think that's so good? Maybe before this trip is over you'll be hoping you met one *goy.*"

Arriving and stepping off Air France onto terra firma Israel was a great emotional experience. I looked—and all around me were my people! Already, they lived like any other nation. You had to be checked in. Your passport had to be examined. You were asked, "Do you have anything to declare?" Only my thanks to G-d that our people had survived to see this!

The people ahead of us were Chasidic Jews. Three or four of them were caught by customs smuggling watch movements. The customs officers called the police, and while they waited, nobody else could be processed.

One of the smugglers said to the customs man who'd caught him, "How did you know?"

"You must not forget," said the customs man, "that our forefathers also stood at Mount Sinai." In other words: We thought as you did—and this time we outsmarted you.

The personnel manager of the Israel Philharmonic was waiting when we got through Customs and Immigration, and was I relieved to see him! After accepting his invitation to do eleven concerts in Israel, I had written asking for my itinerary: an artist likes to know where and when he's going to perform. No answer. I had cabled. No answer. Alice and I landed in Israel not knowing where my first or second or third concert was. So I was glad to be expected and met. As soon as he'd delivered us to our room at the Gat Rimon Hotel in Tel Aviv, however, I asked him, "Why didn't you answer my letter and cable?"

"Ach! We're such a busy people here in Israel."

"Well, I'm from New York and there are some pretty busy people there, too, but they answer questions."

"Well, you know how these things are."

I didn't. Still, I was willing to let it drop if he'd just answer my questions now. It was very hot in the room, so I walked out on the terrace to breathe a little hot air. He followed me out. "Where do I sing?"

He said four times here, three times there, twice here, once there, once there, once there. . . . I said, "That sounds like an awful lot. How many concerts does that amount to?" He said, "Seventeen."

"But my agreement with the orchestra was eleven," I pointed out.

"No, no," he said blandly. "Seventeen, Mr. Peerce."

"I beg your pardon, but it was eleven."

"Seventeen, eleven . . . Eleven, seventeen . . . What's the difference?"

I said, "Seventeen is fifty-something percent more than eleven."

He seemed surprised I could do arithmetic, but he wasn't going to let that change anything. "The figure was seventeen," he went on. "You artists don't have any head for numbers. It's amazing you even remember your music. You're just like all the other artists!"

Thus, in my first hour in the Holy Land of my people, did I become Commando Peerce. I grabbed the man by his lapels and said, "Nobody talks to me that way—in America *or* Israel! Just because a man is one of my own doesn't give him the right to insult me or any other artist. I didn't have to come all the way to Israel to hear this!"

"Don't be angry, Mr. Peerce," he whimpered.

"Please leave him alone, Jan," said a familiar voice. It was Isaac Joffe of the Hurok office, who had traveled with Marian Anderson to Europe and then come to visit a brother in Israel. "Jof" stepped in between us and took over the negotiations. I was still seething. "Tell this guy," I told him, "never to talk to me again."

I did the seventeen concerts because Hurok had impressed upon me the importance of "keeping the local manager happy, John." For the next three weeks, however, I didn't speak to the man. He pestered Alice with "My G-d! What did I say to your husband? I just said what I say to all artists." Alice started to educate him. When we had a week to go and she said he was showing progress, we made up.

After my earliest hours in Israel—first behind smugglers and then up against that manager—I confided to Alice, "You know something? You were right. I'm almost ready to go looking for a *goy.*"

In 1950 in Israel, they had nothing. It was austerity time. Even if you had money, there was nothing to buy with it. If you bought cake, no matter what the flavor, the ingredients were the same: ersatz.

I like sweets after I sing. Following rehearsals, we'd go to the Kapulski bakery in Tel Aviv and look into their dazzling window, like Tiffany's, with one little piece of cake on each doily on the glass shelves, arranged so you'd think you were looking at a gem. My mouth would water, even though I knew that what I'd be buying wasn't cake, but imitation. The white powder on top wasn't sugar; they had no sugar to spare. The eggs they used were not the best; they had no money to buy the best—and besides, eggs weren't available. If you had a million dollars in your pocket, you couldn't buy anything. To one armed with this knowledge, everything tasted okay.

On top of what they, of all people, had suffered in the Second World War, they suffered all these deprivations, but they fought against nature to develop Israel into the most productive nation of its kind, even under the most adverse circumstances. Today, when I'm anywhere in the world—say, Copenhagen—and I pick up an orange that says "Jaffa" on it, I'm thrilled, because I remember how, in 1950, the oranges they grew were terrible. They didn't yet have the know-how. Today their exported citrus fruit wins all kinds of prizes, makes a lot of money, and is the talk of the world.

It makes me think of a story I heard about a Czech journalist, now in Canada, who had been to Palestine right after the war, when the Jewish nation was threatening to be born. He sat in a lone oasis—a café on the very edge of the desert—and an elderly, well-to-do Arab came and sat down next to him. "Tell me," the Arab said, "what do you think will happen if the Zionists take over here?" The Czech, being a journalist, said, "I'm new here. You tell me." "All right," said the Arab. "Do you see this barren desert before us? In months or, at the most, years, it will flower, it will blossom, they will make it into a garden for the whole world—and everybody who is here, Jew or Arab, will prosper. And of course, *we cannot let this happen!*"

Out of that sand, the first part of that old Arab's prophecy was fulfilled. Long before the Six-Day War or the Yom Kippur War or strangulation by oil, I used to wonder: Why all this animosity? Why all this enmity? For when an Arab meets an Israeli, they *do* manage to communicate individually; there *is* some rapport. Then why the hatred? Because the Arab who works in Israel and who comes under Israeli influence and laws—the so-called friendly Arab —enjoys a life almost as good as (if not the same as) an Israeli's. His working conditions are good. He can enjoy life. He is treated more like a human being than he would be by his own sheiks and sultans, who have their people under their thumbs. With all their oil billions, they haven't done a thing yet for feeding their own people. So they hate the Israelis, the Jews, for having brought a little comfort into the desert and shown some of their own people that there is a way out of poverty and starvation. It reflects what the old Arab was saying to the Czech. . . .

Joffe took Alice and me to his brother's place outside Haifa. The man had settled there years before and had developed, with his own strength and own two hands, this beautiful piece of ground. He gave us a tomato to share. He was so proud of it that it tasted better to me than any tomato I'd ever eaten. This man had put his life, his blood, his strength, everything he had, into producing this tomato, much as Toscanini put all of himself into Beethoven's Ninth or Verdi's *Hymn of the Nations*. He was proud of his "orange grove," which was just a couple of trees at that time.

In his own little domain, this man was a millionaire. Every day he learned more that he could do by himself. Every day, with the help of nature, he performed the miracle of making something out of nothing. He was a gentleman farmer who got up at four in the morning to do his day's work. We had come to him at his invitation and he had fed us a cucumber and a tomato. But it was gold to him—and even more than that to us.

Today you can walk into the Tel Aviv Hilton and see the luncheon spread: a buffet such as you've never seen in your life. And that's just the dairy department! You draw your eyes back in your head and go on to the room where they serve the meat. That'll knock your eyes out all over again. And it's all kosher.

In 1950, though, only visiting artists and other luminaries were given coupons entitling them to three meat meals a week (I gave mine away to people who needed meat more than I did) and the Gat Rimon Hotel was the best Tel Aviv had to offer: an old worn-out little piece of property with the toilet down the hall. In the room was a shower, but all you could get from it was a trickle. Once you soaped up, though, the water wouldn't run at all.

I like to sing in the shower. Like everyone else, I find that the acoustics of the bath enhance my voice. If you don't sound good in the shower, you'll never sound good anywhere. There is no such thing as a singer who sounds good onstage and bad in the shower. On the contrary, some people you hear on the stage should be singing in the shower—or should have brought the shower with them.

Anyway, I was singing in the trickle in Tel Aviv when I heard a voice say in English, "Shaddap! Cut that out!"

This was ten o'clock in the morning, so I didn't think I was doing anything terrible. Through the paper-thin wall I shouted, "I'm an American, too, and this is a free country, too, so I'll sing if I want to. Some people even pay to hear me sing." In response came the loudest horselaugh I ever heard.

Later, washed and dressed, I went downstairs. At the desk, I heard a familiar unmusical voice growling at the concierge. He was complaining about "some nut next door who has to sing in the shower and makes so much noise a man can't hear himself think."

The concierge gave me a wink and said, "Do you know who that noisy next-door neighbor of yours is? It's Mr. Jan Peerce of the Metropolitan Opera."

The man gasped and said, "Is that so! He's my favorite singer. So he wasn't kidding when he said people would pay to hear him sing."

The concierge said, "And now I'd like you to meet the man you're complaining about. He's right behind you."

The man whirled around, blushing, but he was fast on the rebound: "I'm terribly embarrassed, Mr. Peerce. What I should have said was: 'Shaddap! It's good, but I don't wanna hear it.' But because I was impolite, Mr. Peerce, I'll let you sing for me without any restriction—free of charge, though!"

I guessed from this that he was a salesman. He represented the Eli Lilly drug company. He was trying to sell antibiotics and other pharmaceuticals to the State of Israel, which didn't have enough money to buy what he thought it should. He told me, "If there should be an epidemic of anything here, only G-d can help them."

"Well," I said, "these are G-d's people."

Of all the curses that have been visited on Israel, an epidemic wasn't one of them. Today their health and medical standards are very high. Back then, the drug salesman and I became pals fast. So I was able to tell Alice that night, "I have found my *goy* and he's a fan of mine."

The Kibbutz from Missouri

The America-Israel Cultural Foundation (A.I.C.F.) raises money in the U.S. to bring about a wedding between the two cultures. It's been responsible for many Israelis' coming to America to study—and quite a few of them have turned out to be international artists: Daniel Barenboim, Itzhak Perlman, Pinchas Zukerman. It has exchange programs, scholarships, and visiting artist programs that send talent not just to the big auditoriums in Haifa and Jerusalem and Tel Aviv, but to the kibbutzim, too.

In 1950, Alice and I were sitting with Judy Gottlieb of the A.I.C.F. in a place called the Kasid, the Sardi's of Tel Aviv—where artists, musicians, and show-business people gathered, especially after performances, to have cake that wasn't really cake with coffee that wasn't really coffee or tea that was colored water. A man came over and Judy introduced him as the cultural director of the big kibbutz Ein-Harod.

"What brings you to town?" I asked him.

"I came to see you," he said. "I was told you're fond of apples, so I brought you a gift." He handed me a paper bag full of apples as he came to the point: "You must know that these apples were grown in our kibbutz —by the hands that will applaud you *when you come to sing for us.*"

This was the first I'd heard of Ein-Harod. It wasn't even on my revised, expanded Israel itinerary. And while apples have been the eternal blandishment of mankind (I hope not half-sour, as these turned out), I was able to say, "Impossible! I have seventeen concerts to do in four weeks."

This didn't faze him. "So when you have a day off," he said, "you'll come and visit us and see how we live and have dinner with us and then you'll sing a few numbers for us. It doesn't have to be a full concert. We'll make it your pleasure as well as ours." When I began to yield, he said, "I'll tell you what! We'll make it on a Saturday night. You'll come and spend the Sabbath with us and then, when it ends, you'll sing a little for us."

Judging by the apples, I came expecting a tiny truck farm at a kibbutz smaller than a *shtetl.* Instead I found a sprawling complex of tractors and barns and barracks at the gateway to the Valley of Israel. After we ate my pre-concert menu of some fruit and *challah* and drank a cup of tea, we stayed in the dining room, for it was the kibbutz's concert hall, too. And our host beckoned to a platform with a piano on it, and said, "It's all yours."

It was very hot. There was no air conditioning. After the first group of songs, the applause was so thin that I barely had time to peel off my jacket before it was time for my second group. I did it in fine voice and finished sweatier and hotter than ever. The only lukewarm thing in that room was the hand I drew.

Knowing I was in good voice, I tried to keep my cool, but I couldn't help wondering what this was about. I took off my tie, but even this didn't improve my reception. After my third set there was an intermission and I asked Alice, "Don't I sound right?"

"You sound lovely," she said, "and they're loving you."

"If that's love," I murmured, "can you imagine if they *didn't* like me?"

When I came out for the second half, I was cussing under my breath and trying to keep from saying anything about pearls before swine. With my shirt unbuttoned and my sleeves rolled up, perspiring plenty and hot under the collar besides, I finished out my program and was glad my ordeal was over.

Then it started: the tumultuous shouting, the rhythmic clapping, the stamping of feet, the whistling and cheering—just as if I'd been a smash hit! They stood up. It almost seemed like a political rally. I was grateful and relieved, but I couldn't help thinking to myself: Why couldn't they have done a little of this before? Why did they have to anger me all evening? Why did I come here? Who needed the apples?

Now they wouldn't let me go. *"More! More! More!"* When I'd done four encores, they mobbed me. Young people, speaking every language, demanded six autographs apiece and asked for my address in America, too.

As soon as I could, I asked our host, "What kind of a crowd is this? First they make you suffer and then they punish you with love."

"Oh," he said, "we have a very discriminating audience. They're not going to go overboard no matter how much they like the first or second group. They need to be shown before they'll embrace you."

"You mean they're from Missouri," I said.

"No," he said, "most of them are *sabra* [native-born] and the rest are from the east of Europe."

I laughed—and explained that Missouri is the "Show Me" state. I came away proud, gratified, and touched. For these were the hard workers of the kibbutzim who built Israel with their hands, harvested those apples with their hands, and gave me their hands only after I'd shown I deserved them.

When I Disowned My Son

When you kick a person out of your life, you find that after a while you can live without him quite easily, whether he's a brother-in-law or a sister or a brother—or even your only son. Without her or without him, without this one or without that one, we go on—until we can't go on any more. I know this well because I disowned my son, Larry, for four and a half years after he married a Gentile girl with two children twenty years ago.

Larry had gone to work for WCPO-TV in Cincinnati, where he met Peggy. He was twenty-five when he and she declared themselves. Everything went dark for me. Life ceased to matter. I lost interest in my singing. My career meant nothing. I withdrew from engagements. I canceled performances. I blamed Alice for what had happened—even though she went out to Cincinnati, followed by our rabbi, David Golovensky, and her two brothers to see Larry and Peggy to ask them to wait. Everybody pleaded with them —until, in reply, they moved the date up and got married sooner. And I, stupidly, told Alice it was her fault for talking with them at all. I told Susan and Joy, "Your brother has been kicked out of the family. He's finished. And if you have anything to do with him, you, too, will be kicked out."

My own father, of blessed memory, kept lecturing me that I was wrong.

He said it was against Talmudic law to cast a son out of your life, that it was my duty to make up with Larry so that he could raise his children in our faith.

I was too sick of heart to listen. I was physically sick, too. If I caught a cold, it was hard to shake it. And I, a pretty strong character who'd never been ill a day in my life, became a hospital patient. The doctors diagnosed internal bleeding and I knew they might be right.

It was in Mount Sinai Hospital that I made a temporary truce—not peace —with myself. I had such strong convictions about my beliefs that I talked to the Lord man to man from my hospital bed. I started out with: "Why me? Why *my* son?" I told him that I hadn't tried to force my beliefs upon my son; I didn't force him to be religious or go against his nature—though Alice says that in my own way I did, just by showing my pleasure or displeasure. Until Larry was sixteen years old, he had a Hebrew teacher—but I didn't mean to hurt him by it. I told the Lord all this. And I said to Him, almost the way Tevye does in *Fiddler on the Roof:* "You are the Power. You are the Master. And if this is what You want and if this is Your way of testing me, I'll still have faith and I'll buy what You've sold me."

It was the only way I could come to the point where I could leave the hospital. I had entered there ready to die. But even when the doctors let me out and said I was physically all right, I was a very depressed man. I was living on another level of existence from myself. I'm a gregarious, fun-loving person. I love to be with people. I love to have people around me. I love to entertain them. I love to eat with them, drink with them, go out with them, have a conversation with them. But after Larry's marriage, I didn't want to see people. I thought they might be laughing at me.

Sometimes they were, I think. I never raised the subject of my son's marriage, but certain people did. I'd pretend it didn't matter to me. I'd just shrug off any mention of Larry and try to relax, but I was standing there at attention with a smile upon my face. Once I simply denied it. A man I knew well came up to me and said, "I hear your son got married."

I said, "Yes."

"Did he marry out of the faith?"

I snarled at him, "What kind of terrible question is that to ask?"

He said, "Well, that's what I heard."

And I said, "If you know the answer, then why do you ask the question?"

"Because I didn't believe it."

"Well, you shouldn't believe it," I heard myself saying, "because you heard wrong." I denied the whole thing. I lied to him, but I hope I made him squirm. People who ask questions like that, when they know the answer, are just twisting knives, enjoying the suffering they cause. This man was a friend—and still considers himself one—but Alice said: "Those people who know, but who don't say anything to you about it, are the ones who understand and love us. Those who have the bad taste to say something—make up your mind you can forget them."

I was ready to die. It was the tragedy of my life. I wanted to sit *shivah* for seven days, mourning for Larry. But Alice wouldn't let me. . . .

Alice Peerce: *I told Jan I would kill him. And from the first day, I never lost contact with Larry and Peggy. I never severed the relationship and I credit myself with saving the situation.*

Right after they were married, they moved to Los Angeles. Larry felt he'd gone as far as he could in Cincinnati. He had trouble getting started on the Coast, but he took a job as a page boy at CBS for $39.50 a week. He told me later that he would look at the list of visitors being shown through the studios. If he saw the name of anybody who knew us, he would switch shifts with someone else, so the guest wouldn't recognize Jan Peerce's son working as a humble page. He didn't want to embarrass Jan, even though he and Jan were on the outs. Once he was guiding a group through the halls of CBS when he saw Vincent Price coming down the hall. We'd met Price through Spencer Barefoot, the San Francisco art and music critic. To the tour's amazement, the guide said, "Here comes Vincent Price!" and disappeared into the men's room.

Larry Peerce: *Another time, a director my folks and I knew from the Russian Tea Room, Alex March, not only spotted me, but followed me when I ducked into the can. I locked the door and stood on the toilet seat until he went away.*

Alice: *Every time we went to L.A., a pal of Jan's named Bernard Wasserman—the kind of friend who's there before you need him—would call up and say to Jan, "While you're working, Jan, how about us taking Alice for lunch and a drive?" Bernard or his wife, Allegra, would pick me up and deliver me immediately to Larry's house. Fifteen months after Peggy and Larry were married, I had twin grandchildren there—a boy, Matthew, and a girl, Louise—and Bernard would leave me with them for two or three hours before calling for me at Larry's again. It was something I couldn't have done on my own, and if I said, "I'm going shopping," Jan was likely to say, "I'll go with you!" He likes to shop when we're out of New York. Jan had already forbidden me to have any contact, but Larry was part of me and I would absolutely not cut him off. Jan never suspected—or if he did, he never asked, because he was all knotted up in one of the worst depressions you could imagine a human being to be in.*

It would have gone on this way—me with my secret visits to my own son—but after four years of it, my brother Walter said to me one day, "Alice, enough is enough! What are you gonna do about it?"

I didn't think. I just said, "I'll do whatever you see fit."

Walter's insurance firm has an office in L.A., so he said, "I'll tell you what. We won't make Jan suspicious. I've been in touch with Larry every time I'm out on the Coast; after all, I baby-sat the boy when I was ten years old. At first Peggy wasn't eager to make up. She felt Jan had offended her too deeply by rejecting her so completely. But now her attitude is maybe a little softer because she recognizes how much it hurts Larry—more and more, not less, as time goes on—and she recognizes how absolutely rigid Jan remains. So now maybe we can at least talk about a reconciliation. . . ."

I asked Walter what Larry thought the possibilities were. He said Larry had told him, with great heartbreak, "I don't think Dad would forgive me."

But Walter had told Larry, "If you do what I tell you, Mother and I will work it out." Larry was willing to give it a try.

Larry used to ring me up whenever I came to the Coast. He'd find out where I was and call me. I wouldn't hang up on him. He'd say, "How are you?" and I'd say, "Fine," and he'd say, "What're you doing?" and I'd say, "Nothing." Then he'd say, "Can I come see you?" and I'd say, "No." But I wouldn't hang up. I enjoyed listening to his voice, even though I wouldn't talk with him. He'd tell me about the twins and I'd say either "I know" or "Thank you" and hang on every word until—well, it was always Larry who said goodbye first. I'd never hang up on him; in fact, I'd just hold on to the phone for a few minutes. . . .

Larry: *When I was calling, I didn't have much hope. I was just giving him another chance to come to his senses, to just let up a little. And each time I came away realizing how much I'd hurt him by marrying Peggy. It had never seemed to me that I'd done anything so terrible, but whenever I called up on the phone, I felt what it meant to him.*

On the next trip, I was making a record of Lerner and Loewe songs with Johnny Green on the Coast. Alice said she couldn't go with me; I should go ahead and she'd come a couple of days later with Walter, who had to make a trip out there, too. Usually Larry would find me on my first day, so I was a little surprised that he hadn't called by the third day—and aware of how much those calls of his meant to me.

I came back to the Beverly Hills Hotel on the third afternoon and Alice was there. She told me Walter had a room upstairs. "Then let me go up and say hello to Walter," I said. Alice went along.

Walter was standing outside in the hall waiting for us. He looked very solemn. He shook my hand, but he spoke to my wife: "The rest is up to you, Alice."

Before I could ask what was going on, Alice said, "Jan, I want to tell you something. Larry's in that room."

"I don't want to go in there!" I said, waving my arms. "I won't talk to him! I don't know him!" All the hurt of four years earlier welled up in me and I think I really meant it.

But Alice said, "You know that isn't so. So Walter and I aren't waiting around for you to say, 'I will.'" With that, Alice threw open the door and then she and Walter walked away from me. Larry was in the room walking toward me. And which way could I go? There was only one way—into my son's arms, two men making up, shedding tears, and both very happy. A father and son who hadn't spoken with each other for four and a half years didn't need words now.

[Rangy, bearded, and rugged, Larry picks up the narrative in late 1975.]

Larry: *Once this happened, it was as though nothing else had ever happened. My wife could never understand it. "How could anybody be that way for so many years and the next day—the same day!—be so changed?" she asked me.*

I told Peggy, "That's my father. It's the way he is with his work, with his creativity, with his family, with his ability to compartmentalize his life. Once something is over, it is over. He is unforgiving, unrelenting, but when he does turn around, it's one hundred eighty degrees." I've tried to take from him his faculty for living one day at a time, moving forward and seldom looking back while keeping the long-range picture in view.

He caught up with (and maybe even surpassed) my mother as a doting grandparent. And he treated my stepchildren, Peter and Susan Black, at least as well as his own grandchildren. One day my wife said to me, "Y'know, Larry, both your parents are really very nice." And I said, "Yes, they always were very nice. It's too bad the situation didn't give us a chance to find it out sooner."

A little later, our son Matthew fell into the swimming pool and almost died. He was in the hospital three days. As soon as we brought him back home, he tried to get into the pool again. We decided to fill in the pool with grass and make a little garden out of it. I called my father to borrow some money and he said, "How much is it going to cost?" I said, "Maybe five thousand dollars." He said, "What the hell are you going to fill it with? Sour cream?" But he came through. He can make your life miserable over five dollars, but when you need him, he's always there.

I never bore any animosity toward him in any way. He and I have an extraordinary relationship, which really didn't start until I was thirty years old. He's really grown up a lot. He's matured quite marvelously.

When I became interested in astrology, I realized that my father is the perfect Gemini, which is the sign he was born under. He is literally twins. I was raised in a home where one night Toscanini came to dinner; it was enchanting and the conversation was fabulous. The next night, some cloak-and-suiter would be sitting on the same chair Toscanini had occupied, boring everybody to death except my father. He seemed to get almost equal pleasure from both.

It was impossible for me to balance this. Here was this man, my father, musically and artistically a perfectionist, living the life of a middle-class Jewish burgher. He read the Daily News *and the* Post; *didn't like the* Times *as much, except for the stock market pages. Not much interest in books, but he would sit down and read a score the way you and I might read a book.*

He is a very private man, but he always has a moment for somebody. He'll always talk to people—not just to boost his ego. I think I got this from him. I care about people, so I give as well as take.

Mother, on the other hand, is terribly bright and intellectual, but she'll bring all her intensity to bear on the most petty thing. Or to her almost violent defense of him. Yet she's always working, criticizing, improving him.

Looking back on our estrangement, I've often thought that the ideal time for a reconciliation would have been when he went to the hospital because of my marriage. But I never knew about it until much later. My mother says that if I'd appeared at his bedside, he would have been convinced he was dying.

Susan Peerce: *I was sixteen when Larry married Peggy. A month later, my sister, Joy, married Bob Wahrhaftig and this left me alone with those two unhappy parents of mine in a house where I wasn't even allowed to mention my own brother's name. It was frightening!*

My father became quiet, moody, with sudden explosions of temper. The three of us would sit alone at the big dining room table and not talk. Then I'd go upstairs and lock myself in my room.

One day I came home from school and Father asked me to drive him to synagogue. When I dropped him off, he asked me to buy some pickles on the way home. At the store, I couldn't remember whether he wanted dill or some other kind of pickle. I bought dill. When he came home an hour later, I'd sliced them and put them on the table for him. He saw dill and he exploded. I'd bought the wrong kind! I was an idiot! How could anybody make such a horrible mistake? The noise that went on over those stupid pickles was something awful. I started crying, ran to my room, and stopped talking to him. That's one thing for a child to do, but he stopped talking to me, too. Two nights later I was up studying for an exam and he came home and didn't even say hello to me.

When I returned from school the next day, Ruby the Butler and our housekeeper, Mary Brown, broke the news to me that Dad was in the hospital. I went there and the doctors said they didn't know whether he would live or die. Then I went into his room and the first thing out of his mouth was to apologize to me about the pickles. And I must say, from that moment on we've been closer and closer. I'd always loved my father and could never reach him until then—when he reached out to me. I really think that was when he began to mellow. It's been smooth going ever since.

In my first year of college, I flunked out. I was really hysterical, but I managed to make a phone call home. And it was my father I called. He said, "Don't worry about it. Look at all the famous men who flunked out of school." I said, "But how are we going to tell Mother?" He said, "We'll figure a way." By the time I came home, she knew. . . .

I've learned to accept him and her. I can openly rebel instead of sitting back and sucking my thumb. I have my own life and it doesn't revolve around them. It's more of a friendship than a parent-child relationship. By the time I was twenty or twenty-one, I knew that this was my mother's life: to be with my father. And this was right, because the children leave the parents anyway. I think what made the difference for me is that I had to knock my father off his pedestal and then put him back within reach. And it all started when Larry married Peggy.

But it was never easy being Jan Peerce's child. In *Growing Up at Grossinger's,* Tania Grossinger, whose mother was a cousin by marriage of the famous Jennie, recalled:

> . . . I suppose the first star I really knew was Jan Peerce, the famous Metropolitan Opera tenor whom I had known, with his wife, Alice, in California. When I came East, I just assumed they would be like my family, and they assumed likewise. It never occurred to me he was "famous" in the celebrity sense of the word until a few months after I had begun to live at the hotel and the Peerces came up with their two daughters, Joy and Susan. People would come over to the dinner table, interrupting Jan in mid-swallow to ask for an autograph and would go up to the girls, no matter where they were, and say, "Are you going to be a singer when you grow up? Do you have as good a voice as your father?" This to youngsters five and eight years old. I saw how badly it affected them, and whenever the girls came up after that we would always seek out someplace private to hide— backstage in the Playhouse, the camp when it was deserted, anyplace—just to get away from the preying guests.

The relationship between Larry and me became, if anything, closer than it ever was before the rift. I was there when a third grandchild, a lovely girl named Amy, was born. And Larry's love for us has developed so much that he's there *before* he's needed—not only by Alice and me, but by his sisters. Whatever was dark is now light.

Nowadays, more and more, I meet men who are going through the same "problem." Most of them don't even know the same thing happened to me. I tell them, "This isn't the worst thing that could happen to you. But the worst thing you could do is disown your child. If the marriage works and you're not part of it, you lose. And if the marriage doesn't work and you're not there to help pick up the pieces, you lose." The main thing to make such a man see is that his child's marriage out of the faith or out of the color is neither unique nor the end of the world. For nearly five years, it *was* the end of my world. But what can a man wish his children except the best of the world they make for themselves?

And since I'm telling you all this, I have to tell you the rest. Do you want to hear the kicker? The marriage of Larry and Peggy broke up in 1972 and ended in the divorce court. And who do you think worked the hardest to keep them together? Of all people, the father who disowned his son and daughter-in-law. What time does for you!

A Medium-Old Faust

I had just turned fifty when I started playing the title role in Gounod's *Faust* at the Metropolitan in 1954. Our conductor, Pierre Monteux, was approaching eighty. In the opening scene, Faust is an old man who wishes to be young again. After a rehearsal, Monteux called me over and said, "Jean, why in the first scene do you walk so stooped? Why do you tremble so?"

"Well, Maestro, Faust is an old man."

"Just how old do you think he is?"

"Oh, I'm not sure, but certainly, er, sixtyish."

"And is that old?"

"In those days it was," I replied quickly. "Sixty was a very old man."

"I will be eighty next year," said Monteux. "I am more old than Faust was. Do I stoop and shake like that?"

"Of course not, Maestro! But look at Faust's beard!" I argued.

"They made a mistake! They should make it shorter. He's not supposed to look like Father Time." Monteux gave me a good-natured dressing down —or rather a shaping up. He implanted in me the idea that Faust wasn't so old and decrepit that he was falling apart. A man in such a condition might be too feeble to even consider a deal with the devil. So my conception changed a little. My Faust never walked stooped again. He could be an old man who walked straight—the way my father did, the way I try to do, the way a lot of old men I see do. He doesn't have to shake—and his voice certainly shouldn't! I retailored my approach to Faust: he's not old old; he's medium old.

Depending upon the staging, it's just as effective—maybe a little *more* credible—when he changes into a young man before the scene is over. Sometimes I'd go behind a screen and pop out as the young Faust from a cloud of Mephistophelian smoke. Underneath the medium-old man's flowing robes, of course, I'd be wearing my young Faust tights. The beard had to be pasted on lightly and have earpieces like spectacles, so that it would stay on but could be torn off quickly.

I've done *Faust* with Cesare Siepi, Giorgio Tozzi, Jerome Hines, and Nicola Moscona as Mephistopheles, and Anna Moffo, Dorothy Kirsten, Licia Albanese, and especially Victoria de los Angeles as Marguerite. The marvelous part of de los Angeles's performance was that I'd stand face to face with her when we did the second-act duet in the garden. She would watch everything I did—every mannerism, every inflection, every nuance, accent, grace note—and repeat it all, exactly as I did it. This not only suggested Marguerite's great love, but proved the soprano's great musical sensitivity. I used to love to sing with her.

Very often, almost traditionally, Faust tends to be the weakest of the three main roles; maybe that's why in Vienna and some other places, the Gounod opera is called *Margarethe.* One Faust in Vienna consistently misses the first high A flat that he sings, but most tenors worry about the high C in the garden two scenes later. After that you can relax; you've cleared the garden wall. But I think you shouldn't be doing the role if you have to worry about the high notes.

What *Faust* needs is a really strong Faust with a voice to stand up to Marguerite and Mephistopheles. It still is Faust's opera. True, he's not the most appreciated guy in the opera—it's harder for him to elicit love from an audience—but if he gives a convincing performance, he can own the place.

Unlike Faust, I wouldn't want to make a deal with the devil to go back forty years. I'll tell you what deal I would like to make with the Lord: That I go on for my allotted number of years *the same way I am.* This, I know, is impossible even to ask for. After all, we all have to get old and there has to be a stopping point. If I were going to make a deal, I wouldn't want to do what I did thirty or forty years ago. It doesn't appeal to me. Not that I didn't enjoy much of the last forty years, but the hardships and disappointments, struggles and mistakes of those four decades I wouldn't care to face again. When I hear people say, "If I had it to do over again . . ." I finish the sentence for them: "You'd do the same!" For if you went back forty years, you'd have to go back with the same mind, the same reasoning, the same logic, the same immaturity you had then. The maturity comes only with experience: you live the experience and you reason your way to maturity. At my age, I'm still trying: hence this book. I'm still praying and trying to improve my situation. But who the hell wants to be young? I don't want to be better-looking than I am now. I don't want to eat anything other than I ate in my first seventy years.

There used to be a very fancy staging of *Faust* at the Met. After the trio at the end of the opera, a see-through scrim would come down and everybody onstage was supposed to be inside it. Marguerite is ascending to heaven, Faust is kneeling preparatory to departure in the opposite direction, and Mephistopheles is clearing his throat happily over what he's accomplished.

It was supposed to make a beautiful picture, but one time I got out of position and wound up kneeling on the audience side of the scrim. All I could do was get up off my knees and ease my way out to stage left as the scene went dark.

Afterward one of my relatives, who was seeing the opera for the first time, came backstage and said, "I want to ask you something. We saw where Marguerite was going and we knew where the devil belonged, but where was it that Faust was going?"

All I could manage was "Offstage!"—and to complete the picture, I told *him* to go to hell.

Hospitality to a Stranger

When I go on the road, I try to eat kosher up to a point. I don't carry a plastic knife and fork with me, but I check in the *Jewish Travel Guide,* and set out with a pretty good list of restaurants, rabbis, or someone in each town who might have the answers I need.

There is no such restaurant in Fargo, North Dakota. But there was a rabbi, and I called him up when I got there one winter Thursday night on a concert tour. "Me, I don't keep kosher," the rabbi said. "I'm Reform. But there are some people here who do. There's one lady who's very good about feeding people who call up with your problem. I don't know what she charges, but I do know that people must be satisfied because they never call back asking me for further advice. Let me give you her name and number."

I phoned the woman from my hotel. She didn't ask my name or anything. She just said, "Well, if you're really hungry and willing to take pot luck—we've already had our dinner, but I'll find something."

I said, "Good. I'll come over in a cab whenever you tell me to."

"Never mind the cab. I'll send my son over," she said. "He'll meet you in the lobby right away." Ten minutes later, a young boy walked up to me and said the car was outside. He, too, didn't ask me anything about myself. All the way to his home, I did the asking: "Are there many Jews here? . . . How many of them are Orthodox? . . . Are they all as kind as your mother?"

He took me into the house through the back door and sat me down in a nice warm kitchen. I waited a minute or two to take my coat off because it can be cold as the devil in Fargo, North Dakota. The mother bustled in —a pleasant middle-aged, Middle Western sort of lady who apologized for having eaten already, ". . . but we've got a leftover piece of chicken and I can heat up the soup."

I said, "Look, anything you have that I can eat, I'm happy!"

She started cooking. Her husband came in, shook my hand, and asked me the first question anyone in his family had asked: Where was I from?

I said New York, and from the stove, his wife commented, "Isn't it nice that a man from New York, who must travel all through the country, observes the dietary laws? What do you do when you're not in a big city like Fargo and there's maybe nowhere you can eat at all?"

"I do the best I can," I told them. "I eat either a piece of fish or a can of salmon or an egg or a vegetable. . . ."

"Oh!" she said. "You're a good man. And what do you do? Are you a traveling salesman?"

"Well," I said, thinking fast, "I sell music."

"How can you sell music?" she wondered.

"You have a symphony orchestra here in Fargo, don't you? Well, I sell them the music they play every once in a while."

"Are you going to be here tomorrow night?" she asked me.

"In Fargo? Definitely. Why?"

"Because, incidentally, there's a kind of a big event that may interest you: a concert."

I played dumb and asked, "What kind of a concert?"

"A singer," she began, "he's from New York, too, so you must know about him. He's a well-known person: Jan Peerce."

Now I was acting—acting astonished: "Jan Peerce? Is giving a concert? Here? Tomorrow night?" When she said yes, I asked, "And you'll be there?"

"Unfortunately, I can't be there."

"Why not?" I said.

"Tomorrow's Friday."

"And you won't go to a concert on the Sabbath?" I guessed.

"No, I'd go," she said, "because I'm very anxious to hear him. But once a month there's an itinerant rabbi who comes to town and holds a service." Tomorrow, she explained, would be the Friday the rabbi prayed Fargo.

"What time does he get here tomorrow?" I asked her.

"Oh, he gets in tonight sometime. He'll call me when he does."

"And what time is Peerce's concert?"

"I think it's eight o'clock. And that's when we have our service."

I didn't have to ask her what time was sundown. I think it gets dark at noon in Fargo in the winter! So I said, "You could hold it a couple of hours earlier if the rabbi said yes and you called your congregation."

"Of course I could. There aren't that many to call," she said—doubtfully. "But still I couldn't go to this Jan Peerce's concert. I don't ride on the Sabbath."

"How far is the concert from here?"

"A mile, a mile and a half," she estimated. "In this weather, to walk a mile isn't easy."

I could believe that, but I was selling music, so I said, "Let me tell you something. The fact that it's cold and that you're not an athlete, that's one thing—but I think you have enough of the pioneer spirit to make it there if you've gotten as far as Fargo. When you tell me about the service, though, that's a tougher proposition, but there's a solution if you can hold it earlier. So I would like to invite you to that concert."

"Why should *you* invite *me* to a Jan Peerce concert?" she wanted to know. "And besides, how can you be sure you can get tickets this late?"

"I'll tell you why and how," I said. "I'm the man who's singing tomorrow night."

Now she was perplexed. "Look here, what are you saying?"

"I'm saying that I'm Jan Peerce and I'm inviting you and your husband and your son to be my guests at my concert if you'll just get there any way you can."

"If you're Jan Peerce," she said, "what are you doing in *my* house?"

"I'm honored to be in your house."

"But I never dreamt a Jan Peerce would be in my house eating my food!" Then she slapped herself hard on the head and said, "So if you're Jan Peerce and you're in my house, what are you doing in my kitchen? Why aren't you in my living room? This is terrible. Myron! Myron!" She called her son, who came running. "Myron, this man is Jan Peerce and you bring him to our house in the car and where do you put him? *You put him in the kitchen!* You should be ashamed of yourself! *We* should be ashamed of ourselves!"

The son took it quite well. He said, "I never heard of Jan Peerce." And when I said, "You'll find out tomorrow night," he said he had a date, and when I said, "Bring your date!" he said he'd promised to take her to a basketball game. He was nice about it, but he knew his own mind. While he and I were having this discussion, the mother ran into the living room to turn on all the lights and the father took my plates away from me and started carrying them in there. So I began to argue with the father, but the mother said, "A Jan Peerce cannot eat in my kitchen. You've got to come into the living room."

I didn't want to budge. "This is your home and I'm glad that you did this for me. Don't worry about me. I'm happy here."

"No, no, please, I can't insult you like that," she said—and before I could say another word, she and her husband were carrying a tray into the living room: a real old-fashioned living room with cellophane on the furniture so it shouldn't get dusty. When I was all set up in there, she took to the phone and called up almost the whole Jewish community of Greater Fargo to tell them the service tomorrow would be at five-thirty so that everybody who wanted could "go hear Jan Peerce, who's sitting in my living room eating dinner." Six or eight people didn't quite believe her, so they came around to see for themselves and I sat up late, talking with my new friends of Fargo. My hostess kept so busy on the phone that the rabbi had trouble getting through to tell her he was in town. He succeeded around midnight.

If she was a heroine of Fargo's Jewish community on Thursday night, she was my heroine and everybody's heroine on Friday, which was even colder and windier than the night before. I dedicated a number to her and I told the audience why. I told how she'd not only opened her door and her kitchen to a stranger without asking who he was, but sent her son to fetch him, and now she had walked a mile in miserable weather because she observes the Sabbath and she had even managed to shift the service so she could be at this concert. I must admit that with one little song, I gave her a reputation as a music lover that half the ladies in the hall had been working at for years. The newspaper did a feature story on her and I still get a greeting card from Fargo every once in a while. It always says: "Thank you for honoring us with your visit."

I remember this woman very well—she lived up to one of the most important teachings of the Talmud, offering "hospitality to a stranger." To extend a hand of friendship to a stranger is one of the most important of the 613 good deeds or *mitzvahs*.

In my own synagogue in New Rochelle, I'm not an officer or a director. But if I do see a stranger I try to make him feel welcome, ask him if there's anything he needs? Like the kind lady in Fargo, I believe we should try to add a little comfort to a stranger—no matter who he is.

Three Potato, Four . . .

During my estrangement from Larry, he had some trouble supporting a wife and twins on his $39.50-a-week salary as a CBS page boy, but then he landed a directing job with KTLA, the Paramount TV station in Los Angeles, doing a show called *Night Court*. By the time we'd been reconciled, Larry was starting to make a name for himself.

For a thousand dollars or so, Larry was commissioned to do eighty-one five-minute television shorts on the great gospel singer Mahalia Jackson. The cumulative title was *With These Hands*. Larry made not only her hands look beautiful; he made her look beautiful. His filming and her singing brought out Mahalia Jackson's great depth of inner beauty. *With These Hands* won a lot of applause and a prize at the Monte Carlo TV Film Festival.

One day Larry had an idea. He called up Alice and asked me to listen in on the other phone. "I'd like to make a film," he said.

Alice said, "Fine! Great!"

"But wait!" Larry added. "I need money."

"How much do you need?" Alice asked.

First he explained that his TV credits and even his prize meant next to nothing in the commercial film world. Then he named the figure: "I need a quarter of a million."

"Two hundred and fifty thousand dollars!" Alice exclaimed. Larry had clearly left the allowance orbit.

I broke in from my end, saying, "That's the kind of money I carry around just for tipping."

But Alice said, "Have you got a story, Larry?"

"Yeah, I've got a story," he said.

"I'll tell you what," I said. "Why don't you fly to New York and sit down and we'll talk about it?"

He came. We sat down. We talked. And he unfolded an interracial love story called *One Potato, Two Potato*. "Oh, Larry," I moaned. "Even if you do manage to make such a picture, how can anybody expect to get his money back, let alone make a little dough? For a first movie, why don't you do something safe?"

"Like what, Dad?"

"A fella meets a girl. They get married. They have children. Their children meet a fella and a girl, get married, have children. That's the kind of film you ought to be starting out with."

"But, Dad, that's been done by bigger people and *more* people! I wouldn't be contributing anything if I did another one of those. But this is something else. I think I've found a way of treating a very sensitive subject."

Now Alice piped up: "You need a quarter of a million dollars? All right. I'll see that you get it. I'll raise it for you." With that, she turned to me and said, "You'll be the first stockholder. You will invest ten thousand dollars. And there'll be a ten percent overcall. If Larry needs extra money, you're in for another thousand."

I hedged. "Wait a minute. Why ten thousand? Why not five thousand? Why do you pick on me for ten thousand?"

Alice said, "Somebody has to be the first, and you're his father." Later, when she and I were alone, she added, "Look, someday we'll be called away —permanently! We'll leave Larry some money then, right? So why not give him his inheritance now, when he needs it? Why wait till after we die? He may not need it then or it may be too late to realize his ambition. He may not appreciate it then. Why leave till later what we can afford to do now?" I still wasn't persuaded, but Alice went on: "How would you like it if he someday told his friends, 'This father of mine, who could have afforded it, didn't want to help me. But for him I might have been.' Be a nice fella, Jan, and do it now. If it works out, fine. If not, not. But he'll be getting his inheritance now, when the living can help the living—not later, when the dead can't help those whose hopes have died."

I squirmed a little, but I couldn't argue with Alice because she wasn't there for me to argue with; she was out raising money for Larry. Not only was I the first to cough up cash for *One Potato, Two Potato,* but when Alice and Larry couldn't raise it all, I persuaded my neighbor and financial counsellor, K. B. Weissman, to post the performance bond.

One Potato, Two Potato was not just the first picture about racial mixing, but it was treated with such sensitivity, skill, and decency that I don't think there's been a film on this subject to match it ever since. I do know that it paid off its investment within a year and a half, and by now it has earned back triple what was put in. It's rediscovered every now and then by a new television generation, and we receive another check when it's been shown. That's why I bring back "The Bluebird of Happiness" again and again, for it's always brand new to the next generation. The strength of any work is to be discovered and rediscovered—and still be relevant to each new generation.

Larry has gone on to make a name for himself as a movie director with an eye for new talent and the film virtues of good novels. In *Goodbye, Columbus,* my brother Mac and I played the two uncles in the carpet business—and Larry also discovered Ali McGraw. That and his other pictures—including *A Separate Peace, Ash Wednesday,* and *The Other Side of the Mountain*—made busy people out of Barbara Barrie, Richard Benjamin, Jack Klugman, and a few others. Another of Larry's pictures, *The Incident,* back in 1968, made Mayor Lindsay and the New York City authorities unhappy because they thought it "misrepresented" the subway as an evil hole in the ground. They wouldn't let Larry's film crews into their subway stations, but he filmed it anyway—with two crews. One crew created a commotion pretending to film a TV commercial, while the other crew unobtrusively went about filming the movie. *The Incident* was truly an underground film.

A Jew in Russia

When Hurok became "Mr. Cultural Exchange" with Russia in the fifties—exporting and importing the best—Isaac Stern was the first instrumentalist to go to Moscow, in 1956. I was the first singer. With the cold war on, I was a little scared, but Hurok and Alice assured me that, going under the auspices of the U.S. State Department, I had nothing to fear.

And I had to admit I was excited about returning to the land where my parents and grandparents were born. I looked forward to visiting the places where they grew up—Horodetz and Hyakuvka, Antipolye and Kobrin—but I learned they were no longer on the map, and could not be located, much less visited. So I said I'd settle for a side trip to Minsk, where Alice's mother was born. But Minsk was off-limits because it is part of the Soviet military-industrial complex. My enthusiasm, such as it was, started to wane.

My reluctance was translated into terms of money. The Russian artists coming here commanded exorbitant fees. Whether they or their government kept the dollars they earned was another matter, but the fees Isaac and I were offered were *not* outstanding. And of whatever we would be paid, we could take home only half in dollars; the rest would be in rubles, which had to be spent or banked in Russia. Still, Alice argued that an international success there would enhance my future bookings and prices back home, and I knew that was so.

The negotiations took a year. When Hurok had the best possible deal, his right hand, Mae Frohman, called my right arm, Alice, and said, "Make up your mind this second: yes or no?" Alice said yes. When I came home, she told me. I said, "What have you done?" Alice said, "Good or bad, let's try it."

Isaac Stern came back from Russia the day before I left New York in June 1956. He called to tell me what to expect: warm and wonderful audiences, but very limited personal contacts. The gist of his advice was: Don't spout off politically. Don't advise people. Don't play games with money. Don't talk to strangers. Nobody will talk to you much either. When you go into your hotel room, whether or not you are being listened to, it would be wise to behave as though you were. I wondered what I was getting into.

In Copenhagen, Alice, Warner Bass, and I boarded an Aeroflot plane with no seat belts and no food, just candies to suck on because the aircraft wasn't exactly pressurized. When we landed in Moscow that night, Warner pointed out the limp parachute dragging behind the plane; it was an "emergency brake" in case the plane's failed—a nice safety backstop that I wish I hadn't seen.

We were met by our official interpreter and guide: a good-looking fortyish woman named Alexandra Alexandrovich, who knew more about American and English poetry than I did. She could recite English poetry by heart, and give facts about New York, Chicago, and San Francisco as if she'd been there, though she insisted she hadn't. She was a well-educated woman, but I saw her flinch when I asked if she knew where the synagogue was in Moscow. "No, I don't," she said, "but *if you want,* I'll find out for you." I said I wanted, but I could tell I'd better not wait for her to deliver an address.

We arrived at the Hotel Metropole at 11 P.M. after seeing nothing, but nothing, on the ride in from the airport. What few lights there were shed no light on Russia; only the absence of light did.

When Alexandra left, Warner, Alice, and I looked at each other and decided that we wanted to do a downtown-Moscow-by-midnight self-guided tour. Searching for the Kremlin, we managed to find the GUM department store. As we window-shopped the unimposing display of canned goods and mentally converted rubles to dollars, I remarked, "For crying out loud, how can anyone afford a can of sardines in this place?"

Out of the dark came a voice speaking perfect Americanese: "Those who want it and those who have it can get it—and not only sardines!"

It turned out to be Marvin Kalb speaking; with him was his brother Bernie. Today both are CBS News correspondents and authors. Back in 1956, Marvin was working as a translator for the U.S. and British governments, while Bernie was visiting from Jakarta, where he was a correspondent. Both being music lovers, they knew me by sight.

"We'd heard you were coming," Bernie said, "and we expected to meet you, but not in front of GUM in the middle of the night!" With that, the brothers Kalb became our tour guides to Moscow by midnight. They showed us not just the outside of the Kremlin, but Gorki Boulevard, the Fifth Avenue of Moscow. Then they took us off Gorki Boulevard to show us the Tenth Avenues of Moscow, too, with houses back of houses, all in utter disrepair. When they delivered us to our hotel, I thanked them and said, "I'd like to see the synagogue."

They said they would take us on Friday. We would take a taxi part way and walk the rest of the way.

The next morning I took my first real look at our hotel room, which had a high ceiling and a piano. It seemed to me that Chaliapin might have once lived there; certainly the piano hadn't been tuned since Chaliapin's day.

Alexandra came for us shortly after 10 A.M. She said she was taking me to see Bialiskowsky, the man who ran Tchaikovsky Hall, where my first concert would be, two nights later. I was eager to see him because, just like the Israelis, he hadn't answered my queries about what, where, and when I would be singing.

Bialiskowsky was a former tenor with a good sense of humor and little command of English. I asked him how the acoustics were in Tchaikovsky Hall. He thought that over for a minute and then he said, "Mr. Peerce, wherever there's a voice, there's a coustic."

I laughed out loud, and later, when his English improved, he started kidding himself, too. By then he had become a great fan of mine and the big *macher* of both Tchaikovsky and Conservatory halls. He especially admired my breath control. Now, whenever we meet in America, in addition to the usual bear-hug greeting, Bialiskowsky slaps my rib cage and says, "You got the voice and we got the coustics."

At our first meeting I asked him which program he wanted me to sing when. I had sent him three, one with a few Hebrew and Yiddish songs. That one wasn't scheduled anywhere in the itinerary. I tried to discuss it with him, but he wouldn't elaborate, so I finally backed off. He sighed with obvious relief.

Later that day, Bialiskowsky gave a reception for us in a czarist palace. All the Russians there drank several shots of vodka apiece, but they didn't throw their glasses against the wall as I expected from the movies. Instead they held them upside down over their heads to show they were empty. Rather than try to match their performance, I would take a sip and set the glass on the table, sorry to disappoint them.

Two nights later, Tchaikovsky Hall was jammed and my usual program went very well. Bialiskowsky must have known what he was doing, I decided to myself.

Russia and Israel had diplomatic relations back in those days. During intermission, the Israeli ambassador came backstage to greet me—and to ask if I was going to sing anything in Hebrew or Yiddish.

"For whom?" I asked.

"At least twenty percent of your audience tonight is Jewish."

"I hadn't known," I said. "I don't have any music with me here. But I do have some Yiddish music in my hotel."

It was a long intermission, so Alice volunteered to go get the music and bring it back early in my second half. Our watchdog, Alexandra, was right there, but suddenly all the limousines and chauffeurs and other services she'd had at her fingertips must have gone on strike, except they don't have strikes in the Soviet Union. The car that had brought us there and was supposed to take us back had disappeared. "The driver must have gone to dinner," she said, though I could have sworn I'd seen the man watching from the wings.

"I'll take a cab to the hotel and back," Alice said.

"There are no cabs in Moscow at this hour," Alexandra insisted.

"Then I'll take your famous subway," said Alice. "Or I'll walk."

"But it's a very complicated thing to do," said Alexandra. "Perhaps you can do that number the next time."

"No, I'd like to do it tonight," I said.

Sensing our determination, Alexandra capitulated. Car and driver suddenly materialized and Alice was back within twenty minutes.

At the end of the program, the crowd applauded, cheered, and stamped for more. The compere—the man who had announced each number printed on the program—asked what I was going to do as my first encore.

"I'm going to do a Yiddish-Hebrew song," I told him. "I want you to tell them that and please don't change the message because my pianist speaks Russian and he'll tell me if you say something different."

"Why should I change it?" he said.

"I don't know why," I said. "I'm just telling you to tell them."

He made the announcement and I could feel the electricity out front and backstage. The number I had picked was a very serious one, "A din-toire mit G-tt" ("A Plea to G-d"), which deals with the oppression of the Jews.

In old Russia there was a rabbi named Levi Isaac, the son of Sarah from Berditchev. And it is said that whenever his people were troubled and oppressed, they would ask him to intervene in their behalf, to speak to the Lord. It is also told that he would enter the synagogue and mount the steps that lead to the Ark and open the doors of the Ark where the Scrolls are and he would address the Lord as if he were there in person. And he would say: What have you got against the children of Israel? What have they done to deserve all this? For a moment he would forget he was addressing the Lord, raise his voice, and say: "Lord, I will not leave this spot unless you do something about it. You must *do* something." Then he would remember who he was speaking to and end with the Kaddish prayer: "Magnified and sanctified is the name of the Lord."

This is the story of the Jewish people—declaring their faith and belief no matter what. I sang it with all the intensity I could bring to it. "A Plea to G-d" was timely in 1956 as it is timely in 1976.

Alice Peerce: *There were Jews in that audience who hadn't heard a Jewish word publicly in thirty-eight years. You could tell who they were. Their backs stiffened. It was both frightening and heart-rending. You suddenly became aware of the Jews in the audience just as they, too, were being reminded of who they were. That encore was the most telling moment in a very important evening.*

When I finished "A Plea to G-d," there were tears and cheers. Much more than twenty percent of the crowd in Tchaikovsky Hall were yelling and stamping. Bialiskowsky was very pleased and therefore Alexandra was, too. So were the ten or twelve people who came backstage and congratulated me specifically on it. That's when I could tell that Jewish encores were in. For in Russia, you don't just go backstage the way friends and admirers of the artist do in the States. You need a special pass to come backstage, so I knew that my well-wishers were mostly official visitors.

Later, in Leningrad, I learned that Hurok's brother was in the audience. Not believing in asking questions when the answer is most likely to be no, I simply sent word inviting him backstage. *Then* I told Alexandra.

"You should have cleared it with me first," she said.

"Clear it with you?" I said. "I have the right to invite him."

"Oh, no, you don't," she said. "You're entitled to an allotment of visitors, but we have to okay each name."

"Allotment? That's the first I've heard of it! I want to see this man. It's a *must!* Do you hear?"

"I don't know if you can."

Well, we knew how to handle Alexandra. I gave Alice a wink and she took up the cudgel, saying, "I'll be out front. I'll bring him backstage personally. And if you don't want him, you'll have to kick both of us out, because I'll be on his arm."

Alexandra backed down. Hurok's brother came backstage. The next time I played Leningrad, I didn't have to ask—he was now on the official list.

Everywhere in the world, even behind the iron curtain, the Fourth of July is a special day: what they call "America's National Day." For everywhere that there's an American embassy, the U.S. ambassador holds an open reception for Americans plus hundreds of friendly or prominent natives. Charles Bohlen was the ambassador to Moscow then. Nikita Khrushchev was just beginning to chip at, if not thaw, the Stalinist ice of the cold war. Khrushchev, Molotov, and Bulganin were there that Fourth of July. "Chip" Bohlen not only introduced us, but interpreted. I found I really had nothing to say to Khrushchev. Just to make conversation, I said, "Mr. Bohlen, would you please tell Mr. Khrushchev that I'm very sorry he did not attend any of my performances."

Khrushchev was playing host to Marshal Tito of Yugoslavia, and having some difficulties in negotiations with him. So I took Khrushchev at his word when he shook his head with a smile and replied, "You tell Mr. Peerce I know his voice. At this time, I have to listen to other voices, but I would much rather listen to his voice than to anyone else's."

I did four concerts in Moscow, one in Leningrad, and one in Kiev. I did *A Masked Ball,* which was revived especially for me, twice in Kiev. I did *Rigoletto* in Leningrad, and after the show there was a party for the cast, which I left around 1 A.M. I caught a couple of hours sleep, and when I came down around 6 A.M. to check out of the Astoria Hotel and leave Leningrad, all the other singers were waiting in the lobby to say goodbye. They had come over right from the party. The camaraderie, if you'll pardon the expression, among Russian artists was truly impressive.

The casts sang in Russian while I sang in Italian, and it worked well. Some of the sopranos knew the duets in Italian, so out of courtesy to me they sang them in that language.

In Moscow I did *Traviata* at the Bolshoi. But for me, the unexpected thrill came at the "dress rehearsal" the morning of the day before the performance. Customarily, the entire Bolshoi company is invited. At first I was surprised to learn that we weren't going to be in costume—which seemed to make it, by my definition, a general rehearsal. When I peeped out through the curtain, however, I saw an audience of some three hundred people—most of them singers, dancers, people who couldn't come to the performance.

At a rehearsal, you generally just walk from place to place to mark your spots and don't sing too much. But facing an audience of fellow professionals, I figured the least I could do was sing full voice. We got through the first act very nicely.

The second act started with Alfredo's aria "De' miei bollenti spiriti"— and that stopped the show. The applause was thunderous, and while I stood there bowing and bowing, Alexandra rushed right onstage to say, "They're shouting *'Bis!'*"

"Get the hell offstage," I hissed at her.

"They want you to sing it again."

"When?" I whispered.

"Right now!"

With that, I whipped off my jacket, threw it on a bench, and opened my collar to signal that I was going to do something informal. The audience understood right away and the applause subsided. I nodded to the conductor, whose name was Chaikin. He started the introduction. I did "De' miei bollenti spiriti" again and drew an even bigger hand.

At the actual performance the next night there were no solo curtain calls, but as I expected, the other singers all turned toward me and applauded. Then they pushed me out toward the footlights, and finding myself in this unexpected position, I instinctively turned around and applauded my fellow artists—which is, I learned later, exactly what protocol dictates.

What I noticed about Russian singers was not just their fellowship, but their total lack of arrogance. Temperament was displayed only during performances, when singers put their all into their parts. Offstage, there were no tantrums, no prima donnas, just artists. Maybe this comes from the fact that singing is a respected profession there, so that artists don't have to show off to attract attention.

On our first Friday night in Moscow, Marvin Kalb took us to the Great Synagogue of Moscow. He called for me right after Alexandra had left, thinking we would spend the evening at the Hotel Metropole. She never had found out where the synagogue was, and kept laughing me off. My eating habits excited even more ridicule. "The food in the Soviet Union is good enough for our Jews. Why isn't it for you?" Questions like hers aren't worth answering, for one knows that the reply won't be heard, understood, or appreciated.

The synagogue was virtually deserted. In fact, if it hadn't been for Marvin and Bass and myself, they might not have had a *minyan* of ten Jewish males. The rabbi, whose name was Schleifer, knew who I was and asked if I would perform the service. We talked in Yiddish and I said thank you, but no: I'd been singing and rehearsing all week. "Perhaps some other time."

"When?" he persisted.

I distinctly didn't make any promises and told him I would be out of town for two weeks on tour. He asked me to sanctify the wine that night by singing the *Kiddush.* It was an emotional moment for me: singing before an almost empty 1900-seat house of worship.

That weekend I went away on tour. Two weeks later, I came back to Moscow on a Friday afternoon. Alexandra, who'd been traveling with us, needed Saturday morning to put her family affairs in order, so I knew we were free until she'd come for us at 2 P.M.

Around nine o'clock on Saturday morning, Alice and I finished breakfast at our hotel and I said, "Now that we have the time and the freedom, how about us going over to the synagogue?"

"Fine with me," Alice said, "if you can remember how Marvin took us there."

We stepped out of our room and—almost as though we'd conjured him up—there was the *shamus* of the Great Synagogue of Moscow waiting in the lobby for us. He wished us a good Sabbath.

"Good *Shabbas!*" we said, and I added, "What a coincidence! We were just thinking we could use a little help finding your synagogue."

"It's no coincidence," he said in Yiddish. "I'm waiting for you. We're waiting for you. They're waiting for you."

"Who's 'they'?" I asked.

"The people. There are hundreds of people waiting for you."

"For me? How come?"

"Well, somehow or other, the word got around that you'd be performing the *musaf* of the service today."

"Who told them *that?*"

"Oh, it could have been the rabbi, it could have been the *gabbai* [the boss of the synagogue], it could even have been me. It could have been any one of the people who were there who heard you say you'd be back. We— I mean, they, or whoever—put two and two together. You said you'd be back in two weeks. Someone asked your hotel and they said you were coming back yesterday, so we figured this morning would be a wonderful opportunity to hear you in our synagogue. Hundreds of people showed up. . . ."

I must say I was dismayed and annoyed. But I wanted to go to synagogue anyway, so I went—protesting all the way that I had no intention of singing at the service.

The *shamus* may have put two and two together to add up to hundreds of Jews, but he had underestimated. By the time we got within a couple of blocks of the synagogue, I could see a thousand people spilling out into the streets around it. The *shamus* opened a path for us, and inside the synagogue they had a chair reserved for Alice upstairs with the women and another for me in a place of honor—where Israeli embassy people sat—near the altar. The Israeli ambassador wasn't there, but he'd sent his regrets and his brother-in-law to this performance I was just learning about.

"Did you ever see such a thing in your life?" the brother-in-law murmured to me. "All these people waiting for you."

"But I didn't tell them I was coming today!" I protested once more.

"It isn't what you told them. They expect you. I don't know what your plans are, but they're expecting you to lead them in prayer. For this is Russia; these are *your* people. I'm not telling you what to do, but it would be terrible if you let them down."

I had my own skullcap. The rabbi and the *shamus* handed me a big prayer shawl. I put it on, walked slowly to the altar, and began to sing. For once in my life, the first phrase was one that I had to work hard to get out. Emotionally, it was a very trying moment. My eyes filled with tears as I looked upon this place filled to overflowing by the Jews of Moscow who had come to hear me pray. But once that wall of emotion was penetrated, I gathered strength and sang my heart out for them.

There was only one slight note of discord in the rest of that long morning. At a certain point in the service, there is a section where they bless the government and its leaders. The *shamus* handed me a card containing the names of Khrushchev, Bulganin, Molotov and other officials. Well, I'm not a rabbi, so there's no reason why I have to bless anybody. I said to the *shamus* very quietly in Yiddish, "You do this part."

"No, no," he said. "The cantor is supposed to do this."

"I'm not doing it," I said. *"You* do it."

The give-and-take went on for some time. The worshipers couldn't hear it, but from our gesticulating they could guess what it was about. Finally he shrugged and capitulated: *"Sha, sha,* Mr. Pirs, don't get angry." So he blessed Khrushchev and I could hear a sigh of relief go through that crowd as I won my fight, which seemed to have become their fight.

After the service, nobody would leave. People outside tried to push in. The crush was so great that the *shamus* made the box in which he stored the precious prayerbooks into a podium for me. There I stood, answering everybody's questions like an American politician.

"Where are you from?" "Don't tell me you were born in America!" "How can an American be so well versed in Hebrew?"

"Look," I said. "America is a very great country with many *yeshivas* and Hebrew schools, with many, many rabbis, and a strong Jewish cultural life." I told them proudly of the religious freedoms we enjoy in America. They in turn took pride in my pride that I was Jewish and I was with them. And in the fact that my mother and father were once two of them. "You see? You see? Didn't I tell you? His parents came from Russia!" From this they took hope as well as pride.

When we finally had to leave, the police were outside, attracted and worried by the unusual throng. On the rim of the crowd stood Alexandra, who'd been called away from her family and must have been properly chewed out for letting this happen. She was looking mightily distressed.

"What are you doing here?" she wanted to know.

"What are you doing here?" I wanted to know.

"Why didn't you tell me you were going to do this?" she moaned. "We would have arranged everything!"

I'll bet! The guide is my shepherd; I should not stray. All I said was: "I didn't even know I was coming here until I started to go."

That afternoon she moved into our hotel with us, and from then on we were together all over Russia. I was still able to get away from her, though. Alice, for example, would ask to see the Hermitage or some other sight in the morning and I would pretend to be sleeping late. Then I would go off on my own.

To this day, I could walk into that synagogue—as I did seven years later—and be recognized and greeted as if I'd been living there all my life. The Jewish community of Moscow and I had shared a great moment together.

My Father in Tiflis

When I went back to Russia in 1963, I returned to the Great Synagogue of Moscow, but this time I wasn't asked to lead a service. In fact, I knew beforehand that I wouldn't be. The Soviet authorities had passed the word to Hurok that no recurrences would be allowed. If they couldn't forbid me to accept, they could prevent my being asked.

The inside of the synagogue had been rearranged physically. The Israeli delegation had a less prominent spot—fenced in, almost like a compound, to isolate them from Russian Jews. Yosef Tekoah, who was later Israel's ambassador to the United Nations, was ambassador to Russia then and he knew that the furor I'd created the last time still lingered in too many official as well as Jewish memories. In any totalitarian system, the officials' biggest fear is crowds. Freedom of assembly is as dangerous to them as freedom of expression.

A new rabbi was there. We both understood why I couldn't lead the service; he seemed very apologetic and I felt much sorrier for him than I did for me.

He did give me an honor, though—the concluding *maftir* and *Haftarah*.* I took advantage of the opportunity and made as much out of it as I would have done officiating at the *musaf* service. It created the same kind of excitement that the *musaf* had in 1956. The congregation was very large, for on Saturday mornings the people come to be together as well as to worship. By the time I stood up to sing, the synagogue had filled.

Despite my own experience, social as well as material conditions in Russia had improved since 1956. All improvements are relative, of course. Thus, in 1963 I heard a joke that my father had heard in czarist Russia and told us on the Lower East Side: "How are things in Russia? Well, I'll tell you. Two years ago was better than three years ago. Last year was better than two years ago. And this year's even better than last year, but it's still no good!"

Certainly the regime had become more skilled at handling visiting artists. They were even letting well-heeled Russians mix with foreigners at the hotels that used to be strictly off-limits to natives. In every deluxe hotel, jazz bands were playing. They were about forty years behind our times, which gave me a certain nostalgia for my Pinky Pearl days of the 1920s. Still, Russia was definitely closing the gap; it had been in another century when I was there seven years earlier.

I couldn't quite understand where a Russian made enough money to eat in some of the fancy restaurants where we were wined and dined, but I was told that a guy would scrimp and save for several months to take his wife out for their anniversary. At least it was possible. And these couples exchanging champagne toasts with us and wishing us well reminded me how wonderful it is when people meet, for warmth can exist even among strangers with no words in common. If we could only find a way to remove the hostility in which politicians wrap nations, their people could be not only warm and friendly to each other, but bound up together.

In Yerevan, in the Armenian part of Russia, a little flag of your nationality is put at your place in the hotel restaurant. Alice and I sat there feeling like Aunt and Uncle Sam. But it was a good idea because it encouraged Russian diners to come over and practice their English on you.

Tiflis (Tbilisi) is the capital of Georgia, the part of Russia where Stalin (born Dzhugashvili) came from. It's a beautiful spot in the Georgian moun-

Maftir in Hebrew means, literally, "dismisser"; *Haftarah* means "finish, ending." The *maftir* is actually the concluding section of the Torah that is read at Sabbath or festival services, as well as the person who recites the blessings before and after it. He also, often, does the *Haftarah*, which is the portion of the Prophets that is chanted and read thereafter. The reading of the *Haftarah* has been observed since the first century and, with its special cantillation, is chanted by a Jewish boy on the Saturday of his bar mitzvah.

tains and I liked the tall, well-dressed chap who met us at the airport and who was assigned to take care of us during our stay in Tiflis.

He was apologizing for my having to rehearse on the same day that I arrived, but pointing out that I *had* been left an extra hour to unpack and unwind and wash up. When he finished outlining my schedule, he asked me where I'd like to go that night and I asked him if there was a synagogue in Tiflis. Very matter-of-factly, he gave me an address. I didn't think I would see him there.

The local orchestra conductor insisted on taking me everywhere and showing me everything. He, his wife, my accompanist, John Wustman, Alice, and I all arrived at the address for the late-afternoon service, *mincha.* The place was crowded and I couldn't understand most of what was going on. I'm an Ashkenazi,* and the Hebrew in Tiflis was very, very Sephardic. When it wasn't in Hebrew, it was in Georgian dialect, for which what little Russian I'd picked up was no good at all. So they had me licked both ways.

I tiptoed over to the *shamus,* who spoke Yiddish. "Oh," he said, "you're an Ashkenazi. You're welcome to stay, but you're in the wrong *shul.*"

"You mean there's another *shul* in Tiflis?" I marveled.

"Yes. Come. I'll take you there." He marched the five of us across three squares to a little synagogue that must once have been a private house. There were far fewer people here, and after *mincha* they sat down to eat a little snack of herring and *kichel* (a small, plain cookie), which is known as the "third meal" in Orthodox synagogues. Jews take every opportunity to say a prayer and sing the praises of the Lord, to make an extra blessing over a piece of cake or an extra *Kiddush* to sanctify some wine. The "third meal" is a special chance to sit and study and discuss Torah. As soon as we entered, all three of us men were invited to sit down and participate.

I had persisted in seeking out synagogues because my father had died a few months earlier and I wanted to say Kaddish for him every day if possible. I found myself sitting next to an elderly man, who was the leader of the synagogue, the *gabbai.* He had a certain softness about him that reminded me of the late Louis Perelmuth. He looked a lot like my father, too. Like my father, who sometimes in the course of a rabbinical discussion would reach into his pocket and produce some notes he happened to have prepared on the subject, everything he said made sense. This made me think I had stumbled onto the ghost of my father.

The service started, and while it was a little different from Henry Street

Ashkenaz means "Germany" in Hebrew. Ashkenazim are the Jews of Central and Eastern Europe. The other main branch of Jewry, the Sephardim, centered about Spain, Portugal, and Southern France. Sephardim tend to speak Ladino; Ashkenazim, Yiddish.

With Pablo Casals.

At the Casals Festival in Prades with the Bach Aria Group. Erich Itor Kahn is at piano, Bernard Greenhouse on cello, and Julius Baker is flutist.

More of the Bach
Aria Group. With
Eileen Farrell,
Norman Farrow,
and William Scheide.
(Whitestone Photo)

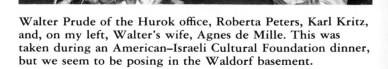

Walter Prude of the Hurok office, Roberta Peters, Karl Kritz,
and, on my left, Walter's wife, Agnes de Mille. This was
taken during an American–Israeli Cultural Foundation dinner,
but we seem to be posing in the Waldorf basement.

Arriving in Tel Aviv, 1967, for the Weizmann–Balfour Assembly. I am
walking with Meyer Weisgal, president of the Weizmann Institute.

At Sherry's in the old Met on November 8, 1954, with Herbert Graf, Dimitri Mitropoulos, and Marian Anderson. *(Sedge Le Blang)*

And, after the same *Rigoletto,* I'm about to be embraced by two female admirers, daughters Joy (left) and Susan.

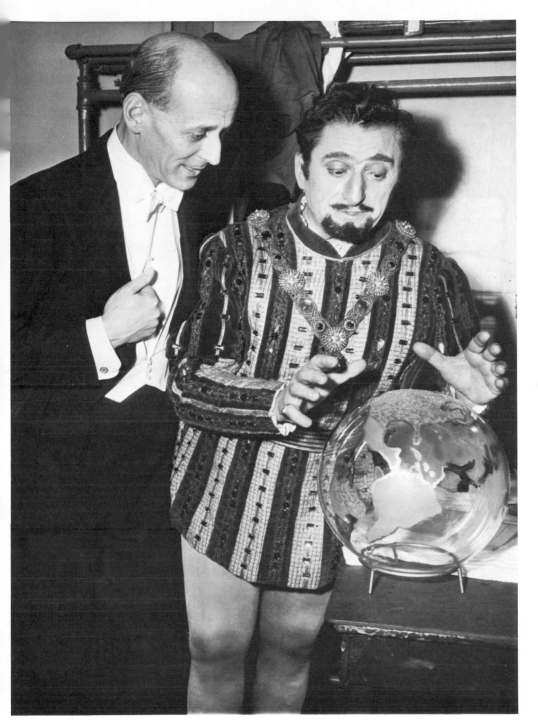

Sir Rudolf Bing and the profligate Duke
shared this view of the world, if no other.

With Susan at
Grossinger's,
September 1960.

Whatever I sing
at Robin Hood Dell,
my Philadelphia
following is likely
to demand "The
Bluebird of
Happiness" as an
encore. (*Jules Schick*)

Passover in Miami
Beach; a Seder at the
Hotel Deauville. On
stage with me, asking
the questions, are my
grandchildren, Joey
Wahrhaftig and
Louise Peerce, and my
grand-niece, Ellen Kaye.

On the set of *Goodbye
Columbus* with my
son, director Larry,
and my co-stars Jack
Klugman and
brother Mac.

With Dolores Wilson and the Kenley Players in Warren, Ohio, on opening night of *Fiddler on the Roof* in the summer of 1971.

With Geraldine Brooks when we did *The Rothschilds* together in 1973. *(Jerry Miller)*

I am a Tevye.

or New Rochelle, I hummed along when I knew what was being sung and tried to learn whatever I didn't know. This fatherly man sitting beside me said in Yiddish, "You seem well versed in things of the synagogue. Where do you come from?" I told him America and he said, "I've met Americans before, but they didn't have your kind of pronunciation."

He asked a few more questions, and when I told him I was saying Kaddish for my father, he said, "Then you have the privilege of chanting the *maariv* [evening] service if you want to and if you know how."

"I think I can handle it," I said, accepting his invitation.

I started very simply. The fatherly *gabbai* stood close, observing me carefully—at first in case I would falter; then in wonder at how easily I did it. But in the part of the service that precedes Kaddish, there is a long line which I just couldn't resist singing out cantorially. When I did, his jaw dropped—and I was satisfied that I had made a hit with this man who reminded me of my father.

As soon as I was finished, he said to me, "With such a voice, who are you? Where *do* you come from?" I told him I had come from America to sing.

"To sing? Oh, you—you are that Pirs who is singing in the opera and then in a concert. Yes, yes, we saw it in the paper. With your picture! Ah, I heard you were Jewish, . . . It was, it was—"

"It was *my* pleasure," I said.

"Well, it was lovely," he said. "Lovely! There is only one thing I regret. It's too bad you weren't here this morning."

"This morning?" I said. "What happened this morning?"

"Oh," he said. "This morning *I* performed the service. And then you would have really heard something!"

I came back the next morning to hear him, but his congregation insisted that I perform the service. Which I did.

The *gabbai* asked me, "You've been traveling all over the world, haven't you, Mr. Pirs?"

I said, "Yes."

"Israel?"

"Many times."

"It must be beautiful in Israel."

"What they've done is beautiful. They've made vineyards out of sand, gardens out of desert. It's a miracle."

He was looking straight at me now. "Of course you know the name of Dr. Herzl?"

"Theodor Herzl?" I said. "Yes, certainly."

"Herzl made a speech years ago," the *gabbai* told me. "He said that the

Jewish people should go there because they belong to Israel. Do you know what? Some went. Some laughed. I am one of those who laughed. Woe to such laughter!"

The old man began to dissolve in tears. "Wait a minute! I want to talk to you!" I called to him, but he had melted into the tiny crowd and had left the synagogue before I could ever again say anything to console that poor, immodest, but humbled man who reminded me of my father.

How Long, O Lord? Forever?

Under the tsars, the Jews of Russia were persecuted, but many were able to emigrate or escape to the outside world, notably the United States. Now, under the Bolsheviks, the estimated 2,345,000 surviving Jews in the Soviet Union continue to be oppressed, but their escape route has been cut off.

Silently, searching their souls, they sit, suffer, wait and wonder.

Into this highly charged atmosphere walked one of the great opera tenors of our time and raised his voice in Moscow's Tchaikovsky concert hall. It was not so much the power of the voice as the power of the words he sang which overwhelmed the Jews in the audience—words which are now certain to spread to all the corners of the vast Soviet empire.

The words, sung in Hebrew, came from the 13th Psalm:

"How long wilt thou forget me, O Lord? Forever?
How long wilt thou hide thy face from me?"

These questions have been weighing for decades on the hearts of Russian Jews. But none would dare voice his complaints to the Lord in public for fear of punishment by the lords of the Kremlin.

It was the son of a Jewish emigrant from Russia who was able to do it for them—Jacob Pincus Perelmuth, better known as Jan Peerce. And the reason he could raise the questions without fear of reprisal by the Kremlin is that his father left Russia so that he might be born on Orchard Street.

—Editorial, *New York Herald Tribune*,
May 14, 1963

The *Herald Tribune*'s editorial was read into the *Congressional Record*. Almost ten years later, on the first Friday in December 1972, I sang to another Russian audience—in Austria at the refugee camp of Schönau: a run-down palace which was the transit point for émigrés going from Russia to Israel. Here they were given clothing, security checks, physical examinations, the medical treatment that most of them needed, and the initial preparation for the culture shock of a new, embattled Jewish homeland after a lifetime of persecution and harassment.

I'd been on a concert tour of Europe, and when I was singing in Vienna, Dr. Aaron Kahan of Israel Bonds had asked if Alice and I would like to see Schönau. We said yes in unison—and so, on that Friday afternoon, we went out there just to see how our fellow Jews looked and felt at this awful yet beautiful time for them in our tragic history.

As soon as we passed the heavily guarded moat, the refugees began to applaud. For a minute I didn't know whom they were applauding. Then I realized it was me.

"We heard your 'Plea to G-d' in Kiev!" "I was in the synagogue in Moscow in 1956!" "Do you remember me from Tiflis?" they greeted me in Yiddish. Sure enough, Aaron Kahan whispered to me that some of them were requesting that I sing for them then and there.

I had brought along no pianist, no piano, and no music. So of course I said yes.

"This being Friday evening," I began, "the best thing I could sing for you is the sanctification of the Sabbath wine: *Kiddush.*"

They jumped at the idea. The people in charge produced a bottle of Carmel, an Israeli red wine with which they'd been supplied at Schönau. So there I stood with a small group of eighty Russian Jews, a few of whom had arrived only that morning on the *Chopin,* * as I chanted *Kiddush.* Some of these Jews were hearing *Kiddush* for the first time. All of them were going to a place where *Kiddush* is sung every Friday night, not just in the synagogue, but in the home. For me, it was a moment packed with deep emotion. For them, it must have been even more profound: I tried to impart a feeling of freedom and give them a send-off that neither they nor I would ever forget.

After *Kiddush,* everyone was happy, but I saw one of them whispering to Aaron Kahan, who began right away: "Jan, they're asking, if it's not imposing on you, whether you would sing a favorite song of yours, a number you did in Russia called 'Raisins and Almonds.' "

"Rozhinkes mit Mandlen" is a simple folk song. In my boyhood, nuts, especially almonds, and raisins were great signs of affluence—particularly if you could afford both of them at the same time. They were for special occasions like a bar mitzvah or the Saturday-morning *ufruf* before a wedding, when the groom visits his father-in-law's synagogue and is called up to the Torah to recite a blessing.

In either event, in an Orthodox synagogue, the women, segregated in

*A so called express, passing through Poland, Slovakia, and Moravia, and favored by iron curtain authorities for deportations to Austria.

the back or the balcony or else concealed behind curtains or peepholes in the wall, have armed themselves with fistfuls of raisins and almonds. As the bar mitzvah boy or bridegroom comes forth, they pelt him with these good wishes of theirs: "May you always be able to afford the luxury of raisins and almonds." Sometimes, when the relatives are unhappy about the groom, they'd rather throw the fists and eat the raisins and almonds themselves.

"Raisins and Almonds" had indeed been one of the most frequent Jewish request numbers during my two trips to Russia. As early as 1958, in his book *Only in America,* Harry Golden had remarked on how "those elderly Jews in the Soviet, cut off from Jewish communal living, folkways, and culture, wanted this great American tenor to sing a folk song to bring them a bit of their past: mother, father, home, and memory."

I have sung with many European and American orchestras and always with at least a piano to accompany me, but rarely at Carnegie Hall or Lincoln Center have I experienced the thrill I felt when I sang "Rozhinkes mit Mandlen" a capella to that gathering of Russian refugees at Schönau. For I was reaching out to my people at a difficult but hopeful moment when they might soon be blessed with sanctified wine and raisins and almonds—and I myself was blessed that I could do this.

Truman, Nixidou and Pius

I didn't meet Harry S. Truman until he was a President Emeritus in 1963. He was supposed to come hear one of my concerts on a Friday night in Kansas City. At the last minute, he couldn't make it. He asked his secretary to call up and tell me. She went on to say: "He has to leave for Philadelphia tomorrow afternoon, but before he goes, he would like to meet you." We made the appointment for 11:45 A.M.

I went to synagogue as usual on Saturday morning. The service started late. I did the morning *maftir.* I couldn't disillusion the younger generation by running out before the service was over—though I was truly tempted to do so when the cantor said, "What Mr. Peerce sang for you now would be classified as a $5,000 *maftir.*" I just bit my tongue, stuck to my seat, and sent a friend out to phone the ex-President of the United States telling him I was running late—and why.

Truman told my friend that his train wasn't until three o'clock, so he'd wait for me as long as he could. I arrived only forty-five minutes late. As I walked into his office apologizing: "Mr. President, I feel terrible about this," he was standing up to greet me. He cut me off with, "Jan Peerce, you were in the right place at the right time doing the right thing. The question was whether to keep the Lord waiting or a former President of the United States waiting. I'm happy to say the Lord won." We spent forty minutes together talking about music, politics, and children, but his first words are what linger indelibly in my memory. No better qualified mortal could have told me I had been in the right place at the right time than this accidental president whose place in history was that he was the right man in the right place at the right time.

Richard Nixon and his family once attended a performance of *Lucia* I was in at the Met. Afterwards, they came backstage to meet me. I'm generally a pretty loquacious guy who has a lot to say to people. But I was struck with silence. There was nothing I wanted to say to this man. I spoke to his wife and daughters. They told me how much they liked *Lucia.* I told them how much I liked *Lucia.* I don't remember whether Nixon was Vice President then or between jobs. Either way, he didn't interest me—whether he was office boy or VP or even President. Enough had happened in the 1940s and 1950s—his campaign against Helen Gahagan Douglas, his handling of Alger Hiss and Joe McCarthy—that I couldn't possibly admire such a man. I didn't think he was honest. I don't think he was even honest to himself. There was a little back room his mind worked in—somewhere behind the White House, the Oval Office, or my dressing room, or wherever we thought we saw him.

Still, I was glad the Nixons visited us because of a conversation Alice and I had right after they left. I began it by remarking: "I'll tell you one fantastic thing. Whatever's in those people's hearts I don't know, but I do know those three women would fight for him to the very last."

Alice asked: "How about your kids? Don't you think they'd fight for you?"

"Would they fight for me if I were like him?"

"No matter what they had in their hearts," Alice told me, "they would fight to save every hair on your head." Over the years, I've learned she was right.

I voted against Nixon all three times I had the chance to. A lot of my friends supported him, particularly the third time, because he was "a friend of Israel." I maintain any other President would have done the same—maybe faster. It was only when he realized Israel was the last bulwark of democracy and our only friend in the Middle East that he helped. Judaism was not a reason for supporting a Nixon—and when I read the transcript of his taped remarks about Jews, I was glad I hadn't.

One of the times I was invited to sing in Nixon's White House I declined when I heard the guest of honor was President Pompidou of France, who was no friend of the Jews. France used to sell Mirage jets to Israel, but then Pompidou decided not to because the Arabs were bigger customers. So I told the Hurok office to tell Nixon to get an Arab to sing for Pompidou. I don't know what Walter Prude at the Hurok office told the White House, but I didn't sing for *their* supper.

Which brings me, as the late Bill Stern might have said, to my audience with Pope Pius XII in the mid-1950s. I was recording *Butterfly* excerpts with Licia Albanese in Rome for RCA Victor. Constance Hope the publicist asked me if I would personally deliver a set of recordings of *Music of all Religions,* including some of my own renditions, for the Vatican Archives. "If so," she added, "I can arrange a private audience for you with the Pope." I told her I would love to, but couldn't go along with the requirements of kneeling and kissing his ring.

"You will not be asked to kneel, or to kiss his ring. He'll just extend his hand and you take it."

This I could do, gladly, so Constance arranged four invitations. In addition to Alice, I asked Albanese and Dick Mohr of RCA to come with us; both were Catholics. When I invited Licia she was annoyed. She said: "Now look, Jan. I know you like to clown around. But my religion is a very serious matter to me, so don't you make jokes about the Pope."

"Would I clown about the Pope?"

"Well, you're teasing me and I don't like it."

"Who's teasing? I asked you to go with me to a private audience I'm having with the Pope."

Finally, Licia looked at me and laughed, "I'm very sorry. I misunderstood. I thought you were trying to be funny."

"You don't give me much credit as a friend," I said. "A friend knows what he can fool around with and what he can't." And I gave her a ticket.

We were staying at the Excelsior Hotel where nobody had paid much attention to us. The management knew I was an opera singer, but, since I've never sung on an Italian stage, nobody had heard of me.

The night before my audience, the Papal secretary came to the hotel and asked for me. He confirmed that the Pope would simply take my hand and he outlined the whole procedure. When he left, the whole hotel staff—which was used to his visits to VIPs—was gawking at me. From then on, I was a celebrity.

The audience went smoothly. The Pope—a small, slight man who spoke English with an accent—had been well-briefed not just on my singing, but on my past.

"Jan Peerce," he said, "you don't sing in Italy enough for me."

"Thank you," I said. "I agree. I don't sing in Italy enough for me, either."

Then he told me we had something in common: "You were a violinist, did you know that I was one, too?"

"Is that so?" I said. "Well, maybe one day, you'll find the time for us to get together and play some duets."

"That would be wonderful!" he said. We stood and talked for ten minutes, but we never did play a duet.

How the Culture Corps Never Got Off the Ground

Maurice Feldman was someone Alice had to sell me on. I'd admired his work as a press agent, but when we first met him in the Russian Tea Room twenty years ago, I could barely understand his English. It was so heavily accented I wondered how this man could deal with the American media.

Alice, however, saw something else: "He has contacts. Jan, I don't want you to take on somebody who has fourteen opera singers, so you'll be the fifteenth. I want somebody who'll believe in you as I believe in you—who'll be dedicated to you. And most of all, this man strikes me as a wonderful human being. I want him! I want such a person to be part of us."

She was right. Maurice was a part of our life, our family, and my career from the time we met him. I learned, from his dealings with the press and the arts, that his Viennese accent was a great professional asset—which may be why it grew thicker during his forty years here. My association with Maurice was at least as personal as it was professional and his slow death at sixty-six in 1976 was not just a personal tragedy, but a loss for many.

Shortly after I returned from my second trip to Russia in 1963, Maurice and I dreamed up an idea based on what both the Israelis and the Kennedys were doing at the time. Israel was sending military, technical, and agricultural advisers, doctors and engineers, to all its neighbors—giving them know-how and making friends. And President Kennedy and his relatives had the Peace Corps going. Maurice and I decided to apply the Peace Corps idea to the arts.

An American artist who goes to Russia or anywhere else arrives, performs, leaves. Much more, however, can be accomplished if you live among the people, share with them whatever you may know, and maybe learn something from them, too. The exchange of ideas can also be the basis of friendships. Let people learn to know you and more often than not, they'll learn to like you.

We were organizing a presentation to be made right to President

Kennedy. Maybe it could be done at the White House by going through channels, but I would have a better chance to approach J.F.K. directly when I would be at the head table with him at a Weizmann Institute of Science fund-raising banquet in December in New York City. Meyer Weisgal, who played a fundamental part in the building of the institute and was Chaim Weizmann's intimate associate, had brought me over to Rehovot several Novembers to sing at the annual pilgrimage on the anniversary of Israel's first president's death.

On Friday, November 22, 1963, I was at home in New Rochelle rehearsing the numbers I would sing for the President: "A Plea to G-d," "How Long, O Lord, Wilt Thou Forsake Me?" "Macushla." Then the phone rang. It was Meyer Weisgal calling. There would be no banquet. The guest of honor was dead.

Lyndon Baines Johnson was the new President. Maurice and I gave him a few months to attend to more urgent matters and then, in early 1964, I wrote a letter to L.B.J. explaining our idea:

> Such a Culture Corps would be on a voluntary basis, but government sponsored and much broader than our present Cultural Exchange Program. It should utilize not only the best-known American artists, but also unknown talent.
>
> The members of the Culture Corps should go all over the world, informing about American ideas, methods, and training, and the payment would be nominal. A commission should decide who would be admitted.
>
> Very often, when American artists perform abroad, the audience consists mostly of the upper classes and the masses are more or less excluded. If our government, through this Culture Corps, could sponsor musical events on a larger basis than has been the case in the past, we could easily reach the man in the street in most countries.

I never received an answer from President Johnson. He must have been concentrating on winning either the 1964 election or else the hearts and minds of Southeast Asia.

Maurice Feldman, being a press agent, knew what to do next. He called the *New York Times,* where Ross Parmenter did a story about the Culture Corps that rated a three-column headline on an inside page. I also sent a carbon copy of my unanswered letter to Senator Jacob Javits, who announced: "This is a splendid idea and deserves careful consideration. I believe it could be developed . . . I am asking the White House for a copy of its reply to Mr. Peerce's proposal."

Perhaps because my Lower East Side neighbor Jacob Javits had grown up to be a Republican, he never received an answer from the White House either. But he did provoke a call from the State Department to me: "We send Harry Belafonte to Africa and Kirk Douglas to Eastern Europe. What is there in the Culture Corps that's different from what we already have?"

I replied, "You have nothing. You have no core. The Peace Corps is working because they live with the people; the minute *that* changes or if *you* lose interest in Washington, it'll dissipate. *Your* artists just fly in and fly out. . . ." I went on to give my Culture Corps spiel for the umpteenth time.

The voice at the other end said, "It sounds interesting. We'll get back to you."

A week later, to my surprise, they did. They asked me to come to Washington. I couldn't manage it because of performances, but I agreed to meet with someone if he could come up to New Rochelle. A few mornings later, a call came from the State Department. A Mr. So-and-so was already airborne from Washington to New York. He would phone me from La Guardia Airport. It was two hours before the call came from La Guardia. I gave him directions. He said he was renting a car and would be there in an hour. Allowing for him to get lost, I budgeted two hours before he and I would set eyes on each other.

Several hours later the next call came. "I'm very sorry, I'm running a bit late, Mr. Peerce, but this car I rented broke down. It's been fixed and I'll be there as soon as I can if you'll still see me."

He sounded almost disappointed when I said I'd wait up for him. Which I did. But after another four hours without any word, I called it a night. I never received another call about the matter from the State Department or anybody else in Washington. Our Culture Corps never got off the ground. That's too bad—and so is the thought that one of our diplomats may still be missing somewhere between La Guardia and New Rochelle.

Cav and Bing

Turiddu, in Mascagni's *Cavalleria Rusticana (Rustic Chivalry)*, is a passionate Sicilian, and from the standpoint of warmth and passion in our likes and dislikes, he and I are much alike. Turiddu loves his friend Alfio's wife, Lola, who was his first love before he went off to the army. He also loves Santuzza, whose reputation he ruined when he found out Lola was fickle. Now he's seeing Lola again—and the whole town knows about it except maybe Alfio, but it isn't long before he learns of it. When Turiddu offers Alfio a drink, Alfio refuses it: "Your wine would become poison in my stomach." Turid-

du's Sicilian blood gets the better of him. He runs at Alfio and bites his ear.
A duel is inevitable.

Turiddu has a premonition of death. He pretends he has had a little too
much to drink. All of a sudden, he asks for his mother's blessing. If I don't
return, he says, take care of Santuzza as if she were your own daughter. Then
he goes out to get killed. You never see him again, but he's had great, great
things to sing—in a short opera that has a lot to say in a very little time.

Cavalleria Rusticana and *La Forza del Destino* are operas that people didn't
expect of me. They were known as dramatic, *verismo* operas. In my own way,
however, I think I proved that a tenor could *sing* a dramatic part.

As I've said, I don't mind taking on a challenge. I can handle it if the
right man's in the pit and I'm careful to control my own emotions, not get
carried away by the music. When it was announced that I was going to do
Cavalleria in San Francisco in 1958, some of my friends thought I was
meshugge (crazy): "You won't do *Aïda,* but you will do *Cavalleria?*"

I had waited until a certain time of maturity when I could handle the
part without straining or injuring my technique. By the time Gaetano Merola
offered Turiddu to me, I had looked it over and decided I could be ready
for it. It was a part that, before 1958, I had turned down in San Francisco
and elsewhere. The Met had never offered me the part; Rudolf Bing had
been there almost ten years.

Rudolf Bing was tall, gaunt, bald, and skinny. Even at his most pious,
to me he looked severe. Claudia Cassidy once described him, walking up the
aisle at intermission of *Faust* in Chicago, as looking more Mephistophelian
than Mephisto. Somehow, whenever I saw him, he reminded me of Ichabod
Crane.

The day I met him in 1949, I'd wandered into Edward Johnson's office
and Johnson told Bing, "I want you to meet our Jan Peerce. We're so proud
of him, we love him."

Bing looked right through me as if I weren't there.

I came home that night and told Alice, "I just met my nemesis."

"What are you talking about, Jan?"

"I'm talking about Bing, my future boss. He's not my friend."

"How do you know?" I told her how I knew. I had seen the look on
Bing's face.

My association with Bing started off on a left foot, probably because I
was such a credit to his predecessor. But I was riding high and involved in
a career that was blooming in spite of him. My first real conflict with him

came when I went in, after my San Francisco success, and told him I'd like to do *Cavalleria Rusticana.*

Bing chuckled and said, "You've got enough to do. What do you want to do that for?" He went on to say, "You know, with all due respect, there comes a time when you and the rest of your generation will have to be replaced."

When I could find words, I said, "Let me tell you a story, Mr. Bing. In November 1941, when I came to this great institution, I was thrilled! You can listen to the recording of the broadcast on that last Saturday afternoon in November if you want; it was a marvelous success. I knew even then that one day I would be replaced here. But by whom? By inexperienced, undeveloped singers? And chosen by whom?"

"Somehow or other," he said smoothly, "you seem not to agree with my choices."

I told him, "I believe that artists should have their careers built and furthered at the Met. But it's not an amateur contest, it's a professional summit. It's not a place where you try things out or give people a chance to gather experience. They've got to be experienced by the time they get to the Met. It's not a school. It's the big league. Set up a school for them, if you want. Or send them out—the way I went out with the Columbia Opera Company, losing time and money at the Music Hall, but gaining experience. But don't have them work out their inexperience on the stage of the Met."

"It's all a matter of opinion, wouldn't you say?" he said in that strange accent of his. He never seemed to make up his mind about what he was: Viennese, *Hochdeutsch,* British, or American. He might go through four or five accents in one sentence. But he had made up his mind that I'd not be Turiddu.

Eventually he explained, with an air that told me the interview was over, that the young must be given every chance and "in order to get these people to stand by, mature, and eventually take over, we have to make it worth their while. I can't give them nothing, so I'd like to give them a *Cavalleria* from time to time."

"That's the trouble!" I exploded. "You think Turiddu is a role for beginners. There are impresarios in this world who give the wrong roles to youngsters. That's why, by the time they're thirty, they're in vocal trouble. That's why they have a wobble at the age of thirty-five so bad you can't listen to them."

"And whom do you blame for that?" Bing purred. "Isn't it their teaching?"

"No," I said. "Not only their teachers, but critics, conductors, and all the people around the theatre, and particularly the impresarios!"

I left his office, cussing him under my breath and hoping the Lord would deliver my cuss on a Saturday. (Bing managed to fill the role of Turiddu without me all season.)

The next season, when Robert Herman, Bing's right hand, called me in to discuss which operas I'd do, I found *Cavalleria* headed the list. I also noticed who my Santuzza was: Giulietta Simionato. Like Novotna, she was not only a terrific singer, but a great actress. In this part, she was fabulous. I recognized what Bing was trying to tell me: "You want a party; we'll give you a real funeral. We'll put you up against the best Santuzza in the business." What Bing may or may not have known is that a Novotna or a Simionato is so good that not only do you rise to the occasion, but she helps *you* look even better! Turiddu became one of my most gratifying parts just from working with Giulietta, responding to every move she made, and above all, meeting her on her own level.

To bring off Turiddu, you have to know what you're doing vocally. You also have to generate a certain passion and heat. Santuzza is a role that tends to bring out harshness in too many sopranos. When the chemistry works between a good Turiddu and Santuzza, however, *Cav* becomes a great, great opera instead of a mere curtain-raiser to *Pagliacci*.

Simionato used to have an acting trick in *Cavalleria*. During a dramatic scene in which Santuzza pleads with Turiddu not to leave her, when I began to move away from her, she would hook her arm around mine so that she would be dragged along with me, singing her pleas. It was very effective.

Later, Zinka Milanov, Eileen Farrell, and Martina Arroyo were wonderful Santuzzas to me. Martina Arroyo was the busiest I've ever seen, thanks to Franco Zeffirelli's planting of a whole Sicilian village on the vast stage at Lincoln Center. She raced in and out, grabbing, lurching, skidding, falling. The staircase was an even greater obstacle to her. Once she actually broke an arm. Another time, she fell with such a hard thud that as soon as the curtain fell, I asked if she was all right. "Oh, yes," she said sweetly. "I have a cushion of tush"—which is the Harlem version of the Yiddish *tuchis*.

From the beginning, Rudolf Bing was the most private and least friendly man I'd ever met. He walked through the corridors of power looking straight ahead, never saying hello to anyone, even when someone was right in front of him and had to get out of his way. The man who doesn't greet anybody is, in my opinion, invariably insecure.

Later Bing thawed a little. Somebody must have told him he should try to upgrade his image. He used to favor the dancers. They were his pets. He knew all their birthdays and I sometimes saw him feeding the boys and girls their birthday cake in person.

Bing ran the Met for twenty-two years (1950–1972), and I worked for him eighteen of those years. Of all his sins, the one I most condemn him for came early, when he failed to defend the old Met as a landmark. Perhaps the blame should be shared by the Metropolitan's board of directors. To this day, nobody knows why they were so anxious to tear down the old Met at Thirty-ninth and Broadway, but determined they were. Bing must have gone along partly because he was attracted by the snob appeal of a new $47 million house. Even if they needed the new house, the old Met—with its dust and dirt and worn-out paint on the walls and broken chairs—could certainly have been made into something grand. I think Bing wouldn't let the old Met stand because he didn't want any competition.

In 1972, when Bing's memoir *5000 Nights at the Opera* was published, somebody brought it to me and made me read some of it.

There, in the next-to-last paragraph of Chapter One, Bing's ghost, Martin Mayer, writes that when everybody was speculating about the next general manager of the Met, Edward Johnson had playfully tossed out the names of four singers: "John Brownlee, Lauritz Melchior, Jan Peerce, Charlie Kullmann. . . ." It was just a joke, but for a man like Bing, maybe I represented a threat.

I have been asked if I would have taken the job if it had been offered to me. I wouldn't have been interested. My career was going very well and continued to in spite of Bing. This to me was more of a challenge and an accomplishment than that of any pious martinet who ran an opera company, ran it into the ground, saddling his successors with a white marble elephant of an opera house that became a full-time problem in itself. John Dexter, the Met's new director of productions, has been quoted as saying that the ultimate salvation of the company would be to tear the house down and start again on a sensible scale.

What's wrong with the Met? You listen to the administrators, and the more they talk about their financial problems and labor troubles, the more they forget that the quality of the shows has deteriorated. That's worse than anything else! Too much time and money are spent on fanfare and flashy productions, but hardly anybody is looking out for the quality of the performances or picking the proper people to sing the proper roles.

The trouble, as with Bing when he didn't want me to sing *Cavalleria,* is that administrators aren't musicians. Their choice of vocalists leaves something to be desired. This has been a chronic condition since the Bing years. A good administrator must surround himself with trustworthy experts who know music better than he does. Such people are plentiful in New York, but Bing felt more at home with sycophants. As it was, during Bing's regime the European meanness of booing and claques was imported to the Met on an organized basis. (Everything was priced: applause upon entrance, applause upon exit, applause after inferior rendition of aria. One could buy twenty-five or fifty or a hundred dollars' worth of noise. In Bing's own book, he admits to having "hired a claquer" for the night of February 5, 1959, when Leonie Rysanek made her debut replacing Maria Callas in *Macbeth*. The claquer shouted, "Brava, Callas!" on Bing's assumption that this would win enormous sympathy for Leonie. He guessed right, but Rysanek didn't ever need such artificial respiration.) The worst part of the Bing years was that he had a claque right in the front office—paid to tell him everything was perfect and could only be made more perfect.

Casting directors and executives often didn't seem to know the difference between what a singer *could* sing and what he or she *should* sing. They would send anybody out to sing anything, throwing them to the lions and maybe hurting the voice or the singer's confidence.

Miscasting knew no bounds in the Bing years. In *Don Carlo,* the Met had baritones rather than basses singing the Grand Inquisitor, which calls for the blackest and deepest of voices. Or a deep bass singing the baritone part of Wotan. Many "name" singers were allowed to pick roles that they shouldn't have even considered.

This Bing Revolution, alas, has permeated other opera companies. Today it falls upon the artist to resist—to know what he can and cannot do. Whether anyone is strong enough to keep saying no is something else again. The pressure to accept a role when it is offered is hard to fight. But you can't build a reputation on a foundation of the wrong roles. You're living beyond your means singing *Aïda* and *Turandot* when you should be singing *Rigoletto, Traviata, Lucia,* and *Bohème.*

The Great White Hope of the Met

The Cincinnati Zoo Summer Opera used to be a fun palace for me. It was the kind of al fresco place where I could ask a soprano to hold my Coke bottle backstage while I went out and did my death scene. The peacocks never shouted me down, for they preferred tenors to coloratura sopranos. Bats, moths, and, especially, pigeons posed greater problems. But Bob Weede and I did more than one memorable *Rigoletto* there. We also did *Traviata, Lucia,* and *Tosca.*

Back in 1953, the pigeons used to get into one's hair. There was also a chubby kid who used to hang around rehearsals. He knew every word, every note of every score we did. With *Rigoletto,* he used to tell you what you were going to do wrong even before you did it. He used to be attracted to my voice and this uninvited attention particularly vexed me, so I used to chase him away, saying, "Get out of here! You annoy me." At the end of one season, he handed me a gray autograph book with multicolored pages and asked me if I would sign it. I didn't much cherish the kid, but I did write something nice in it even as I was thinking: Good riddance!

I didn't make the connection when I went to the Meadow Brook Music Festival in Rochester, Michigan, fifteen years later to do a concert version of *Rigoletto* with Cornell MacNeil, Roberta Peters, and Ezio Flagello (doubling as Sparafucile and Monterone). I had asked who was conducting and been told by Hurok: "James Levine [pronounced La-vine], one of the great new prospective talents in conducting." I'd never heard of him, but I looked forward.

Cornell, Roberta, and I were taken from the Detroit airport to the rehearsal building, where someone was playing *Rigoletto* more beautifully than I've ever heard from a piano. "Gee whiz," I said, "I don't know anything about your conductor, but you've got a great pianist. Who is he?"

"That's James Levine," our host told me.

I said, "No kidding!"

Cornell MacNeil seemed perplexed. "Don't you know Jim Levine, Jan? He says he knows you very well."

I could have sworn I didn't know him from Adam Levine—even after we walked in and this stocky, bushy-haired fellow I was sure I'd never seen before jumped up from his piano bench, ran over, and embraced me, saying, "Jan! What a great day this is! It's a moment I've always dreamed of." I looked at him. He looked at me. "Don't you recognize me?"

"No, I'm sorry," I said. "Where did I meet you?"

"At the Cincinnati Zoo Opera," James Levine answered, producing a gray autograph book with multicolored pages and opening it to one that said, in my handwriting: "To James Levine, a worthy colleague: Wishing you great success in your future. Jan Peerce, July, 1953."

I looked at him closely. "Do you mean to say that you're that pesky kid?"

"I was," he said, beaming.

"Then you see?" I said. "I knew something."

That kid grew up to be not just a great talent, but a wonderful man: sweet, lovely, knowledgeable, and warm. A *Wunderkind* pianist before he was eleven, he studied form and analysis, structure and style, for the next eight years with Walter Levin, first violinist of the La Salle Quartet in Cincinnati. He fulfilled all the undergraduate requirements at Juilliard in one year.

Since 1964, James Levine had been working as assistant to George Szell, a cold but honest man and a great conductor of the Cleveland Orchestra.

Even after all these years, *Rigoletto* was a revelation to me when I did it with James Levine. Later, doing *Don Giovanni* at Severance Hall in Cleveland, he inspired Flagello, Ramon Vinay, Italo Tajo, and me to a performance that was the nearest in my experience to what Toscanini used to accomplish. Levine had all of us singing over our heads. He had us making music, not competing with him or our fellow artists for glory. He used the orchestra as part of an ensemble. It didn't overpower the artists. Nobody tried to be a prima donna. When you make music and strive to make music, particularly when the music is Mozart's, you become an ensemble that can't be beat. James Levine has the faculty of putting it all together.

In 1970, I was booked to do a recital at Severance Hall. Before I could line up my pianist, a mutual friend in Ohio called me to say James Levine would like to accompany me, if I wouldn't mind.

"Mind?" I said. "I'd be honored!"

He and I gave one of the best concerts of my life. I've always had a soft spot for Jimmy: as autograph seeker, musician, performer, and man. And apparently our high regard is mutual, for he wrote to me in 1973: "This is the first chance I've had to write and tell you how much I enjoyed your Carnegie Hall concert! . . . Jan, it's very difficult to put into words how exciting it was to hear you sing like that! The sonority, rhythm, diction, style, enthusiasm, and communication were fantastic as ever. . . ."

[James Levine was interviewed November 17, 1975, at Le Poulailler Restaurant, opposite Lincoln Center, during the celebration of Roberta Peters's twenty-fifth anniversary with the Metropolitan Opera.]

James Levine: *To me, Jan Peerce is really a phenomenon among singers of today in general and tenors in particular. First of all, no other tenor in our time has had a career of over forty years singing leading roles. Also, his incredible technique, diction, rhythm, enthusiasm, and stylistic élan are unique.*

For several years, I taught a class at the Cleveland Institute of Music. The subject was "Musical Style and Interpretation." Obviously, a lot of time was spent discussing singing. I made it a point each year to devote one whole class period to a lengthy discussion of Jan's artistry along with selections from his recordings.

Another explanation for his fantastic vocal longevity is that he never agreed to sing anything that he didn't really feel was right for him at that particular time. This included refusing offers from Toscanini on occasion—something which should be a lesson to many young singers who try to function as exceptions to the natural physical laws of vocal development and end up with very short, insecure careers.

No other singer of our time has been equally at home with the Bach Aria Group, on the recital stage, at the Metropolitan Opera singing Verdi, singing the Beethoven Ninth with Toscanini, doing Fiddler on the Roof *on Broadway, singing in* shul, *or singing* The Star-Spangled Banner *in Shea Stadium on opening day.*

In 1976, at age thirty-two, James Levine became music director responsible for artistic decisions at the Metropolitan Opera. He's probably the best thing that ever happened to the Met and I hope this is a good thing that's happened to Jim. When I worried that he might bog himself down in paper work and negotiations, he assured me that he won't even have a desk at the Met and that he'll conduct an average of three performances a week seven months of the year. And I'll be rooting for him, because he has great conducting talents like those conductors of thirty or forty years ago who are legends now.

Boris Was a Baptist

The six-foot-six American bass Jerome Hines was not only one of the outstanding Boris Godunovs of our time, but an ardent Baptist who liked to missionize and proselytize—even when he was singing *Boris* in Russia. He brought in new Baptists right and left.

On tour with the Met in Dallas, we sang *Don Giovanni* together. He and I were standing outside the Fair Park Auditorium, going to different parties and waiting for the cars coming to fetch us. He stood next to me— or rather, towered over me—as we congratulated each other on the night's work. To kill time, he started talking about new members of his church. "Do you know," he said, "we now have one of your coreligionists: a very nice man."

"Is that so?" I said.

"Yes, and we're very happy to have him."

"That's fine."

"He sure is a great addition to our movement."

"I'm sure," I said.

Then Jerry began to extol the virtues of Baptism. The more he went on, the more I felt he was directing his remarks at me for more than conversational purposes. So I said, "Listen, Jerry! I want to tell you something. The fact that you have one of my coreligionists as the newest addition to your church is all right with me. That you're happy with him is also okay with me. But look, if you're telling this to me for any other reason, let me assure you: *Me you won't get."*

He slapped me on the back just as my car came. "Don't worry, Jan," he said, "we'll get you yet."

As I disappeared into the Dallas night, I added, "Don't call me and I won't call you."

The one time Jerome Hines had the last word with me was on the morning of July 22, 1952, when I was rehearsing *Traviata* at the Cincinnati Zoo Opera with a lovely soprano named Lucia Evangelista. At two o'clock that morning, Lucia and Jerry had been married in Indiana.

When they broke the news to me, the three of us were strolling in the park. I asked Lucia the usual question I ask a bride: "Why did you marry a bum like this when you had me around?"

Before Lucia could give the first of ten easy answers, Jerry cut in: "Look, Jan. Take away my amazing stature and physique, my handsome face, my gorgeous voice—and what have you got?"

"Yes," I agreed. "What have you got?"

"Jan Peerce," he said.

And Peerce Was a Monk

Verdi's *La Forza del Destino* was the other opera I had trouble persuading Bing I should sing. He knew me as a lyric tenor. The part of Don Alvaro has to be sung both lyrically and dramatically. When I say "dramatic," I mean "with great intensity."

Eventually I won my chance—but not until 1962 at the Met. I did it only twice there and twice more on tour. But I think of Don Alvaro as one of my finest parts. *Forza* is a very rewarding opera with good parts for everybody. I have sung it with Leonard Warren and Robert Merrill as Don Carlo di Vargas; Eileen Farrell and Martina Arroyo as his sister, Leonora; Jerome Hines and Cesare Siepi as Padre Guardiano; and Salvatore Baccaloni and Fernando Corena in the fine character part of Fra Melitone.

As soon as the tenor walks out, he begins singing great stuff, and it goes on all evening, so you'd better have your upper voice working.

In the beginning, Leonora's about to elope with Alvaro when her father, the Marquis of Calatrava, tries to stop us. Not wanting to fight my future father-in-law, I throw down my pistol, which, of course, goes off and kills the Marquis. Bedlam breaks loose. I go one way and Leonora another. From then on, I'm a hunted man. She goes to a convent and I wind up in a monastery. Before I get there, though, I'm a Spanish soldier fighting the Germans in Italy under an assumed name. So is Leonora's brother, and naturally we're in the same regiment. By the time we come together, I've saved Carlo from death at the hands of some drunken soldiers. He and I swear eternal friendship. This is on the eve of a battle. I am wounded offstage, but brought back on to sing one of the greatest duets ever written for two men: "Solenne in quest' ora" ("In this solemn hour"). I think I'm dying, so I give my friend Carlo a sealed packet, which he is to destroy upon my death. But Carlo has already begun to suspect that I am the killer of his father, whom he has sworn to avenge. In the same bag as the packet he finds a picture of—good G-d! —his sister Leonora.

Though I'm nearly dead, I escape to a cloister and disguise myself as a monk. There I do penance, though I know I'm not guilty. But Don Carlo finds me, taunts me, insults me, and finally goads me to a duel. With that, we rush offstage to fight. I wound Carlo near a hermit's cave and when the dying man calls for a priest, I go to the cave of this "holy man"—only to discover that he's a she and she is Leonora. She rushes to her dying brother's side, offstage, and he stabs her mortally.

Leonora now staggers back onstage. I'm very remorseful, pleading with her not to leave this world. She doesn't listen, so she leaves. The music in her death scene once inspired me to remark at a rehearsal, "Y'know, this is so beautiful, it must be Jewish."

Jan Peerce as a man of the cloth in big white robes and a little yarmulke (skullcap) was bound to elicit a reaction. My own was simple: I always have respect for a part. Offstage, I won't kneel in St. Patrick's or even in the Vatican to the Pope himself, but onstage I will do what the role calls for.

One of the two *Forza*s I sang at the Met was a benefit for a synagogue. Afterward a man came back to my dressing room and began, "Mr. Peerce, I was of the impression that you are an observant Jew. How can you play that part in the last act?"

"What has this got to do with playing the role?" I said. "First of all, I'm acting. Second of all, if you *must* know, I have something that counteracts my robes and my cross. Underneath, I'm wearing my *mezuzah.*"

He was impressed but I went on. "Why are you complaining to me? If you're so fussy, why don't you complain to your synagogue? Tell them not to book this particular opera for their benefits. They could have booked *Traviata* or *Don Giovanni!* They could have booked a dozen operas where nobody makes the sign of the cross."

"Oh, they couldn't have done that," he said.

"Why the hell not?" I demanded.

"Because I'm the program chairman and this was the only opera I've never seen you in."

At *The Golem* with Maria Callas's Mama

Abraham Ellstein was a very dear friend of mine from my early music days: a fine musician, composer, conductor, arranger. He conducted my records of *Yiddish Folk Songs* and *Cantorial Masterpieces* and composed for me a cantorial masterpiece called "V'-li-rusholayim ircho" ("And to Jerusalem, Thy City, Return to Mercy"). Whenever I needed a new composition or arrangement, I'd call Abe. Invariably he'd sound harassed: "Jan, I'm so busy right now. Why did you have to call me at this particular time? I can't do it. But tell me what I'm missing out on. What was it you wanted?" I'd tell him. He'd say, "Well, I'll try it, but you may have to wait two or three weeks, maybe longer." And I could rest assured that next morning he'd call up to say it was ready.

When Abe made an opera out of the great play *The Golem,* he wrote it with me in mind for the rabbi, but I declined the honor. I told Abe, "Even before I hear it, I can't do it. I can't learn an opera for just a few performances, particularly when it's not for the Met." The tenor the New York City Opera did get, Jon Crain, turned in a fine job when I attended the premiere March 22, 1962, at the City Center on West Fifty-fifth Street.

At intermission, someone told me, "Maria Callas's mother is here tonight and she'd like to meet you."

"Gladly," I said. I was taken to a swarthy woman, whose first words to me were: "You're very short, aren't you?"

She certainly brought up the right subject, didn't she? For a split second, I dreamed I was auditioning for Earl Carroll's *Vanities* in my elevator shoes instead of attending the premiere of Abe Ellstein's *The Golem.*

I said, "There are lots of shorter men in this world, madam."

"But you *are* short."

"I beg your pardon, I am very tall."

"How can you say you're tall?"

"How can you say I'm short?" Thirty years earlier I might have burst into tears, but now I heard myself saying to Maria Callas's mother: "Do you know, madam, that from where I stand, I look down upon you?"

The funny thing is, I felt good. Maria Callas's mama had liberated me. I'd said those words before—about how tall I was—but always I'd been telling them to myself, no matter whom I was addressing. This time I believed them and I'd told the world!

A Riot in Trinidad

Phil Schapiro used to be a trumpet player at the Metropolitan Opera. A big, strapping guy who never tells the same dirty joke twice, he went into managing talent—and one day, he came to me and said, "Jan, the government of Trinidad would like to buy your services."

"For what?" I said. "To spy on Tobago?"

"No, I'm representing Tobago, too. I've been producing a series of concerts for the Trinidad-Tobago Public Library—three a year. So far we've had artists like Miriam Makeba and the Porgy and Bess Singers, but now we'd like to vary the menu, starting with you."

The price was good, so off I went. The audiences in Trinidad and Tobago were very well dressed, polite, and enthusiastic. They were not very familiar with my program of oratorio, German lieder, French chansons, English songs, and operatic arias, but they liked what they heard—and its freshness to them imparted a new freshness to my rendition of what is considered "standard" fare. When, during the applause, they started shouting for "The Bluebird of Happiness," I was glad to oblige and was pleasantly surprised that my "Bluebird" had arrived there before I did.

I gave one concert in the Naparima Bowl in San Fernando, Trinidad; three in the Queen's Hall in Port-of-Spain; and one in Tobago at the prime minister's request. During the intermission at the Naparima Bowl, an East Indian woman came backstage and asked me to "please sing one of your Chasidic numbers."

"A Chasidic song?" I asked in amazement.

"Mr. Peerce," she said, "I have every one of your records."

So I did "Sha, Stil" as an encore. When she came backstage again, I thought she would kiss me. Instead she said, "May I take your hand?" When I gave it to her, she slipped a ring off one of her fingers and onto one of mine. "I give you this ring," she told me. "We are now wedded. We are friends for life." Alice was the first to congratulate us. I still cherish the ring.

After a performance in Port-of-Spain, Alice asked Phil Schapiro if we could see a little night life. Phil took us over to the other side of town to the wharf area. We went into one of those interchangeable joints where sailors gather from all over the world.

The three of us squeezed into a corner upstairs. Phil had rum and Coca-Cola; Alice and I had Cokes. Two sailors began to fight. A couple of dancing girls in abbreviated costumes came out and exposed their talents.

Another sailor tried to grab both of them, but two civilians jumped him and one of them had a knife. The fight that started now was just like what you see in the movies. Two men who'd had nothing to do with either incident, but had just been sitting at a table talking, suddenly started slugging each other. All over the joint, big and little fights started up and merged into half a dozen brawls, any one of which was wilder and bigger than anything I'd anticipated. Sailors threw chairs. Natives threw tables. There was yelling and screaming. Men smashed half-filled bottles to use as weapons. Tables were overturning, glass was flying, and even John Wayne would have screamed for help.

Phil Schapiro kept his managerial cool, but said, "I think we ought to be going, Jan and Alice." By the time we reached the stairs, whistles were blowing and sirens were wailing. As we maneuvered down the long, steep staircase to the streets, the police rushed up, swinging their clubs at everything that moved. This was not long after I'd torn my tendon in Lisbon, so I was a little slower than Alice and Phil. By the time I was three-fourths of the way down, we were smelling smoke and I had to hug the wall to let in police reinforcements and firemen. Another few steps and I could almost see civilization when a big, swarthy, unshaven, tough-looking guy loomed up before me and blocked my way. I side-stepped to my right; he side-stepped to my right. "Just a minute!" he said.

I was in a terrible hurry, but for him I had a minute because I could see he was a man not to be argued with. So I looked down at him as calmly as I could and waited to hear what he had to say to me, which was: "Aren't you Jan Peerce?"

I gave him a one-word answer: "Yes."

"Isn't this great!" he exclaimed. "What a break for me!"

"Oh, for me, too," I said.

"Mr. Peerce, would you give me your autograph?" he said. He produced a pen and a pad. The ham in me was such that, even while fleeing for my life, I asked him how he spelled his name and signed mine with, in between, this message: "Having a riotous time, glad you were here."

I Am a Tevye

When I was sixty-seven, at the end of 1971, I made my Broadway debut— as Tevye in *Fiddler on the Roof.* It was Alice who opened my eyes to the opportunity. Six years earlier, we had watched Zero Mostel do Tevye. We'd loved the show and laughed at Zero. Somewhere in the first act, Alice poked me in the ribs and whispered, "Zero is great, but you could do this role, too, Jan. *You* are Tevye."

We were lucky to have tickets, but I had some reservations. Sholom Aleichem's milkman was not a clown. Playing Tevye, you don't have to roll your eyes to get laughs. Or, worse still, roll your belly after singing "If I Were a Rich Man." Or, worst of all, slosh milk on the stage: a disgrace to his religion as well as his profession.

Thinking about that evening later, I decided Alice was right. I *am* a Tevye. I do have conversations with the Lord much the way Tevye does. I had a grandfather who was a Tevye living in Russia under the same conditions that Sholom Aleichem wrote about in the book upon which *Fiddler* is based. My father was a Tevye, too, in his way of life.

There is so much of Tevye in me that when Tevye turns his back on the daughter who marries out of the faith and speaks the line "Can a man deny his own child?" I see and hear and remember the four and a half years when I disowned my son.

It was four or five years before anybody asked me to do *Fiddler on the Roof.* Managers only thought of Tevye in the Zero Mostel image. But Phil Schapiro, who had taken over managing the popular side of my career (which Hurok didn't handle), persisted. He tried summer theaters and was told: "We'd love Jan Peerce in a one-man show, but he's not Zero Mostel."

"No," Phil would say, "but he *is* Tevye."

Or the managers would ask if I could act. "Coming from the Metropolitan Opera, he probably can't."

Phil would say, "Jan Peerce doesn't have to act to do Tevye."

Finally John Kenley—chief of the Kenley players in Warren, Pennsylvania—took me on as Tevye for a five-week tour of Ohio in the summer of 1971. It was wonderful to do it away from New York in cities where not everyone had seen Zero Mostel as Tevye. I gave my own performance.

To me, Tevye was a simple family man, a godly man. Everything G-d dictated, Tevye tried to live up to. He wasn't a clown, or a wisecracker, but a man who talked seriously to the Lord. With my co-star Dolores Wilson, the best Golde any *Fiddler* ever had, teaching me all the tricks of the Tevye trade, the show was a great success. All over the East and Midwest, music circuses and tent theaters that season found room to schedule Jan Peerce in *Fiddler on the Roof.* I did seventy-two Tevyes during the summer.

Phil Schapiro: *After one of Jan's opening nights in Ohio with* Fiddler, *the cast party was in the back room of an Italian restaurant, where the food was all pizza and sausage and scampi and spaghetti in clam sauce and all kinds of things Jan* *wouldn't eat. Everyone was having a good time, including Jan, who has a better time at parties than most people because he ignores the food and concentrates on conversation. Suddenly the power failed and the lights went out. Everybody staggered around lighting matches and looking for candles. People had trouble finding food at the buffet. People with food had trouble finding their tables. After ten minutes of this, someone had a great idea: "Maybe they don't know about this up front."*

Someone else made his way out of the private room into the main restaurant, where the lights were blazing and everyone was happy. The headwaiter replaced a fuse. When the lights came back on in the back room, everybody heaved a sigh of relief— except two people: Jan Peerce and the man he'd been talking to during the blackout. Jan's eyesight was pretty poor by then and he had gone right on with the conversation without being much bothered by the absence of light. As for the other man, he was so interested in whatever Jan had to tell him that they both had carried on just as if nothing had happened.

Meanwhile, back on Broadway, Harold Prince was looking for a seventh Tevye to follow Mostel, Luther Adler, Herschel Bernardi, Harry Goz, Jerry Jarrett, and Paul Lipson in the original production. He was also looking for "a name Tevye" who might prolong the run until the middle of 1972, when *Fiddler* would play its 3,225th performance and pass *Life with Father* as the longest-running show in Broadway history. Phil Schapiro had been prodding Prince to put Peerce and Tevye together. Hal Prince sent one of his agents to check me out at a performance at the Shady Grove Music Fair in Rockville, Maryland. The report came back that I was okay. Later Hal Prince told me it was the first time he'd ever hired a singer he'd never met or seen perform. I asked him how come he took me without an audition. "I collect your records," he replied.

Phil Schapiro: *I wanted 100 percent star billing for Jan, which Prince agreed to. His people did it in the ads and on the posters, but they said Jan couldn't be billed on the marquee. Ever since they had moved to the Broadway Theater, their agreement with all the other Tevyes had been no performer's name on the marquee, just the title,* Fiddler on the Roof. *It was an institution, bigger than any name. Besides, there was an agreement with the authors and the director, Jerome Robbins, and with Hal Prince himself, that if* anyone's *name appeared on the marquee, then* everyone's *name had to appear on the marquee.*

You don't have to be a kid to dream of your name in lights on Broadway. I could never have broken the news to Jan that the marquee wouldn't say "Jan Peerce in Fiddler on the Roof." *But no matter how I argued, Prince's office invoked that binding written agreement.*

I thought there had to be some way we could get Jan's name up on that marquee. I thought it was ridiculous to hire Jan Peerce and then not advertise him in lights.

They kept saying "No way" right into the "finalization" session, the last meeting before the contracts would be shown to Jan. I said I wanted to read that binding agreement one more time. They read it aloud to me: "If anybody's name appears on the marquee, then everybody's name appears."

"All right," I said. "I don't want Jan's name to appear on the marquee. I want it to appear in lights above the marquee." Which is how Jan Peerce's name appeared on Broadway in lights, in big lights. You could look uptown and downtown at night and you might not see the name Fiddler on the Roof, *but you did see* JAN PEERCE *in fifty-million-watt illuminated letters. Nobody had ever thought of that.*

I was surprised how little preparation was asked of me on Broadway: a few private rehearsals with a choreographer and then, from 10 A.M. to 5 P.M. on the day I opened, just one rehearsal with the whole company of this well-oiled machine I was joining. Fortunately, Boris Aplon—who had been playing Lazar Wolf the butcher on Broadway for five years—took me aside and gave me the same kind of orientation Dolores Wilson had given on the road. Boris has been a crony of mine to this day.

When I stepped out on the stage of the Broadway Theatre on December 14, 1971, there were a few ghosts in the wings, but I did my own Tevye. I did the Sabbath song with cantorial embellishments and I did everything else with fidelity to Sholom Aleichem and Tevye. In the *New York Times,* Clive Barnes wrote that "Mr. Peerce sings the role better than any other Tevye I have heard"; that I made the music of *Fiddler* sound "both more operatic and more Jewish than it has ever sounded before. Mr. Peerce is the kind of singer who can make every day a holiday."

While *Fiddler on the Roof* was my first experience doing a legitimate musical eight times a week, it was no sweat at all for one who used to do four or five shows *a day* at Radio City Music Hall. True, the Music Hall shows weren't full-length, but the schedule was much more demanding. After my *Fiddler* performances, I was in the theatre an hour longer than everybody else in the show because so many spectators came backstage to greet me. Alice had to train the stage doormen to let everybody through. I like to see people after a show. I like to talk to people. That's part of what live audiences are all about.

The theatre was such a holiday for me that I've spent every summer since then touring in one show or another: *Fiddler* or *The Rothschilds* or a musical version of Leo Rosten's *The Joys of Yiddish,* which was called *Laugh a Little, Cry a Little.* It had book and lyrics by Arnold Horwitt and some lively music by Gary Friedman. I had hoped *Laugh a Little* would be the vehicle to bring me back to Broadway, in a part I would create. But while the show broke a record or two on the summer circuit in 1974, it was not for New York. Book trouble. Making a musical out of a dictionary, however delightful, has that hazard.

Playing the immigrant grandfather on the Lower East Side in *Laugh a Little,* I had my memories of my father to supply whatever was missing in me. I didn't have to take lessons to know those characters' natures. Rothschild, however, took a little more acting. I mean, his was a family with whom I don't readily identify. The struggle for power and riches is not what my life was about. But in his lust for power, Rothschild used his money in a very positive way: for Jewish education. You have only to go to Israel and see what his family accomplished there—planting vineyards and cultivating land, building old-age homes and synagogues—to respect him and his ambitions. True, the character was neither kindly nor as noble as Tevye. He was tough at the core. I found him easy to play.

There was a scene in *The Rothschilds* where Metternich insults him and Rothschild gives a shake of the head as if to say: "There'll come a time, Tom Rooney, when you'll be happy to let me buy you a cup of coffee." This I could carry off, for *this* was me, too.

I wasn't in *Fiddler on the Roof* when it broke the Broadway record, however. My contract had to have all kinds of escape clauses for previous concert commitments and options, and the publicity from *Fiddler* caused everybody to exercise his option now rather than later. Of course, when I got to these concerts, everyone wanted selections from *Fiddler.* Back on Broadway, though, I was disappointing a lot of people who showed up expecting Jan Peerce and found someone standing in for me. So at the end of April 1972, I bowed out and Paul Lipson came back to do the part.

The Lubavitch Experience

Lubavitch was a village in Russia noted for the orthodoxy of its Jews two hundred years ago, despite czarist persecution. By orthodox, I don't mean just the retention of ancient rituals, but the twin aims of devotion to G-d in heaven and living decently on earth. The word *Lubavitch* itself means, in Russian, "City of Brotherly Love." The Chasidic movement that originated in that Russian village now has half a million members around the world, with a headquarters and a chief rabbi (the *rebbe*) on Eastern Parkway in Brooklyn. Nowadays, at a summer camp in the Catskills near Liberty, New York, Lubavitch is working with American kids and one hundred young refugees from Communist Russia—aged five to twenty—who are just now learning the Judaism for which they and their parents were persecuted.

I had always known that Chasidism meant simple faith, joyous worship, and everyday pleasures as well as mysticism, prayer, and a certain fanaticism. But it is perhaps symbolic that my daughter Joy's son, Joey Wahrhaftig, was the one who introduced me to Lubavitch and made me a Chasid in 1972, when he was seven.

A friend of mine in San Francisco called me up and said, "I wish you had been at the Chabad House in Berkeley on Simchath Torah. You would have seen your little grandson dancing on a table with a tiny Torah clutched to his breast. You should have seen him dancing and singing his love to the Lord!"

Simchath Torah is the day the Jews celebrate receiving the five Books of Moses; but I had to ask what a Chabad House was. I was told it was the name of Lubavitcher headquarters.

The next time I was visiting the Wahrhaftigs I asked Joey to take me to Saturday-morning services at the Chabad House near the University of California campus at Berkeley. When we arrived around 9 A.M., the young rabbi greeted us and I expressed surprise that the services hadn't started yet. He explained that on Friday nights, after the service, they hold rap sessions with the college students and other youngsters. They talk about G-d, Torah, and today's problems—their own as well as the world's. "These sessions last until two or three in the morning," the rabbi said, "so we start later the next morning—I mean, the same morning, actually."

This gave me a chance to snoop around. The rabbi said I was welcome to. The whole house had eight rooms. In some of them were kids, most of them still teen-agers, some sleeping off drunken binges and drug trips. The graduate student looking after the place was as straight and serious as could be.

Back upstairs, someone else was waiting for services to start. He wasn't dressed for *shul*—he wore tattered jeans, an old shirt that looked slept in for three days, and a matching growth of beard—but he was eager, in fact fidgety, for it to begin. I asked him what he was doing here and the question seemed to startle him.

"I—well, I—I go to school here. At Berkeley."

"But what brings you to *this* house?"

"Oh, don't you know what these people do?" he said, finding his tongue. "If I hadn't met these people or hadn't found out what this house stands for, I'd be dead or in jail or in the loony bin or in the gutter where they found me."

I said, "That's quite a statement for a young man to make."

"I was doing things I shouldn't," he went on. "Drugs had a great appeal to me, but then I met these people and they helped me away from all that. I don't use drugs anymore. I'm not freaked out, and what's more, I'm starting to come back to my own religion, my own people. I've got a long way to go, but I'm enjoying it."

The service started. It was very simple. The rabbi talked about Torah and the portion to be read that week, but it all fell under the heading of learning, not an oration on current events. (For the affairs of the world, the men's club meets on Tuesdays; the Sabbath is for the service of G-d.) Thanks to the mustache I had grown to go with my beard in *Fiddler on the Roof,* nobody recognized me, but as a stranger in their midst I was called up front to chant the *broche* (blessing). I did not sing.

Before I was ready to leave, though, I was invited to stay for lunch— and there I found out how big a role music plays in the life of Lubavitch. Joy had come with Alice to meet Joey and me, but they stayed for lunch, too. Men and women sat apart. Lubavitchers don't shake hands with women. When Alice extended her hand, the rabbi didn't embarrass her, but he didn't shake it either. He told her his name was Chaim Drizin. He was all of twenty-three at the time, but he is one of the wisest men who ever figured in our life—particularly in the crisis that came a year or so later.

After that lunch there was a little dancing—but the men danced with men and the women with women. At first it didn't look right, but within a few minutes it was the most natural thing in the world to me. The type of dancing they do—horas and folk and square dances in groups: happy dances with religious feeling—don't call for intimacy of the sexes. If they sing a song, it's about the beauty of worshiping the Lord, not about the banalities of the day or even the love of man and woman. So there I was dancing with my grandson and thirty or forty other boys and men. When I looked across the room, there was Alice dancing joyfully with Joy and a dozen other women.

The music they sang was a great revelation to me, for it was in the great tradition of Chasidic song: the *nigunim,* it is called. Through song, the Chasid transcends his material condition to reveal the inner state of his soul. So long as the melody lasts, while the notes are being sung, the singer can rise to new levels of inspiration. For a singer, doing *nigunim* is not just a performance, but an experience. For a listener, there is transport in sharing the express longings of another soul.

Since the reflecting of a soul transcends mortality, Chasidic songs work without set forms or rules that would limit the potentials of the melody. In their most classic form, the *nigunim* are wordless, although many of the basic melodies have been adapted to the Psalms or the prayerbook. To many a Chasid, words express only the superficial: that which is profound defies verbalizing. "The tongue is the pen of the heart," one Chasidic saying goes, "but melody is the pen of the soul."

The early Chasidim composed melodies themselves, but if they detected a "holy spark" in any of the folk songs of the areas in which they lived, they incorporated it into their own melodies. Some of the *nigunim* are sung in Russian and even English as well as in Hebrew and Yiddish. One chabad (an acronym on the Hebrew words for "wisdom, learning, and knowledge"), a Chasidic song without words, is an adaptation of martial music played by Napoleon's troops when they invaded Russia in 1812. To this day, this same song represents the sense of mission and victory each Chasid feels when he serves his Creator. Sung with fervor, it is thrilling.

Just imagine, at this stage of my life, the thrill of discovering a whole new art form that had been in my bones and my roots when I was born! Before that wonderful afternoon was over, somebody at the Chabad House had realized that the man they were treating deferentially because he was Joey's grandpa also had something to share with them. Rabbi Drizin put the Lubavitcher chief of West Coast operations, a senior citizen of thirty-three, Rabbi Shlomo Cunin, in touch with me and I came back a while later to "light the lamp of Judaism," in a program called "A Chasidic Experience" that Lubavitch held in San Francisco—at the Masonic Auditorium, of all places.

I never formally joined the Lubavitch movement; I just *am* a Lubavitcher. I came away from that great Sabbath of my life deeply affected. I had been among young people who thought the way I do—in a world where I had begun to feel like an anachronism. More important than this, they struck me as absolutely truthful. They were as honest and liberal as I would want them or any of my people to be. Lubavitch preaches religion and orthodoxy and teaches dedication, but Lubavitchers don't criticize or berate you. When you see them stopping other Jews on the street, all they're asking them to do is don the *tefillin* to reaffirm their faith each day. Even if one just puts them on and says the quickest blessing for each, the Lubavitchers are happy, for it's a giant step toward religion. They don't look to find fault with you. They are tolerant. In this regard, their approach to religiosity is different from that of other Chasidic groups.

There is one Chasidic sect in New York that doesn't recognize Israel as a nation because Israel is man-made—the Messiah has not yet come to create a Jewish state. One night their young followers burned an Israeli flag in a street in Brooklyn. Watching this on television with horror, Alice and I both spoke the same words: "Thank G-d for Lubavitch!"

The Lubavitcher *rebbe*, Menachem Mendel Schneerson, believes that inasmuch as the Jews in Israel are one and G-d is one, even if you want to wait for the Messiah, the Jews need that place now. True, the *rebbe* would like to see the reestablishment of the Temple and of serving G-d the way Jews did in the old days. Until then, though, he looks to Israel with love.

What appealed to me most of all about that first Sabbath at the Chabad House in Berkeley was how the Lubavitchers reached out to others: not just to those within reach, which is easy to do, but to some of those sleeping downstairs and the disheveled boy upstairs, who had been picked out of cracks in walls. It was the human connection that overwhelmed me. Lubavitch receives calls from parents whose kids have just begun to rebel or who already hate them, don't write, get lost, or disappear. The police can't help these parents, but Lubavitch very often finds them. It doesn't end there. Lubavitch raps with the kids in their language and turns them on to religion. The Lubavitchers' patience knows no bounds and their understanding beggars comprehension.

Passover

Passover is the Jewish holiday I enjoy the most. As a boy, there was nothing about Passover I didn't like—except the spring cleaning. You painted your apartment for Pesach just as you bought something new for the New Year (even if only a "remnant" from which a blouse or knickers could be made). Yom Kippur was a fast and Passover was a feast—a Seder, a combination of worship and banquet. So even when my mother churned up dust and put us to work beating rugs, and ordered us to walk on air so as not to mess her floor, we obeyed almost cheerfully, for we knew Passover was near.

What I especially liked about Passover on the Lower East Side was the grown-up feeling I had when, sitting between my father and my grandfather, I asked the four questions, sang the *Kiddush* and listened to them discuss the meaning of the Passover Seder and how the Jews were freed from a life of slavery. Although the form and sequence of the evening is prescribed, the give-and-take of the discussions is not, so my father would say to me, "Can you give me a translation of this?" or to Mac or Sender, "What do you think of that?" Our sister, Sara, would be brought into the discussion, too, for Passover is one time where girls play a part. Each time, I felt not just pride, but emotional strength.

Years later, Alice had been reading a so-called fiction by Thomas Mann
—I think it was *Joseph and His Brothers*—who had the patriarch Jacob living
with a concubine. In the middle of the night, when she came upon this, Alice
asked me, "Is this true?"

"I think so," I said.

"I don't believe it!" Alice insisted.

"You don't have to take my word for it. Ask Papa tomorrow when he
comes to visit."

The next day, Alice told my father what she'd been reading.

My father listened, looked around to make sure nobody else was there,
leaned close, and almost in a whisper, said, "It's true. He had two of them:
Bilhah and Zilpah. But don't talk about it."

I disagreed with my father. In the Jewish religion, we have nothing to
hide. It's all there in the Bible. That's why we always invited Gentiles to
partake of our Passover feast, to share our ritual with us, and even to pick
up the *Haggadah* (the Passover narrative) and read one part or another of
it. Francis Robinson, the assistant manager of the Metropolitan Opera, was
such a regular at our Seders that all the Jews at the Met used to check with
him as to when Passover began. At our Seder, when I finished chanting a
cantorial *Kiddush* to sanctify the wine, I'd ask Francis to stand up, wearing
the skullcap we gave him, and read the English translation. Francis was so
moved that tears would roll down those pink cheeks of his while he read.
Later he told me, "Jan, you honor me so by letting me say those precious
words."

So it went from Seder to Seder, from Passover to Passover, our interest
rarely flagging and our hearts and minds and palates always looking forward
to the next encounter. Once Leonard Bernstein said to me, "I hear you have
a wonderful Seder." So I invited him.

Our Seders in New Rochelle used to be for some fifty people. Lenny
came on the second night because our first night was strictly for family and
relatives; the second was for family and friends. Maestro Bernstein proved
to be very well informed on his Judaism. He knew all the small print and
black dots. It was a wonderful evening in which Lenny explained a lot to us
and we explained a lot to him. He also ate with great zest—particularly
Alice's matzo balls and gefilte fish. Alice still used to make her own in those
days. She bought and cleaned and prepared the fish by hand, not through a
grinder. The poundage of fish filets chopped up per Passover Seder was an
important statistic to us: fifty-five pounds was the record.

After the Seder was over, we adjourned to the living room. Leonard
Bernstein gravitated to the piano and began to play beautifully. He played
a melody, saying, "Remember how we used to sing this on Passover?" just

as if I'd been his boyhood chum in Massachusetts. "Sure," I said, "but we didn't sing it the way you're playing it." Then I sang it my way and he played it my way. To return the favor, he played it his way and I sang it his way.

Among the many others who have come to our Passover Seders are Steve Lawrence and his wife, Eydie Gorme, Tania Grossinger, Roberta Peters, Robert Merrill, Sol Hurok, Walter Prude, Mae Frohman, William Scheide and Herbert Barrett, the Bach Aria Group's concert manager, Joseph Machlis, the writer, and Mr. and Mrs. Ernest Heller, patrons of the arts. But for the past nineteen years, I have spent my Passovers in Miami Beach, conducting Seders in hotels there. The last fourteen Passovers have been at the Deauville. Some two thousand guests come to share the first night of the holiday with me, and another two thousand (though many are repeaters) show up for the second night's Seder. Morris Lansburgh and Sam Cohen and family, who own the Deauville, arrange relatively cozy tables for six, eight or ten in the vast Napoleon Room. At the beginning of the festivities I ask the guests to imagine they are home at a Seder. "Each table has its own family. The most important part of Passover is that it's a family holiday."

We don't have a rabbi. I do the reading, narrating, and explaining, and lead the praying in Hebrew and English. The guests read and sing with me. I don't skip a word—no matter how long it takes. We start at 7:30 P.M. and it goes on until almost midnight. With the help of a choir led by Barnett "Bob" Breeskin, who conducts the Miami Beach Symphony, we sing joyously. I'll lead the singing of a rhythmic song like "Dayenu," which means "It Would Have Been Enough." As part of the Seder I also sing a song from the Warsaw Ghetto uprising: "Ani maamin" ("I believe"). I don't sing that song, I cry it, for I feel the Jews who were killed there are worth our tears at Passover: they died for us in modern times.

The service ends with the words: "May we celebrate again in peace and liberty. May the year ahead bring redemption to Israel and Jerusalem and to all mankind. Amen." Or as it has been condensed in the minds of Jews all over the world: "Next year in Jerusalem. Amen."

Rosh Hashonah at the Concord

Ever since my leg injury ruled out the three-and-a-half-mile hike from my home to my synagogue, I've been coming to the Hotel Concord in Kiamesha Lake, New York, for Rosh Hashonah and Yom Kippur. Entertainment director Phil Greenwald—the man who shattered Catskill tradition, for better or for worse, by replacing salaried "special staff" entertainers (like Dean Martin, Buddy Hackett, and Robert Merrill when he was Morris Miller) with imported stars doing one-night stands—always books me there for a mixed program of classical cantorial and Yiddish music in between the two Highest Holy Days of our religion, so I stay the whole ten-day period.

On the first night of the Jewish New Year, the Catskill resort's Imperial Room nightclub is made into an Imperial Synagogue. All the tables are taken out and replaced by tiers of chairs. Earlier in the day or week, guests have arrived not just from New York City, but from Cincinnati, Detroit, Canada, Aruba, and Paris. The nightclub begins to look like the United Nations General Assembly, but it *is* a synagogue. It has a congregation of strangers, but when people worship together it doesn't take them long to get to know each other. After all, they're there for the same purpose. A certain air of friendship forms, even though you don't chat inside the Imperial Synagogue and the decorum is high. People listen to Rabbi Simon Cohen and Cantor Herman Malamood and actually participate. Some of the guests really do know each other, because they've been coming for years. There is the custom —a beautiful one—that when you finish the service, everybody wishes a Happy Holiday to each other. A Happy New Year.

Some may knock this atmosphere as "commercial" or "pseudo-religious," but what I see is a very pious, serious attitude. The Imperial Synagogue at the Concord is Orthodox-Conservative: the service is Orthodox, but the men and women can sit together—or, if they want to, they can go to opposite ends of the vast room.

At the Concord, which is the world's largest year-round hotel (capacity: 3,200), everything is done on a grand scale, but everything is done right— and that applies to religion, too. If you're devout, you can start worshiping at eight every morning of the year in the small chapel off the lobby, where they have a rabbi-in-residence, Sol Saphier. What the Concord offers me is a centralized, convenient place where I won't be tempted or forced to ride on the High Holy Days. And, as for the legendary orgies in the dining room, there's nothing wrong with partaking of good kosher food, except, of course, on Yom Kippur.

My Friend Gene

When I was just growing up in the concert business, I did one of my earliest Ninth Symphonies in New Orleans with Eugene Ormandy and the Philadelphia Orchestra. In seeing fit that I should be part of his great aggregation, he honored me and I served him well for it.

A few years later, though, he honored me again by asking me to sing the Verdi *Requiem* with his orchestra. But all his intermediaries could offer me for four performances was $1,000 or $1,200, a fee that took the edge off the invitation, for I felt I was being asked to pay for the privilege of singing with him. Be that as it may, I simply told the intermediaries, "For that kind of money, the answer is no."

The next time Ormandy and I met was in the foyer just inside the stage door of the old Met. He asked me, "What's the matter, you don't like to sing with your friend Gene? You start turning me down?"

"C'mon, Gene," I said, "when you offer me this kind of money . . ."

"Is money everything to you, Jan?"

"No," I said, "money isn't everything, but I didn't hear that *you* took a cut in salary to do Verdi's *Requiem.*"

With that—and with no hard feelings on my part—we went our separate ways. A few years later, Fredric R. Mann, the Philadelphia philanthropist whose name is on the Mann Auditorium in Tel Aviv, came to me and said, "Jan, I was at a meeting and I don't know whether I should tell you this." Well, when someone begins that way, you know that nothing in heaven or on earth is going to stop him from telling you. Sure enough, Mann went on: "But I think I've got to tell you, Jan, because you're my friend. At this meeting, your name came up. But that man Ormandy dislikes you so much that as soon as you were mentioned, he said, 'No,' just like that. I asked him why and he said, 'I don't like his vibrato.' "

I began to laugh. I said to Mann, "You go back and tell him his baton has a faster vibrato than I have in my singing." Later, though, I started to stew about it and wanted to write Ormandy a letter, but Alice talked me out of it. Still, I will never deny that the man is one of the greatest conductors the world has ever known. The world, which includes you and me, owes him our ear and our respect, but he owed me a little professional respect, too.

From Toscanini and Rachmaninoff and "Bravo" Bruno Walter and Fausto Cleva to Bernstein and Ormandy and James Levine, I've now done all the talking I'm going to do about the conductors whose autographed faces hang on my wall in New Rochelle, where they can't get at me. But I have a few concluding generalizations about the breed.

When a conductor tries to be a nice guy, as a rule the orchestra falls apart. The New York Philharmonic was never in worse condition than when it had two nice men directing it: Dimitri Mitropoulos, a beloved man who spoke to G-d every day, and Sir John Barbirolli, another nice guy the musicians danced all over. A conductor doesn't have to be really mean, but if he can't rule efficiently, he had better get nasty.

At my age, I reflect sometimes on the long life of conductors. Their secret is in the old saying: They drink human blood.

Imagine what an outlet it is for a man to stand with a stick in his hand and a body of one hundred men and women before him whom he must drive and mold and dictate to and implant reactions in until they respond as one, meeting his standard, producing the sounds *he* hears in his head. However you look at this and whatever you call a man who strives and drives this way, I am sure that such a form of expression and the possession of such power has great influence upon his existence.

You and I believe in driving ourselves and our families and maybe our employees to meet certain standards we have. But as soon as a conductor walks out onstage or into the pit, the musicians cease tuning their instruments or chatting and there is a hush. The audience feels it, too, though they break it with applause. This is power—when his presence alone dictates such an atmosphere. No dictator could ask for more.

The maestro takes a stance that he hopes will be appealing to the crowd, particularly because he's going to be seen from behind. He must have force, command, and a straight back. Then all of a sudden, at a given signal, the orchestra responds to him as one—and it had better be right. Right according to him! The fact that they may have done it one way for Toscanini or Fritz Reiner doesn't mean anything. You've got to give it to him *his* way.

I try to understand such individuals, but I'm glad I'm not one of them. I have never worried about power. I'm just glad to be on the stage. I have always felt that while I'm up there, I can express myself in beauty of song. If I do what I think is right and it works, that is my power. The only forces I have in my arsenal are beautiful expression and projection to try to reach an audience as an artist.

6

The Eye and I

An Optical Tragedy

I have alluded in passing to injuries, accidents, and bad eyesight. Now the time has come to weave back and then forward again in time, focusing on the optical tragedy that cost me my operatic career.

Vision had always been a problem for me. I was born nearsighted. When I was four, a bed fell on me, cutting my head just above my left eye.

Like all kids, I was a pretty nosy guy who liked to put his hands where they didn't belong. On Madison Street, we had so many relatives and boarders and so little space that we kept one bed standing up against the wall when it wasn't in use. Playing with it one day, I tipped it over—and the result was both a disaster and a miracle.

I don't remember any of it, but my mother used to tell me how they rushed me to Beth Israel Hospital while she pressed the skin together to keep it from bleeding. With the help of a neighbor, I was carried two blocks to Beth Israel Hospital.

In those days, you took your chances whenever you went into a hospital. Quite a few doctors on the Lower East Side weren't graduates of medical schools.

But I was very lucky; back in 1908 on the Lower East Side, I received as clean and expert a job of eye-area surgery as I could have hoped for. There was no permanent damage except, if you look very closely, a scar—more like an indentation—running diagonally across the bridge of my nose. And I still had better vision in that left eye than I ever had in my right eye.

As we age, our eyesight tends to weaken. Extremely nearsighted people, however, can really feel it deteriorating from month to month or even week to week. In my forties, I put my optometrist to work on me and he brought my vision up half a point here, half a point there—but he and I both knew that it wasn't going to stay better, or even just as good, for long. My doctor, William Feinbloom, would console me by saying that after all, I could still read a newspaper or a book or music. Then he would show me people in his waiting room who could barely see. This was small comfort, for I feared I would be one of them one day—and I almost ended up worse off than that.

I began to sense that people were noticing how bad my sight had become. When casual acquaintances would suddenly take my arm when we were crossing the street, it wasn't because *they* needed *me*. To make matters worse, my eyes could no longer handle the contact lenses I'd worn since 1938, and so, offstage, I had to wear glasses with lenses as thick as the bottom of Coca-Cola bottles.

It used to be that appearing with glasses would have limited my career. Luckily, Steve Allen made his mark on television at the right time for me. In the early days of TV, people who had to read on screen would either squint or wear contact lenses. Came the revolution—when Steve Allen did a talk show wearing horn-rimmed glasses. He was so popular that some people who wanted to seem as witty and intellectual as Steve Allen wore spectacles with blank glass in them. For me, Steve Allen meant that I could go on the *Tonight* show or give concerts wearing the glasses I needed. On the opera stage, I could just barely see enough.

My sight continued to go from bad to worse. I started complaining to Alice that she must have done something to the lighting in our house, particularly in the living room. She denied everything. "Then you must have changed the shades," I told her.

"These are the same shades we've had for a dozen years, Jan."

"But the room is darker, it's browner."

"I haven't changed anything, Jan. Maybe you're changing."

I wouldn't admit anything *new* was the matter. Alice consulted an architect, who looked around our high-ceilinged living room and suggested unobtrusive floodlighting. I was willing to spend the money, but I didn't relish the idea of making my living room into a stage set.

Finally I had to admit to myself that my sight was fading fast. Whenever

I stepped out of the house into clear sunshine, my vision washed out. On-stage, certain lights obliterated my vision. Reading at home, I could manage by pushing my glasses up and down, jockeying for position on what I was reading.

The eye doctor suggested I try reading without my glasses—holding whatever I was reading way up close. It worked, but everyone who saw this became convinced I was going blind. And perhaps I was—for the time came when even this didn't work.

In March 1965, I gave a concert with the Detroit Symphony Orchestra in Ford Auditorium. John Finlayson wrote a rave notice in the *Detroit News*, but he wondered why "the soloist sometimes buried his face disconcertingly behind the music he scanned. Acceptable or not, this technique gives the audience the feeling of looking in on a rehearsal."

I had developed a cataract on my right eye, which was not unusual for a man in his sixties. The head of a great institution's ophthalmic department told me I had nothing to fear from cataract surgery. He explained to me how little was involved and how quickly it could be done. The risk was barely one in a hundred, but to improve even those odds, he would do the operation himself. We set a date in June 1967. I went in and he operated.

Man proposes and G-d disposes. I was that one in a hundred. While I was unconscious on the operating table, something went wrong and this world-famous eye surgeon slipped me a blinkeroo.

Alice Peerce: *As I came in the door of the hospital room, Jan was there, but much more unconscious than I expected him to be. Later I learned that when something terrible happens, the doctors lower the blood pressure.*

The great surgeon was there, too. Very crisply and tensely, he told me, "Your husband had a hemorrhage. If it had been anyone but him, I would have thrown the eye out." It took me a while to realize that it was the eye that had hemorrhaged. He even said that he had "saved the eye," but that didn't mean he had saved Jan's sight. It just meant that when the question arose during the operation whether to remove the eye or leave it in Jan's head, he did him the favor of letting him keep a nonfunctioning eye.

Since 1967, I have been sightless in one eye. I wear a plastic shield over my right eye—it's not a glass eye, for my own right eye is in my head—painted to match the brown of my left eye.

I didn't find out the bad news right away. They kept me sedated on medications and advised Alice not to tell me. But it seemed to me that the period of convalescence was stretching out a lot longer than the doctor had told me it would. I still wasn't allowed to sit up or get out of bed. I said to

Alice, "Tell me something. Is there anything wrong with the way I'm recovering?"

"Oh, no," she said. "You're recovering nicely, Jan." In the back of my mind, though, she didn't sound quite as happy as she should.

"This may sound stupid or foolish," I persisted, "but did anything happen to me during the operation?"

"What do you mean, Jan?"

"I just have the feeling that this slowness is caused by something out of the ordinary."

"What could have been out of the ordinary?"

"I don't know," I said. "Like the doctor making a wrong move or me falling off a table."

"Ridiculous!" she said. "How can you even think of a thing like that?"

"Stranger things have happened," I said weakly.

Alice's brother Sidney knew what I had, just as I knew what he had. (Sidney died of cancer two months later.) He phoned me every day from his sickbed to tell me that everything would be all right and it could be a lot worse. This made me wonder, too. Finally I said to my wife, "It's gnawing at me, Alice. I *must* know what's the matter with me. Either I have a tumor of the eye or I have a tumor of the brain."

Hearing this, Alice sent for the surgeon. In his presence, she told me, "The eye hemorrhaged during the operation. You've lost the sight of your right eye, Jan."

Then the doctor spoke: "You know, Mr. Peerce, we must take the good with the bad. And bad things do happen. In your case, it was something unforeseen. People who are nearsighted have flabby retinal tissue, especially when they're in their sixties."

It seemed to me that he might have foreseen this. But as he went on about fate and how such an accident happens once in ten thousand cases, I wanted to say that in my case, it was one eye out of two. Still, I felt almost relieved: it wasn't a tumor! It was a lesser evil. So as the doctor discoursed on my evil eye, I kept my one good, unbandaged eye not on him, but on Alice's face. She didn't crack a tear. She saves her crying for behind the scenes, and had already done it. Now she would be strong once I was ready to face up to what had happened.

No Farewell at the Met

I didn't like it. I was unhappy about it. But what could I do about it now? Instead of cutting my throat, I got out of bed as soon as I could and went back to work. Unfortunately, at the Met, it didn't work—for Mr. Bing had been importing from Europe the new scenic fashion of platforms and darkness. Narrow steps, plenty of curves, dim lighting, and dark backdrops did nothing to help me.

In *Rigoletto* at the Met, the Duke of Mantua makes a very theatrical entrance down a long staircase in the first act. While the orchestra plays the introduction, the tenor must run down the steps and start singing the minute he's on level ground; the music is timed that way. Ever since I ripped out a tendon in Lisbon three years earlier, I'd had trouble making that cue—and sometimes I'd started singing halfway down the stairs. Now I went to the director and said, "Look, you'll have to think of another way. I'm finding it difficult."

Even when a director is your long-time friend, he'll bristle at that. You're interfering with his creativity. But I persuaded him. Much as he didn't like it, I came in from under the staircase, but at least I arrived on time. And in the scene where the Duke is scheduled to climb another staircase for a brief exit—to make way for a ballet—I just disappeared behind a pillar and hid there throughout the dancing.

Onstage, I used to wear built-up boots with high heels, to give me that extra inch in height and ego which my vanity demanded. (I used to wear elevator shoes in the street, too. By the time Maria Callas's mama took her potshot at me, I no longer did—and do you know something? When I took them off for good, I felt taller than I ever had.) Now I couldn't risk elevator boots on the stairs of the Metropolitan's stage either.

Don Ottavio was the role that taught me I couldn't make it at the Met on one eye—particularly a left eye that wasn't ever that great and where I could guess another cataract was beginning to form. I never fell, but I had to take strict precautions. Don Ottavio becomes less of a don when he has to hesitate on stairs and make sure he's standing on terra firma. All my intensity was focused on something irrelevant (yet highly relevant) to the role: my condition. Will I make it? What will happen if I don't make it? Sooner or later, this would affect my performance. More than anything else, however, it was already affecting my state of being.

I recognized this, but said nothing. Alice was the first to speak of it. One night on the drive home to New Rochelle, she said, "Jan, when you walk down those steps, you're actually groping in the dark."

"I have to look down to see where I'm going," I admitted.

"It's too much of a price to pay," was all Alice said.

She was right. I finished out the 1967–1968 season and didn't renew my contract.

I will always miss the beauty of appearing in opera. I will always miss the warmth of participating in opera. It is an art form, even when a good many singers don't treat it as such, using it as a medium for making a big noise vocally and histrionically. I believe there is as much beauty in doing an operatic performance as there is in giving a recital—and there should be just as much art in singing Puccini or Verdi as there is in singing Schubert and Brahms.

Bing's underlings at the Met wanted to give me a farewell party, a big send-off, maybe even a gala evening, but I refused it all and they didn't push the issue. Today I might feel differently, but a decade ago my leaving the Met —even for optical, rather than vocal, reasons—was enough to threaten my concert bookings and maybe even the Broadway career that Alice and Phil Schapiro were working toward for me.

The same with age. Back in late 1966, barely half a year before my operation, I had celebrated my twenty-fifth anniversary with the Met. Incidentally, what do you think the board of directors of the Metropolitan Opera Association gives a singer who lasts a quarter of a century on their stage? A plaque you can show off? A photo of a role you did in a silver frame? No; a travel clock, which a number of singers I know have left behind in hotel rooms.

I haven't lost mine; I cherish it as a memento. I don't take it on the road with me, however—because it doesn't work. The alarm doesn't ring.

But the Lord Said Yes

So in one respect, I was in Toscanini's class: he had had bad eyes, too, and ears that could pick out instantly which instrument was doing something wrong. When I had minus-twelve vision in my one remaining eye, I was more aware than ever of every sound from every part of the orchestra, more than some conductors, even with my back turned to the musicians. One conductor remarked upon this, saying, "Jan, you must have eyes in your ears."

Maybe my hearing was improving, but the sight was not. Working without the right eye didn't interfere with my concertizing or my ventures into musical comedy, but as the years passed the left eye began to worsen, leading to an event that shouldn't happen to anyone.

As ocean liners stopped crossing the ocean, big ships like the Holland America line's *Rotterdam* went on week-long Caribbean and Pacific cruises for music lovers, with vocalists such as Jerome Hines, Roberta Peters, Anna Moffo, Mary Costa, and myself; pianists such as Gina Bachauer, Eugene

Istomin, and Jerome Lowenthal; and violinists such as Daniel Heifetz and Ruggiero Ricci. Musicologists Boris Goldovsky, Martin Bookspan, and Robert Sherman served as panelists; and as cellist there would be Christine Walevska, wife of Exprinter tour organizer Fred Mayer, the founding father of this floating conservatory. Each artist gave a concert one night and then we would all combine for a gala performance on the last night at sea. Sometimes I doubled in brass as the nightly master of ceremonies. For this work I was paid a handsome fee and given a free cruise for Alice and myself.

I had just played a particularly successful Festival of Music on the High Seas engagement aboard the Sitmar liner *Fairsea* in October 1973. My concert calendar was so heavy that we'd had time only to join the cruise in Puerto Vallarta and disembark in Los Angeles. We visited Larry and his children, Matthew, Louise and Amy, and then flew up to San Francisco for a reunion with Joy and Bob and our grandson Joey.

After the usual hugging and kissing at the airport, my Joy drove my Alice and me to the Wahrhaftig home in Orinda. I am a creature of habit, so as soon as I crossed the threshold, I wanted to put my coat into the closet and my shaving kit into the bathroom. As I have many times before, I walked toward the closet, which was down a three-step staircase that I knew as well as I did my own name.

For some reason, such as faulty vision, I stepped down one step and missed two. I found myself flying in the air and making a turn of some kind. I yelled, "Oh, G-d, no!" But the Lord said yes and I landed on the stone floor. I tried to lift up. I tried to turn. But my left side wouldn't move.

Alice and Joy, who'd been unloading the car, came running. "No, no," I told Joy. "Don't touch me. Alice, I'm hurt. Call a doctor!"

Joy called the office of Drs. Ben and Jess Shenson, two well-known brothers and friends of mine who practice together in San Francisco. They advised Joy to get an ambulance and they'd meet us at St. Francis Hospital in the city. They took an X-ray, which showed a clean, straight, perfectly classic fracture of the left femur, the big bone between knee and hip that is supposed to be the strongest bone in the body. It carries most of the weight. The doctors told me so many good things about this wonderful bone I felt quite ashamed of having gone and broken it—particularly when they went on to talk about surgery.

The hospital recommended a good young doctor. With all due respect to good young doctors, Alice thought I should have a more experienced man. She called her brother Walter back east, with his insurance and medical connections, and he called back in half an hour to say that the doctors back east agreed on the man to do the job in San Francisco: a Dr. Floyd H. Jergesen.

I began to pray that he wasn't on vacation, but luckily Dr. Jergesen had just come back. Alice reached him by phone. He came right over, confirmed that I needed an operation, and set it up for the following day.

I went into surgery. I came out, I woke up in intensive care, and by the time I was wheeled back to my room, everybody was happy. I wasn't feeling too much pain, even as the anesthetic wore off. The doctor was happy with the result. He told me the X-rays showed that the operation was a success: everything in place, everything fine.

The only assurance he couldn't give us was how long the recuperation would take, though he estimated that a complete recovery—without my having to use cane, walker, or wheelchair—might take four months. This was a long time, particularly with all the bookings I had lined up. Alice insisted that we cancel them. So I found myself in the position of Oscar Levant, who is said to have once put an ad in a music magazine: "Oscar Levant available for a limited amount of cancellations." I was worried about all the commitments I couldn't fulfill. Still, when I'm sick or incapacitated, I try not to cry over spoiled bookings: I concentrate my mind and body on getting well.

At this I was coming along famously. On Tuesday, Wednesday, and Thursday, the doctor spoke in exclamations: "Fine! Great!"

On Friday, I felt very good in the morning. I chatted with Alice, chatted with the nurse, and tried to watch a little TV, on which I couldn't seem to concentrate. Lunch was a tuna fish sandwich.

In midafternoon, I began to feel a little indigestion, a little heartburn. "Gee whiz," I told Alice, "I shouldn't have eaten that tuna."

"Go on," said Alice, who'd tasted some of mine. "You always eat tuna and it was very good."

A couple of hours later, the heartburn had been joined by a pain on the right side of my body. I asked for a doctor to come look at me.

St. Francis is a beautiful new hospital, superbly equipped, but it isn't a medical center; it's more of a hotel. Each doctor comes in and takes care of his own patients. St. Francis doesn't have medical students and doesn't have too many residents. Late on a Friday afternoon in October, a doctor was hard to come by on the premises.

There was one fellow in a white jacket hanging around. He was a nice, helpful chap, but he was at a total loss about what could be bothering me. Then Alice called the Shensons, but they had a waiting room full of people and acted as if I was acting up: you know, temperamental artist, a tenor, demanding attention, probably complaining about imaginary pains. "Now, Alice," they kept saying in their most soothing manner, "now, Alice."

Alice insisted that one of them come look at me. While we were waiting for him, the pain grew worse and worse. The nurses and the man in white kept taking my temperature, blood pressure, and pulse every time I complained. "Your pulse is fine. Your blood pressure is great—like a young boy's. And you have no fever."

"I'm *not* well. There's something wrong with me. Can I be having a heart attack on the right side?"

"You're not having a heart attack, Mr. Peerce."

Just then a young doctor, filling in for one of the long-weekending physicians, walked by and heard the commotion. I'd never seen him before and I've never seen him since, but he just walked in my bedroom door and sensed what was wrong.

"Mr. Peerce," he said, "I'm going to put a nasogastric tube in your throat. I promise you it won't hurt your esophagus if you'll just take a breath and bear with it." It quieted me down, relieving the pressure and the pain.

By the time the Shensons arrived, the young doctor had said I needed a surgeon. The chief surgeon of the hospital was called. All four doctors agreed I had a stress ulcer. This is a fairly normal complication of my kind of operation. Why they hadn't told me about this possibility or thought of it sooner and why medical science hadn't taken precautions against it I don't know to this day. Nevertheless, for all its fancy names, it was what they used to call in the old days a perforated peptic or gastric ulcer.

Luckily, it didn't seem to be in a dangerous spot. The chief surgeon said to Alice, "Look, I'm going to operate right now. I'm sure the perforation is where I think it is and you have nothing to worry about: just a simple sewing-up job."

Alice said, "And if it's not where you think it is?"

"Well, if it's in the lower bowel, then pray for your husband and pray for me. But let's go on the first premise." Back to the operating room I went. The perforation was exactly where he'd thought. Also, knowing I was a singer, he did me a big favor: he went in at a very low angle, so the diaphragm didn't get into any trouble and my breathing apparatus wasn't affected.

When I got out of that one, everyone was happy. I was sorry it had to happen and that I'd spoiled a couple of doctors' long weekends, but we all agreed that under the circumstances, it had worked out very well. All the experts told Alice, "He's going to be fine now." I thought so, too. I thanked the Lord for taking care of me. My convalescence went well and they said, "Now look, Mr. Peerce, we've got to get you moving."

"Fine with me," I said. They instructed my nurse, Nancy Monahan, to put me through my paces in a wheelchair. "Now we've got to put some strength into your hands," they said. So Nancy Monahan stopped pushing me around and told me to go wheel my wheelchair myself. Which I did—dropping in on everybody on the floor and making my rounds like a doctor. Every day in every way I was feeling better and better.

I had been in St. Francis Hospital nearly a month when I began to feel a little pain in my right side. By now I was a resident diagnostician, so I decided that maybe I'd been driving my wheelchair a little too hard and developed a strain. I went easy, but I still had this pain when one of the Shensons came in the next morning, examined me, and said everything was fine.

"You know, doctor," I said, "I have a little pain."

His ears pricked up, his mind went to work, he looked quizzical, felt around the area of pain, and said, "Let's listen to your chest." Then he whisked me down to X-ray. The report came back that I had a pulmonary embolism—or in simple, frightening English, a clot on the right lung!

They called in a chest man, who confirmed the diagnosis. He told me what was needed: a strong anticoagulant drug called heparin for nine or ten days. As a singer with a lung clot, I had no time to feel sorry for myself. I simply nodded my head and said, "When do we start?"

They began to feed me heparin intravenously, like glucose, through my hand. The next day all the doctors went away—Dr. Jergesen to a seminar to deliver a paper; the chief surgeon to Houston to visit his friend Dr. Denton Cooley; the chest man to Puerto Vallarta to soak up some sun—so I should have known something would happen.

Sure enough, in the afternoon I began to experience gas pains. The medics on hand took me down to X-ray. After they'd read the pictures, they kept me around. Meanwhile doctors started to come and go: various colleagues of all the missing specialists and then both the Shensons. I sensed something important was going on. I began to feel some of the vibrations I'd felt after my cataract surgery, so I said, "Don't tell me I need another operation!"

They didn't tell me. While I was thinking (growth, blockage, clot, coronary), they held a full consultation and decided nothing serious was happening *yet,* but it bore watching.

From then on, the tide turned. The pains stopped a day or two later. In another week I showed improvement and then I went off heparin for Coumadin. When I was finally allowed to get out of bed, I'd almost forgotten I had a bum leg.

A Religious Experience

[While Jan Peerce lay in St. Francis Hospital going from crisis to crisis, another drama was resolving itself in the same room. Alice Peerce tells of her religious regeneration.]

Alice: *Two of the things I think brought Jan and me together in the beginning were that each of us was the oldest in the family and the only child who observed the dietary laws. I was a very straight-laced young girl. I didn't wear décolletage and my mother used to predict I'd marry a rabbi.*

Jan never, never deviated from his prayers or the dietary laws. At the table, the other world didn't exist for him. But I was more curious. After our three children were growing up and we were traveling all around the globe, I always wondered: "I would like to know what *that is that* they're *eating."*

"So ask," Jan would say.

I knew, however, that I would really like to experience *the answer.*

I still remember the first time I ate a piece of chicken I wasn't supposed to. I don't think it tasted any different from any other chicken, and if it did, it was because my heart was in my mouth, too. I was positive I wouldn't wake up the next morning— that I'd die in my sleep. So I lay awake all that night waiting for something to happen to me—convulsions at the very least. When dawn found me alive and reasonably well, except for the effects of insomnia, I tried again—and again and again.

I never brought myself to eat pork. The family repulsion for it was too ingrained in me, and besides, Tania Grossinger got trichinosis once. But I did eat and enjoy shrimp.

I had eaten that first forbidden chicken at a women's luncheon. All my friends advised me, "You're crazy if you tell Jan. Eat his way at home and your way outside when he's not with you and he'll never know." But I said, "I haven't lived that kind of life with Jan and I'm not going to start now having secret affairs with food."

Jan's first reaction was shock. I didn't change one thing in our house, but I did go on eating the other way outside the home. In front of Jan I never ordered shrimp or anything else that I knew would upset him. But I did order chicken and roast beef that I knew and he knew weren't right.

Around 1967, when Jan lost his eye, I started to think that it really wasn't very nice of me to sit in an airplane and eat whatever the airline was featuring, while Jan ate the specially packaged meal. Jan had adjusted to the point where he seemingly took no notice, but it was not a situation in which I took any pride.

I had food for thought when I helped out at the Russian Tea Room for six months after my brother Sidney's death that same year. Walking around greeting people and doing everything I used to see my father and brother do, I went through all the motions on the outside while inside I was working on this dilemma. Suddenly, I woke up one day and I was an observer again: no pain, no strain, no more guilt.

Then in late 1973, I found myself crying beside the empty bed of a husband who was in surgery for the second time in a week. With me was Chaim Drizin, the young rabbi from the Chabad House in Berkeley who had helped make Lubavitchers out of Jan and me a year earlier. It may not be proper for a married woman more than twice his age to confess she loves a twenty-four-year-old rabbi, but I did and I do love Chaim. Through the tears and the sobs, I was saying to him, "If I could only do something! If I could only do something!"

Chaim said to me, "Why don't you talk to G-d?"

"What do you mean, talk to G-d?" I asked. "I pray to Him when I light the candles."

Chaim said, "No, Alice. I mean you should make a bargain with G-d. You should actually tell Him you'll do this if He'll do that."

"But what could I do?" I wondered. "I've never really done any harm to anybody. I accept people as they are."

Chaim said, "G-d will think of something else. Then you do it."

Then it occurred to me: "There is one thing I could do. I could observe the Sabbath —to its fullest!"

"Would you?" Chaim asked softly.

"Yes," I said. "I would do anything."

"Then do it," Chaim said, "if you want to."

Having made this Sabbath deal with G-d, I proceeded to violate it right and left for a few days. My sister, Maye, and my brother Walter and his wife, Selma, had flown out to the West Coast, because we weren't sure just how serious Jan's embolism was. His life could have been over in a matter of days or even hours. And all his troubles seemed to be coming toward sundown on Fridays.

Toward midnight on the Friday of his embolism, they told us we had to leave the hospital. I had already told Walter and Selma and Maye and Joy about my vow. Joy had booked me a room at a hotel seven blocks away, for Friday night only. She wouldn't let me walk there and I wouldn't ride, so—arguing back and forth in the lobby—we agreed that Joy and Maye would follow me in the car while Walter and Joy's husband, Bob, who is six feet two, would walk with me. But now the security guard, who was unlocking the front door of the hospital for us, suddenly shut it again. "Mrs. Peerce," he said, "I am not letting you out of this building because I will not be responsible for any of you walking through this neighborhood at night. There was a man and a woman stabbed together out there just a few weeks ago. . . . I won't let you out!" So I had to come up with a solution that was acceptable to him, too. But what about

Him? I had just given my pledge to G-d and here I was about to break it. If Jan died a hundred years later, I would blame myself. Finally, all I could think to do was shrug and say, "I'll tell you what, Joy. I'm going home with you. By car."

The next night, Chaim came to see us in the hospital—not only because he loves us and would have come anyway, but because he had to report to the Lubavitcher rebbe *and his able deputies, Rabbi Abraham Shem Tov and Rabbi Yehuda Krinsky, back east at least once a day on Jan's condition. He could see Jan was doing a little better, but that something was wrong with me.*

"Chaim," I began, "there's something I want to tell you."

He cut me off with: "One thing I must tell you first, Alice. Don't . . . have . . . guilt."

I looked at him closely and asked, "Do you mean you know what happened?"

"I don't know," he replied, "but I'm asking you not to bear any guilt. You will do what you have to do at the right time."

For the next three weeks of Jan's hospital stay, I went back and forth by car on Fridays and Saturdays as well as all other days. I will never forget how Chaim helped me by telling me not to have guilt or how a black security guard wouldn't let a woman, escorted by two healthy men, walk seven blocks through San Francisco for fear of a stabbing. What terrible times we live in, but wonderful people live in them with us!

Since then I have observed the Sabbath unfailingly. If I thought I was religious then, I know I am now.

My Sabbath observance must be a little hard on Jan when I miss a performance on the Sabbath. He always feels happier knowing I'm out front and he likes it when I come backstage to tell him the truth about how he's doing. He also worries whether I'm safe wherever I am. Still, he has never complained.

How I Booked Hurok's Funeral

Sol Hurok was never the same after his office was fire-bombed, on January 26, 1972, because he was bringing Soviet artists to this country. A lovely young girl named Iris Kones, who worked for him, died in the blast, thirteen people were injured, and Hurok himself was carried from the blaze wrapped in his fur coat. The firemen thought he was dead. The medical reports say he suffered from smoke inhalation and recovered quickly, but I say he died a little. Certainly, he never completely recovered from the shock.

I visited him soon after that in his Park Avenue apartment. Amidst all the lavish furniture and gorgeous paintings, he looked particularly wan as he sat there in his bathrobe. The fright was still with him, and no matter what we talked about, he kept coming back to the explosion: "Och! John! How do you like what happened?"

I didn't like it at all and I was even sorrier to see how it had weakened him. Not only was he feeling sorry for himself, which was debilitating, but also this was, at the age of eighty-three, his first real look down the tunnel.

Even so, his death a little more than two years later was shockingly sudden. He had lunch with his associate, Walter Prude, and the guitarist Andrés Segovia. They were selling Segovia on the idea of accepting the same concert cruise I was doing. Segovia was going to Spain anyway; why not get a paid trip by giving one or two concerts during the journey and enjoying eight or ten days of vacation en route, plus a fee?

Once Segovia said yes, Hurok excused himself to go to a meeting with David Rockefeller of the Chase Manhattan Bank. It probably had to do with underwriting another cultural export or import. Rockefeller's office was on the seventeenth floor of 1 Chase Manhattan Plaza. Hurok's limousine went instead to 1 New York Plaza, a few blocks away. Hurok rode up to the seventeenth floor of the wrong building and collapsed. At the hospital, he was pronounced dead of a massive heart attack.

We heard about it half an hour later from Shelley Gold of the Hurok office. At first, almost like condolence calls, other friends and colleagues phoned us to ask: "Is it true?" or "Isn't it terrible?" But Walter Prude called up with a more urgent question: "Jan, did you know of any affiliation Hurok had with a synagogue or a Temple?": "Is it true

As close as we were to Hurok, none of his so-called children ever penetrated very far behind "papa's" amiable façade. He certainly never denied he was Jewish and I had always assumed he possessed some modest religious leanings and maybe even membership in some synagogue. Years earlier, he had mentioned going to *Kol Nidre* at B'Nai Jeshurun, a Conservative synagogue on Eighty-ninth Street and West End Avenue; another time, he said he'd been at Temple Emanu-El. Nowhere along the line had I ever had occasion to question him about his religion—not that it was any of my business anyway.

I mentioned Temple Emanu-El and B'Nai Jeshurun. Walter Prude said, "We have called both and they said he had no affiliation with them. We asked them if they would handle the burial and the funeral service, but they both said no. They deal only with members and can't take outsiders—not even Hurok."

A man must be mindful that when the day comes for him to bid farewell to this world there must be a place for him to be buried and a place for him to be buried from. That's why synagogues have burial societies and Jewish cemeteries have family plots. It's not something you can shop around for after you've gone. I could tell by the way Walter Prude just hung there on the phone that he was hoping I could suggest something or use my influence. I knew plenty of rabbis, but I didn't know any one of them who would alter the rules of his house for me or Hurok.

"You've told me about the places that are refusing," I told Prude. "Why don't we come up with a place that'll be happy to have him?"

"Where's that?"

"I'll tell you, Walter. This man has done more than enough for music and culture, so how about Carnegie Hall? With a religious ceremony, it would be exactly the right idea."

Walter Prude jumped at it, but being a manager, he tried to "improve" upon it: "Jan, that's a great idea! But how about Lincoln Center?"

"Lincoln Center?" I said. "Now you're becoming ostentatious." Besides, I knew that Carnegie Hall wouldn't say no. Hurok's client and friend Isaac Stern, who had saved Carnegie Hall from being torn down, was now its president. Julius Bloom, the executive director, was also a friend of Hurok's. And Hurok belonged there.

The next question was: What kind of ceremony? Walter Prude asked if I would sing. I don't like to sing at funerals, but I've done a couple in my life: when Abe Ellstein died and when Bruno Walter's wife died. So I told Walter Prude to find out first what Hurok's family wanted. Meanwhile I would work on locating a notable rabbi who would be willing to perform in Carnegie Hall. But I wouldn't arrange it until the family approved of the idea.

The rabbi who agreed to do the service was Dr. Bernard Mandelbaum, who used to be President of the Jewish Theological Seminary and was now on the board of directors of the America-Israel Cultural Foundation. I rang up Rabbi Mandelbaum and, without giving him any hints, asked him if he'd be available to do me a favor. He said yes. Then I called the Hurok office to find out what the family thought. As was to be expected, the agents were negotiating instead of deciding. One relative said, "No rabbi! He wasn't so religious." The only detail they seemed to agree upon was that Jan Peerce should sing at Hurok's funeral.

I picked up the phone and called Hurok's daughter, Ruth. She was relieved to hear from me. I told her I would sing only if the funeral was done properly. She said, "Anything you say!"

"Then what I say is this: I will sing 'The Prayer for the Dead.' You can ask Isaac Stern to play. I also feel you should have a rabbi—not Orthodox, not Reform, but Conservative. The rabbi and I will wear skullcaps. If you want it otherwise, let someone else make the arrangements."

That was how Carnegie Hall became Sol Hurok's synagogue on Friday morning, March 8, 1974. More than 2,600 mourners came to look at Hurok's coffin, blanketed with deep red roses, on the bare stage. Rabbi Mandelbaum spoke briefly and beautifully—reading from the Bible about young David playing the harp for King Saul. Isaac Stern, with a nod to the coffin, played Bach's B-minor Partita. Then he walked over to the coffin and touched it gently. Marian Anderson delivered the eulogy: "He launched hundreds of careers. He magnified thousands of others. And, in the process, he brought joy and a larger life to millions. He made not ripples, but waves. He went beyond his own shores."

When Marian Anderson sat down, I came to the podium and asked the audience to stand. I sang out the first low, wailing notes and then my voice rose to the uppermost reaches of the house that Hurok had filled many times over. As I sang, I heard not my voice, but his voice on another Friday saying: "Now go home, make Kiddush over your sweet red wine . . . and kiss Alice. You are a member of the Metropolitan Opera Company!"

That's all there was to it. When it was over, eight pallbearers wheeled the coffin away as a big white curtain came down slowly on the life and death of Sol Hurok, impresario.

An Optical Illusion

Recovery from my California injury and hospitalization was rapid. I was doing concerts five weeks after I left St. Francis, which was three weeks after I was discharged from rehabilitation therapy at Mount Sinai in New York. At home I did bicycle exercises, and in June 1974, when I celebrated my seventieth birthday, the doctors gave me a clean bill of health. Everything was completely healed.

As we get older, when one threat recedes, another is always waiting on the runway to move up. In my case, the retreating and the advancing threats collided and exploded one grim night that summer in Westbury, Long Island.

The cataract forming on my "good" eye had left me with twenty-percent vision. I had read in the papers that the greatest advances in modern medicine lately have been in ophthalmology: laser beams to weld detached retinas back in position and the ultrasonic cryogenic (freezing) probe for removing cataracts. The inventor had done wonders for the vibraphonist Lionel Hampton, who had given a performance the day after cataract surgery. At the time I had thought: Maybe there's something in this for me. Such is human shortsightedness, however, that I didn't clip the item or write down the doctor's name.

Thank G-d for my son Larry! He read something similar and immediately started nosing around. He had a medical consultant working on one of his movies. "Oh, sure," the doctor said. "The Kelman Method. You don't even have to stay overnight at the hospital. That's the method we use at Santa Monica Hospital."

Dr. Charles D. Kelman, a low-key, boyish man in his early forties, examined me in his space-age modern office on East Fifty-eighth Street in Manhattan that June. He advised me to have the operation as soon as possible. Medically speaking, the cataract was ready for removal, because it was dense and interfering with my vision. But he said two things that made me doubt him for many—too many—months.

The first was: "Mr. Peerce, if everything goes the way I anticipate, not only will we save your eye—with the help of G-d and assuming that your retina is intact, I know it's going to be fine—but you will then have twenty-twenty vision or near that."

"Twenty-twenty vision?" I said. "I never had twenty-twenty vision in my life, even *with* glasses."

"That's the rule of the game," he said. "With people as nearsighted as you, the eye compensates when we remove the cataract. If a person with normal vision is operated on for a cataract, he becomes rather farsighted and needs glasses or lenses to bring him back to his natural twenty-twenty. But coming from where you've been, the worst that could happen would be twenty-forty vision."

When you're concerned with saving an eye, it's hard to believe you'll see better than ever before. But a cataract operation, like certain hearing operations, can "restore" something that you didn't have before.

The second doubt arose when Alice asked what the odds were of anything going wrong, since I had only my left eye to gamble with.

"I would say," Dr. Kelman answered with some caution and deliberation, "there are ninety-eight chances in a hundred of everything going perfectly right."

My heart sank. The eye surgeon who'd given me the blinker for a right eye had estimated ninety-nine percent. This one seemed to have doubled the risk.

Actually, he was just being cautious. Detached retina is the two-percent risk of cataract surgery. Nevertheless, I told Kelman I had a show to do that summer, but I would call him when it was over. Kelman understood what I was thinking. I told him, "When the time comes, doctor, it'll be you and you alone. Until then, the show must go on."

We opened *Laugh a Little, Cry a Little* in Paramus, New Jersey, at the Playhouse on the Mall. We moved to Philadelphia's Playhouse in the Park, where we broke the house record by grossing $90,000 in two weeks, according to the treasurer, who had the remarkable name of Alan Ross Kosher. The following Tuesday, we opened at the Westbury Music Fair on Long Island, to a $106,000 advance sale.

Although I've been superstitious ever since I whistled in my dressing room and was cut out of the opening show at Radio City Music Hall, one superstition I've avoided and detested is the "Break a leg!" traditionally uttered to an actor before a performance. Me, I believe a good simple *"Mazel tov!"* or "Good Luck!" is much more civilized. I know that somebody who says "Break a leg!" to you—and somebody always does—means well, but I don't have to like it. It also depends on who is saying it; if it's your understudy, chances are he really means it.

On our second night at Westbury, after a couple of people had told me to "Break a leg, Jan!" I obliged.

Westbury is theatre-in-the-round, which means exits and entrances via the aisles. Three times that night, I traveled up and down the aisles on foot. What I particularly like about theatre-in-the-round is the contact I have with people. They actually greet you in the dark, and while I don't see them and can't acknowledge them, I greatly appreciate them. That night, a voice I recognized from past shows and concerts said, "God bless you always, you're so wonderful!" I couldn't nod or turn around because I was watching my step and thinking of the next lines I had to speak (they were being revised from night to night).

For my fourth exit, I found myself facing an aisle that looked unfamiliar. We had started there only the night before, but I knew I was in the wrong place. Still, I had to make my exit, and judging from the happy, enthusiastic faces I could see looking up at me, it seemed to be only a four- or five-inch drop. When I had one foot off, I knew I was in trouble, but I couldn't pull back. The illumination and my own eye had played me a trick. It was a fifteen-inch drop, and as I went over it, I sat down hard on the left leg, the one that had been through hell in San Francisco.

I felt shock. Then I felt pain. But I actually stood and took two steps up the aisle, holding onto the railing by the seats. Then Phil Schapiro, who had been sitting in an aisle seat right near my disaster, scooped me into his arms and carried me up the aisle: a 160-pound baby in the arms of his 250-pound manager.

The show was interrupted for just fifteen seconds. Then Jerry Jarrett, one of the Tevyes who had preceded me in *Fiddler* on Broadway and who had a role in *Laugh a Little,* picked up a script and started reading and singing my lines. It all happened so fast and so smoothly that a few of the three thousand people in that audience thought my marvelous pratfall was part of the show. The others knew better.

In the audience was a theatre party of Long Island doctors, all on call with their little bleeper radios. Seeing what had happened, half a dozen of them came backstage—so I had every kind of specialist on hand for consultation. But there was pandemonium.

Alice had fought her way backstage by then. The Little General took charge of the chaos. If you've never heard someone shout "Shhhh!" ask Alice to do it for you sometime. *"Shhhh!"* she shouted. "Just a minute! Everybody leave Jan alone! I'll tell you what's going to be done here."

At those words, everybody looked to her and she had restored order to my life. Now she turned to me in the wheelchair they had placed me in and said softly, "Jan, how are you? Do you have much pain?"

The pain seemed to be waning, so I said, "No. I think I'll be able to do the second act."

The police doctor, who had begun to assert his authority as the medic in charge of my dressing room, whispered to me, "Mr. Peerce, you're either kidding or you're out of your mind."

"No, no," I said. "Look. I can stand up." With that, I lifted myself out of the wheelchair and stood the way I had after wrenching a tendon in Lisbon —with my leg turned out in sort of a concert pose.

"Do you stand that way always?" the doctor asked.

"No," I said, "just frequently."

Even I had to laugh at my remark. Everyone else in that room did. The trouble was I could stand that way, but I couldn't walk.

Instead of going back onstage, I was strapped to a chair and carried out of the Westbury Music Fair to an ambulance. It was intermission by then and half of the spectators were in the parking lot waiting to find out what was happening to me. Some just looked; others wished me well as I passed them. And I'd say "Thank you," though when one of them said "Bravo!" I wondered what I had done to be cheered that night. I must have looked as guilty as I felt. Ahead of me I could see the police ambulance's red light circling and I felt a little like a bank robber who'd just been nabbed and wounded in the act. From the minute I'd stepped off the deep end of that stage, I'd known that whatever I was getting was good for a month or six weeks at least. That would be my sentence.

As I made my exit, one man was producing an old Italian gesture I'd learned from *Cavalleria Rusticana:* thrusting forth two fingers as if to push away the devil or ward off the evil eye that had deceived me into my fall.

With four doctors—three of them orthopedists—in attendance, the ambulance took me to Syosset Hospital for X-rays. The break was two or three inches below the old break; the metal plate that had been installed in San Francisco had protected me from a lot of the pain I was just beginning to feel. The orthopedists all agreed that I needed surgery now to take out the old plate and put in a new one to cover both breaks.

They offered to do the job right there in Syosset, but I asked to be taken to Mount Sinai Hospital in Manhattan. The reason I gave was that my own physicians are all affiliated there. Over and above that, it was tradition with me by now. When I get hungry, I've learned to eat in certain restaurants. When I get sick, I go to Mount Sinai.

Back into the ambulance I went—with Alice and one physician along. Alice's brother Walter had phoned the director and reserved a private room for me. But when the ambulance pulled up, there wasn't one. There were exactly two beds available in the whole Klingenstein Pavilion. One was in pediatrics with three kids. The other was upstairs with three old men. I settled for the old men as roommates; they're quieter.

At dawn, I learned that one of the men had trouble with his esophagus and couldn't swallow. Another had blood trouble, which involved tapping his backside and backbone. I never found out what the third one had, but he was the sickest and most lifeless of all. As I looked around me, I said, "Lord, thank You for just breaking my leg!"

After surgery I woke up in my private room without even realizing I'd been operated on. Around me were my Alice and my Susan, as I'd expected —and my Larry and my Joy, who had flown in from the Coast as soon as they'd heard the news. I couldn't believe any of it—let alone that the operation was over and it was a success. "But," I acknowledged, "whatever it was, it doesn't hurt." The pain came later.

My own doctor, Dr. Marvin Levitt, took the offensive in his approach to me on a day when I was down: "What're you unhappy about, Peerce? So you broke a bone! At least you know that bone mends."

"Some consolation!" I snorted. "It would have been a greater consolation if nothing had happened. Or if the X-ray had shown it was just a bruise, that would have been the *Peerce de résistance.*"

He couldn't fight repartee like that, so he said, "Your bone is already mending even while I'm talking to you, while you're sitting around feeling sorry for yourself. It's a nothing you've got, Jan! Do you want to take a walk down Cardiac Row with me? So smile, be happy, and pray that you get well soon."

"I'm praying," I assured him.

"And you *will* get well soon. You will sing and perform and make people happy and that'll make you happy, wealthy, and wise again."

But when you're down, you listen only for what goes unsaid. "You mean," I responded, "I'll never dance again?"

Within a week after my operation, the doctors had me in therapy, doing exercises and getting ready to walk. The therapist to whom I was assigned knew who I was and said, "It'll be an honor to work with you, Mr. Peerce."

"Thank you," I said. "I wish I could be honoring you under other circumstances." With that, we got to talking. He mentioned that he'd studied music and I mentioned that he had the same last name as the Italian baritone Renato Capecchi.

"I'm not related to him," therapist Capecchi told me, "but I did study with a man you may remember because he always spoke well of you: Louis d'Angelo."

"Oh!" I gasped. "That is one very noble name in opera." Louis d'Angelo, born 1888 in Naples and died 1958 in Jersey City, appeared no fewer than 1,490 times at the Met as well as 461 times on tour. He did smaller character parts, but he was the greatest scene-stealer on the operatic stage. He didn't have to lift a finger to steal a scene. His slender, aristocratic appearance alone riveted your attention. In *Rigoletto,* he was a courtier who would stand there with his arms folded while Leonard Warren as the anguished jester pleaded to be told what I, as the Duke, had done with his daughter. Cold and lean and haughty, d'Angelo would just stand there— nobility looking right through riffraff and not even seeing poor Rigoletto— and this would steal the scene. D'Angelo's was a commanding presence, and when I say he stole scenes, I'm only saying that he helped put the story into perspective and not just focus it on the star performances. I told Capecchi all this, adding, "When you see his children, give them my love and be sure to tell them what I said about their father."

Capecchi put me to work walking between two parallel bars. He showed me what to do. You lift up out of your wheelchair, you stand up, and with the strength of your arms, you jump a step ahead, landing on your good leg. With him showing me the way, we must have traversed the parallel bars a dozen times before I sat down in the wheelchair.

While Capecchi made me rest, some fellow patients began to look over the newest Olympic entrant in their midst. An elegant blue-haired dowager, wearing costume jewelry with her hospital pajamas while trying out a new hip, said to me ever so prissily, "Am I correct in surmising that your name is Mr. Jan Peerce?"

"Yes," I said, "you are correct."

"Oh, my dear Mr. Peerce, it is indeed a pleasure and an honor to meet you."

"But sometimes we meet in the funniest places."

"I must admit," she went on, "that when I read about your misfortune in the *Times*, it occurred to me that we might meet. But where we meet is rather unfortunate, I daresay."

A much less pretentious, but not too perceptive-looking man joined us on the bench and asked me, "Where do I know you from?"

I don't like to play that game of exchanging picture postals, so I said, "Why should you know me?"

"I've seen you many times and I should know who you are. I would say you're some kind of television personality."

"You're right to some extent, but mostly I'm a singer."

"Oh, no," he said. "That you can't be. With that mustache and those glasses, and you're only—"

I would have let him finish the dissection before telling him off, but the elegant dowager with the new hip couldn't contain herself. *"Schmuck!"* she shouted. "Don't you know Jan Peerce when you see him?"

That was my 1974 debut in therapy. I was in the hospital for three and a half weeks. Then, barely a month after my accident in Westbury, I rejoined *Laugh a Little, Cry a Little* at the Valley Forge Music Fair. When I came back to rehearse, Peter Howard, who was conducting the orchestra, played my own "Hail to the Chief"—"The Bluebird of Happiness." The chorus sang it to me and I joined in. You don't think I'm ever going to hear "The Bluebird of Happiness" played without singing it, do you?

Throughout the show's tour—which took me to Baltimore, Washington, and back to Westbury for a return engagement in September—I played the part in my rented droshky: a wheelchair. The part of the immigrant grandfather lent itself to the wheelchair—particularly at the end, when the family moves from the Lower East Side up to Jerome Avenue and I have to say, "Oy, vot a *shlep* it's gonna be to go down to *shul* every *Shabbas.*" All the more meaningful for a man in a wheelchair, playing a grandpa who'll always keep going to the same synagogue. As one critic wrote, "If the circumstances hadn't been in the news, I would have taken it for granted that the part was written this way."

The Miracle of My Eye

When Dr. Charles Kelman read about my accident in Westbury, he was on vacation in California. He felt very bad. His administrator, Joseph Lizerbram, called Alice to convey his and Dr. Kelman's sympathies. In the conversation that ensued, Alice had an idea and Lizerbram got back to Kelman with

it. Then he called Alice at Mount Sinai to tell her that Dr. Kelman was willing
to interrupt his vacation to fly in and operate on my cataract while I was still
in my hospital bed. His equipment, which is about the size of a small refrigerator, can be transported in a station wagon. Alice put me on the line and had
Joe repeat the proposal. Dr. Kelman was willing, but I wasn't. I practically
snarled at Joe:

"You mean while I'm in the hospital, so it shouldn't be a total loss, I
can have my eye done, too? And what do you do for an encore? Take out
my appendix?"

That's how much I wanted to think about any more surgery.

By this time, I couldn't read the newspaper (I couldn't even see the
losses I was taking in Wall Street); I couldn't read the lines of my show (Alice
would read them to me and cue me until I knew them); and though I could
still read sheet music up close, I couldn't see anything when it was on the
piano. I could "fake" it by learning everything by heart, which I'd been
doing for some time.

After the show had finished its tour, I began to think in terms of the fairly
immediate future: Where was I headed? I could no longer take any job where
I had to read something onstage, the way one does with an oratorio. For my
Passover booking the next March in Miami, I had a lot of reading to do. True,
I knew much of it by heart, but I would still have to have the *Haggadah* before
me and give my guests at the Deauville the page numbers to turn to.

I called up my friend Dr. William Feinbloom, who is one of America's
leading experts on the shortsighted and nearly blind, and asked him if there
was any alternative to surgery. Bill said that neither he nor anyone else knew
of any.

Alice consulted one more expert—the Lubavitcher *rebbe,* Menachem
Mendel Schneerson. The *rebbe* said, "Do you have a friend you trust who is
also a doctor?"

"Bill Feinbloom," Alice answered without hesitation. "But we've already asked him and he's urged us to go ahead."

"Go back to him," the *rebbe* advised, "and ask him to go see three other
doctors about your husband's case. Whatever two out of three decide should
be your choice."

We asked Bill to submit my case to arbitration by his peers. When we
came back from a trip to Florida, he had an answer ready:

"Alice and Jan, I saw six doctors instead of three. Three are old and
three are young. All six say you should be operated now. All three of the
younger men are for your having Kelman do it. Two of the three older men

are absolutely in favor of Kelman, too. The oldest man, though, thinks it would be advisable to have it done not by Kelman, but *conventionally*—the way it was done before."

This verdict, of five out of six, decided me. I canceled a trip to Israel and made a date with Dr. Kelman for surgery on Tuesday, November 5, 1974.

With conventional cataract surgery, the surgeon makes a 180-degree incision in the cornea, grasps the lens of the eye with forceps, and pulls it out of the eye. With forceps, however, the danger is that the instrument can rupture the lens and ruin both the operation and the eye. The danger is greater where the eye is totally lacking in elasticity, as was the one I lost. And this method requires many stitches to put the eye back together after cutting it in half.

Kelman's "cryogenic probe" is an instrument that, upon touching the lens of the eye, freezes some of it to form an ice ball. This ice ball becomes part of the probe, serving as a sort of handle for removing and replacing the lens.

The second innovation of what is known as Kelman's Phaco-Emulsification and Aspiration Cataract-Removal Technique is the instrument used for the surgery itself. This is a needlelike drill (inspired by the ultrasonic drills dentists now use) that vibrates at 40,000 strokes per second to draw up the cataract, each fragment of which is sucked away by a pump. It requires only one stitch.

Kelman himself does ten operations a day, on Mondays and Wednesdays. But he asked me to pick a different day of the week because of the special circumstances attending a patient who had already lost an eye through cataract surgery. He would do just me and one or two other special cases on that day.

Kelman does most of his surgery at the Lydia Hall Hospital in Freeport, Long Island, where two operating rooms and a rooftop helicopter pad have been set aside for him. The two operating rooms enable him to do operations one right after the other instead of waiting for the room to be vacated and cleaned. The helicopter, which he pilots himself, spares him "three hours a day in the pure carbon monoxide poison of commuter traffic" to and from his office in Manhattan. The Long Island Rail Road doesn't work for a number of reasons—one of which is that the Long Island Rail Road doesn't work, and another being that the crosstown trip from Penn Station on the West Side to Kelman's office on the East Side can be a commute in itself. His helicopter lands at the heliport on Thirty-fourth Street at the East River. On the way in, he radios for a cab, which is waiting when he lands. His time is too valuable to be wasted in traffic. A couple of times a month, he flies himself to a hospital in New Jersey to do guest surgery there, and once a month he operates at Manhattan Eye and Ear Hospital. He makes video tapes of every operation in case there is anything to be learned from replaying it. He has done 3,500 operations thus far using the Kelman Method.

Kelman's instrument costs upward of $25,000. Some 350 of them are in use by hospitals across America and as far away as Germany, Israel, and Japan. In his "spare time," he is a singer, composer, and a particularly accomplished saxophonist and clarinetist. Every year or so, he rents Carnegie Hall and gives a benefit concert—with guest stars onstage and the cataract crowd filling every seat at prices up to one hundred dollars—to equip a needy hospital somewhere in the world with the Kelman Method, including personal training of its doctors with the instruments. The March 1, 1975, concert was for a hospital in Israel that treats young soldiers with traumatic cataracts brought on by fighting.

The day I'd elected for my eye surgery was Election Day, 1974. On Election Eve—that is, Monday afternoon, November 4—I went to Kelman's office on East Fifty-eighth Street to be pretreated with eye drops and chauffeured to the hospital in Freeport. There was only one other patient making the trip: William B. Williams, the disk jockey, who was also having a cataract done by Kelman.

We rode out in an airport-type limousine that can hold a dozen patients. Williams and I made a lot of nervous conversation about everything but our eyes. I could see he was more nervous than I was, so I interrupted the chitchat to say, "Are you taking the local anesthetic?"

"No," he said, "I'm taking general."

"I'm a coward, too," I told him. Then we talked about nothing but our eyes.

We drove up to that charming little hospital and were offered champagne. I said, "No, thanks. I'll celebrate another time—I hope." But this reception was in keeping with Kelman's concept of "a happy experience." He truly believes that with present-day technology, cataracts can be fun. And this treatment is extended not just to Jan Peerce and William B. Williams. The next day, when the limousine delivered ten patients who were Joe Blows and William B. Nobodys, they were offered champagne and a fancy supper, too.

We were shown to our rooms. Everybody danced around me. Nurses kept coming in and greeting me personally. They were all prepared for me.

The anesthetist, a fine young man, came in and said, "I'll take good care of you. My mother is a fan of yours. Don't worry, Mr. Peerce, you'll be all right."

The whole place was warmer than Mount Sinai or any other hospital I've ever dropped or fallen into. Lydia Hall is a happy hospital—too happy, in fact, to be a hospital; it's more like a laboratory on a new frontier of science. Everybody who works there is involved in what he or she is doing. And what they're doing is showing signs of remarkable success. It was like being in a hit show.

The last voice I heard that night, aside from my own, praying, was Dr. Kelman's. He phoned to wish me a good night's rest.

"Thank you," I told him, "but it's more important that *you* get a good night's rest.

"Well, in your honor, I'm going to go to sleep early tonight," Kelman assured me.

I was awakened at six-thirty in the morning. Alice appeared soon thereafter. She and Larry, who'd flown in from the Coast for the occasion, had stayed at a motel in Long Island. Now they walked part of the way with me as I was wheeled into surgery with a prayer on my lips—and my one dim eye soaking up the sight of my loyal wife and my lost-and-found son in case this was to be my last look at them.

The young anesthetist joined us and that was as far as Alice and Larry could go. "I don't have to say to you 'Be calm,' " the anesthetist told me as we entered the operating room, "because you're halfway under already, thanks to sedatives. But you can still hear and do everything I ask you to. It won't be long before Dr. Kelman will be with you."

With those words, in walked Kelman.

"Did you have a good night's sleep?" I asked him.

He laughed and said yes. Then he said, "We're going to be ready for you in a couple of minutes. Just relax. We're almost ready to go." With that, his sound system began to play Tony Bennett singing "I Left My Heart in San Francisco." Considering what I'd almost left in San Francisco the year before, I began to pray that I wouldn't leave my sight in Freeport. The last thought I remember before going under was: Why the hell should he play Tony Bennett when he could be playing me?

Dr. Kelman: *It might have overstimulated both of us. I don't use Muzak because I believe it's noise pollution. And for working, I prefer to use the same music over and over again. When I listen to fresh music, it takes away a certain amount of my concentration on the operation. I mean, I might get excited about a chord change.*

At my concert in Carnegie Hall four months later, when both Jan and William B. Williams appeared with me, Willie Williams told one of his favorite jokes: "The day Dr. Kelman operated on Jan Peerce and me . . . well, you haven't lived until you've had your eye doctor—in the middle of the operation!—lean over and hum 'Stardust.' Meanwhile, on the next table, some guy is doing Kol Nidre!"

Jan Peerce had one of the hardest cataracts—not especially difficult, but hard like a diamond—that I've ever operated on. It took longer than any operation I'd done in three or four years. The actual "emulsification time" it takes for the vibrating needle to break up and suck up the cataract is usually one or two minutes, followed by sewing up and washing hands. In Jan's case, it took almost ten minutes. This meant I had to sit there, looking at the cataract under magnification of ten or fifteen times under a microscope, while holding my hand absolutely motionless for ten minutes. It's one of the greatest exertions in the world.

Otherwise, thank G-d, it was an average operation: uneventful, with no surprises, no complications. When you live with cataracts day in and day out, you become somewhat inured to the effects of what you're doing. But when Jan Peerce came to me, he could barely count fingers. He was certainly legally blind—much worse than legally blind. And in his case, there was so much more riding on the operation than usual that I was tuned in on all my channels. When it was over, I was so elated that he'd done so well and he and his family were so happy that I just felt good being a part of it.

[Alice Peerce later watched the video tape of Jan's operation.]

Alice: *What I saw on the screen was like an Arctic ice floe of a blur. The needle went in, made a crack, and then, after the big crack in the blur, I began to see little cracks in the ice floe. Suddenly, the lens was clear and bright—like a sunrise. Just like that. It's like watching sepia tone on TV and then it opens up into bright, vivid color. Jan had been living with those dull browns and grays for so long that his vision had adapted to it. It was the most miraculous thing.*

I have no recollection of the operation or the recovery room. When I awoke, my left eye was covered, but I felt I was in my own room. A voice spoke the second I stirred. "Jan? This is Dr. Kelman. I'm going to take the cover off your eye."

He lifted it and that was when the miracle happened for me.

I looked at him and exclaimed, "Dr. Kelman!" Then I looked at my wife and said, "Alice!" Then I looked right at my son and said, "Larry!" That was when we all knew the operation was a success, for Larry was standing at the far end of the room, where I would not have been able to see anybody the day before. And this was without eyeglasses!

Dr. Kelman didn't have to tell me, but he said, "Everything went well and you'll see better than you ever did in your life." And he was right. Now I can see people in the tenth row orchestra when I'm giving a concert.

I didn't even have to stay in bed that day of my surgery. I was up and down and up and around. After a while, I could visit with William B. Williams, who had been operated after me, and was recovering just as fast. Ninety-nine percent of the patients just take the local anesthetic, which means even quicker recovery (they can go home the same day) and fewer complications, though I had hardly any aftereffects.

The next day, after Kelman had done his ten new operations, Williams and I were ready to go back to Manhattan for some finishing touches in the doctor's office. Kelman offered us a ride in his helicopter. Williams accepted. I declined. I'm not afraid of helicopters—having flown them from airport to airport—but I prefer to be piloted by professional pilots, not by a sky surgeon. So I took the limousine, which came right in on the expressways and over the Queensboro Bridge. And do you know something? I reached Kelman's office before Kelman and Williams, for their taxi was stuck in traffic almost an hour between Thirty-fourth and Fifty-eighth streets.

They had some drops and a pair of glasses ready for me at Kelman's office. It turned out I didn't really need the glasses except for protection and reading, but I thought that people wouldn't recognize me without them. As it was, a lot of people didn't recognize me in my new horn-rimmed glasses *without* the Coca-Cola lenses!

I didn't even have to wear a patch on my eye. Kelman gave me a little metal patch with holes to see through; I put it on only when I went to bed, so I wouldn't rub the eye when I slept. I had to wear it every night for four weeks.

Just before he discharged me from his office and told Alice to take me home, Dr. Kelman turned the corners of his mouth down and murmured rather sheepishly, "I have something I must tell you, Jan."

I thought: Uh-oh. Here comes the kicker.

"You know, Jan," Kelman went on solemnly, "I told you I went to bed early on Monday night. Well, I lied to you. I sat up until midnight reading medical papers."

The pent-up sigh of relief—for much more than this confession—that I emitted was practically a howl. "Well," I finally said, "it beats nightclubbing. But if you want a night on the town tonight, Charlie, it's on me!"

All in My Head

In all fairness, I must confess that after the miracle of my eye, I kept getting a pain in my head at night. After studying his video tape and reexamining me, Kelman could find no reason for it—except perhaps some unidentifiable traumatic reaction. The operation was still a success. I started taking Percodan, a real painkiller, which enabled me to sleep two hours and then wake up with the same headache. I was afraid to take another pill; I might start relying on it. So with a certain concentration on my part and a strong desire to lick it, the pain went away—and has been gone ever since, thank the Lord.

I can't put my finger on why or how I licked it. I just told myself: "Peerce, you've always been a good sleeper with good sleeping habits. Who wants to sleep in the daytime because you didn't sleep at night?" Anyway, it was all in the head.

After my leg operation a quarter of a year before my eye operation, I had also grown attached to my cane. But in early 1975, when we were on a trip to Europe, Alice started nagging me about this. I insisted I couldn't get around without my stick. "What do you mean, you can't?" she yelled at me in a Paris hotel room. "Are you going to go through all your life wearing a cane?"

It was that phrase "wearing a cane"—like an ornament—that enraged me. I threw my cane—though not right at her. It hooked itself onto the clothes rack and Alice laughed.

"All right!" I said to her, trying to keep a straight face. "I won't use the cane! But it's on *your* head."

"So it's on my head," she said. "It doesn't hurt."

On her head, I didn't need to use the cane anymore.

Alice has always been there when I needed her—sometimes before I knew I needed her. Sometimes she says to me, "Jan, you lean on me too much." I tell her that isn't so; it's just that I trust her greatly. She's not always right, but even when she isn't, I know she's being wrong on *my* side.

Before Dr. Kelman brought me back from the legally blind, Alice used to sit with me until I learned the lines I couldn't see in the script. I had the worst trouble with *Laugh a Little, Cry a Little*—partly because the lines kept changing with each rewrite, partly because I was depressed about my eyes and my leg, but mostly because I was creating this part. I've learned operas in foreign languages. I've learned a Japanese folk song. I've learned Tevye and I've learned Rothschild. But all those were parts that others originated, or sounds I had heard, while here were words on paper waiting for me to bring them to life. No matter how long we sat and studied and fed each other dialogue, the lines wouldn't come. Whenever I did learn them and thought I knew them, twenty minutes later I couldn't think of them to save my life. I began to wonder if old age had finally caught up.

I took it out on Alice: "You got me into this goddamn thing! Why did you? I didn't need it! I don't need it! I can't do it!"

Alice gave it right back to me: "So give it up! If you feel I got you into something, I'm sorry. I thought I was doing you a favor instead of letting you sit around. I didn't think you were ready to retire."

So I said: "Look here. Listen to this speech and see if you like the way I do it."

She made a suggestion, I disagreed, and we were back in business again.

Now that I can see the lines, it doesn't take me long to learn a part— or relearn Tevye, as I did the summer of 1975 for a tour of *Fiddler* in the West and Midwest and again the summer of 1976 in Honolulu. And now that I can see better with one eye than I ever did with two, there is nothing to keep me out of opera—except who is looking for a seventy-two-year-old tenor going on seventy-three?

I had an offer to open a new culture complex in San Jose, California, in *La Bohème.* I accepted—and promised that I'd bring down the house. Unfortunately, before I could get there, the roof caved in, and they hadn't found the money to rebuild it.

Then I had another offer: to do *Traviata* with the Peoria Civic Opera Company—and I took it. A lot of people didn't think a seventyish Alfredo would play in Peoria. They couldn't see me at this age as a dashing, impetuous youth of twenty-three or twenty-four. Hell! I didn't even look twenty-three or twenty-four when I was twenty-three or twenty-four! I certainly didn't in 1941, when I made my debut at the Met in *Traviata* at thirty-seven. I wasn't that juvenile and neither was anybody else in the opera. I thought I wouldn't look young enough for Alfredo in 1975, but I knew I would sound young.

We did a concert version in Galesburg and a full performance in Peoria. Jerry Klein wrote in the *Peoria Journal-Star:*

> He was here last season in a concert. He won an ovation then and he won one last night again at the Scottish Rite Cathedral, not because he is a symbol or a name, but because he sings with such strength, such appeal and such sheer magnificence. His is one of those grand voices from the great days of

opera that is quite able to reach the farthest extremes of almost any hall without microphone. Even from the back of the Scottish Rite stage, where other singers' voices tended to disappear into the flies, his boomed forth grandly.

Critics are critics and audiences are audiences. The important thing still is to keep the local manager happy. I knew that they loved me in Peoria when the Civic Opera asked me back to do *Lucia* and *Cavalleria Rusticana* in 1976.

Larry flew in to Peoria from the Coast to hear me sing. Let him tell you what he told me.

Larry Peerce: *First let me tell you what I didn't tell Dad—that once he stepped into those magic boots he bought for fifty dollars thirty-five years ago, he was Alfredo. That was backstage, before the opera. Onstage, well, in the directorial trade we have an expression for a commanding presence: an actor or actress "takes stage." I have to tell you that in Peoria that night my father "took stage."*

What he wants me to tell you about is something that happened in 1941, which he didn't remember until I reminded him of it. I was eleven then and I've remembered it all my life. Splendid in my navy blue suit, I was at the Met on the Saturday afternoon he made his debut in Traviata. *And I was backstage right after the performance to soak up my father's glory. A man with white hair, Edward Ziegler, the assistant general manager of the Met, rushed into the dressing room talking telegraphically in headlines, almost like the sign that went round the Times building in Times Square: "FABULOUS! NEXT YEAR! OPENING NIGHT AT THE MET! PAGLIACCI! YOU!"*

And my father said, "Thank you very much, Mr. Ziegler, but no, thank you."

I was astonished and so was Ziegler: "What do you mean, Mr. Peerce? You're turning down a tenor's dream! Why?"

My father said, "I could sing it and I could sing the hell out of it. But I think, if I did, I couldn't do Traviata *this well ten, twenty, thirty years from now."*

I looked and listened. Later, when I was old enough to understand, I was deeply moved that a hotshot tenor on what should have been the biggest ego trip of his life could think that far ahead about his technique and artistry as well as himself. I must have understood a little of it from the moment he said it. I never got over it in terms of how I have to treat my own talents and abilities and creativity over the long haul. Every time I've been tempted to yield to a studio or the fast buck, I've looked back on that scene.

So almost thirty-four years after that moment in his dressing room at the Met, I was asked to give a toast at the party in Peoria. It embarrassed him. For after telling this story, I proclaimed that I love him as my father, worship him as an artist, and thank him for that moment in 1941 which had more effect on the rest of my life than anything else that ever happened to me.

EXUBERANCE MARKS RECITAL BY PEERCE

BY PETER G. DAVIS

Jan Peerce, 71 years old next week and still going strong, gave a recital in Alice Tully Hall on Sunday night with Allen Rogers accompanying at the piano. Time and nature have been kind to Mr. Peerce, for he is still recognizably the same tenor that he was 40 years ago.

The program was the sort of thing that Mr. Peerce has always enjoyed singing—operatic arias, traditional Hebrew and Yiddish songs and show tunes. Of course there were differences—the timbre of his voice has dried out considerably and there is not much variety or color to the tone, while the breath control is not quite what it was. Still, Mr. Peerce shrewdly minimized these liabilities wherever possible, concentrating on generalized interpretive exuberance and a secure top register to carry the operatic portion of his recital.

In matters of technical control and expressive warmth, the tenor was at his best in the cantorial selections. As for sheer entertainment, Mr. Peerce's unbuttoned delivery and chatty description of four Yiddish songs were nonpareil and left the audience clamoring for more. The concert was a benefit for FREE, Friends of Refugees of Eastern Europe.

—*New York Times,*
Tuesday, May 27, 1975

FOOLING MA NATURE

BY BILL ZAKARIASEN

Outside of witnessing an important debut or the premiere of a great new composition, there's nothing more gratifying in the business of music criticism than hearing a performer hold on to his art and technique beyond a time theoretically dictated by Nature.

Tenor Jan Peerce, who sang in Tully Hall Sunday night, will be 71 years old this June 3. While no one —even he himself—could claim he sang with all the freedom, or all the notes, he possessed 30 years ago, the solid foundation of his voice remained intact.

Peerce was singing Bononcini's "No, O Dio" years before Baroque scholars told us the way they thought it should be sung; if his scholarship remains at variance with theirs, his fabled breath control would be a joy in the music of any period. He sang the "Traviata" aria with the same perfectly-timed rubato he learned from Toscanini.
. . .

There were of course encores, including "If I Were a Rich Man," and Peerce gloated: "I haven't had such a standing ovation since last Sunday! G-d willing, I'll sing this same program for you right here in Tully 20 years from now."

Don't put it past him.

—*Daily News,*
Tuesday, May 27, 1975

I gave a concert in Amsterdam not long ago and an old singing colleague of mine, Paolo Goren, an Israeli who's now a cantor, came to my dressing room and paid me the usual backstage compliments, telling me I'm singing even better than the first time he heard me, twenty years ago—all good things to hear from another singer, but if you're smart, you let them go in one ear and out the other. That is, until he wished me the old Talmudic blessing of may you live to 120 years, and then added, "Jan, your voice is in such wonderful shape that when you die your voice will have to be buried at a later date."

Unfortunately, in too many cases involving singers who don't sing correctly or don't have the proper schooling or proper handling or self-discipline, the voice goes prematurely. This shouldn't be. According to science, the voice is one of the last parts of the body that should go. As a man grows older, he may get round-shouldered or stoop or falter in his steps or his hands may shake, but the voice should stay relatively strong. Aside from healthy vocal cords, breath is the best foundation for good singing. My outlook is that a person who sings correctly should be able to sing as long as he can breathe.

Sometime in the forty-eight remaining years that the Talmud and Cantor Goren have allotted me, I think I may have to face up to the end of my singing career. I won't wait until my voice doesn't sound good. I am courageous enough, knowledgeable enough, and truthful enough to know when I can produce to the point of success. With Alice around, closer to me today than ever before, I know she'll be the first to tell me when I'm not producing. So I don't worry about self-deception.

I've sung with artists who were sailing along for ten years or more on tricks, on reputation, on pity, on emotions they once roused. But I'd sooner die than walk out onstage and produce echoes.

I've had a good life and I'm too much of an egomaniac to tolerate my not doing well enough. If that ever happens, I'll bow out, saying just one thing:

"My dear G-d, I have no complaints. You've been wonderful to me. I've had a great life and I want to thank You and thank the people who made all this possible."

ACKNOWLEDGMENTS

In addition to nearly four years of interviews with Jan Peerce and others mentioned in this book, the following secondary sources were drawn upon: B. H. Haggin, *The Toscanini Musicians Knew* (New York: Horizon Press, 1967; interview with Jan Peerce on pages 107–119); William E. Wiener Oral History Library of the American Jewish Committee, uncorrected transcript of Jan Peerce's 1973 interviews-in-depth by Janet Bookspan; Leo Rosten, *The Joys of Yiddish* (New York: McGraw-Hill, 1968), for defining (and spelling) my terms; Museum of Modern Art for screening and rescreening the film of Toscanini's *Hymn of the Nations* at my behest; and Robert J. Wayner, editor, *What Did They Sing at the Met?* (New York: Wayner Publications, 1971), for statistical reference.

I also gratefully acknowledge the invaluable help provided by Mrs. John DeWitt Peltz and her associates at the Metropolitan Opera Archives; Dr. Lothar Knessl and Frau Lolly Muller of the Vienna State Opera, who exposed me to every French and Italian opera Jan Peerce ever sang; the late Maurice Feldman, who brought Jan and me together; Gene Mack, Leonard Sloane, and Philip Spitzer; Valerie, Monica, and Enka Levy; Kitty Benedict, an editor who truly edits; and that walking encyclopedia of civil law and opera lore, Herbert Rosenberg.

—A. L.

Vienna, 1976.

Index

About the Author

Born in New York City in 1932, educated at Brown University and Columbia Graduate School of Journalism, Alan Levy has been a reporter, and since 1960 a free lance writer. He is the author of many books, including *Good Men Still Live!* and *The Culture Vultures* (written as the result of his experiences as an investigator for President Lyndon Johnson's Carnegie Commission on Educational Television). His interests range far and wide from cultural affairs to travel, to personalities and politics. In 1967, Levy took his wife and two daughters to Czechoslovakia where he worked with the film director Milos Forman. While there the Levys lived through an historic time: the Prague Spring of Alexander Dubcek and freedom, followed by the brutal intervention of the Russians in August 1968. In 1971, Levy and his family were expelled and deported to Vienna, where they now live. His book about this experience, *Rowboat to Prague,* has come to be considered the definitive book about that country's hope and tragedy. Since his enforced return to the West, Alan Levy has stayed "alive, proud and sane" doing writing for *The New York Times Magazine,* the Sunday edition of *The New York Times,* and many other publications.

Alfredo *in*
La Traviata

Cavaradossi
in Tosca

Pinkerton
in Madama Butterfly

Don Jose
in Carmen

Alfredo
in La Traviata

Richard
in A Masked Ball